KLUWER EUROPEAN LAW LIBRARY – 1

THE LEGAL ELEMENTS OF EUROPEAN IDENTITY

KLUWER EUROPEAN LAW LIBRARY – 1

THE LEGAL ELEMENTS OF EUROPEAN IDENTITY

EU Citizenship and Migration Law

By

Professor Elspeth Guild

University of Nijmegen, Partner, Kingsley Napley, London

KLUWER LAW
INTERNATIONAL

Published by
Kluwer Law International
P.O. Box 85889
2508 CN The Hague
The Netherlands

Sold and distributed in North, Central and South America by
Aspen Publishers, Inc.
7201 McKinney Circle
Frederick, MD 21704
USA

Sold and distributed in all other countries by
Extenza-Turpin Distribution Services
Stratton Business Park
Pegasus Drive
Biggleswade
Bedfordshire SG18 8QB
United Kingdom

ISBN 90–411–2304–0

A C.I.P. catalogue record for this book is available from the Library of Congress.

Printed on acid-free paper

Printed in the Netherlands

Table of Contents

Series Editor's Foreword

No one would put a question on a contractual clause to an expert of criminal law. However this is what happens on a daily basis to those brave enough to call themselves European law specialists. Nowadays, there is virtually no area of the law which is left untouched by either European legislation or by the case law of the Community courts. It is thus impossible to keep abreast of every development, making specialisation essential. As for the 'law-consumers', everyday work and study requires constant reflection and enquiry as to whether there is a directive or a recent judgment of the European Court of Justice which might affect the outcome of a certain case, or influence how a certain thesis can be developed.

The *Kluwer European Law Library* is born out of a very simple but ambitious idea: to provide a series of 'state-of-the-art' publications focused on specialised areas of EU law, which could be truly used and not simply placed on a remote shelf.

Boldly, the series has been baptised 'library' by the two members of the scientific committee of this project, Bruno de Witte and David O'Keeffe, and in the Aristotelian sense this means gradually covering all the possible ramifications of EU law. This is very well, but there is already a myriad of publications dealing with the same topics. Why another series? And what is the difference? It is always good to start with the practicalities. The library will offer svelte albeit exhaustive books at very affordable prices. This policy decision, for which full credit should be given to our publisher, should make the future books easily accessible to students and lawyers alike. It is hoped that the library could become a useful instrument, not only for those already involved in Euro-related work, but also for those who do not work on a daily basis in this field and yet may be in need of a reliable and clear text on specific topics. As for the substance, it is for the reader to judge and not for the editor to say. Just two modest remarks which are probably mere 'self-post-its'. Firstly, the topics selected are highly specific and original, and such, they are not intended to be a kind of 'nutshell textbooks' but a series of valuable short monographs. Secondly, the library does not have a targeted audience. Just good law books, which will be read by academics, students and practitioners alike.

Finally I would like to thank everybody who is involved in making this series happen, in particular Karel van der Linde at Kluwer and Andrea Cordwell James at King's College London.

Andrea Biondi
London, July 2004

Preface

This book plots the construction of identity and citizenship in European Union law. The central question which I address in the chapters which follow is: how is a European identity being created through the adoption and interpretation of immigration and citizenship laws by the European Union. While the focus is on the European Union and the interplay among the Member States in the creation and development of a legal framework of immigration and citizenship, this history can only be told in tandem with the development of immigration and citizenship rights as human rights which has been taking place at the same time in the "other" Europe – that of the Council of Europe – through the European Convention on Human Rights.

The construction of a European identity is a field which has been much discussed by both political scientists and international relations academics over at least the past 20 years. This literature is rich and deeply informative about what kind of Europe is emerging and why. However, the divide between jurists and political scientists has tended to be substantial in the field of "Europe" particularly in this area. While very informative books have been produced on the black letter law, such as K Hailbronner's[1] and S Peers'[2] work, the cross-over between law and the political science perspectives has been less well charted. In this book I have sought to remedy this shortcoming of the literature. The course of EU identity measures regarding individuals is one of a gradual transformation of immigrants in nation states (i.e. migrant nationals of the Member States) into citizens without a state (in the form of citizens of the Union). This has been coupled with an increasing legal differentiation between these new "citizens" and other immigrants – those from third countries. These are issues which can only be understood through a multidisciplinary approach. Thus the chapters here are structured around the EU legal measures but with reference to and seen in the light of the major theorists on European identity including Habermas, Koskenniemi, Sandholtz and Stone Sweet, Caporaso and Žižek.

In the introduction I start by examining the concept of Europe from the perspective of the definition of the state using Weber, Beck and Giddens as guides. Into this

---

1   K Hailbronner, *Immigration and Asylum Policy of the European Union*, Kluwer Law International, The Hague, 2000.
2   S Peers, *EU Justice and Home Affairs Law*, Longman, London 2000.

framework, I address the question of the individual and his or her identity as attached to the state or as arising from supra-national law. Chapter 1 considers the meaning of the border as regards identity in the form of citizenship and immigrant status. When the EU starts to shift the border outwards in the form of the Single Market, what are the consequences for the individual's identity. The work of J Torpey provides the point of departure. In Chapter 2, I examine the meaning of citizenship in the context of constitutionalism, including the EU constitution. What does it mean and what are the rights of citizenship, both in the context of the literature on constitutions and the construction of "Europe"? This discussion is then followed in Chapter 3 by an examination of the content of citizenship of the Union, using the work of T H Marshall as a guide. Chapter 4 examines the residence–citizenship nexus. The relationship of the legal concept of citizenship to a specific territory is complex and contested in Europe. Here Habermas provides the important connection with the development of thinking in political science.

Chapters 5 and 6 deal with central concerns of the citizen/migrant: the right to security of residence and protection against expulsion or exclusion and family reunification. In Chapter 5 I assess what some consider the Achilles heel of citizenship of the Union, the continuing power of the Member States to expel or exclude citizens of the Union who are nationals of another Member State both from the territory and from certain economic activities. The extent to which these powers are consistent with the principle of equality among citizens is highly contentious. Further, the continuing focus on the border as the place of security against terrorism, even in an Internal Market raises important questions about whether there is variable geometry of rights in the common space. Chapter 6 examines EU family reunification law both for citizens of the Union and third country nationals under the directive adopted in 2003.

The development of migration rights as human rights in the European Convention on Human Rights is plotted in Chapter 7. Caporaso's three analytical tools for understanding the Europeanisation of the politics of identity provide assistance in understanding the interface between the EU and the ECHR in the development of rights of migration and State obedience. In Chapter 8 the move from citizen to third country national in EU law is explained from the perspective of those who are in between the two concepts: the third country nationals whose work, residence or social rights in the EU are protected by agreements between their state of nationality and the EU. The development by the EU legislator and interpretation by the ECJ of these rights is an important part of the variable geometry of being an "immigrant" in Europe. Chapter 9 then sets out the new powers in immigration and asylum inserted into the EC Treaty in 1999 with a five-year deadline for the implementation of many of them. Schedules of adopted measures in the fields of immigration, asylum, borders and irregular migration as at 1 March 2004 are included as well as an analysis of the important aspects of each measure.

Sandholtz and Stone Sweet examine how the process of integration creates its own dynamic which sparks new political arenas and thus qualitatively changes the nature of politics. In light of their work, I examine in Chapter 10 the development of the new EU international relations policies of enlargement, the Wider Europe and the Doha round of WTO negotiations as it impacts on immigration. The future of EU immigration law seems as much bound up in the external policies of the EU as with the policies being pursued in the context of Justice and Home Affairs. Mikkeli characterises the idea of Europe as an identity which is structured around the difference of the other, be it skin colour, religion, culture or whatever. I examine in Chapter 11 the consequences of the adoption of measures against racial and other discrimination at the EU level with immigration law and policy. To what extent is Mikkeli proved right or wrong in law by the approach of the EU legislator towards racial discrimination? Chapter 12 examines the directive on long term resident third country nationals adopted in November 2003 in some detail. I set out in this chapter the provisions of the directive and their context. Žižek's work on Europe's fascination with the Real and the Other provides the prism through which to examine the wider significance of the directive.

The conclusion seek to bring together some of the main themes of the book, concerning the legal framework of identity in Europe. The intersecting and conflicting policies, approaches and venues is among the most startling of aspects of this work. It will be some time before the meaning of the legal elements of identity in Europe will become clear. Not only must clarification be awaited from the European Court of Justice but also from the European Court of Human Rights. The decisions of the highest courts in Europe alone will not provide any final answer on European identity. The most important test is whether the people of Europe embrace the concept as it is developing and accept its legitimacy. To understand this process, our colleagues in political science and international relations are indispensable.

I would like to thank a number of people for their help and support throughout the period of writing and revising this book. First, I must thank Didier Bigo of Sciences-Po for his endless and selfless help in discussing political science theory with me. Kees Groenendijk and Paul Minderhoud of the University of Nijmegen, Carol Harlow of the LSE and Ryszard Cholewinski of the University of Leicester provided me with might need legal criticism on some chapters which are much improved as a result. Andrew Neal of Keele has been a most careful and patient help, reading all the chapters and editing them for me. There are many other persons, too numerous to mention, who have assisted me greatly with their discussion, insight and ideas. Finally I must thank the European Commission Framework V programme ELISE and Framework VI programme Challenge which have both provided me with financial support to enable me to finish this project.

Table of Cases

European Court of Justice

European Court of Human Rights

National Courts

UK

International Court of Justice

Abbreviations

CAT	UN Convention against torture and other cruel, inhuman or degrading treatment or punishment 1984
CEEC	Central and Eastern European Countries
ECHR	European Convention on Human Rights
ECJ	European Court of Justice
ECmHR	European Commission of Human Rights
ECtHR	European Court of Human Rights
EU	European Union
ICCPR	International Covenant on Civil and Political Rights
JHA	Justice and Home Affairs

Introduction

Identity and the Individual in Europe

This book is about European citizenship and migration law.[1] The subject immediately presents a number of questions and issues about its scope. Europe, citizenship and migration all require some delineation and definition. However the definition is only possible through the gradual examination of the law and its framework in Europe. What is central to the ideas in law and practice of citizenship and migration is that they are ways of classifying types of identity and belonging in respect of individuals. Belonging to what, however, is one of the questions which is pivotal to this book. Definitions of the state, whether by Weber,[2] Giddens[3] or Tilly,[4] involve a territory, people and a political class/administration exercising authority. The term European citizenship and migration law begs the question of the state. What "state" of Europe is the territory within which these categories of belonging and separation apply?

In classic state theory, the state, through its bureaucracy, embraces the citizens to provide protection in various forms and to extract resources.[5] In law this is expressed as a relationship between identity, in the form of citizen versus foreigner, borders, as the container within which the state bureaucracy operates, and legal order, which provides the rules of the relationship.[6] I shall examine each element as it relates to "Europe": territory, people and the political class/administration. The first focus as

---

1 This text is complete as at 1 May 2004. The article numbers used in respect of the EC Treaty take into account the changes made by the Nice Treaty. The corresponding article numbers of the EU Constitution are those agreed in June 2004 and as posted on the Statewatch website.
2 M Weber, *Economy and Society*, vol 1, Ed Roth G & Wittich C, University of California Press, Berkeley, 1978.
3 A Giddens, *A Contemporary Critique of Historical Materialism*, vol 2, *The Nation-State and Violence*, University of California Press, Berkeley and Los Angeles, 1985.
4 C Tilly, *The Formation of Nation States in Western Europe*, Princeton University Press, Princeton, 1975.
5 G Noiriel, *Etat, nationalité et immigration vers une histoire du pouvoir*, Belin, Paris, 2001.
6 M Albert, D Jacobson, Y Lapid (eds), *Identities, Borders, Orders*, University of Minnesota Press, Minneapolis/London, 2001.

regards Europe is on the European Union.[7] However, an important second framework of the concept is the Europe of the Council of Europe, which I shall also consider. I will then return to the question of identity and the use of the categories of citizen and immigrant to denote different relationships of the individual and the state within Europe. In this second part of this chapter I will consider which state or supra national entity is entitled to claim a right to control identity in so far as it relates to the right to enter and live in a certain territory and to enjoy equal treatment with the most privileged class in that territory. The extent of the Member State's right to control these two aspects of identity must be negotiated with the claims of the European Union and the Council of Europe. Each of these fields will be analysed separately. In every case I have sought to use practical examples from law and jurisprudence to illustrate the complex dynamic which is currently being played out in Europe in this field.

The Territory

There is uncertainty at the heart of the physical territory which comprises Europe. As Walker puts it – Europe is not where it is supposed to be.[8] The narratives of size and emergence as regards 'Europe' which place it in a mould of territorial or vertical forms of authority do not properly explain the transformations occurring as a result of integration. Instead he suggests that the use of images of shifts from fragmentation to integration and common identity demand renewed emphasis on pluralisms and differences. At the same time that a common EU citizenship is developing rights, so diversity has been elevated to a positive attribute and goal in the EU.[9] In these transformations, according to Walker, "citizenship is becoming functionally disaggregated, migrations multiply communitarian attachments, and while the liberal political theorists blithely assert their faith in the rational and self-identical individual, everyone else is becoming used to a world of multiple and overlapping identities/subjectivities."[10] This framework of multiple and overlapping identities is central to understanding the meaning of citizenship and migration in Europe.[11]

---

7   For the sake of consistency I will refer to the European Union or EU irrespective of the time period unless the transformation of the European Economic Community into the European Community and the European Union which took place as a result of the entry into force of the Maastricht Treaty in 1993 is central to the sense of the point being made.

8   R B J Walker, 'Europe is not where it is Supposed to be' in M Kelstrup and M Williams, *International Relations and the Politics of European Integration*, Routledge, London, 2000, pp 14–32.

9   The preamble to the EU Constitution expresses the contrast: "convinced that, thus 'united in its diversity' Europe offers [the people] the best chance of pursuing, with due regard for the rights of each individual ..."

10 R J B Walker, supra pp 27–28.

11 Here, too, the first paragraphs of the preamble of the EU Constitution expresses this complex relationship between migration and citizenship: "Conscious that Europe is a continent that has brought forth civilisation; that its inhabitants, arriving in successive waves from earliest times, have gradually developed the values underlying humanism: equality of persons, freedom, respect for reason."

The three 'Europes' with which I work are the Council of Europe, the European Union and the Member States of that Europe which make up the two supranational entities. All three levels have undergone major transformations in the last twenty years. State dissolution and succession following the end of the Cold War have changed the entities of sovereignty and indeed the meaning of sovereignty. Countries that seemed stable have transformed themselves, as in the case of Germany, which absorbed a previously independent state thus changing itself dramatically. The accommodation of territorial claims in support of nationhood among various groups in Europe has led to the recognition of entities as states even where there are only very weak state institutions, as is the case in respect of a number of the successor states of the former Yugoslavia. Many of these new states have sought to join "Europe" in its various collective configurations. For example, the Europe of the Council of Europe doubled after 1991, Armenia and Azerbaijan now forming its eastern border.

The enlargement of the European Union has also been a story of continuous change of territorial identity and borders. Starting with the inclusion of Denmark, Ireland and the UK in 1972, the (then) European Economic Community continued to expand to include all of Southern Europe except the former Yugoslavia by the mid 1990s and the Nordic states except Iceland, Liechtenstein and Norway by the end of the decade. In 2004 the EU expanded to include ten countries: four Central and Eastern European countries (CEECs), the Baltic states, Slovenia and two Mediterranean islands. According to the agreement reached in Copenhagen 2002 this will be followed by a further enlargement to Bulgaria, Romania and Turkey. President of the European Commission, Romano Prodi, indicated in a speech in November 2002 that enlargement may eventually include the five Western Balkan states as well.[12]

In tandem with the EU's enlargement has been its intention to efface intra-Member State borders for certain purposes. The Schengen Agreements were developed around this theme and integrated into the EU in 1999.[13] The meaning of borders among the Member States and their place, as regards sovereignty, has become increasing fragmented and difficult to identify.[14]

The People

The relationship between citizen and migrant slowly stabilised in Europe following the completion of decolonisation is once again in flux. An investigation of citizenship must be the starting place in any consideration of migration, as it is only against

---

12 ECSA World Conference 2–5 December 2002, Brussels; European Commission Communication on the Wider Europe COM (203) 104 final.
13 I have extensively analysed this aspect in E Guild, *Moving the Borders of Europe*, Inaugural Lecture, Nijmegen, 2001.
14 K Groenendijk, E Guild, P Minderhoud, *In Search of Europe's Borders*, Kluwer Law International, the Hague, 2002.

the background of who "belongs" in law to the state that one can determine who the "other" is. The settlement of European state citizenship laws has had an uneven history.[15] For instance, in the UK the relocation of citizenship laws in the light of the independence of former colonies is found in the British Nationality Act 1948. Immigration rights, however, were only formally separated from citizenship in 1973 when the Immigration Act 1971 came into force.[16] Until the reorganisation of UK citizenship law in 1981, there was one status: citizenship of the UK and colonies. But from 1973 only those holders of the citizenship who acquired it in certain ways, primarily either by birth in the UK (as opposed to the colonies) or by ancestral link had the right to enter, remain and exercise economic activities in the UK. In 1981 a new British Nationality Act once again brought about a convergence of citizenship and residence rights by redefining citizenship into a series of new categories only one of which carried immigration rights. The redefinition of citizenship in the light of decolonisation was finally complete. However, the exclusion of one category of British national, British Overseas citizens, from any residence right anywhere continued to perturb the scene.[17] The question of belonging spilt over into the EU domain when, in 1999, the European Court of Justice was required to adjudicate on whether citizenship of the Union could compensate for the defect in the status of British Overseas citizen by guaranteeing a residence right.[18] Less messy, and in the view of some commentators less unfair, solutions were found in other European states to accommodate the end of empire. Portugal for instance chose the method of a cut off date – all those persons born in former colonies before a specified date retained Portuguese citizenship. All those born afterwards did not obtain it.[19]

Control over the creation and extinction of citizenship rights is a highly sensitive area closely linked to sovereignty. I will return to this in the next chapter when considering citizenship of the Union in greater depth. In theory, states have sought to keep a close guard over the power to create citizens or extinguish that status. However, transformation of borders and perceptions of borders have consequences for the citizenship identities of individuals. For instance, the category of citizen of the Union is enlarged dramatically when new states join the EU. Persons who were aliens viewed with suspicion, such as Czech Roma, must be transformed into citizens of the Union without the application of nation state mechanisms of conferment of citizenship – i.e. registration, naturalisation or acquisition by birth.

---

15 P Weil & R Hansen, *Nationalité et citoyenneté en Europe*, La Decouverte, Paris, 1999.

16 The separation of citizenship and immigration began in the 1960s with a number of very inelegant and frankly racially discriminatory measures. Order was only brought to the field in 1973. See I Macdonald & ors, *Immigration Law and Practice*, 5th ed. Butterworths, London, 2001.

17 The status of British Overseas nationals under the Immigration Act 1971 and the British Nationality Act 1981. Only in 2003 was the anomalous status ended when this category of British was given residence rights in the UK.

18 The ECJ held that it could not C-192/99 *Kaur* [2001] ECR I-1237.

19 R Manuel Moira Ramos, 'Le droit portugais de la nationalité' in B Nascimbene (ed), *Nationality Laws in the European Union*, Butterworths/Giuffre, London/Milan, 1996 pp 599–628.

4

The Political Class/Administration

There are many levels of bureaucracy in Europe tied to substantially different forms of democratic legitimacy. In each of the fields of Europe considered here, there are democratic institutions and dedicated civil servants. Their relationships with one another are increasingly interconnected.[20] The nation state level has the most clearly plotted system of democratic legitimacy and bureaucracy though substantial differences may be observed. Its legitimacy is founded on forms of representative democracy which permit the claim of government by the people.[21] The European Union, however, is comprised of multiple democratic and administrative parts with different qualities. On the level of the treaty divisions, there are parts which have international legal personality, parts with law making capacities, parts over which a binding judicial dispute resolution mechanism applies and parts to which none of the above apply. The settlement reached at Amsterdam in 1997 and continued in Nice in 2000 provided a treaty basis where a traditional first pillar of the Union was made up of the original EC Treaty with law making powers and the European Court of Justice to resolve disputes and interpret the treaty and institutional divisions of power. The second pillar, the European Foreign and Security Policy, was subject to rather different rules which do not engage law-making powers and were not susceptible to the jurisdiction of the Court of Justice. The third pillar, on Justice and Home Affairs was a hybrid between the first and second pillars as regards its constitutional structure. The collapsing of the pillar structure by the second Rome Treaty agreed in 2004 has modified the difference of political and administrative organisation but not beyond recognition.

The democratic legitimacy of the arrangement has come under substantial scrutiny.[22] The twin pillars of legitimacy in the Union are on the one hand indirectly elected via the intermediary of the governments of the Member States, that is to say through the Council of Ministers, and on the other hand directly elected through the European Parliament. The two institutions frequently find themselves in competition as to which has the greater authority, though clearly the Council as the law making body has the greater power.

The mechanisms for making operational the European Union are also fragmented. On the one hand there are central institutions in Brussels and elsewhere with responsibility for drafting, adopting and ensuring the implementation of EU law. However, these institutions are small in comparison with national bureaucracies and

---

20 D Bigo, *Polices en Reseaux*, Presse de Sciences-Po, Paris, 1996.
21 The claim is always subject to doubt as to the extent of its legitimacy – see C B MacPherson, *The Real World of Democracy*, OUP, Oxford/New York, 1974.
22 See in particular, D Beetham and C Lord, 'Legitimacy and the EU' in A Weale and M Nentwich, *Political Theory and the European Union*, OUP, Oxford, 1998; D Beetham and C Lord, *Legitimacy in the European Union*, Longman, London, 1998.

their role is only rarely direct implementation. The functioning of the Union implies the cooption of the administrations at the national level, whether in the form of the civil servant or the judge, to act as a faithful EU administrator when within the competences of the Union.[23] The Brussels based institutions only provide direction and control. One of the more popular theoretical tools for describing the Union is as a new form of governance rather than strictly an international organisation which is unusually powerful or an emerging federal state.[24] The development of a new EU constitution over the period 2002–2004 raises fresh doubts about whether the theoretical tool of a new form of governance actually corresponds to the reality.

The Council of Europe also has institutional structures and bureaucracy but these resemble more those of an international organisation than any new form of governance. However, it too has a bifurcated democratic structure. On the one hand the Committee of Ministers plays part of the role of the Council in the EU as the body competent to adopt treaties, open them for signature and to take other legislative acts. Its membership is composed of the delegated members of government of the participating states. On the other hand, there is the Parliamentary Assembly, which is composed of delegates from the parliaments of the member States. The competition for legitimacy between the two is less shrill than in Brussels though it could be pointed out that the Parliamentary Assembly enjoys a rather substantial degree of popular sympathy, at least among those who are aware of its existence.

In both the case of the Council of Europe and EU, the existence of a bureaucracy with a supranational judicial structure changes the quality of legitimacy this level of governance commands. As mechanisms for giving authority in the resolution of disputes, the existence of supranational judicial structures bring the legitimacy of judges to governance projects. This legal legitimacy, independent from the Member States, is perhaps the central feature of both the Council of Europe and the EU which elevates both of them beyond the usual status of international organisations. I shall return to this point in due course below. The degree of change at the heart of the relationship between territory, people and political power/administration at the moment in a space loosely called Europe is impressive. This relationship in law is, inter alia, called citizenship and immigration.

Sovereignty and Individual Identity

Where are the decisions on identity in Europe made? Where are the borders of identity and the rules of the legal order which determine the relationship of identity and

---

23 F Mancini, 'The Making of a Constitution for Europe' CMLRev 26:595 (1989); C-224/01 *Köbler* ECJ 30 September 2003 where the ECJ in effect held that if national courts are so deferential to national administrations that they fail correctly to apply EC law then the state itself will be responsible in damages to the individual who suffers loss as a result.

24 H & W Wallace, *Policy Making in the European Union*, 4th Edition, OUP, Oxford, 2001.

the border? These are questions of citizenship and migration. That there are many different types of answer to the questions is apparent from the degree of political dispute there is in this arena. The field of immigration and asylum was so contentious in the EU's 1990/1 inter-governmental conference that a whole separate treaty was created to provide a framework within which it could be discussed – the Treaty on European Union.[25] The creation of citizenship of the Union in 1993 by the Maastricht Treaty was one of the reasons for the rejection of that Treaty in the first Danish referendum on it. The second referendum was won only after concessions had been made to reinforce national sovereign control over citizenship.[26] In the following years the debate did not go away. At the 1996 inter-governmental conference immigration and asylum were only inserted into the EC Treaty on the condition of an opt out for three Member States and under substantially modified procedural rules which weakened the control of some of the European institutions over the field, in particular the European Commission and the European Court of Justice. Only now in the EU Constitution has the field been largely 'normalised', that is to say brought within the normal procedural rules of the EU.

Citizenship of the Union also changed the relationship of nationals of the Member States to migration in the controversial field of asylum. The 1996 intergovernmental conference agreed a protocol to be attached to the Treaty, providing that nationals of the Member States are presumed ineligible for refugee status in any other Member State.[27] The effect of deploying the term 'citizen' made possible (if still controversial) the presumptive exclusion of international protection obligations, i.e. the UN Convention on the status of refugees 1951 and its 1967 Protocol. At the time of the 2004 enlargement of the Union, one of the detriments of citizenship of the Union which passes immediately to nationals of the new Member States is their exclusion from asylum in any Union state. The benefits of citizenship of the Union, in particular the right of free movement is delayed for up to seven years.

The Individual and Identity

The question who am I? and who is entitled to say? is at the heart of the changing structures of Europe. The concept of identity in Europe is in transition: it is a space within which many competing interests and actors are seeking dominance, recognition, acceptance or validation. Immigration, European integration and globalisation,

---

25   Of course the Treaty on European Union also provided a venue for the development of a European foreign and security policy.

26   G-R de Groot, 'The Nationality Legislation of the Member States of the European Union' in M La Torre, *European Citizenship: An Institutional Challenge*, Kluwer Law International, the Hague, 1998 pp 115–147.

27   Protocol 6 TEU, Protocol on asylum for nationals of Member States of the European Union.

to name just a few forces, are challenging established concepts of identity but at the same time providing new solutions to the question of belonging. Conceptualising the challenges to citizenship has led in a number of directions. Soysal posits the transformation of citizenship from a state to a supranational status of belonging as a result of the development of supranational human rights treaties.[28] Jacobsen similarly sees citizenship as a status the importance of which is diminishing in favour of increased rights for migrants.[29] Sasken and others also develop thinking on citizenship in this direction bringing into the equation the changes which globalisation, in the form of movement of persons, is entailing.[30] At the heart of these discussions is the question of sovereignty. This attribution of the state in traditional political science theory depends on the link not only with the defined borders of the state but with the allegiance of the citizen. When critical rights for individuals escape the state, the meaning of citizenship is transformed. The power of the state to define the difference between citizens and immigrants and the rights each of them will hold, which is often considered as central to sovereignty, is less and less clearly attributable to the state. Even the theorist of sovereignty, Agamben, ties sovereignty and the constitutional settlement within the territory to the power to determine the differences between the citizen and the foreigner.[31] The question what is citizenship will be addressed in greater depth in the next chapter, here suffice it to note that in international law and in particular in international human rights law, the one right which applies to citizens as opposed to those rights which may also be open to non-citizens is the right to leave and enter the territory of citizenship and the right to live there. The state is precluded from expelling its citizens.[32] Thus in international law, recognition of the link of allegiance finds expression first and foremost in the right to enter and reside. Most people in the world are divided into citizens of one or other country which is "responsible" for them. That country must accept them back when they prove undesired in another state. International law uses as a key to the operation of international relations the attachment of the citizen to the state and the separation of the citizen from the immigrant or foreigner. This key provides a starting point in the consideration of identity in Europe.

---

28 Y Soysal, *Limits of Citizenship, Migrants and Post-national Membership in Europe*, University of Chicago Press, Chicago, 1994.

29 D Jacobsen, *Rights Across Borders: Immigration and the Decline of Citizenship*, John Hopkins University Press, Baltimore, 1996.

30 S Sassen, *Losing Control? Sovereignty in an Age of Globalisation*, Columbia University Press, New York, 1996.

31 "In the system of the nation-state, the so-called sacred and inalienable rights of man show themselves to lack every protection and reality at the moment in which they can no longer take the form of rights belonging to citizens of a state" G Agamben, *Homo Sacer: Sovereign Power and Bare Life*, Stanford University Press, Stanford, 1998, p 126.

32 In Europe this finds expression in articles 2 and 3, Protocol 4 European Convention on Human Rights. The same right is found in article 12 International Covenant on Civil and Political Rights 1966.

Identity and the Nation State

There are three inter-related fields which regulate identity in Europe. First are the nation states of Europe, those sovereign states recognised within the international community. Exactly where the territorial limits of the states of Europe are to be found is unclear. Some would include all countries west of the Urals; others would place Europe in a wider or narrower framework. Some clearly European states include overseas territories in their national definition. Thus the little Caribbean island divided into Sint Maarten and Saint Martin belongs respectively to the territories of the Netherlands and France. The ambiguity at the heart of the EU discussed above about the limits of Europe has not helped to clarify this issue. Another European development, the fall of the Berlin Wall in 1989, must also be explained in part through the relationship of citizenship law to territory. This event, which symbolised the end of bipolarity occurred, inter alia, because the constitution of the Federal Republic of Germany (FRG) recognised as its citizens not just the majority of persons born within its territory but also those Germans in the GDR (the old East Germany). In order to exercise their citizenship right to move to and live in the FRG, Germans in the East faced two problems – access to the territory which was increasingly difficult after the building of the Berlin Wall, and acquisition of a FRG passport. When in the summer of 1989 the Hungarian border guard failed to deny admission to Germans from the East nor to prevent them from leaving to the West, access to the territory of FRG was possible. The FRG consulate in Budapest was willing to issue passports to East Germans more or less on demand. The result was to consign the Wall to history. However, if the FRG constitution had not acknowledged these persons as citizens but instead had defined them as foreigners seeking asylum or to immigrate, there may have been quite a different turn to the events of the Summer and Autumn of 1989 in Berlin.

The process of state succession has also placed strains on definitions of citizenship. The dissolution of the former Yugoslavia and the war which ensued particularly in Bosnia-Herzegovina presented enormous challenges as regards identity and citizenship. The definition of individuals on the basis of religion became linked with citizenship, rights and exclusion. Part of the fragmentation of citizenship and the rights attendant on it was the flight from and partial return to the former Yugoslavia of several million persons between 1991 and 1999. The consequences of state succession on the former Yugoslavia in terms of citizenship are still not fully clear. Relatively relaxed approaches to the issue of passports by the newly formed succession states in the early 1990s masked or possibly resolved the uncertain status of belonging of many people from the region. Passport issuing practices at the newly established consulates of the successor states, particularly in Europe, to persons who fled the conflict tended to correspond to the sympathies of the personnel that had been rapidly recruited to staff the new consulates. Citizenship laws often take at least two generations to reveal their true consequences. A passport is only evidence of the status of the holder as a citizen; should the holder not in fact enjoy in law citizenship status, the passport of itself cannot compensate for that lack. Thus new citizenship laws in any state create uncertainty for a substantial period of time.

The contingencies of citizenship in the Western Balkans will not, in the short term, impact directly on citizenship of the Union itself; not so, however, as regards the Baltic states which become Member States of the Union in 2004. The creation of new states in the Baltic region has given rise to tensions about citizenship particularly in respect of the Russian minority population that had taken up residence there after WWII. The exclusion of this minority from citizenship in Estonia in particular and to a lesser degree in Latvia has been the subject of concern in the European Union and the Council of Europe.[33] Estonia adopted a citizenship law which restricted automatic acquisition to persons linked to the territory before the Soviet annexation, i.e. persons who held Estonian citizenship before 16 June 1940 and their descendants. This meant that 28% of the population resident in the territory was excluded from citizenship.[34] According to the Estonian authorities, these persons are "Russians" thus should be given passports by the successor states of the Soviet Union. The question of just how possible this is remains cloaked in administrative uncertainty.[35] In practice, however, few members of the Russian minority in Estonia have sought to exercise such a possibility. They consider themselves part of Estonia and their identity to be tied to that state. To accept that they are foreigners or immigrants by obtaining Russian passports would mean they would be required to obtain residence permits from the Estonian authorities who would not necessarily view the applications favourably.[36] They would also be subject to expulsion from the territory which the minority considers to be home. The same issue arises also in Latvia but to a lesser extent because the proportion of the population affected is less substantial.[37]

This problem will follow these two states into the EU. The result is that a local citizenship conflict is thrust into the territory of citizenship of the Union through enlargement. This is by no means a minor issue. The disparity between Estonians and non-Estonians resident on the territory will be magnified by the acquisition by

---

33 European Commission, *1999 Regular Report on Estonia's Progress towards Accession 1999*, pp 11–12; Open Society Institute *Minority Protection in Estonia* Monitoring the EU Accession Process: Minority Rights 2001.

34 European Parliament Task Force "Enlargement", *The Russian Minority in the Baltic States and the Enlargement of the EU*, Briefing No 42, Luxembourg 1999.

35 Y Sungurova, *Care for Migrants in Russia: Present Situation and Proposals for Future*, paper presented at the 8th Conference of the International Association for Studies in Forced Migration, Chiang Mai, Thailand, 5–9 January 2003.

36 The 2000 Observations of the UN Committee on the Elimination of Racial Discrimination regarding Estonia indicate some of the continuing problems. As the country rapporteur pointed out, the definition of a minority for the purpose of integration efforts in Estonian law is limited to those holding Estonia citizenship. Thus non-citizens living in the country were ignored. UN Press Release 17 March 2000.

37 It is somewhat ironic then that the first successful claim before the ECtHR of a breach of the right to private and family life in article 8 ECHR by a family of Russian extraction expelled from the Baltic states was against Latvia: *Slivenko v Latvia* ECtHR 9 October 2003.

the former of Union citizenship rights. The latter group will continue to be excluded. As effectively stateless persons, this group will not enjoy free movement rights for economic purposes. The indefinite delay in the accession treaty for the lifting of the 'Schengen' border then means that persons in this category will be effectively blocked in Estonia.[38]

The importance which both institutions of the EU and Council of Europe have placed on the adoption by the Russian Federation of inclusive citizenship laws in the 1990s shows just how central the questions of citizenship and migration are. The control by the nation state of the definition of citizenship is exercised through its nationality laws – the mechanism for automatic acquisition of citizenship being the most important. So long as acquisition of citizenship depends on a specific act by the individual it remains precarious. The state can contest the act of the individual seeking to establish the right to citizenship. Automatic acquisition is the means by which the state defines who fully and wholly belongs to the state and is not required to take any specific steps in order to activate or acquire the right. The tension between citizen and immigrant is played out in this territory of belonging. The nation state's control over that definition in the EU has been carefully reserved notwithstanding the potential consequences to the whole of the EU.[39]

The example of Germany is again instructive. Aussiedler – those persons of German descent who were living for many generations in Central and Eastern Europe and the former Soviet Union – acquired German citizenship automatically by virtue of their parentage according to the German constitution. This acquisition is not dependent on any contingency beyond presentation of the documents showing the ancestral link. When the Berlin Wall fell, itself in part a victim of citizenship laws, these Ausiedler started to come to Germany. Their numbers exceeded 200,000 per annum for a substantial part of the 1990s.[40] However, many of these persons did not speak German and lacked links with contemporary Germany. They were, to some extent, the subjects of Benedict Anderson's imagined communities, participating in a vision and understanding of Germany which generations of separation from the state had transformed into an identity no longer recognizable in the state itself.[41] About this identity

---

38 The question of the Russian minority in the Baltic states was raised a number of times in the Dutch Parliament. First, on the abolition of the so called grey list of states on the mandatory visa country list (i.e. those countries which some Schengen countries had on their mandatory visa requirement list but others did not) in 1999, the issue of the Russian minority was raised (Tweede Kamer vergaderjaar 1998–99 19 326, nr 212); then again the issue was raised in the Dutch Parliament on the discussion of accession of the Baltic states in 2000–1 (Tweede Kamer vergaderjaar 2000–2001 23 490 nr 167) by Mrs Albayrak with an anodyne reply by the minister (Tweede Kamer vergaderjaar 2000–2001 23 490 nr 182).

39 There is only a weak reference in the Tampere Conclusions from the European Council meeting in that city in October 1999 to opening national citizenship to third country nationals in the Union. The European Court of Justice, however, has shown itself particularly sensitive to the possibility of abuse by Member States of citizenship laws see C-192/99 *Kaur* [2001] ECR I-1237.

40 K Groenendijk, 'Regulating Ethnic Immigration: the case of the Aussiedler' New Community 23(4) 461 1997.

41 B Anderson, *Imagined Communities*, Verso, London, 1996.

group, Groenendijk recounts an anecdote from Kiev, Ukraine, where in 1998 the German community of the city invited a Ukrainian minister to address their group. The minister agreed on condition that he would address them in German. The invitation was not pursued not least because of concerns as to whether the majority of the group would be able to follow a presentation in German.[42]

Thus throughout the 1990s Germany was the destination country of hundreds of thousands of persons annually who needed language training, social and economic integration. These people were classified as citizens rather than immigrants in law, notwithstanding their contested links with the country and culture. Because an essential element in 20th century citizenship thinking is that there is equality among citizens, the newcomers were equal rights holders in the society.[43] Furthermore as German citizens they were also entitled from their arrival in the Union to enjoy free movement rights as citizens of the Union to move and take work anywhere in the combined territory.

In the post war boom in Germany from the 1950s to the 1970s, substantial numbers of Turkish workers migrated to fill labour shortages.[44] Notwithstanding substantial efforts to prevent their long-term settlement, many stayed permanently in Germany and brought their families there. German citizenship law, however, provided no mechanism for facilitated or automatic acquisition of citizenship for this group.[45] Thus they and their families including children born on the territory remained Turkish nationals. The arrival of substantial numbers of Aussiedler in the 1990s revealed a mismatch between citizenship and residence on the territory which became unsustainable. In 1999 a new law was proposed (and passed in amended form in 2000) to provide citizenship to the generation of Turks (and other immigrants) born in Germany or who arrived there at a very young age. However, the option of automatic acquisition of citizenship without further measure was rejected. Under the 2000 law, although persons born in Germany to parents who have lived there lawfully with a specific residence status for more than seven years acquire citizenship automatically at birth, if this is not confirmed by the individual between the ages of 16 and 22 the status will normally be lost. Thus for this group there is only a contingent right to citizenship. The difference between the two categories of persons – Aussielders and immigrants – is important. One group is admitted to citizenship automatically, which brings with it a right to equal treatment. The other group is grudgingly acknowledged.

---

42 K Groenendijk Pallas Conference 2001, Nijmegen.
43 As Agamben notes "And one of the few rules to which the Nazis constantly adhered during the course of the 'Final Solution' was that Jews could be sent to the extermination caps only after they had been fully denationalized (stripped even of the residual citizenship left to them after the Nuremberg laws)." Ibid p 132. I will return to the question of citizenship and equality in chapter 3.
44 S Castles, 'Globalisation and the Ambiguities of National Citizenship' in R Baubock & D Rundell, *Blurred Boundaries: Migration, Ethnicity, Citizenship*, Averbury, Aldershot, 1998 pp 37–54.
45 B Nascimbene, *Nationality Laws in the European Union*, Butterworths/Giuffre, London/Milan, 1996.

A further difference between the two groups also indicates how the classification of really "belonging" and "newcomer" is structured in law. This difference is found in the legal treatment of dual nationality. Those who are born dual nationals, such as the Aussiedler, are not required to abandon their other nationality in order to exercise their rights as German citizens. But those who are the children of immigrants and who accordingly under the 2000 Act have only a contingent right to citizenship must renounce any other nationality they have and prove they have done so in order to confirm their status as Germans. It would appear that their allegiance to the state is considered weakened by the retention of another citizenship though the same fact of dual allegiance for Aussielder does not have this effect on identity.

Identity and the Union

The next field in which identity is controlled is the European Union – the supranational body established by six European states commencing in 1957 and which encompassed 15 Member States up until May 2004 and 25 thereafter. In the next chapter I will look at the linkage of immigration and citizenship in the law of the European Union. Some initial observations are, nonetheless, justified here. First, immigration law has been regulated at the EU level since the entry into force of the first treaties. It has been an objective of the original European Economic Community to achieve free movement of persons. Specific rights of entry, residence and protection from expulsion came into full force for Community nationals in 1968 so long as they were exercising an economic activity. While the language of the treaties has not changed, the way in which the right to move, reside and work is perceived and promoted has changed. While the Italian worker in Germany or France in 1968 was seen as just another immigrant,[46] the development and interpretation of the right of residence and work in Community law in the 1970s and 1980s transformed the individual from an immigrant subject to national discretion into a rights holder not dependent on local immigration laws. The substitution of the phrase "free movement of persons" for the term "immigration" has been part of the shift of thinking away from the citizen/immigrant divide into an intermediary state as regards the movement of nationals of the Member States within the EU territory. Each time the EU expands this division is challenged. The most recent enlargement of 2004 bringing into the Union most of the Central and Eastern European countries (CEECs) is a good example.

The identification of insiders and outsiders is increasingly modified by legal measures adopted at the European level. These measures give rights to individuals upon which they are then entitled to rely to defeat the exercise of national law or

---

46 S Castles with H Booth and T Wallace, *Here for Good, Western Europe's New Ethnic Minorities*, Pluto Press, London/Sidney, 1984.

discretion. For instance, in EU law, nationals of the Member States are entitled to work and reside in the territory of any Member State. An economic migrant who is a Portuguese national has an entitlement to entry, stay and economic activity anywhere in the Union, which gives that individual strong legal elements of identity. Those elements are governed exclusively at the European level where the political debate is about how to encourage such economic migration.[47] Notwithstanding the development of the discourse of citizenship, EU immigration rights have been extended to nationals of third countries through bilateral agreements using the same framework. The EEC Turkey Association Agreement 1961 is the oldest such agreements still in force and which provides a basis for security of work and residence for Turkish nationals in the Union. The agreements with the Maghreb countries guarantee social security rights for their nationals. The Europe Agreements with the CEECs provided for free movement for the self-employed.[48]

When the first agreements between the EU and the CEECs were signed in the early 1990s, in the thinking of the Member States, nationals of Poland, Hungary etc. were clearly in the category of foreigners when in their own states and immigrants when they found themselves on the EU territory. The transformation of thinking from, for example, Poles as immigrants when in the EU to Poles as nationals of a Member State and entitled to free movement follows the acquisition of rights by these persons. While enlargement seemed a distant prospect in the mid-1990s, the recognition that nationals of the CEECs had migration rights was hotly contested. The example of the right of establishment (the right to self-employment for natural persons) is instructive. In the Europe Agreements a right of establishment for natural persons was included. The main pressure for this right was from businesses in the EU wanted access for their employees and contractors in the developing markets to the east. When nationals of the CEECs started to exercise their right of self-employment in the EU Member States there was a substantial degree of resistance by the administrations – greater or lesser depending on the state.[49] The perception of CEEC nationals within the Member States as "immigrants" and therefore excluded from free movement rights meant that there was a comprehension gap for officials between migration rights in an EC agreement with a CEEC and the exercise of national discretion over entry, residence and expulsion of immigrants. In the first case that was decided by the European Court of Justice on these migration rights, seven Member States intervened on behalf of the defendant state seeking to defeat the recognition of supranational migration rights by CEEC nationals.[50] It is a credit

---

47 Commission Communication on Citizenship of the Union COM (1998) 403; Commission Communication on Free movement of workers – achieving the full benefit and potential COM (2002) 694 final.
48 For the new Member States these agreements were replaced by the accession treaty. However, for Bulgaria and Romania they still provide important rights, see chapter 8.
49 A Böcker & E Guild, *Implementation of the Europe Agreements in France, Germany, the Netherlands and the UK: Movement of Persons*, Platinum, London, 2002.
50 C-63/99 *Glozsczuk* [2001] ECR I-6369.

to the Court of Justice that it did not cave in to this political pressure but interpreted the right of establishment in the agreements in accordance with its existing jurisprudence in the field. It found that the right had as a corollary the right of entry and residence on the territory for nationals of the CEECs seeking to exercise self-employed activities. The effect of this decision was to change the status of CEEC nationals from immigrants to holders of the right to move across borders.

Identity in the Larger Europe

The Council of Europe is composed of 45 countries in the region. All the Member States of the European Union are member States of the Council of Europe. A condition of membership of the later is that states sign and ratify the European Convention on Human Rights (ECHR) and accept the permanent jurisdiction of the European Court of Human Rights not least in respect of complaints by individuals against the state. Through the European Convention on Human Rights and other conventions, the Council of Europe has become an important actor in regulating identity. The claim of an individual to entry and residence has gradually gained ground in the realm of human rights law in Europe largely due to the ECHR. As regards identity, the fullest legal expression of inclusion is nationality; of exclusion it is expulsion with a prohibition on return. In between there is a spectrum of legal elements such as security of residence, the right to engage in economic activities, the right to equal treatment, etc. against which identity as a legal expression can be gauged. These elements are increasingly determined or circumscribed by supranational legislation. In this way the arbiter of identity through rights is changing.

Article 1 ECHR requires that the rights of the convention be secured for all persons within the jurisdiction of the signatory states. Thus human rights cannot be reserved for own nationals of a state and a lesser level of rights extended to immigrants and foreigners. However, from there to the acknowledgement of residence rights as human rights is still a substantial step. There is no provision of the original ECHR expressly refers to foreigners as regards migration rights. It is not until Protocol 4 was adopted that specific, if limited, protections for foreigners were included. However, two provisions of the ECHR: article 3 – prohibiting torture and article 8 – guaranteeing the protection of private and family life have served as a base for the development of migrants' rights as human rights. These provisions have been interpreted by the European Court of Human Rights (ECtHR) as requiring parties to the ECHR not only to grant rights to their own nationals but also to grant rights to foreigners, including residence.

The landmark decision of the ECtHR in 1985 on article 8 family rights is often considered to be starting point of supranational control over residence rights.[51] The

---

51 *Adbulaziz, Cabales & Balkandali v UK* [1985] Ser. A 95.

UK sought to impede or prevent the migration of foreign husbands to join their wives in the UK. It adopted legislation which restricted the possibility for women, either British or settled in the UK, to bring their foreign husbands to live with them. Men in the UK were not subject to the same handicap as regards their foreign wives. While the ECtHR rejected the right to family reunification as inherent in article 8, it found the provision engaged and thus the discrimination on the basis of gender unlawful. This case was followed in 1988 by a second decision on immigration and the meaning of family life in article 8, *Berrehab*,[52] where the efforts of the Dutch authorities sto expel the Moroccan father of a Dutch child resident with his Dutch mother in the Netherlands were held to breach the individual's right to family life. For the first time in the European legal framework an immigrant succeeded in establishing a right to residence as a fundamental human right contrary to the opinion of the state (including the courts of the state).

Article 3 ECHR and its interpretation by the ECtHR as limiting the power of states to expel foreigners has been the subject of substantial controversy. The prohibition on torture contained in the provision was first interpreted by the ECtHR as applying also to return of a person to a country where there is a substantial risk of torture in 1989.[53] In this first case the ECtHR found that the prohibition on torture contained in article 3 applies also where a state, in this case the UK, was intending to extradite a foreign national to the USA where there was a substantial risk that he would suffer death row syndrome (which would constitute torture according to the ECtHR). The application of article 3 to asylum seekers followed very shortly in a case against Sweden.[54] However, it was not until 1996 that an individual successfully challenged his expulsion (as opposed to extradition) from Europe on the basis of article 3 and the real risk that he would be subjected to torture in his country of origin.[55]

The engagement of a European supranational court in the protection of asylum seekers contrary to political and judicial opinion within the nation state has been controversial. While European states have from time to time called for a review of the main international instrument which constrains them to protect refugees, the Geneva Convention, the fact that the judicial interpretation of the convention remained within the state has blunted opposition. The protection of asylum seekers under that convention is tied to the obedience or resistance of national judges.[56]

---

52 [1988] Ser. A 138.
53 *Soering v UK* [1989] Ser. A 161.
54 *Cruz Varas v Sweden* [1991] Ser. A 201.
55 *Chahal v UK* [1996] ECtHR Reports 1996-V.
56 The fact that the supreme courts of different European states have interpreted the protection provided by the convention differently is evidence of this. The difficulty which the institutions of the European Union have had in finding a common notion of a refugee for the purposes of a proposed directive on minimum standards for the qualification and status of third country nationals and stateless persons as refugees or as persons who otherwise need international protection OJ 2002 C 51 is tied to the different balances which state institutions in the Member States have given to protection of asylum seekers.

When the definition of protection of asylum seekers escapes the national level not only as regards treaty commitments, but in respect of their interpretation by supranational courts, the legitimacy of contrary positions at the national level is greatly reduced. A good example of this comes from the UK. The ECtHR interpretation of the duty of member States to protect asylum seekers so infuriated a British Prime Minister that he called for the UK to withdraw from the ECHR in January 2003.[57] However, he was immediately advised by his senior civil servants that such a move was likely to be held to be illegal by the national courts.[58] The intertwining of the national and supranational has circumscribed the state in respect of its power to refuse access to its territory of persons seeking asylum.

Thus the insertion of migration rights into the framework of human rights has also brought about a change to the nature of identity. The legal expression of this in Europe is through the ECHR where on human rights grounds, non-nationals may gain a right of residence and protection against expulsion.

Conclusions

The rights of residence and equality of treatment are at the core of identity and indeed citizenship. They are the marker between citizen and immigrant reflecting a fundamental element of state formation and maintenance. A right of residence is an essential element in the control of identity as it is the legal expression of the individual's relationship to the territory and the state. The right to control that relationship is currently divided among three levels of governance in Europe. From the perspective of the individual, his or her status as a rights holder in respect of identity is determined by the level of governance which regulates his or her rights, in particular, of residence and protection from expulsion.

The right to define identity is shared among these bodies, though the balance is changing. The nation state controls who are its nationals but remains answerable to the supranational bodies for the interpretation and definition of their rights and access to other territories. In the legal expression of the right to control identity can be found the tension of different identities and different levels of engagement on the part of individuals and states to identities. There is continuous overlap between identities which are shared and expressed simultaneously. The appeal to one identity in law can have the effect of undermining or overruling the rights and duties associated with identity at another level. In this sense, Walker's insistence that European integration can only be understood through an examination of multiple and overlapping

---

57 P Wintour, 'Blair warning on rights treaty' The Guardian, January 27 2003. G Jones, 'Blair ready to pull out of asylum deal' Daily Telegraph, January 27 2003.

58 A Travis 'You can't quit treaties, Blair warned' The Guardian February 6 2003.

identities/subjectivities is evident in the development of European citizenship and migration law. Separation of the fields is not sustainable. The German immigrant in Portugal is still a citizen of the Union, subject to the jurisdiction of the ECJ. He or she is also within the jurisdiction of a member State for the purposes of the application of the ECHR. National law may still is some areas apply to him or her. The interconnection of the fields in law will be considered in greater depth in the chapters which follow.

Chapter 1

Borders and Citizenship

I have set out in the introduction the parameters of the discussion on identity, orders and borders which is central to understanding European citizenship and migration. In the next chapter I will look at the rights attendant on citizenship of the Union. Here I will look further into the relationship between citizens and borders in the European Union. The dividing line between the citizen and the foreigner is the border, either the territorial border for those states which accept the principle that birth on the territory gives rise the automatic acquisition of citizenship (ius soli), or the border of the legal order for those states which use the principle of belonging to the ethnicity as the basis of citizenship (ius sanguinis).[1] The consequence of being a citizen of the state in international law is the right to cross the territorial border to enter the state and live there.[2] Citizenship of the Union, however, is a status which is attached to a supranational entity which is not a state, the European Union. Its borders are intrinsically related to the borders of the Member States and have varied dramatically over time, in particular as a result of enlargement.[3] The consequence of being a citizen of the Union is the right to cross the territorial borders of many states, subject to limitations. The nature of these borders is central to the development of EU citizenship.

Separating Citizens from Foreigners

For the relationship of the individual and the border to be determined, a process of identification must take place. Until a person is identified as having the citizenship

---

1   See the introduction for a substantial discussion of these categories in the context of the Baltic states.
2   For instance article 13 International Covenant on Civil and Political Rights 1966; article 3(1) ECHR.
3   See chapter 10 on this subject.

of one state or another, his or her status as a rights holder is indeterminate. As a citizen, the individual is entitled in international law to be present on the territory of the state. As a foreigner, the state is entitled (subject to international commitments) to expel the individual. The lawfulness of expulsion, however, is dependent on establishing the individual's citizenship to the satisfaction of three parties: the state seeking to expel, the state of alleged citizenship and the individual.[4] For the individual and the state, one of the most cogent pieces of evidence of the success of the citizen-state relationship is an internationally recognised passport. Two examples from the state's perspective are: the disappointment of the Palestinian Authority in the late 1990s and early 2000 that it was unable to convince a substantial part of the international community of the validity of the travel documents which it issued to those persons it defined as its people; the preoccupation of many Member States in detecting forged passports – in particular their own.[5] For the individual, the threat by the state to withdraw a passport is linked primarily with his or her criminal behaviour (or in the case of children their protection). The passport has become both an important symbol and practice of citizenship.

The Definitions

A series of categories indicate different relationships between the individual and the state. All of the categories are premised on the ability to determine the borders between states and the position of the individual in relation to them – whether this is overt or implied. Each category is subject to a different state response. The state acknowledges the different categories of individuals by issuing different documents which indicate their status.

1. citizen: this group is defined by national law, commonly contained in constitutions; as a term, it is most evident by its absence in international human rights conventions. The state normally issues an identity document as evidence of citizenship;[6]
2. national: in this concept there is an inference that the relationship between the individual and the state is recognised beyond the borders of the state; the

---

4   Recent developments in the EU reduce the need for the individual's consent or the consent of the country of citizenship. The settling of readmission agreements with third countries which require the third state to take back a person of any or unknown citizenship if he or she has travelled from that state to the EU is intended to reduce the dependence of Member States on third countries of origin in the process. M Schieffer, 'Community readmission agreements with third-countries – objectives, substance and current state of negotiations' EJML, 3(2003) forthcoming.

5   An EU project, Rio IV, has this specific purpose, see EU Presidency Report to SCIFA: *Report on the implementation of programmes, ad hoc centres, pilot projects and joint operations*, Council Document 9535/03 12 May 2003.

6   The UK is exceptional among the EU Member States in not having a state system of identity cards.

national is the citizen viewed from outside the state.[7] When the International Court of Justice was required to consider a case of dual nationality it found that "according to the practice of States, nationality constitutes the juridical expression of the fact that an individual is more closely connected with the population of a particular State. Conferred by a State, it only entitles that State to exercise protection if it constitutes a translation into juridical terms of the individual's connection with that State."[8] This definition has since been used in the Council of Europe's Convention on Nationality 1997 where nationality is defined as "the legal bond between a person and a State and does not indicate the person's ethnic origin."[9] The document which evidences status as a national is an internationally recognised passport.

3.   resident: this is a neutral term as regards citizenship – citizens may be residents but not necessarily, similarly non-citizens may be residents or not; residence may be a legal or factual term: an individual may be legally or illegally resident; further, within the legal sphere, it may be defined very differently depending on the field, for instance a person may be classified as resident for tax purposes but not resident for social benefits purposes;[10] while the document issued to legally resident non-citizens in many Member States is called a residence permit, in fact it relates more closely to the status of migrant/immigrant than to that of resident.

4.   migrant/immigrant: in an attempt to achieve a coherent content to the concept of a migrant, the UN, in 1998, provided a new definition of "international migrant." The definition is divided into long-term and short-term migrant. The first is a person who moves to a country other than that of his or her usual residence for a period of at least a year, so that the country of destination effectively becomes his or her new country of usual residence; a short-term migrant is a person who moves to a country other than that of his or her usual residence for a period of at least 3 months but less than a year except in cases where the movement to that country is for purposes of recreation, holiday, visits to friends and relatives, business, medical treatment or religious pilgrimage.[11] The UN Convention on the protection of the rights of all migrant workers and members of their families defines its subjects as "a person who is to be engaged, is

---

7   For instance, articles 1 and 2 Convention on certain questions relating to the conflict of nationality laws 1930 provide that each State is entitled to determine under its own law who are its nationals. Any question as to whether a person possesses the nationality of a particular State is to be determined by national law of the State.

8   *Nottebohm Case (second phase) Liechtenstein v Guatemala* ICJ Reports, 1955.

9   Article 2(a) Council of Europe Convention on Nationality 1997.

10   For instance, section 55 Nationality, Immigration and Asylum Act 2002 provides that asylum seekers resident in the UK in certain circumstances are outside the scope of social benefits; this does not change their tax liability as residents in the event that they take employment.

11   See SOPEMI 2000, *Trends in International Migration*, OECD, Paris, 2000 pp 295–301.

engaged or has been engaged in a remunerated activity in a State of which he or she is not a national;"[12] the document which the host state issues to the migrant or immigrant is a residence permit. Surprisingly, in a number of EU states persons who are categorised as illegal by the state are also issued documents relating to their presence on the territory. The best known example is the *duldung* in Germany.

5. alien/foreigner: this term is "migration" neutral; thus a person who is not a national and who does not come within the various definitions of a migrant may be either an alien or foreigner. Aliens appear in international human rights instruments but without definition;[13] "foreigners" like "citizens" are noticeably absent. An alien or foreigner is unlikely to have separate documentation from the host country. When in the territory of another state he or she is likely to be in possession of a national passport. However, the alien or foreigner may have recorded in his or her passport a document issued by the host state, for instance a visa, a stamp permitting entry onto the territory or the equivalent.[14]

6. person/individual: this category is radically different from the others above as the differentiation which is being made is between human beings and other animals or objects.[15] The "belonging" of the individual is not to a state but to the human race. The "person/individual" is the holder of most human rights in international law.[16] The person can also be stateless in international law that is to say a person who is not considered as a national by any state under the operation of its law.[17] This category goes beyond the state, though the issue of birth certificates may be considered a form of evidence of this status.

Within this series of categories I will examine the EU citizen who is both a citizen and a national depending on the perspective from which he or she is viewed. He or she may be a resident either in the state of origin or elsewhere in the Union. He or she will also be a migrant if living in a Member State other than that of his or her

---

12 Article 2 UN Convention on the protection of the rights of all migrant workers and members of their families 1990.

13 For instance article 13 International Covenant on Civil and Political Rights 1966 "An alien lawfully in the territory of a State Party to the present Covenant ..."

14 The Commission proposed the inclusion of biometric data on visas for third country nationals in the form of facial images as a primary biometric identifier and fingerprints as a secondary biometric identifier. It could be argued that the value of the passport as the internationally recognised document of identity of the individual is diminished by the creation of a secondary system of identification by the state which the individual intends to visit. European Commission Press Release IP/03/1289, 24 September 2003.

15 The right to life is a good example of this: article 6(1) International Covenant on Civil and Political Rights 1966 states "Every human being has the inherent right to life."

16 For instance article 2(1) International Covenant on Civil and Political Rights 1966 provides that "Each State party to the present Covenant undertakes to respect and to ensure to all individuals within its territory and subject to its jurisdiction the rights recognised in the present Covenant, ..."

17 Article 1(1) UN Convention relating to the status of stateless persons 1954.

nationality. The citizen of the Union can also be an alien within the territory of another Member State for the purpose of claiming rights in international law. Finally, the citizen of the Union will also always be a person in international human rights law wherever he or she may be living.

The Legitimate Means of Movement Across Boundaries

What is the role of the border in the relationship of the state with the citizen? Torpey suggests that a central part of the formation of modern states is their need to expropriate the legitimate means of movement across certain spaces and boundaries.[18] This need arises from the nature of the modern state as a defined territory with a defined membership governed by a bureaucracy which is able to identify both the territory (and protect it) and the members (and protect them). However this protection is to be provided, the state must identify the object and it is to this process that the difference between citizen and non-citizen is central. When a state establishes a border guard which has as its job to check people entering and/or leaving the country, it is, in effect, seeking legitimacy to control movement of persons across its borders. The claim will only be effective if those crossing the border accept its legitimacy or, if they do not, the state has the power to exclude them.

Europe is littered with disputed borders where the legitimacy of controls is not accepted. The fall of the control of the Green Line between the Greek and Turkish parts of Cyprus in April 2003 presented exactly this dilemma.[19] As the Greek community had never recognised the partition of the island, when the separation of the communities suddenly ended the government was faced with a quandary: did they have the power to apply controls on persons and (whether or not the answer was positive) should they insist on passport controls on persons leaving the Greek part of the island to go to the Turkish part? Concern about the security implications of the opening of the border took priority over political positions against the separation of the island: passports are required and checked. However, the fact of the Greek Cypriot authorities undertaking passport checks at the Green Line has undermined the principle that the island is in fact one state with one people. The state's imposition of a claim to a legitimate control over movement of persons through the examination of identity documents at a fixed territorial point has brought with it the appearance of delineating sovereignty.[20]

For the EU, the greatest disputed border is that of the internal market. From 1987 the Member States inserted into the EC Treaty the objective of elimination of

---

18   J Torpey, *The Invention of the Passport, Surveillance, Citizenship and the State*, Cambridge University Press, Cambridge, 2000 pp 4–5.
19   Council of Europe Secretary General: *Europe Must Support National Reconciliation on the Island*, Press Release 25 April 2003.
20   I will return to this example from another perspective in chapter 10.

border controls on the movement of goods, persons, services and capital among themselves.[21] The objective was to complete this internal market area by the end of 1992. The UK became increasingly concerned, as the deadline approached, that it would have to abandon its border controls on persons arriving from other Member States, an action which would be particular difficult politically.[22] By 1999, this dispute was resolved by an opt-out for the UK (Denmark and Ireland also obtained opt-outs) contained in a protocol to the treaty (and now to the Constitution) permitting the UK to continue to apply its border controls on movement of persons arriving in the UK from other Member States. For the other Member States, the establishment of the internal market as an area without internal border controls did not change Member State sovereignty over their borders, nor did it change the position of their borders in international law. What it did was change the control of those borders. Among the matters which have become clear in the Union is that borders where systematic checks by border guards on persons crossing them do not take place cease to have symbolic importance as places of differentiation. The focus of sovereignty becomes the border of the bureaucratic state.[23] I shall return to the issue of the bureaucratic state later in this chapter when looking at sovereignty, citizenship and the extraction and allocation of resources.

Moving Across which Borders?

Torpey does not claim that states effectively control movement of persons across boundaries, only that the claim to control the legitimacy of movement is central to the state. In order to claim such a power, the state must be able to distinguish between different parts of the population – those who belong and those who do not. The mechanism for doing so is the allocation of citizenship and the issue of identity documents which enable the state to identify its people as opposed to the 'others'. The right and the power of the state to identify individuals has had different histories in Europe. Torpey follows in some detail the history of identity documents in Europe from the Roman era to recent history including WWII and the use by the Nazis of identity documentation to stigmatize Jews.[24] One of the difficulties, however, with Torpey's analysis is that it focuses on the passport as an identity document to differentiate the foreigner from the citizen. The most substantial use of identity documents (including but not limited to passports) in Europe has been and

---

21 Article 14(2) EC/article III-130(2) EU Constitution.
22 House of Commons Home Affairs Committee Report, *Migration Control at External Borders of the European Community*, Session 1991–92.
23 J Crowley, 'Where Does the State Actually Start? Territorial Control in the Contemporary Governance of Migration' in D Bigo and E Guild, *Controlling Frontiers: Free Movement into and within Europe*, Ashgate, Aldershot, forthcoming.
24 Torpey, ibid pp 131–143.

continues to be as internal documents. The state's ability to control the population on its territory does not start or finish at the border but is internalised.

The EU right of free movement of persons is assimilated, in this regard, to movement of the individual within the state in so far as it may be exercised as regards the crossing of the (uncontrolled) intra-Member State border by a person in possession of either a valid identity card or a passport.[25] The principle that movement within the state is lawful only when an individual is in possession of an identity card is present in German and French law. The international law requirement that everyone lawfully within the territory of a state shall have within that territory the right to liberty of movement and freedom to choose his or her residence[26] can be made subject to an internal identification document which authorises the movement. An internationally recognised passport is the requirement for the crossing of the borders of sovereignty. The merging of the two regimes in EU law indicates the ambiguity of the EU internal border/Member States' sovereign borders with one another.

A further mixing of internal identity control measures and external ones takes place in EU law with the ECJ's decision in the case of a Greek national resident in Germany.[27] Mr Giagounidis, a Greek national, arrived in Germany with a valid passport which subsequently expired. The Greek authorities would not renew it for him in Germany. He did have a Greek identity card but its validity was limited to the territory of Greece. The German authorities refused his application for an extension of his residence permit as he did not have a valid passport and thus was not lawfully resident in Germany under national law. The ECJ rejected the German government's argument that it could demand a valid passport in respect of Mr Giagounidis before acknowledging his right of residence. It held that "a Member State is obliged to recognise the right of residence within its territory of [Community national workers] when they produce a valid identity card, even if that card does not authorise its holder to leave the territory of the State in which it was issued." Thus the documents of control which a Member State produces for internal purposes must be given the same force externally within the EU.

The right of free movement of persons, however, in EU law is compatible with the right of the sovereign state to information regarding the whereabouts of the population on its territory. For the ECJ there was no incoherence between the two principles. It held that "by creating the principle of freedom of movement of persons and by conferring on any person falling within its ambit the right of access to the territory of the Member States, for the purposes intended by the Treaty, Community law has not excluded the power of the Member States to adopt measures enabling the national authorities to have an exact knowledge of population movements

---

25 Article 3(1) Directive 68/360, now consolidated in Directive 2004/38.
26 Article 12(1) International Covenant on Civil and Political Rights 1966.
27 C-376/89 *Giagounidis* [1991] ECR I-1069.

affecting their territory."[28] Such measures are, of course, related to identity documents. The right of the Member States to have precise knowledge of population movements is not limited to movements across the borders of sovereignty. It includes movement within their territory. However, the two aspects are dealt with by the ECJ as similar if not identical for the purposes of the lawful power of the Member State and the compatibility of measures with EU law.

The EU obligation on the Member States to issue identity documents and passports follows logically from the power of the EU to subsume the control at the border of sovereignty with the control of identity within the state. Where movement within the state and movement across Member State's borders is to be qualitatively similar if not the same as regards the degree of control which the state can exercise, the EU must also have the power to coerce the state into issuing the relevant documents or else fail to make good the promise to the individual that he or she has a right to move. "Member States shall, acting in accordance with their laws, issue to such nationals, or renew, an identity card or passport, which shall state in particular the holder's nationality."[29] By this provision, the EU obliges the Member States to determine who are their citizens and to document them. By virtue of the creation of a right in EU law to leave one Member State and take up residence in another, the EU has acquired the power not only to determine the validity of identity documents but also to oblige Member States to issue them (though the Member State retains the right to determine who gets an identity document certifying possession of citizenship).

The state's refusal to issue or return to one of its citizens an identity document may be an act of state coercion if the individual needs the document to carry on normal life. The success of the bureaucratic state in creating administrative borders to the enjoyment of private life and access to public benefits may be measured by the importance of identity documents to the citizen. The state's act to deprive an individual of identity documents may be justified on the basis of a criminal conviction or the risk which the individual constitutes for the state, but will be measured against the degree to which effective administrative borders have been put in place. This question of the lawfulness of state coercion in retention or refusal to issue identity documents has not come up before the ECJ but it has done so before the ECtHR as an issue relating to respect for private and family life under article 8 ECHR. Two Russian nationals were detained and released four times over a five year period. During this period, the passport of one of them was held by the authorities. As the Russian national explained, the failure to have an internal passport meant that she was in breach of national law concerning identity papers and was unable to carry on normal activities. Having had no success at the national level, she sought relief from the ECtHR on the basis that the deprivation of her passport constituted a breach of

---

28   C-118/75 *Watson & Belmann* [1976] ECR 1185.
29   Article 2(2) Directive 68/360, now consolidated in Directive 2004/38.

her right to private life under article 8.[30] In reviewing the facts surrounding the application of the internal passport, the ECtHR found that in everyday life, Russian citizens must prove their identity even when performing basic daily activities such as exchanging currency or buying train tickets. The ECtHR noted that the passport was essential for finding employment or receiving medical care. Accordingly, it held that "The deprivation of the passport therefore represents a continued interference with the applicant's private life." As a citizen, Smirnova had to have a passport to carry out daily tasks. The act of the state to deprive her of the passport was not assailable at the national level. However, her status as a "person" in human rights law provided her with a right to have an internal passport. This internal purpose is perhaps more significant than Torpey's focus of control on the external border. While the symbolic consequences of the border of sovereignty are greater, for the individual the internal "border" and its control may constitute a fundamental part of private life.

Borders, Movement and Property

Kostakopoulou argues that historically the right to move within the territory of the state is fundamentally linked with the concept of ownership of property.[31] In so far as individuals were the property of other individuals in their capacities as slaves or serfs, their right to move was controlled by their masters. With the end of slavery and serfdom, the individual is no longer the focus of the control of movement through a limitation based on his or her status, rather the focus is on the territory. Within private spaces, individuals may control entry and exit, for instance into their fields or houses or corporate premises based on the rules of property law. The status of the individual as a rights holder regarding access to private spaces is limited to specific groups, such as family members, co-owners and possibly lenders against the property.

As regards the modern state, one aspect of movement of persons (and the state's right to control and prevent movement) is the carving out of a private space on the basis of property rights which the state enforces. The state has international obligations to protect the right of property owners against forced entry into their property and respects the right of the property owner to peaceful enjoyment of his or her property.[32] However, an analogy between the right of the property owner to control who enters his or her home and that of the modern state in the exercise of border controls is untenable because it elides two very different concepts: the population of the state and the occupants of a household. The small group of persons, usually defined in law

---

30 *Smirnova v Russia* ECtHR 24 July 2003.
31 D Kostakopoulou, 'Unweaving the Threads: Territoriality, National Ownership of Land and Asylum Policy', EJML (2004) forthcoming.
32 For instance, article 1 Protocol 1 ECHR contains such a right.

and practice, for instance, as a family, are all well known to one another and to one extent or another have made a positive choice to live in the same dwelling and share intimate life. There is no inherent principle of equality among members of a family nor any principle of governance of the family within itself. The state, however, is comprised of large numbers of persons who do not share the link of family and of whom only few have a real choice about whether they live in the state or not. Notwithstanding theories of citizenship that are based on ethnicity, the modern state's relationship with the individual rests on a bureaucratic allocation of belonging evidenced through identity documents. There is generally no option to the citizen to leave the state and set up his or her own separate state, recent examples of state succession or radical devolution notwithstanding.[33] Similarly, the principle of equality among citizens and the mechanisms of democratic governance indicate fundamental differences which render the analogy unworkable.

There is, however, a continuing aspect of "property" ownership of the state in the treatment of the citizen through the issue of documents of identity. The state certifies the individual's right to be on the territory which is bounded by its borders of sovereignty. Within that territory, most EU states exercise a right to control the identity of the citizen not only through the issue of documents but also in the name which the individual is entitled to use. The state's right regarding the name of an individual, or to certify the individual's identity, has, in some respects, an element of possession or property. While the citizen may chose the name of his or her child, the state is entitled to place limits on that choice so that it corresponds to the state's rules on identification. So long as the citizen and the state remain within their borders, the question of names will be one of national law tempered, if at all, by human rights considerations. When the citizen leaves the state to reside elsewhere in the EU, the state's control over the identity of the individual is modified by EU law.

Turning to the state's right to control the identity of its nationals in human rights law, the ECtHR considered a claim of a breach of the right to respect for private and family life, article 8, by a French couple who wished to give a name to their child which was rejected by the French authorities.[34] Under the law in force at the time, only specified names could be recognised by the authorities as acceptable for the purposes of official documents, including birth certificates. The family wished to give their child a name which was not specified and the state authorities refused to register the child's name as requested, instead giving the child another, permitted name. The ECtHR accepted that forenames are a means of identifying people within their families and communities and thus come within the ambit of family life, and as personal and emotional matters also come within the ambit of private life. However, the ECtHR found that as the family were permitted to use the preferred name for the

---

33 N Walker, 'Beyond the Unitary Conception of the United Kingdom Constitution?' PL 384 (2000) 394 et seq.
34 *Guillot v France* ECtHR 23 September 1996.

child in their private sphere and were only required to use the official name for public purposes, the interference with private and family life was not so severe as to constitute a breach of article 8. The ECtHR accepted that there could be a fundamental difference between an individual's public and private identity. So long as within the private sphere the individual is entitled to use his or her preferred (unofficial) name, the state is entitled to oblige the individual to accept an official identity consistent with its rules on names.

A somewhat different result was reached by the ECJ when faced with a similar question. A mixed nationality couple, one Spanish the other Belgian, who were resident in Belgium had two children. The children's surnames were registered by the Belgian authorities with their father's surname, Garcia Avello. However, the parents registered the children's surname at the Spanish Embassy in Belgium as Garcia Weber, incorporating the mother's surname as well as the father's. The parents then sought to change the Belgian registration of their children's surnames to correspond to that accepted by the Spanish authorities. The Belgian authorities refused on the basis of national law. The parents appealed against the refusal, *inter alia* on the basis that it constituted a breach of their (and the children's) rights as citizens of the Union. Eventually the Belgian Conseil d'État referred the matter to the ECJ.[35] It is interesting to note that in a case which seems rather state specific, in fact two Member States, Denmark and the Netherlands, intervened to support Belgium.

The first issue which the ECJ dealt with was whether the matter was wholly internal to one Member State and thus outside its jurisdiction. Although the children were dual Belgian/Spanish nationals and had been born in Belgium and had never lived anywhere else, the ECJ found that the situation did come within its competence. On the merits of the case, the ECJ found that "although, as Community law stands at present, the rules governing a person's surname are matters coming within the competence of the Member States, the latter must none the less, when exercising that competence comply with Community law ... in particular the Treaty provisions on the freedom of every citizen of the Union to move and reside in the territory of the Member States."[36] Therefore, Belgium was prohibited from restricting the effects of the grant of nationality of another Member State by imposing an additional condition for recognition of that nationality with a view to the exercise of Community rights. In effect, the ECJ held that the different treatment of dual Belgian/Spanish nationals resident in Belgium as regards their registered names in comparison with Spanish nationals resident in Belgium without the handicap of dual nationality constitutes discrimination in the enjoyment of citizenship rights and thus is contrary to EU law. While the reasoning of the judgment leaves much to be desired (not least because the ECJ found direct discrimination on the basis of nationality and then went on to consider justifications) it is important regarding the state's right to

---

35 C-148/02 *Avello* judgment 2 October 2003.
36 C-148/02 *Avello* judgment 2 October 2003.

"appropriate" children as its citizens and thus to submit them to its laws on names. The fact that the children are within the territorial border of the state and within the bureaucratic border of the state (i.e. citizens) does not necessarily permit the state to apply its laws on names to them. Where the parents object and are able to claim an alternative system of naming for their children on the basis of their relationship with another Member State, their right as citizens of the Union rather than as citizens of the state gives them the option to choose. The state's property interest in the children is diminished though the children's relationship with the border remains unchanged.

Borders, States and Resource Extraction

The disputed border of the EU's internal market also reveals another important feature of its position between or around the state and the citizen. It may be useful to return to Torpey's border for a moment: the need to define the border and control it arises from the purpose of the modern state to protect the territory and the people. So long as the border remains a border of sovereignty for the purposes of resources, the state is still recognisable as the source of protection. The UK, a Member State with a reputation for tending its sovereignty garden with particular assiduity, has highlighted in its White Paper on the Inter-Governmental Conference 2003 the centrality of resources to sovereignty. The UK government confirmed that it would place taxation and social security among the issues of greatest importance for it in the discussions and in respect of which it would not move towards greater EU competence.

One of the central interests of the state is the extraction of resources. The consolidation of territory depends on a successful system for financing the project. The mechanisms for resource extraction engage the people who are on the territory. If one considers briefly that first documented expression of dissatisfaction with the King, the Magna Charta in 1215, by far the vast majority of the demands of the barons against the King relate to practices of resource extraction which the King had been exercising and which the barons considered illegitimate. Of course, the majority of the resource extraction systems challenged in the Magna Charta are historically bound (it takes a leap of the imagination to understand demand 7 – no one shall perform a greater service for a knight's fee than is due therefrom). The modern European state relies on taxation of individuals, natural and legal,[37] to finance their policies.[38] As tax authorities are well aware, the greatest chance of success of the

---

37 A breakdown of taxes and social contributions by economic category of the tax base in the EU indicates that labour accounted for 23.8% of GDP and capital accounted for 7.4% of GDP on average across the EU in 1997. European Commission, *Tax Policy in the European Union*, Brussels 2000 p 27.

38 The European Commission expressed this as "Taxation is central to national sovereignty, for without revenue governments cannot conduct policy." European Commission, *Tax Policy in the European Union*, Brussels 2000 p 3.

state to acquire funds is to act at the place of greatest weakness of property rights. When money is in motion, at the point of transfer there will be a moment when it has left the ownership of one individual before it arrives at the other. It is here, whether temporally or figuratively, that the state usually exercises its taxation power. Thus movement of money (or liquid resources) rather than the nationality of individuals is central to effective tax collection. For example, the successful assessment of tax on wages depends on cooperation with employers. Personal taxation accounted for between 23% of GDP in Denmark to 6.5% in Greece over the period.[39] In other economic exchanges, tax is assessed at the place where the goods or services and the money change hands. The EU tax, value added tax, applies in the second circumstance. All the machinery for the successful extraction of the tax, however, rests at the national level.[40] In any event, the nationality or immigration status of the taxpayer is irrelevant. Among EU Member States, indirect taxes in total accounted for between 17.5% of GDP in Luxembourg and 11.1% of GDP in Spain in 1997.[41] The third source of state income is social contributions.

In respect of their own citizens, EU states usually seek to extract taxes on all their income, irrespective of where it arises. This method depends on the control of the citizen and his or her identity. If the citizen is rooted in the state and engaged economically, socially or politically within the state, he or she may be coerced into providing information about income gained elsewhere and required to contribute a part of that income to the state. The principle of taxation on worldwide income can only operate where the state has a grip on the individual which is sufficiently strong as to create a reasonable possibility of extracting the resources. When citizens move, however, problems are created. The strength of the link of the individual to the state of citizenship is diminished and the capacity and legitimacy of the state of citizenship to extract and enjoy resources from the individual is challenged. Of course, international agreements among states help them retain control over their citizens' incomes. The EU has two directives in force concerning mutual assistance by the authorities in the field of direct and indirect taxation.[42]

Things may look somewhat different from the citizen's perspective. The national of one country who is receiving income in another country, in principle will be taxed twice on the same income if both sets of rules apply. The responsibility for the double tax burden can be presented as the result of the individual's choice to move. Movement, in itself, may be undesirable from the state's perspective as regards taxation. However, where the individual moves between states with linked economies and strong trading relationships pressure from the private sector is put on

---

39 European Commission, *Tax Policy in the European Union*, Brussels 2000 p 24.
40 The comment here is not intended to underestimate the problems and issues which arise in VAT. The Commission proposed a directive to replace the VAT directive (COM (2003) 397 final) which addressed in the explanatory memorandum a wide variety of issues to be resolved.
41 European Commission, *Tax Policy in the European Union*, Brussels 2000 p 10.
42 Directives 79/1070 and 92/12.

the states to rationalise their resource extraction. Thus double taxation treaties between European states seek to resolve the conflict between states as to which is entitled to tax income – on the basis of the source or citizenship. At the EU level little has been done on this front other than a proposal for a directive on taxation of savings income which would ensure a minimum level of taxation on interest income paid in each Member State to individuals who are resident for tax purposes in another Member State.[43]

As citizens of the Union have a right to move and reside anywhere in the territory of the Union, a new tension as regards the rules of resource extraction comes into play.[44] If the individual has a right to move, is there a commensurate duty on the state to give relief in respect of double taxation? This problem has begun to trouble the ECJ in a series of cases relating to the tax consequences of the exercise of a right to free movement. Mr Gilly, a French national, and Mrs Gilly, a German national lived in France but Mrs Gilly worked in Germany as a civil servant. They were both assessed for taxes on income in France. However, under German law, civil servants working in Germany, even where resident in another state are liable to pay full taxes in Germany. A double taxation treaty between France and Germany which regulates the taxation of nationals resident in the other state otherwise on the basis of taxation in the country of residence is inapplicable to public sector work. Mrs Gilly was accordingly taxed in both countries on her income. The ECJ noted that although the Union has an objective of avoiding double taxation there has been no unifying or harmonising measure adopted for this purpose. On the question of discrimination, the ECJ refrained from attacking the taxation systems of either Member State, noting only that there were provisions for allocation of tax credits so that the individual circumstances of someone in the position of Mrs Gilly could be taken into account in assessing (i.e. reducing) her tax liability in one of the states.[45] The trepidation of the ECJ in this field has been the subject of comment elsewhere.[46]

As regards the issue of the EU border and the citizen, there is clearly a variable geometry at work. While a citizen of the Union has the right to live and work anywhere in the Union and the territorial borders of the Member States cannot be an obstacle, the borders of the legal orders of the Member States continue to apply. Thus as regards resource extraction, the Member States' legal orders are permitted to continue to hold the citizen on the basis of his or her nationality of the state after he or she has moved to another Member State. The Member State of the individual's residence is permitted to apply its territorial border to resource extraction from the same individual.

---

43 The final version following the Opinions of the Parliament and Economic and Social Committee is at OJ 2001 C 270 E.

44 A van der Mei, *Free Movement of Persons within the European Community: Cross Border Access to Public Benefits*, Hart, Oxford, 2003 pp 2–18.

45 C-336/96 *Gilly* [1998] ECR I-2793.

46 D Martin & E Guild, *Free Movement of Persons in the European Community*, Butterworths, London, 1996.

Borders and Protection – Identifying Rights Holders

In the preceding section I have examined the role of the border as regards how Member States identify and claim "their" people for the purposes of resource extraction. The other side of the coin is the provision of protection. The state also owes duty to provide protection.[47] Here the Member States are quite careful about who is included in the category of persons to whom the duty is owed. Only those persons whom the state has claimed and identified are eligible for the full benefit of systems of protection devised by the state. A clear example of this is in respect of social security. The majority of social security systems in Europe are organised around a mix of two principles – citizenship and contribution, the so-called Bismarkian principle, and residence, the so called Beveridge principle.[48] The EU is responsible for coordinating social security systems across the Union for the purpose of achieving free movement of persons.[49] However, the link between the right of the citizen to move across the EU borders and the right to claim social benefits is fragile. In an amended proposal for a directive on the right of citizens of the Union and their family members to move and reside freely within the territory of the Member States, the Council has inserted a new limitation on access of citizens of the Union to social benefits. Article 13a(1) provides that "Union citizens, other than workers, shall have a right of residence provided for in Article 6a, as long as they do not become a burden for the social assistance of the host Member State ... (2) An expulsion measure cannot be the automatic consequence of recourse to social assistance."[50] Thus while the Union citizen may be required to pay taxes he or she will not necessarily have access to social benefits if he or she is not a worker. The possibility of expulsion across the (uncontrolled) territorial border is the result of the citizen seeking to cross the "benefits" border. Here again, the border of free movement and the border of protection have a different geometry. I will return to the relationship of social protection and citizenship of the Union in chapter 3.

Conclusions

Citizenship and the right to move across borders are both intrinsically connected and oppositional in the EU. As Torpey contends, the categorization of individuals into

---

47 I will only consider here social protection to the exclusion of defence policy.
48 See also K Sieveking, 'The Significance of the Transborder Utilisation of Health Care Benefits for Migrants', M Sakslin 'The Concept of Residence and Social Security: Reflections on the Finnish, Swedish and Community Legislation' and P Minderhoud 'The Dutch Linking Act and the Violation of Various International Non-Discrimination Clauses', EJML 2 (2000) pp 143–201.
49 C-95/99 *Khalil* [2001] ECR I-7413.
50 Council Document 11807/03; 29 July 2003.

citizens and non-citizens is central to state formation: the fixing of the borders and the people. The relationship of the border and the citizen derives legitimacy from the principle that the state has responsibility for "its" people as regards extracting resources and providing protection. The success of both these operations depends on the identification of the citizens and the control of movement across borders both territorial and of legal orders. Citizenship of the Union presents a series of challenges to traditional thinking about the control of borders and their significance. The documentation on the basis of which the control of territorial borders is carried out, identity documents and passports, have taken on new characteristics. They are no longer systematically checked at the intra-Member State territorial borders (with notable exceptions) but they are central to the borders of the legal order – for instance checks within the territory, access to benefits. The Member States are no longer entitled to refuse to issue identity documents or passports to their citizens who wish to cross the borders (except on the basis of public policy, public security or public health) nor are they necessarily entitled to determine the identity of their citizens, for instance in the form of their names.

As regards resource extraction and allocation, the Member States' power to include in the case of the former and exclude in the case of the latter has become increasingly divorced from the territorial border. The right of the citizen to move across the border has not been accompanied by a right to pay taxes only once or a right to receive social benefits. In both cases the border of the bureaucratic state has adjusted to include or exclude individuals irrespective of the territorial border.

Chapter 2

Citizenship of the Union

The category of "citizen" is defined in relation to a border of sovereignty, providing the central tool to differentiate between the citizen and the foreigner. Citizenship of the Union presents certain challenges to this view of the citizen and the state, not least as it is a citizenship which does not attach to a state and which guarantees the citizen rights across a number of borders of sovereignty. In the two chapters which follow this one, I consider the legal nature of citizenship of the Union in light of two influential citizenship theorists, T H Marshall and J Habermas. First, however, it is necessary to examine the rights of citizens of the Union as contained in the treaty/Constitution.

Creating Citizenship

Child of the 1993 Maastricht Treaty, citizenship of the Union has been the subject of intense legal and political debate even before it came into existence.[1] Article 17 EC began the section with a resounding claim: "Citizenship of the Union is hereby established." This idea of a new citizenship was not welcomed by all the people of Europe with resounding enthusiasm. In order to enter into force the Maastricht Treaty had to be ratified by all Member States some of which were required to poll their citizens in a referendum on their views. When Denmark held its first referendum on the Treaty on 2 June 1992, a "no" vote succeeded with 50.7%. It is somewhat problematic for the principle of liberal democracy for a state's government to act

---

1   S O'Leary, *The Evolving Concept of Community Citizenship*, Kluwer Law International, the Hague, 1996; Weiner also plots the history of the concept of citizenship of the Union finding its antecedents, *inter alia*, in the Addonino Report to the European Parliament of 1984 A Wiener, *"European" Citizenship Practice: Building Institutions of a Non-State*, Westview, Boulder, 1999.

explicitly contrary to the will of the people after they have been asked their opinion in a referendum. Thus although a second referendum would be required, before this could take place a compromise towards the concerns of the Danish people had to be found. Denmark presented a document to the Edinburgh Council Meeting 12 December 1992 where it noted seven points central to the negative vote, *inter alia* citizenship of the Union on which it sought compromises.[2] The Council adopted a decision which sought to address the issues of Denmark including citizenship of the Union, stressing that citizenship of the Union in no way takes the place of national citizenship and "the question whether an individual possesses the nationality of a Member State will be settled solely by reference to the national law of the Member State concerned."[3] This decision was supplemented by a four paragraph unilateral declaration by Denmark which commences: "citizenship of the Union is a political and legal concept which is entirely different from the concept of citizenship within the meaning of the Constitution of the Kingdom of Denmark and of the Danish legal system." A second referendum held in May 1993 succeeded with 53.2% of votes in favour of ratifying the Treaty. In November 1993 the Maastricht Treaty came into force and citizenship of the Union came into existence.

Citizenship Versus Multiple Citizenship?

Notwithstanding the vehement reaction of the Danes to the concept, what is surprising as Shaw has noted, as regards the 1993 provisions on citizenship is just how limited the rights of citizens are.[4] At the national level, citizenship is attached to the idea of constitutional settlements which, by and large, consist of the nuts and bolts of the legitimacy of governance, branches of government, division of powers, means of selection of rulers etc. and the rights of the citizen. The French constitutionalist, Badinter, expresses this idea rather elegantly: constitutions are the expression of a certain idea of political power which finds its legitimacy in its founding principles.[5] In order to seek to understand this citizenship of a non-state, I will examine the provisions as originally inserted into the EC Treaty in light of citizenship norms which were developing simultaneously within the Council of Europe. I will also seek

---

2 The most important issue, according to the Danish Government, was economic and monetary union in respect of which an opt out for Denmark was negotiated. Danish opposition to monetary union has continued. A referendum on whether to join monetary union was held there on 28 September 2000. On this occasion 53% of the Danish people voted no (Denmark in the EU www.eu2002.dk).

3 Conclusions of the Presidency: Edinburgh 12 December 1992, Annex I: Decision of the Heads of State and Government, Meeting within the European Council, Concerning Certain Problems Raised by Denmark on the Treaty on European Union.

4 J Shaw, *Citizenship of the Union: Towards Post-National Membership?* Jean Monnet Working Paper, Jean Monnet Center, NYU School of Law, New York, June 1997.

5 R Badinter, *Une constitution européene*, Fayard, Paris, 2002.

to place the issue of citizenship of the Union and in particular the EU constitution's treatment of citizenship rights in the wider framework of international human rights conventions.

After declaring its existence, EU citizenship provision states: "Every person holding the nationality of a Member State shall be a citizen of the Union. Citizenship of the Union shall complement and not replace national citizenship. Citizenship of the Union complements but does not replace national citizenship." This means that from the entry into force of the Maastricht Treaty all nationals of the Member States have two citizenships – that of their Member State and that of the Union. At this point the difference between citizenship and nationality is important. To what extent is it the same thing to have two citizenships or nationalities? There is no clear answer to this question in international law.[6] A detailed analysis of citizenship policies which engaged many of the foremost experts in the field uses the two terms interchangeably.[7] In so far as the terms citizenship and nationality may be used to express the same concept, citizenship of the Union gives every citizen of a Member State a second citizenship.

As Aleinikoff and Klusmeyer point out, there is a global hostility to dual citizenship.[8] In Europe this has been expressed in the Council of Europe's Convention on the Reduction of Cases of Multiple Nationality and on Military Obligations in Cases of Multiple Nationality 1963. The principle of the convention is found in article 1(1) – nationals of the parties who acquire of their own free will the nationality of another party shall lose their former nationality. "They shall not be authorised to retain their former nationality." Of the 25 Member States, 12 had signed and ratified the convention, one had only signed (Portugal) and 12 have done nothing. Of those, 10 are new Member States,[9] only Finland and Greece among the pre-2004 Member States have not signed the convention.[10] Thus there was a fairly wide consensus among EU states that the convention was valuable.[11] As an increase in transnational contacts and family formation took place in the years following the signature of the convention, it became increasingly difficult to police the system. Aleinikoff and Klusmeyer consider that over recent decades (including following the

---

6   See chapter 1 where I consider the two terms.

7   "Historically, state laws and practices have varied widely, yet citizenship regimes of liberal democracies have generally featured the following elements: birthright citizenship, routes to citizenship through naturalisation, disfavour of dual nationality, and policies that limit certain rights to citizens." T Aleinikoff and D Klusmeyer, *Citizenship Policies for an Age of Migration*, Carnegie Endowment for International Peace, Washington, 2002 p 2.

8   T Aleinikoff and D Klusmeyer, *Citizenship Policies for an Age of Migration*, Carnegie Endowment for International Peace, Washington, 2002 p 22.

9   The Czech Republic, Cyprus, Estonia, Hungary, Latvia, Lithuania, Malta, Poland, Slovakia and Slovenia.

10 Council of Europe: http://conventions.coe.int/Treaty/EN/searching.asp?NT=043 as at 11 November 2003.

11 This is notwithstanding the fact that among the states which had signed and ratified are a number which permit multiple nationality without restraint such as Ireland and the UK.

opening of the convention for signature) "[n]ew practices that tolerate or foster dual nationality, however, have sprung up without close scrutiny or without systematic attention to the full implications of the changed practices."[12] In Europe at least, the lack of scrutiny or attention can certainly not be laid at the feet of the Council of Europe.

In reaction to these developments and in light of the intention of the convention, the Council of Europe adopted, in 1977, a protocol to it, providing that parties inform one another wherever a national of one party acquires the nationality of another. The objective of the protocol was to give the parties to the convention the power to regulate these practices through a common obligation of information. However, by November 2003 only five Member States had signed and ratified the protocol,[13] a further three had signed but not ratified,[14] while 15 had done nothing.[15] Of those Member States which have ratified the protocol, the vast majority did so in the 1970s and 1980s. In the 1990s only Belgium ratified (1991) and since then Sweden is the only Member State to ratify it (in 2002). Thus interest among the Member States to exchange information on the multiple nationality practices of their citizens (or persons about to become such) appears to be quite limited.

In February 1993 (slightly more than eight months before the entry into force of the Maastricht Treaty and the creation of citizenship of the Union) the Council of Europe adopted a further protocol to the convention reversing the principle against dual nationality. It inserted the following wording into article 1: "where a national of a Contracting Party acquires the nationality of another Contracting Party on whose territory either he was born and is resident, or has been ordinarily resident for a period of time beginning before the age of 18, each of these Parties may provide that he retains the nationality of origin." Clearly, the objects of this protocol are the children of Europe's migrant workers of the 1960s and 1970s who arrived at a young age or were born in their parents host state. These young people have been the subject of a wide variety of legal measures regarding their residence at national level[16] and a whole class of human rights challenges before the ECtHR (see chapter 7). As a side issue, the risk that in the event that citizenship of the Union became a "real" nationality it would conflict with the principle of the Council of Europe convention was in theory diminished. In any event, the EU Member States have yet to show any enthusiasm for the protocol. 22 have neither signed nor ratified it. The only three which have done so are France, Italy and the Netherlands.

---

12 T Aleinikoff and D Klusmeyer, *Citizenship Policies for an Age of Migration*, Carnegie Endowment for International Peace, Washington, 2002 p 22.
13 Belgium, Denmark, Luxembourg, Netherlands, Spain, Sweden and the UK.
14 France, Germany and Portugal.
15 http://conventions.coe.int/Treaty/EN/searching.asp?NT=095&CM=8&DF=.
16 K Groenendijk, E Guild and H Dogan, *Security of Residence of Long Term Migrants: A comparative study of law and practice in European countries*, Council of Europe (English and French) Strasbourg, 1998.

The attention of the Council of Europe to the field but from a completely different perspective reinforces the impression that citizenship of the Union was not intended or seen by the Member States as constituting a "real" citizenship. Although Denmark was moved to spell this out in a declaration (see above) the others considered it implicit in the provision. Indeed, a number of EU states which retain the principle against dual nationality, such as Austria, Germany and Sweden were not perturbed by the acquisition of a second citizenship (that of the Union) by their nationals.[17] Nor are they the Member States which have signed and ratified the protocols to the Council of Europe convention. No doubt the fact that acquisition and loss of the citizenship are controlled through the national citizenship is central to this complacency.

Acquisition and Loss

The rules of acquisition and loss of citizenship of the Union rest firmly with the Member States, according to the Edinburgh Declaration of 1992. It stressed that whether an individual possesses the nationality of a Member State or not is a matter to be settled exclusively by the state concerned in accordance with its national law.[18] As I have noted in chapter 1, these rules differ substantially among the Member States – from a system of ius sanguinis only recently amended to include an element of residence in Germany to a system of almost pure ius soli in Ireland where birth on the territory is sufficient to confer citizenship.[19] However, this does not mean that Member States are unencumbered by international obligations in respect of acquisition and loss of citizenship. In fact the Member States have been particularly active in limiting their power to determine acquisition and loss rules through international commitments.

The acquisition and loss of citizenship has troubled the international community, in particular at the end of each of the world wars. After the first war, within the context of the League of Nations, two measures were adopted in 1930. First, the Convention on Certain Questions relating to the Conflict of Nationality Laws 1930 sought to resolve a series of outstanding issues in particular regarding the nationality of women and children. As recognition of an independent legal status for women became widespread, so rules on their automatic acquisition and loss of citizenship on marriage became unacceptable. The convention sought to protect the nationality status of women from the negative effects of citizenship laws which confer on or

---

17 See T Aleinikoff and D Klusmeyer, *Citizenship Policies for an Age of Migration*, Carnegie Endowment for International Peace, Washington, 2002 p 28.

18 Conclusions of the Presidency: Edinburgh 12 December 1992, Annex I: Decision of the Heads of State and Government, Meeting within the European Council, Concerning Certain Problems Raised by Denmark on the Treaty on European Union.

19 B Nascimbene, *Nationality Laws in the European Union*, Butterworths/Giuffre, London/Milan, 1996 pp 1–20.

deprive them of nationality on the basis of their husband's status. Secondly, the convention contains provisions to regulate the citizenship of children, whether legitimate or illegitimate, with a view to diminishing their risk of being stateless. A second 1930 measure, a Protocol relating to a certain case of statelessness in 1930, provides for a child born to a woman with the nationality of the state of birth to acquire that citizenship where the child's father is either without nationality or of unknown nationality. After World War II, statelessness was again a substantial issue resulting in two conventions within the United Nations, one in 1954 and a second one in 1961 (which only limped into force in 1975) both aimed at reducing the incidence of statelessness. Married women were again the subject of their own convention in 1957. The common feature of all these measures is that they aim to set a threshold for acquisition and loss of citizenship in the international community. Specific focus on stateless persons resulted from concern about displaced persons who were excluded from participation in any community because of a lack of belonging to anyone. Women and children were the subject of specific measures as a result of the gradual individualisation of members of a family as separate legal entities distinction from the adult male considered to be the head of the family.

While the 1930 convention enjoyed limited support in Europe with seven signatures from the current Member States[20] out of a total of 19 signatories, the Protocol of the same year was even less successful, only France, Germany, Italy and the UK signed up out of a total of 6 parties. Some of the post WWII conventions have been somewhat more successful: the convention on the Nationality of Married Women has been the most popular with 70 parties. Among the Member States, 15 have ratified it,[21] (one Member State, the Netherlands, ratified and then denounced the convention in 1993) a further two, Belgium and Portugal, signed but have not ratified.[22] The 1954 statelessness convention comes next in popularity with 49 parties of which the Member States account for 15[23] while in respect of the 1961 stateless convention, out of 26 parties 11 are Member States though France has only signed and not ratified the convention.[24] Thus when the EU Council declared the sovereignty of the Member States as regards acquisition and loss of citizenship, it failed to note that this sovereignty of many had already been restricted by international commitments. A new rush to limit sovereignty as regards acquisition and loss of citizenship resulted from the crumbling and ultimate demise of the USSR and serious concerns of a new age of statelessness in Europe.

---

20 Belgium, Cyprus, Malta, the Netherlands, Poland, Sweden and the UK.
21 Austria, Cyprus, the Czech Republic, Denmark, Finland, Germany, Hungary, Ireland, Latvia, Luxembourg, (the Netherlands signed ratified and then denounced the convention effective from 16 January 1993), Poland, Slovakia, Slovenia, Sweden and the UK.
22 UN Website: as at 5 February 2002.
23 Belgium, Denmark, Finland, France, Germany, Greece, Ireland, Italy, Latvia, Luxembourg, the Netherlands, Slovenia, Spain, Sweden and the UK.
24 The other Member States are: Austria, the Czech Republic, Denmark, Germany, Ireland, Latvia, the Netherlands, Slovakia, Sweden and the UK.

In the context of the Council of Europe, steps towards a common system of acquisition and loss of citizenship began in the 1970s (again with the rights of women and children at the forefront) in the form of resolutions and recommendations from the Committee of Ministers and the Parliamentary Assembly.[25] 1989 changed the discussion. By 1993 a committee was charged with preparing a draft text for a European Convention on Nationality. The push for such a convention came directly from the need for the new democracies in Central and Eastern Europe and succession states of the former Yugoslavia and USSR to draft nationality laws. Concern to avoid statelessness and to protect the rights of persons habitually resident on the territories were crucial. The resulting convention was opened for signature in 1997 (thus post-dates citizenship of the Union). At article 4 it sets out the principles of nationality of which there are four:

1. Everyone has the right to a nationality;
2. Statelessness shall be avoided;
3. No one shall be arbitrarily deprived of his or her nationality;
4. Neither marriage nor the dissolution of a marriage between a nation of a State party and an alien, nor the change of nationality by one of the spouses during marriage, shall automatically affect the nationality of the other spouse.

In these principles are found the core obligations regarding acquisition and loss of citizenship which had begun their development with the 1930 convention. The Council of Europe convention goes on to provide a set of minimum rules on acquisition of nationality: children acquire the nationality of their parent(s) subject to limitations; foundlings and children who would otherwise be stateless acquire the nationality of the state where found or born; there must be rules permitting the naturalisation of persons lawfully and habitually resident on the territory for ten years (maximum); states must facilitate acquisition of nationality for: spouses of their nationals, children of their nationals, persons born and residing on the territory or who have been residing before the age of 18, stateless persons and refugees.[26]

Article 7 of the convention limits states' powers regarding loss of nationality: "A State Party may not provide in its internal law for the loss of its nationality *ex lege* or at the initiative of the State Party ..." except as set out in the sub-paragraphs (a)–(g). These include voluntary acquisition of another nationality; fraudulent acquisition; voluntary service in a foreign military force; conduct seriously prejudicial to the state's vital interests; lack of a genuine link where a national is habitually

---

25 Explanatory Memorandum to the European Convention on Nationality 1997, http://coe.int.Treaty/en/Reports/Html/166.htm.
26 Article 34 UN Convention relating to the status of refugees 1951 (and its 1967 Protocol) requires the Member States, all of whom are signatories, to facilitate the assimilation and naturalisation of refugees. This includes expedition of applications and a reduction as far as possible of charges and costs.

living abroad; where children no longer fulfil the requirements; adoption of a child where it acquires another nationality as a result.

By 11 November 2003, 17 Member States had signed the convention and seven had ratified it.[27] This is fairly impressive in view of the fact that the convention was only opened for signature in 1997. Eight Member States have not yet committed themselves to the convention.[28] The question which is raised by this activity to limit sovereignty regarding citizenship is the extent to which it has or may have consequences for citizenship of the Union. I shall return to this question in chapter 4 from a different perspective when considering the jurisprudence of the ECtHR and ECJ on Member State citizenship. Suffice it here to note that the ECJ has held that a Member State can define the concept of "national only if it has due regard to Community law."[29] However, Community law includes fundamental rights which form an integral part of Community law. In its search for these fundamental rights, the ECJ has had regard to other conventions which the Member States have signed and ratified (indeed, even to treaties which not all Member States have ratified). It is not impossible that the Convention on Nationality may, in due course and on further signature and ratification by Member States, take a place as an aid to the interpretation of the lawfulness of acquisition and loss of citizenship of the Union.

Rights and Duties

Article 17(2) EC/article I-10(2) EU Constitution provides that "Citizens of the Union shall enjoy the rights conferred by this Treaty and shall be subject to the duties imposed thereby." The rights which the citizen of the Union has by virtue of that citizenship apply only when he or she is outside his or her Member State of underlying citizenship. Citizenship of the Union provides to individuals rights which are not applicable on the national territory of their citizenship. Thus the retention of the source of national rights comes only from national citizenship. This will become clear as we consider the rights in more detail. As Finer, points out, the principle of rights and duties is deeply rooted in constitutional settlements.[30] Considering the constitutions of five countries – USA, USSR, Germany, France and the UK Finer notes that the recital of the rights tends to be easier than that of the duties. Even the rights are by no means clear. Bellamy provides one explanation why this may be

---

27 Those which have ratified are: Austria, Denmark, Hungary, the Netherlands, Portugal, Slovakia and Sweden; those which have signed but not yet ratified are: the Czech Republic, Finland, Germany, Greece, Ireland, Italy, Latvia, Malta and Poland.

28 Belgium, Cyprus, Estonia, Lithuania, Luxembourg, Slovenia, Spain and the UK.

29 C-360/90 *Micheletti* [1992] ECR I-4239.

30 See S E Finer, *Five Constitutions: Contrasts and Comparisons*, Penguin, Middlesex, 1979, pp 82–86.

when he divides citizenship into juridical, which defines citizenship by rights, and political, defined by the mechanisms by which the negotiation of what is the political take place.[31] The juridical approach leads to clearly defined rights which in turn give an advantage to the judicial branch which is responsible for their interpretation; the political approach is less clear on the wording of rights, instead specifying the political structures within which disputes are negotiated and thus privilege parliaments.

When one looks in detail at the rights in EU law, these rights are generally either applicable to all persons on the territory (such as to the abolition of sex discrimination or the protection of working conditions) or are acquired by nationals of the Member States only when they move from one Member State to another as in respect of the right to free movement of workers, of establishment or provision and receipt of services. Even where citizenship of a Member State was not a specific requirement of EU law for the enjoyment of a free movement right for economic purposes (i.e. workers), the Court of Justice found it to be an implicit requirement.[32]

The EU Constitution highlights the tension of rights held by virtue of being within the jurisdiction and rights which are dependent on citizenship of the Union. In Title II, Fundamental Rights and Citizenship of the Union, article I-9 provides that the Union shall recognise the rights in the Charter which constitutes Part II of the Constitution. In any event, it goes on to specify, the ECHR rights are fundamental rights for the purposes of EU law and constitute general principles thereof. Article I-10 then sets out the citizenship rights (to which I shall return one by one below). Part II of the Constitution incorporates the EU Charter of fundamental rights and at articles II-99–106 and sets out the rights of the citizens of the Union. However, articles II-101–104 apply not only to citizens of the Union but also to "every person" or "any natural or legal person." Thus article II-101 provides that "every person" has the right to good administration; II-102 provides that "any citizen of the Union, and any natural or legal person residing or having its registered office in a Member State" has a right of access to documents; II-103 gives the same group a right to the services of the European Ombudsman; II-104 assures the right to petition the European Parliament to this same group. Thus only the electoral rights, free movement and residence and diplomatic and consular protection are actually limited to citizens of the Union only. Articles II-69–72 provide powers to adopt legislation to give effect to the Part I rights.

---

31   R Bellamy, 'Constitutive Citizenship versus Constitutional Rights: Republican Reflections on the EU Charter and the Human Rights Act' in T Campbell, D Ewing and A Tomkins, *Sceptical Essays on Human Rights*, OUP, Oxford, 2001 pp 17–39.
32   C-230/97 *Awoyemi* [1998] ECR I-6781.

The Right to Move and Reside

Article 18 EC provides the first right: "Every citizen of the Union shall have the right to move and reside freely within the territory of the Member States, subject to the limitations and conditions laid down in this Treaty and by the measures adopted to give it effect." In the EU Constitution this changes slightly in that article I-10(2) first indent provides the right and article I-10(3) sets out the limitations "these rights shall be exercised in accordance with the conditions and limits defined by the Constitution and by the measures adopted to give it effect."[33] The right to move and reside presents most clearly the tension inherent in citizenship of the Union. Is it a citizenship of one territory, that of the European Union, or an immigration status that permits the crossing of sovereign borders? The right to move and reside as a territorially bounded right is clearly expressed in international human rights law regarding the interior space of a state. Article 12 International Covenant of Civil and Political Rights 1966 provides that "everyone lawfully within the territory of a State shall, within that territory, have the right to liberty of movement and freedom to choose his residence." Restrictions are only permissible where provided by law, necessary to protect national security, public order, public health or morals or the rights and freedoms of others and are consistent with the other rights contained in the ICCPR. What is a right to everyone lawfully within a territory in international human rights law becomes a right for citizens of the Union within the territory of the Member States. Thus the position of the citizen of the Union is assimilated to the position of any human being, including the foreigner, in international human rights law.

If the territory of the Union is that of all the Member States and the nationals of the Member States are citizens of the Union, one might argue that the citizen must have an unrestricted right to move and reside within the EU. This would be consistent with the Human Rights Committee's interpretation of article 12 ICCPR: "Everyone lawfully within the territory of a State enjoys, within that territory, the right to move freely and to choose his or her place of residence. In principle, citizens of a State are always lawfully within the territory of that State."[34] Thus the scope of permissible restrictions on the movement within a state of its citizens cannot include, at least in principle, a legal regime which permits the citizen's presence to be unlawful *per* se. Citizenship of the Union may be criticised as lacking a fundamental quality in this regard. The early jurisprudence on citizenship of the ECJ has indicated that the right to enter any part of the territory of which one is a national is not a right attendant on citizenship of the Union.[35] These citizens can still be expelled from one Member State on the basis that they are nationals of another Member State and have offended

---

33 The limitations on the right of free movement are considered in depth in chapter 5.
34 UN Human Rights Committee General Comment No 27(67), 2 November 1999.
35 C-348/96 *Calfa* [1999] ECR I-11.

against the Member State of residence's sensibilities regarding public policy, public security and public health.[36]

Article 18(2) EC/article III-125 EU Constitution provides a power to the Community to take measures to achieve the right of free movement. Nonetheless, the right is directly effective according to the ECJ in *Baumbast* (a case to which I will return later in chapter 6).[37] In that case the ECJ found the provision sufficiently clear, precise and unconditional to regulate the relations of the individual and the state directly. In 2001 the Commission proposed a directive to give effect to the rights of citizens of the Union.[38] The proposal takes as its starting place the existing secondary legislation on free movement of persons and seeks to rationalise and consolidate it. For example, different family reunification rules exist for different categories of migrant citizens of the Union. The proposal would provide uniformity. It would abolish the duty on migrant citizens of the Union to obtain residence permits issued by the host Member State. Thus the control of the host state over the identification of persons on the territory would be diminished. The Commission proposed that power of the Member States to expel would also be curtailed where the individual has lived four years or more in a host Member State.[39]

Finally in article 18(3) EC/EU Constitution III-125(2) a protection for the national competence in respect of identity documents and social security is reserved: "Paragraph 2 shall not apply to provisions on passports, identity cards, residence permits or any other such document or to provisions on social security or social protection." The harmonisation of the appearance of passports has been achieved though non-binding measures which have been applied by the Member States. Identity cards remain as different as the legislation of the Member States can devise. Though agreement has been reached on a common residence permit for third country nationals (see chapter 9). Thus it would appear that identity documents for citizens is a more sensitive sovereignty issue for the Member States than residence documents for third country nationals even where those permits have the same legal effect of confirming identity and residence status as identity documents. This sensitivity about identity documents appears to support Torpey's thesis regarding the importance of passports and identity documents to the formation and existence of modern states. He argues that there is a fundamental necessity of the nation state to be able to identify its nationals and exclude the nationals of other states in order to protect only those from whom it has extracted resources in order to provide protection.[40] The fact that the Member States excluded the EU from this field may indicate sovereignty concerns.

---

36   C-348/96 *Calfa* [1999] ECR I-11.

37   C-413/99 *Baumbast* [2002] ECR I-7091.

38   COM (2001) 257 final of 23 May 2001.

39   For a critical view of the proposal see the Immigration Law Practitioners Association Response to proposed EC Directive on the Rights of Citizens of the Union and their Family Members www.ilpa.org.uk/submissions/reunion.htm.

40   J Torpey, *The Invention of the Passport*, Cambridge University Press, Cambridge, 2000.

Social security and social protection are dealt with elsewhere in the EC Treaty – at article 42 EC/article III-136 EU Constitution and in the implementing legislation of article 39 EC/article III-133 EU Constitution – free movement of workers. Thus the exclusion of this field from citizenship of the Union can be seen as a protection of the competence in another part of the Treaty. It can also be seen as an attempt to exclude the principle of equality of treatment among citizens from the sensitive area of the re-distribution of resources. One of the most contentious forms of protection which the state provides is this social form. I shall return to this aspect in the next chapter when looking at T H Marshall and the development of citizenship theory and the jurisprudence of the European Court of Justice.

Political Rights

Article 19(1) and (2) EC/article I-10(2) indent 2 EU Constitution provide the rules for political participation of citizens of the Union:

"1. Every citizen of the Union residing in a Member State of which he is not a national shall have the right to vote and to stand as a candidate at municipal elections in the Member State in which he resides, under the same conditions as nationals of that State. This right shall be exercised subject to detailed arrangements adopted by the Council, acting unanimously on a proposal from the Commission and after consulting the European Parliament; these arrangements may provide for derogations where warranted by problems specific to a Member State."

"2. Without prejudice to Article 190(4) and to the provisions adopted for its implementation, every citizen of the Union residing in a Member State of which he is not a national shall have the right to vote and to stand as a candidate in elections to the European Parliament in the Member State in which he resides, under the same conditions as nationals of that State. This right shall be exercised subject to detailed arrangements adopted by the Council acting unanimously on a proposal from the Commission and after consulting the European Parliament; these arrangements may provide for derogations where warranted by problems specific to a Member State."

When inserted into the Constitution this has become "Citizens of the Union shall enjoy the rights and be subject to the duties provided for in the Constitution. They shall have ... the right to vote and to stand as candidates in elections to the European Parliament and in municipal elections in their Member State of residence, under the same conditions as nationals of that State;"

The implementing measures for the two aspects of voting rights – municipal and European Parliament have been adopted by the Council Directive 93/109 regarding the European Parliament and Directive 94/80 concerning municipal elections. It is worth noting that the right is limited to the electoral rights to two levels – municipal and European Parliament – which leaves the national level limited to nationals of the state (or otherwise as the state itself may chose). Article 25 ICCPR recognises and protects the right of every citizen to vote and be elected within their state. Should citizenship of the Union comply with this requirement as a "genuine" citizenship, then access to political rights at the national level would also be required. In General Comment 25 adopted in 1996, the UN High Commissioner for Human Rights clarified article 25 as follows "No distinctions are permitted between citizens in the enjoyment of these rights on the grounds of race, colour, sex, language, religion, political or other opinion, national or social origin, property, birth or other status." To exclude citizens of the Union resident outside their Member State of nationality from voting rights at the national level would appear to constitute discrimination on the basis of national origin.

The creation of a right to vote at the municipal level created substantial controversy and challenge in Belgium and France on the ground that mayors play an important constitutional role at the national level.[41] The concepts of electorates and citizens are not necessarily the same but in traditional constitutional theory electorates include all citizens meeting the criteria (e.g. age, residence etc.).[42] In the context of citizenship of the Union, this overlap is not complete – the citizen of the Union can only exercise electoral rights when outside his or her country of nationality. The exercise of electoral rights within the state of nationality are not regulated in any way by the treaty. The Commission has produced three reports on citizenship of the Union, the most recent in 2001.[43] The 1994 European Parliament elections were the first where citizens of the Union resident outside their Member State of nationality could vote in the Member State where they lived. Only 5.9% of those eligible did so. The 1999 European Parliament elections saw an increase on that figure to 9%. The Commission suggests that the very low turn out rate is the result of lack of interest in two Member States with large numbers of resident citizens of the Union who are not nationals, France and Germany. Apparently if the apathetic response of citizens of the Union in those two states is taken out of the equation for the first election the participation rate would jump to 17.3%. No information is provided about participation of citizens of the Union in municipal elections. It would appear that the effort to incorporate a form of democratic legitimacy into citizenship of the Union has not, so far, proven terribly attractive to its subjects.[44]

Whether foreigners should have a right to vote and stand for election in municipal elections had been under discussion for some time in the Council of Europe before citizenship of the Union was introduced. In 1992 the Council of Europe opened for

---

41 C-232/97 *Commission v Belgium* [1998] ECR I-4281.
42 S E Finer, ibid p 68 et seq.
43 COM (2001) 506 final 7 September 2001.
44 Another explanation may be that the registration requirements of Member States for citizens of the Union from elsewhere are sufficiently onerous as to act as an obstacle to the exercise of the right.

signature a convention on the participation of foreigners in public life at the local level. The specific reasons for the convention, according to the preamble, are three:

1. Foreigners on the national territory are a permanent feature of European societies;
2. Foreign residents have the same duties as citizens at local level;
3. The active participation of foreigners in the life of a local community contributes to prosperity, improves integration and enhances the possibilities of participation in local public affairs.

The convention has a fairly complex structure of which chapter C is of particular interest. Article 6 in chapter C provides for parties which opt into it to grant foreign residents the right to vote and stand for election in local authority elections on the same requirements as nationals after five years residence on the territory. There is an exception at article 7 for the right to stand for election should a signatory state wish to limit the right and there are exceptions in respect of emergencies provided for in article 9. The convention provides in chapters A and B for association rights and consultative bodies for foreigners. Among the 25 EU Member States, four have ratified the convention[45] and a further three have signed it.[46] This can hardly be said to constitute overwhelming support for the convention after ten years. Nonetheless, the principle of chapter C of the convention – the right for foreigners to vote at the local level, became one of the political rights of citizens of the Union.

Diplomatic Protection

Article 20 EC/article I-10(2)(b) EU Constitution provides that "every citizen of the Union shall, in the territory of a third country in which the Member State of which he is a national is not represented, be entitled to protection by the diplomatic or consular authorities of any Member State, on the same conditions as the nationals of that State. States shall establish the necessary rules among themselves and state the international negotiations required to secure this protection." This is particularly interesting from the perspective of state formation. What the Union is seeking to do here is to impose on the international state system recognition of the right of citizenship for its nationals. Thus the diplomatic representations of the Member States are treated as all representing the interests of the Union. Thus a duty is placed on them to protect all citizens of the Union in compliance with the principle of equality of citizens. However, for this principle to apply outside the territory of the Union – which is the only place where this obligation is placed – the agreement of third countries is necessary. Should the third country in which the individual citizen of the Union finds him or her self not agree, then the individual will be at the mercy of his or her own nation state coming to his or her assistance.

---

45 Denmark, Finland, the Netherlands and Sweden.
46 Cyprus, the Czech Republic and the UK.

Article 21 EC/article I-10(2)(d) EU Constitution inserts as a citizenship right, a right which in fact applies in respect of all persons, natural or legal in the Union – the right of petition. "Every citizen of the Union shall have the right to petition the European Parliament in accordance with Article 194. Every citizen of the Union may apply to the Ombudsman established in with Article 195. Every citizen of the Union may write to any of the institutions or bodies referred to in this Article or in Article 7 in one of them languages mentioned in Article 314 and have an answer in the same language."[47] The right to remedies is formulated as a citizenship right though in fact it is a right which applies because of interaction with the institutions in the Union or presence on the territory. Finally, Article 22 provides for the Commission to report to the Parliament, the Council and the Economic and Social Committee every three years on the application of these provisions.

Conclusions

When citizenship of the Union was established, a very limited number of rights were attached to it: (1) the right to move and reside subject to the conditions set out in the treaty; (2) the right to vote and stand as a candidate in municipal and European Parliament elections in a Member State other than that of his or her nationality if he or she resides there; (3) the right to seek help from the consular authorities of another Member State when in a third country; (4) the right to petition the European Parliament and Ombudsman (though this right is also given to third country nationals and so cannot truly be considered a citizenship right). What is striking about all of these rights is that they only apply to immigrants. When a person is in his or her home state, the rights have no effect. Thus the meaning of citizenship of the Union when considered from the perspective of fundamental freedoms is as a citizenship which only gives rights to persons outside their state of nationality. The only exception is the right to petition the ombudsman but in reality that is a right given to third country nationals as well. The EU constitution does not extend or develop these rights substantially.

However, this may be understandable not least as citizenship of the Union has not been a building block of legitimacy of the Union until very recently. It has not been a central element of the constitution in which it appears. The EC and EU Treaties form the central elements of the constitution of the Union. However, the process of constitutionalisation of the EU is one which has been cautiously developed primarily in fields far from citizenship.[48] Commercial adventures have been much more pertinent to the development of the central constitutional principles of the

---

47 This wording has been slightly changed in the EU Constitution, but the right continues to exist.
48 The key theorist on this subject is Joseph Weiler whose book, *The Constitution of Europe*, is central to any discussion of this kind: J H H Weiler, *The Constitution of Europe* (Cambridge University Press: Cambridge: 1999).

Union, such as direct effect and supremacy of EU law.[49] From the start of the project in 1957 until the transformation in 1993, individuals enjoyed rights primarily as a result of their exercise of economic activities – as workers, self-employed or service providers or recipients. Further, the rights which individuals gained through the treaty from work were only available to them if they were immigrants in another Member State. Thus the right to family reunification in Union law only comes into existence when the individual carries on his or her economic activities in another Member State.[50] The right to immigrate to any other Member State which the treaty provides to nationals of the Member States was and continues to be central. But the rights of the individual in EU law still depend largely on the individual having exercised that migration right.[51]

---

49 These principles were enunciated by the European Court of Justice in 6/62, *Van Gend en Loos* [1962] ECR 1; 6/64, *Costa v ENEL* [1964] ECR 585.
50 Article 10 Regulation 1612/68 – there can be continuing effects if the family return to the home Member State C-370/90 *Singh* [1992] ECR I-4265; very recently there has been a further extension C-60/00, *Carpenter* [2002] ECR I-6279.
51 These comments are in respect of rights which attach to citizenship rather than those which are generally available to anyone living in the Union – such as health and safety rules or consumer protection.

Chapter 3

Equality and Citizenship

Equality remains one of the central issues where the concept of citizenship stubs its toes. So long as the idea of citizenship remains defined as freedom guaranteed through the rule of law, the problem of equality is limited to equality before the law.[1] In liberal democracies, the triptych of territory, people and constitutionality (as bounded governing authority) constitute the state. The importance of constitutionalism to the meaning of citizenship has been well described by Preuss in the following terms: "to live under a constitution means the individual is not to be merely the object of domination but is to be recognized as a person vested with rights; to live in a nation, to be a member, i.e. a citizen of this nation; not to be alienated from his or her fellow man and from the community into which he or she is born; to enjoy equal civil rights and liberties ..."[2] Citizenship provides a single legal status to all the members of the polity but does not resolve the question of socio-economic, political and cultural inequalities.

Citizenship in democracies does not, however, mean equality among citizens in a number of fields. For instance, majority rule in democracies does not necessarily result in political power being harnessed in the interests of the less fortunate.[3] Indeed the increase in inequality in many parts of the Western world belies the position of some theorists that "democracies will normally work to serve the less fortunate segments of the population, thereby promoting 'positive' or 'social' rights and more generally, social justice."[4] The mechanisms of equalising distribution lie within

---

1   P Magnette, *La Citoyenneté*, Bruylant Brussels 2001 p 182.
2   U Preuss, 'Constitutionalism – Meaning, Endangerment, Sustainability' in S Saberwal and H Sievers (eds), *Rules, Laws Constitutions*, Sage, New Delhi, 1998, pp 173–174.
3   For instance in the UK, 1 in 3 children were living in poverty in 1992/3 compared with only 1 in 10 children in 1980; see Justice Submissions to the UN Committee on Economic, Social and Cultural Rights, November 1997. In 2002, the UK government confirmed that it was (still) targetting child poverty (The Guardian, 'Blair backs redistribution of wealth to end child poverty' 18 September 2002).
4   C Offe, 'Homogeneity and Constitutional Democracy: Group Rights as an Answer to Identity Conflicts?' in S Saberwal and H Sievers (eds), *Rules, Laws Constitutions*, Sage New Delhi, 1998, p 190.

the power of the authorities – taxation and social security being among the foremost. The choice of laws to adopt in these fields will have consequences regarding the strengthening or weakening of the principle of equality before the law in economic privileges and social power. Where the principle of ownership of property takes precedence over the principle of redistribution of wealth, the one will be transposed into law in respect of which the principle of equality will apply. The other will not be, or will be incorporated into law as a weak right and thus engage only in a limited way, if at all, the principle of equality. The result will be economic inequality among citizens consistent with the principle of equality as expressed in law. The adage that the right to protection of private property applies equally to the pauper and the duke but is rather more interesting for the latter encapsulates this conundrum.

The more comprehensive the vision of equality the more contentious becomes the protection of the property rights of the individual against the principle of economic equality. In 1950, T H Marshall sought to address this problem through three questions:

1. Is it still true that the basic equality, when enriched in substance and embodied in the formal rights of citizenship, is consistent with the inequalities of social class?
2. Is it still true that the basic equality can be created and preserved without invading the freedom of the competitive market?
3. What is the effect of the marked shift of emphasis from duties to rights?[5]

The gradual acquisition of political rights in the UK in the 19th century was accompanied by increasing agitation for socio-economic rights.[6] Socio-economic rights enter into direct conflict with the rights of contract and possession of property. The way the state regulates that conflict is a reflection of the nature of citizenship in that state. This tension is central to the fall from favour of the Magna Charta as the source of fundamental rights in the 1960s. The majority of the rights which the Magna Charta promotes are those which protect property and the rights of ownership against the right of the state to extract resources in various fields. Thus in a period of increasing agitation for a new balance between socio-economic rights and civil rights, the Magna Charta is more easily called in aid by those opposing an extension of socio-economic rights. At times such as the beginning of the 21st century when liberty of the person and habeas corpus are in question, the attraction of Magna Charta increases.[7]

---

5   T H Marshall, *Citizenship and Social Class*, CUP, Cambridge, 1950 p 9.
6   N Timmins, *The Five Giants, A Biography of the Welfare State*, Fontana Press, London 1996.
7   T Bingham, 'Personal Freedom and the Dilemma of Democracies' International and Comparative Law Quaterly, Volume 52, Issue 4, October 2003, pp. 841–858.

In the modern state, resource extraction is linked to and justified by redistribution of resources and the diminution of economic disparities. As the idea of equality moves into the space of citizenship its field becomes contested. J S Mill's work on liberty throws this question to the fore – the right to liberty as a negative, the lack of interference coupled with state protection of the lack of interference with various rights, not least property accumulation and ownership, does not lead to a reduction of inequality between citizens.[8] The 19th British century constitutional expert, Bagehot considered it inappropriate to extend the franchise to the lower classes as, in his opinion, they lacked understanding and learning.[9] This definition of citizenship as a set of rights contingent on a requisite degree of economic well-being to the exclusion of the poor and ill-educated places equality in the field of class and class distinctions. The shift to a concept of citizenship tied to membership of the nation state finds its theoretical framework in Marshall. The development of the welfare state marks a shift towards a different conception of the citizen. Marshall illustrates the development with the example of the gradual universal provision of education as necessary to create a citizen capable of informed electoral choices. Thus the extension of the franchise demands the education of the citizen and the true exercise of citizenship rights demands that the state take responsibility for the education of the citizen.

When Marshall divides citizenship into three parts, civil, political and social, he engages centrally with the problem of equality and citizenship. It is important to remember when considering Marshall that his work is about the UK. While he refers to other countries in Europe, his quest to understand citizenship is highly coloured by the UK experience. Nonetheless the force of his way of imagining citizenship remains seminal.[10] Citizenship according to Marshall is "a kind of basic human equality associated with the concept of full membership of a community, or, as I should say, of citizenship ..."[11]

Marshall, Civil Rights and Citizenship of the Union

Marshall defines the civil rights necessary for individual freedom as liberty of the person, freedom of speech, thought and faith, the right to own property and to

---

8   J S Mill, *On Liberty and Other Essays*, OUP, Oxford, 1998.

9   "The mass of uneducated men could not now in England be told 'go to, chose your rulers;' they would go wild; their imaginations would fancy unreal dangers, and the attempt at election would issue in some forcible usurpation. The incalculable advantage of august institutions in a free state is, that they prevent this collapse." W Bagehot, *The English Constitution*, OUP, Oxford, 2001 p 27.

10 Crowley notes the risks attendant on the wide application of Marshall not least in the light of Marshall's rather specific views on the kind of social cohesion upon which the principles of citizenship shall apply: J Crowley, 'The national dimension of citizenship in T. H. Marshall' Citizenship Studies 2(2) pp 165–178. Notwithstanding this risk I shall, nonetheless, review, in this chapter the extent to which Marshall's approach can provide insights into citizenship of the Union.

11 T H Marshall, *Citizenship and Social Class*, ibid p 8.

conclude valid contracts, and the right to justice.[12] He notes that the right to justice is a different type of right from the others in that within it the concept of equality is inherent. Notwithstanding what the underlying subject matter of a legal dispute may be, access to the justice system and due process of law in an undifferentiated manner is essentially an equality right unlike the right to own property.[13] His insistence on the engagement of the institutions of justice, in particular the courts, in constituting this first step of equality in citizenship deserves consideration. By the championing of the liberties of individuals against inter alia, parliament, the courts gain a legitimacy which is central to their power. He takes for granted the independence of the judiciary though he recognizes the importance of the institutions of justice, the existence of an independent bar etc.

In the economic field, Marshall posits the first basic civil right as the right to work, in the sense of following the profession of one's choice in the place of choice and subject only to legitimate demands for preliminary technical training.[14] The right of free movement of the citizen presupposes that the individual is not the property of another person. The right to enter into a contract of employment, to move freely to do so and to accumulate wealth if possible from doing so are thus inherent in citizenship.

Does Marshall's construction provide any assistance in understanding citizenship of the Union? In the preceding chapter I have set out in detail the rights which are attendant on citizenship of the Union. In the light of that chapter I will compare Marshall's vision of citizenship with Union citizenship. The first right of citizenship of the Union arises from the inclusion in the EEC Treaty in 1957 of the right of free movement of workers together with the mechanisms for cross recognition of diplomas.[15] The rights in articles 39–49 EC/articles III-18–30 EU Constitution apply to workers, persons moving for the purpose of searching for employment, the self-employed and those intending to set themselves up in self-employment and service providers and recipients. No economic criteria can be placed on their exercise; for example, the individual who moves cannot be required to have a particular amount of money or health or any other kind of insurance. Provided that the individual has effectively exercised the right, he or she is entitled to equal treatment with nationals of the state in all areas related to economic activity including, for instance, social welfare.[16] I shall return to these rights below in more detail. Thus the economic free movement right in EU law predates the creation of formal citizenship by more than 35 years but remains the right best known and most central to the status. It corresponds to Marshall's first set of citizenship rights, the right to work at the place of one's choice.

---

12 T H Marshall, *Citizenship and Social Class*, ibid p 10.
13 He recognises the need for a system of public funding for legal matters both criminal and civil in order to achieve in practice this equality and he examines the development of the UK legal aid system from this perspective.
14 T H Marshall, ibid p 16.
15 Articles 39–49 EC/article III-133 EU Constitution; Regulation 1612/68 and Directive 71/148.

Political Rights Deriving from Civil Rights

The second set of rights which Marshall considers fundamental to citizenship are political rights. In his view citizenship rights at the end of the 18th century were defective because political rights were limited to a small oligarchy defined by economic status. He plots how the extension of the franchise in the UK followed economic grounds, moving gradually from the right attached to certain types of property ownership to one attached to the individual as a citizen irrespective of property ownership. Thus political rights were, according to Marshall, a secondary product of civil rights.[17] They only gradually became attached directly to citizenship. A parallel could be drawn with the development of citizenship of the Union. The political rights of citizens of the Union are only activated when citizens have moved from one Member State to another. If the right to move for employment is the centre of the civil rights to which political rights are initially attached so too in the Union it is the right to move which precedes the right to vote. The search for a better economic status through the crossing of EU borders is the trigger for political rights. Then they are limited to the right to vote and stand for election in municipal and European Parliament elections. However, the starting point of political rights is the right to move to another Member State.

The rights of free movement of workers, the self-employed, and service providers and recipients are immigration rights. They are available to nationals of other Member States.[18] As such their exercise is subject to conditions regarding the exercise of the right. For instance the work-seeker must have a real prospect of finding a job in the host Member State.[19] The worker must carry out an economic activity for remuneration in a relationship of subordination and that activity must be genuine and effective.[20] The worker must have housing available for his or her family in the host Member State.[21] The self-employed must carry out economic activities other than in a relationship of subordination.[22] The service provider and recipient must also be carrying out economic activities, though for the recipient of services using tourist facilities has been found sufficient.[23] These obligations are not self-evidently part of the citizenship right of movement unless they can be implied from the phrase subject to the conditions and limitations which qualify the free movement right.

---

16 Article 7(2) regulation 1612/68.
17 T H Marshall, ibid p 20.
18 Article 39 EC/article III-133 EU Constitution provides for free movement of workers, however, the European Court of Justice has interpreted this provision as applying only to nationals of the Member States and family members even where their third country nationals, C-230/97 *Awoyemi* [1998] ECR I-6781.
19 C-292/89 *Antonissen* [1991] ECR I-745.
20 53/81 *Levin* [1982] ECR 1035.
21 Article 10 regulation 1612/68.
22 C-268/99 *Jany* [2001] ECR I-8625.
23 186/87 *Cowan* [1989] ECR 195.

In 1990 three directives were adopted which extend the right of free movement for nationals of the Member States who are not economically active.[24] Under the directives, pensioners, students and the otherwise economically inactive must be economically self-sufficient to the level of social security in the Member State and must have health insurance for all risks in order to enjoy a right of residence in another Member State. A substantial controversy arose over the legal bases of the three directives, which were adopted under the power *to take measures not specifically foreseen by Community law where necessary to achieve the objective.* After a successful legal challenge by the European Parliament,[25] the legal basis of the students' directive was changed to article 12/article I-4(2) EU Constitution, the general non-discrimination provision. Of course where an individual has moved in an economically inactive capacity he or she is free to take up an economic activity thereafter. If he or she does so, the restrictions on economic self-sufficiency can no longer apply, as they are contrary to Community law on the free movement of the economically active. Thus according to the 1990 secondary legislation, a citizen of the Union who is not economically active can only move and reside when he or she is unlikely to be a burden on the social security or protection system of the host state.[26]

Following the creation of citizenship of the Union, much discussion took place on the meaning of the right to move and reside in article 18 EC/article III-125 EU Constitution and in the light of the 1990 directives. The addition of the qualification that the right is subject to the limitations and conditions laid down in the Treaty and by the measures adopted to give it effect appears to limit the right to the pre-existing free movement rights in the Treaty – i.e. for economic purposes or as economically self-sufficient under the directives. As an individual only accesses the right to vote and stand for election as part of Union citizenship when residing in a host Member State, there is no franchise right without the economic right unless the link between economic self-sufficiency and residence is broken.

Cutting the Civil Right-Political Right Link?

The controversy regarding the application of the economic sufficiency requirement in respect of the free movement right for the economically inactive moved into the judicial field as individuals who did not fulfill the economic requirements sought nonetheless to enjoy a residence right as citizens of the Union. Should the European

---

24 Directive 93/96 on students; Directive 90/365 on pensioners and Directive 90/366 on the economic inactive but self-sufficient.
25 C-295/90 *European Parliament v Council* [1992] ECR I-4193.
26 Only after the individual has been a worker/self-employed persons in a Member State and becomes unemployed is he or she entitled to equal treatment in all social advantages, include social security and protection benefits (Article 7(2) regulation 1612/68).

Court of Justice have followed the more restrictive approach recommended by a number of Member States,[27] that the right to move and reside of citizens of the Union could only be exercised in accordance with the existing secondary legislation on the matter, then political rights in the Union would have remained, in Marshall's terms, a "secondary product of civil rights". In the first case which came before the Court of Justice on the substance of the right of residence of a citizen of the Union, *Martinez Sala*, a Spanish national resident in Germany sought a child rearing allowance. This was refused as she did not have a residence permit. She applied for a residence permit but this request was refused on the basis that she had no right in EC law to reside on the territory as she was not a worker, nor was she self-employed, nor did she have sufficient resources to support herself without social assistance. Ms Martinez Sala appealed against the decision and the domestic court referred to the Court of Justice, *inter alia*, the question of Ms Martinez Sala's right to reside. The Court did not take this occasion to confirm directly that article 18(1)/article III-125 EU Constitution has direct effect.

Instead, the ECJ held that as Ms Martinez Sala was not subject to an expulsion decision and could not be made subject to one because of Germany's commitments under a Council of Europe convention,[28] she was, thus, lawfully on the territory of Germany in her capacity as a citizen of the Union. The fact that she did not have a residence permit was not decisive as "for the purposes of recognition of the right of residence, a residence permit can only have declaratory and probative force ..."[29] I shall return shortly to this case as regards the second issue – her claim to the social benefit. What is important here is that the residence right is tied to a citizenship right by the ECJ to the exclusion of the limitations and conditions which are placed on it when it is exercised as an immigration right. Although the ECJ did not find that the residence right was inherent in the citizenship right, it took the first step.

The Court of Justice, starting with the *Sala* judgment, interprets the citizenship right of free movement as qualitatively different from an immigration right. According to the ECJ, the individual enjoys the right directly and any restriction which is placed on it must be justified to a high level by the Member State. The right of a citizen of the Union to rely directly on his or her status as such to enjoy a right of residence irrespective of the conditions of secondary legislation is expressly recognized for the first time by the Court of Justice in a 2002 decision. In *Baumbast*,[30] an economically inactive Community national had taken up residence with his third country national spouse and their children in a Member State (the UK) other than that of his nationality (Germany). Paradoxically, Mr Baumbast had moved from

---

27 See for instance the positions of the French and British governments intervening in C-184/99 *Grzelczyk* [2001] ECR I-6193.
28 European Convention on Social and Medical Assistance, 11 December 1953.
29 C-85/96 *Martinez Sala* [1998] ECR I-2691.
30 C-413/99 *Baumbast* [2002] ECR I-7091.

Germany to the UK to take up a job but the company which employed him went into insolvent liquidation. He then took up employment with a variety of companies outside the Union while his wife and children remained resident in the UK. The family applied for residence permits to continue residence in the UK but these were rejected on the basis that the UK authorities were not satisfied that Mr Baumbast was resident in the UK or that he fulfilled the requirements of the residence directive (specifically the health insurance requirement). Mr Baumbast appealed against the decision and the national court referred the issue of the Court of Justice.

In respect of the right of a citizen of the Union to continue to reside on the territory of a host Member State, the Court replied "As regards, in particular, the right to reside within the territory of the Member States under Article 18(1) EC,[31] that right is conferred directly on every citizen of the Union by a clear and precise provisions of the EC Treaty. Purely as a national of a Member State, and consequently a citizen of the Union, Mr Baumbast therefore has the right to rely on Article 18(1) EC."[32] In effect, the Court of Justice disapplied the qualifying economic conditions for residence of the secondary legislation (it spent some time unraveling the health insurance requirement) on the basis of the principle of citizenship of the Union, but also making reference as well to the principle of proportionality. I will return in chapter 5 to the question of expulsion and citizenship of the Union which remains one of the quandary issues of the status. What is important to note at this point, is that the political right of franchise as part of citizenship of the Union is being detached from economic conditions. With each step the European Court of Justice in interpreting the right of residence of citizens of the Union reduced the financial criteria in favour of a wide definition of the residence right of the citizen. The right to vote is attached to the right to reside in so far as a citizen of the Union can only exercise it as a Community law right when resident in a Member State other than that of his or her nationality.

Marshall, Gellner and the Transformation of Social Rights

Marshall turns to social rights as the final step in the development of citizenship in the 19th and 20th centuries. It is in this sphere that he sees the question of equality as most pressing. He plots the development of social rights and their association with membership of communities or associations. He outlines how, at the height of the 19th century in the UK, poverty became instrumentalised through law to divorce social rights from citizenship rights. He describes how the poor lost their civil right of liberty of the person through internment in workhouses exclusively because of

---

31 See chapter 2 for the wording.
32 C-413/99 *Baumbast* [2002] ECR I-7091.

their poverty. As a result in law they also lost their political rights. Thus the failure of the state to redistribute goods resulted in fundamental inequality in the essence of citizenship and the loss of all three sets of citizenship rights – civil, political and social for the poor as Marshall points out.

The relationship of equality and citizenship thus finds its point of maximum conflict in the area of social class. Marshall accepts that social class and citizenship are antagonistic mechanisms of social organization "the rights with which the general status of citizenship was invested were extracted from the hierarchical status system of social class, robbing it of its essential substance."[33] Until social rights become part of citizenship, the inequalities of developing capitalist societies in Europe did not conflict with the principle of equality in citizenship. The core of citizenship was in civil rights, which according to Marshall are central to a market economy.

The anthropologist Ernest Gellner describes the same process somewhat differently when analysing the rise of nationalism. He outlines the transformation of Western societies from agrarian, where solidarity is within classes, to industrial where solidarity is built into the concept of the nation. According to his analysis, cultural affinity in agrarian cultures is not based on an idea of common national origins but on position in the hierarchy. Survival depended on access to resources which take the form of surplus food production. Access to this surplus food depends on a hierarchical relationship to those holding power – thus barons had more interest and solidarity with barons who were in a similar relationship of access to resources than with peasants who might be regarded as almost a separate species. According to Gellner, the transformation from agrarian to industrial societies required a reformulation of the central organising principle from hierarchy within the meaning of the agrarian world – i.e. who gets access when to the surplus food supplies, – to technocracy and with it a different understanding of boundaries and solidarity.[34] Marshall's citizenship and Gellner's nationalism share a function as organising principles in society – the transformation from class solidarity to a definition of a project beyond class alliances, citizenship for Marshall, nationalism for Gellner.

Civil rights give the individual the power to be an independent economic unit in the economic struggle, as Marshall puts it, and thereby make it possible to deny him or her social protection.[35] Because the individual has the right to move and reside and work, he or she should be able to support him or herself. The argument goes that the community does not need to provide social protection for those who can work for themselves and make a living. Marshall challenges this view by considering the fairness of the conditions of work in a society like that of the UK which in the 19th century privileged the owners of capital in comparison with those without.

---

33   T H Marshall, ibid, p 30.
34   E Gellner, *Nationalism*, Phoenix, London, 1997, p 96.
35   T H Marshall, ibid p 33.

He describes a history of the slow development of social rights out of the trade union movement and campaigns for workers' rights. He is continuously drawn back to the field of judicial dispute resolution and the issue of access to justice as a civil right which regulates all the others. Access to the institutions of due process is controlled by financial capacity. The gradual development of legal aid schemes to assist the poor in the funding of legal disputes is a critical part of the development of the idea of social rights as citizenship rights. Citizenship and its claim to equality is a tool by which social inequality can be diminished through the establishment of a state duty of provision of social benefits, coupled with access to a mechanism of enforcement.

Marshall accepts that the development of the social component of citizenship interferes with the operation of the competitive free market.[36] The establishment of a system centred on rights, including social rights – health, housing, income etc., which are justiciable and require redistribution of wealth by the state has become tied to the content of citizenship through the principle of equality. There is an inherent tension within the right to contract, accumulate and retain wealth. The imposition of collective labour negotiations, state regulation of income replacement schemes and taxation all challenge the right to property acquisition and retention. The articulation of this tension in the rights of citizenship is, for Marshall, one of the challenges of his century.

Social Rights and Community Law

The demand for increasing social equality as part of citizenship and the resistance to these claims finds central expression in citizenship of the Union. When one considers the express rights of citizens of the Union (see chapter 2) not only do they apply only to the migrant, a point I stressed both here and in the previous chapter, but they are limited to very minimal civil and political rights, i.e. the right to move and reside, and political rights at the European Parliament and municipal levels only. Marshall's third category, the social rights, find no place whatsoever.

Instead, social rights were incorporated into the EC Treaty in article 42/article III-136 EU Constitution from the very beginning, providing for coordination of social security across the Member States. Given expression in regulation 1408/71, the Community's provisions on social security are designed to give effect to free movement of workers. The fundamental differences in the social security systems of the Member States and the fact that these differences are particularly resistant to change means that co-ordination in the field was necessary.[37] The system does not

---

36 T H Marshall, ibid p 81.
37 For a detailed discussion see R Cornelissen, '25 Years of Regulation (EEC) No 1408/71; Its Achievements and Its Limits' in *25 Years of Regulation (EEC) No 1408/71 n Social Security for Migrant Workers*, Swedish National Social Insurance Board & European Commission: Stockholm 1997.

require Member States to provide insurance or benefits of any specific risks though there has been a concerted effort by the institutions and the Member States to move towards a more uniform system of social cover regulated at the national level.[38]

European social security systems come in two main models: (1) the Bismarkian system of funds which are state controlled, financed by contributions (though the state contributes on behalf of those who are not financially able to do so) and provide insurance against specified risks such as unemployment, illness etc. The protection against the risk is calculated on the basis of income and contribution;[39] (2) the Beveridge model which is based on general protection of those resident on the territory rather than an insurance system.[40] The EC enters into the framework of social security because of the consequences of national rules for migrant workers.[41] Thus co-ordination of social security was one of the first areas to be the subject of secondary legislation in this field (now the main secondary legislation is Regulation 1408/71 which has been amended many times) and has given rise to very substantial amounts of jurisprudence from the ECJ. There are three main principles to Community social security legislation:

1. Nationals of one Member State cannot be discriminated against in comparison with own nationals of the state; thus for instance qualifying residence require-ments for social benefits are unlikely to be lawful as they will offend against the non-discrimination rule as own nationals are more likely to fulfil them than nationals of other Member States; [42]
2. An individual may be affiliated to only one social security system at a time – normally this should be that of the state in which he or she works but if the intended work in the host Member State is likely to last less than 12 months (with the possibility of renewal for a further 12 months) then the individual should remain affiliated in his or her home state (article 14 Regulation 1408/71[43]); thus contributions should be continuous and only in one state at

---

38 I have discussed this at some length in 'How Can Social Protection Survive EMU? A United Kingdom Perspective', ELRev, 25:1(1999), pp 22–37.

39 K Sieveking, 'The Significance of the Transborder Utilisation of Health Care Benefits for Migrants', M Sakslin 'The Concept of Residence and Social Security: Reflections on the Finnish, Swedish and Community Legislation' and P Minderhoud 'The Dutch Linking Act and the Violation of Various International Non-Discrimination Clauses' EJML 2(2000) pp 143–201.

40 For a fuller explanation see N Timmins, *The Five Giants: A Biography of the Welfare State*, Fontana Press, London, 1996.

41 For a general discussion of immigration and welfare see M Bommes & A Geddes, *Immigration and Welfare: Challenging the borders of the welfare state*, Routledge, London 2000.

42 C-90/97 *Swaddling* [1999] ECR I-1075.

43 "1(a) A person employed in the territory of a Member State by an undertaking to which he is nor-mally attached who is posted by that undertaking to the territory of another Member State to perform work there for that undertaking shall continue to be subject to the legislation of the first Member State, provided that the anticipated duration of that work does not exceed 12 months and that he is not sent to replace another person who has completed his term of posting." Regulation 1408/71 has been replaced by Regulation 883/04.

a time.[44] To make sure that the contributions are effective, the Regulation requires that contributions made in different Member States be aggregated for the purposes of calculating the level of benefits;

3. An individual is entitled to export his or her benefits to any other Member State. The most commonly exported benefit is health benefits where individuals travel on holiday within the Union.

The regulation on social security only covers nine fields: (1) sickness and maternity; (2) accidents at work; (3) occupational diseases; (4) invalidity benefits; (5) old age pensions; (there has recently been an extension to supplementary pension schemes) (6) survivor's benefits; (7) death grants; (8) unemployment benefits; and (9) family benefits. The three rules apply to all these kinds of benefits whether or not they are financed by contributions, paid by employers, social insurance institutions or public administrations. While the regulation contains a list of risks to which it applies, it is limited to social security not social assistance. Further, Member States may seek to exclude certain benefits by enumerating then in an annex (subject always to the interpretation of the ECJ).

It is important in the context of citizenship rights to note that the system is tied to article 39/article III-133 EU Constitution – free movement of workers. An individual must have moved from one Member State to another, or at the very least been affiliated to the social security systems of more than one Member State, to be able to enjoy the benefit of the system.[45] Thus the formal system of social security coordination is attendant on the status of being a worker (the self-employed are also covered by a separate regulation).

The second source of social security or assistance rights of citizens of the Union comes from article 7(2) regulation 1612/68 (now consolidated in Directive 2004/38) which implements the free movement right. This provision guarantees to workers and their family members equal treatment in social and tax advantages. As regards social rights, it has been the legal base for the extension of social assistance benefits to migrant workers, nationals of other Member States. Under the equality principle, the European Court of Justice has found that social benefits as wide as travel reductions for large families are social advantages which must be made available to migrant workers from other Member States.[46] However, again this source of social rights is based on status as a worker and not incorporated into citizenship, other than indirectly.

---

44 It does not matter whether a person is employed in one Member State and self-employed in the other. If the social security system does not provide additional protection to the individual it is not permissible for the second state to demand social security contributions C-53/95 *Kemmler* [1996] ECR I-703.

45 C-95/99 *Khalil* [2001] ECR I-7413.

46 32/75 *Cristini* [1975] ECR 1085.

Social Rights and Citizenship of the Union

It is in the field of social rights that the Court of Justice has begun the substantive interpretation of citizenship of the Union. If we return to the *Martinez Sala* case, what the applicant is seeking is a social right from which she is being excluded because of her nationality. She cannot benefit either on the basis of regulation 1408/71 nor on the basis of article 7(2) regulation 1612/68 as it has not been established that she is a worker or has been one in the recent past. Apart from those exceptions, the reservation of social benefits for own nationals is based on the principle that equality is for citizens. It is the citizens who pay for the benefits and who are entitled on the principle of equality among citizens to equal access to the benefits.[47] Thus the exclusion of non-nationals who did not pay into the system (or even if they are not part of the mechanism of equality) is justified. Applying this reasoning to .citizenship of the Union, Ms Martinez Sala ought to be entitled to the benefit expressly on the ground of her right to equality.

Article 12 EC/article III-123 EU Constitution states "within the scope of application of this Treaty, and without prejudice to any special provisions contained therein, any discrimination on grounds of nationality shall be prohibited." This general expression of equality predated the arrival of citizenship of the Union into the Treaty by over 35 years. When citizenship of the Union was added, there was no immediate relationship drawn between the two provisions. They were contained in separate parts of the Treaty, though, of course, article 12/article III-123 EU Constitution is a general principle of all Community law and thus was well known as a transversal provision which applies in all spheres of Community competence.

As regards Ms Martinez Sala and her claim to a German social benefit even though she is not a citizen of Germany, the ECJ would need to take a number of steps before article 12/article III-123 EU Constitution could apply. First it found that the unequal treatment came within the scope of the Treaty because Ms Martinez Sala had a right of residence as a Spanish national living in Germany, notwithstanding the fact that the right to be in Germany came from outside EU law. Unless a nexus with Community law were present, there would be no EU aspect to which the non-discrimination principle could be applied.[48] Thus the existence of a residence right which brought Ms Martinez Sala within the scope of article 18(1)/article III-125(1) EU Constitution was critical to the ECJ's right to apply article 12/article III-123 EU Constitution.

---

47 This, of course, raises the issue of taxation and social contributions of non-nationals, which I looked at in the preceding chapter.
48 A particular cogent example of the need for a Community law nexus is apparent in C-60/00 *Carpenter* [2002] ECR I-6279.

Secondly, article 12/article III-123 EU Constitution applied directly to her as there is no specific provision of the treaty which protects her right to equal treatment in this field (in fact this could be read as a criticism of the provisions on citizenship of the Union themselves which failed to incorporate a right to non-discrimination). The non-discrimination right of article 12/article III-123 EU Constitution can only apply if there is no specific right to equality within the Treaty. So, for instance, article 12/article III-123 EU Constitution will not apply to nationality discrimination as regards working conditions of EU migrant workers because the specific provision expressly regulates the field.

Thirdly the treatment accorded to Ms Martinez Sala, on the facts and evidence constituted unequal treatment in comparison with German nationals. The exclusion of Ms Martinez Sala from German child rearing allowances was based on the fact that she did not possess a specified residence permit. It was not expressly based on her nationality as Spanish nor as non-German. Nonetheless, the effect of the legislation was disproportionate on nationals of other Member States who are required to have residence permits to access the benefit. Own nationals, of course, cannot be required to seek residence permits.

Fourthly, the discrimination, because it is based on her nationality could not be justified. Here the ECJ left open the possibility that a Member State could seek to justify such unequal treatment, noting, "in any event, nothing to justify such unequal treatment has been put before the Court."[49] Finally the Court concluded that Community law precluded a Member State from requiring nationals of other Member States to produce documents issued by the state itself and not required from own nationals in order to access social benefits. Thus the right of residence inherent in citizenship of the Union begins to give rise to a right to social benefits.

The issue of equality and citizenship came back before the ECJ in 2001 when Mr Grzelczyk, a French national studying in Belgium, sought a social benefit to finance the final year of his studies. The Belgian social benefit, the minimex, had been the subject of more than one reference to the Court of Justice, after the last of which the Belgian authorities removed a discriminatory residence requirement for access to the benefit.[50] The Belgian authorities paid Mr Grzelczyk the benefit for a period but when the local authorities were not reimbursed by the federal authorities they cut off Mr Grzelczyk's benefit. The local court referred only one substantive question to the ECJ – does citizenship of the Union together with the prohibition on discrimination on the basis of nationality mean that Belgium must pay Mr Grzelczyk the benefit? Although at first appearance this case seems rather Member State specific, four Member States not otherwise involved in the case intervened, as did the Council. All of these interveners, with the exception of Portugal, argued against

---

49   Para 63.
50   249/83 *Hoeckx* [1985] ECR 973; C-326/90 *Commission v Belgium* [1992] ECR I-5517.

Mr Grzelczyk. The position of the French Government encapsulated the issue best: "the idea that the principle of equal treatment in the matter of social advantages should be extended to all citizens of the Union when at present it applies only to workers and members of their families would amount to establishing total equality between citizens of the Union established in a Member State and nationals of that State, which would be difficult to reconcile with rights attaching to nationality."[51]

This position indicates the heart of the issue – the Member States argue that the extension of social rights to non-citizens is inimical to the justification for social benefits themselves as a form of mutual protection society for a community. In doing so they fail to mention that foreigners resident in a state are equally obliged to pay taxes as any other member of the community. Instead, they insist that social rights are justified on the basis that they are limited to equality among citizens to the exclusion of foreigners, even resident foreigners like Mr Grzelczyk who had been paying taxes throughout the period when he worked in Belgium. Social benefits, according to the Member States, are part of the system of solidarity on which the state achieves the loyalty of the citizen and seeks to establish the legitimacy of resource extraction from them. To extend these rights to non-nationals destroys the basis for the rights. The failure of the Member States to differentiate between non-resident foreigners and resident foreigners is one of the weaknesses of the position.

In the case, all the parties agreed that there was only one basis on which Mr Grzelczyk was being discriminated against – nationality. The Court, for the first time, interpreted the place of citizenship of the Union in the developing constitution of the EU. It stated "Union citizenship is destined to be the fundamental status of nationals of the Member States, enabling those who find themselves in the same position to enjoy the same treatment in law irrespective of their nationality, subject to such exceptions as are expressly provided for."[52] It is not yet entirely clear what the ECJ meant by fundamental status or indeed how citizenship of the Union might acquire such a relevance. The fact that this statement is central and will gradually transform the nature of belonging in Europe seems, however, highly likely. Further, Mr Grzelczyk did win his right to the benefit.

In the third case where the relationship between citizenship of the Union and the right to non-discrimination in social benefits is central, the ECJ takes another step in the same direction.[53] Ms D'Hoop, a Belgian national, finished her secondary studies in France then continued her education in Belgium where she applied for a social allowance. Her application was rejected on the basis that under the conditions for the provision of such allowances the student must have completed her secondary studies in Belgium. The ECJ first considered the case under Community secondary legislation relating to the children of migrant workers and found that it did not apply.

---

51   C-184/99 *Grzelczyk* [2001] ECR I-6193.
52   C-184 *Grzelczyk* ibid Para 31.
53   C-224/98 *D'Hoop* [2002] ECR I-6191.

The key issue, according to the ECJ, was that Ms D'Hoop was seeking a social benefit from her country of nationality, Belgium. It was refused because she and her family had immigrated to France (and then come back to Belgium). Because she had not completed her secondary studies in Belgium she was not eligible for the benefit. What this kind of legislation does is handicap people who migrate. They are punished for having left the state (and potentially, at least, the state's resource extraction mechanisms) and when they return they are subject to requirements to complete residential periods before they can again access social benefits which are tied to citizenship rights.[54] The loyalty of own nationals who migrate can be questioned through the application of limitations afterwards on their access to social rights.

The principle that Community law on free movement does not apply where the activity is wholly internal to one Member State was argued by the Belgian Government as relevant to the situation of Ms D'Hoop. The ECJ rejected this position stating "a citizen of the Union must be granted in all Member States the same treatment in law as that accorded to the nationals of those Member States who find themselves in the same situation. It would be incompatible with the right of freedom of movement were a citizen, in a Member State of which he is a national, to receive treatment less favourable than he would enjoy if he had not availed himself of the opportunities offered by the Treaty in relation to freedom of movement."[55]

Conculsions

In *D'Hoop*, the ECJ took forward the place of citizenship of the Union which it had begun in *Grzelczyk* stating that such inequality of treatment is contrary to the principles which underpin the status of citizen of the Union, that is, the guarantee of the same treatment in law in the exercise of the citizen's freedom to move. The language of the ECJ is that of equality before the law, the principle which Marshall found as central to the acquisition of other rights. The right which the ECJ is securing is a social one, the latest and most highly contested of the citizenship rights. Equality as a principle of Union citizenship can compensate for the lack of equality which a state accords to its own nationals who have migrated to another country. The right of the state to penalize its citizens for abandoning the state to seek their futures elsewhere (and contribute to other states' social benefits systems) is qualified if not extinguished by the interpretation the ECJ gives to citizenship of the Union as a right to equality in social rights.

---

54 Similar UK legislation relating access to benefits to a test of habitual residence was introduced in the 1990s in order to prevent benefits tourism as it was seen from nationals of other Member States, but in fact hit mainly British nationals who had been abroad. The European Court of Justice found that legislation to offend against the right of free movement: C-90/97 *Swaddling* [1999] ECR I-1075.

55 C-224/98 *D'Hoop* para 30.

The problem with which this chapter began was that of equality and citizenship. The tension between a principle of equality at the heart of citizenship and the continued acceptance of very substantial economic inequality within a community does not find resolution easily. The use of the principle of equality among citizens to expand social rights from the territorially controlled nation state to the European Union has been contentious. The number of interveners in *Grzelczyk* is indicative of this.

Marshall's premise that citizenship must be expanded to include social rights is borne out in the development so far of citizenship of the Union. As Member States are obliged to grant social benefits to citizens of the Union from other Member States (or their own citizens on their return) the social content of citizenship is enlarged. It is curious to note that out of the three important cases on citizenship of the Union and social benefits two relate to students. Marshall's argument that social citizenship is closely linked with the development of universal education which is a prerequisite for the extension of the franchise finds an echo here. It is in paying for the education of the citizen that Member State resistance to social citizenship has arisen before the ECJ.

There is, however, another perspective to the development of European social citizenship. Gellner's argument on the rise of nationalism depends on the transformation of political boundaries into a new configuration of the homogeneity of culture. The acquisition of citizenship rights and in particular social rights is central to the legal definition of individuals as within or outside a homogeneous culture. The role of high literacy and education-linked culture as key to the social transformation of societies towards a citizenship-based concept of solidarity is the second element to the emergence of nationalism. If Gellner's position is correct, and the two features which he sees as central to the rise of nationalism are appearing in EU citizenship law, the question must be examined whether this is also laying a foundation for the development of negative aspects of nationalism at the EU level.

Chapter 4

The Residence/Citizenship Nexus

The rights and duties of citizens are contained in the constitutional settlements of the state and the people. The content of such settlements may vary substantially from one country to another. For example, even the right to be a citizen is subject to completely different rules in different European countries. In Germany the voluntary acquisition of the nationality of another state together with a declaration of allegiance to that state is sufficient to extinguish German citizenship.[1] The same act by a British national has no such consequence.[2]

These two different perspectives on citizenship can be categorised as nationalist, where ethnicity and the borders of its citizenship are tightly linked, or republican – a social contract model of citizenship linked to voluntary membership. Habermas seeks to reconcile these two concepts of citizenship in the context of European integration.[3] The transformation of Europe and with it the logic underlying citizenship demands some degree of co-existence between these rather different perspectives of belonging. A new unifying principle is needed to make sense of citizenship in the face of regionalism and indeed globalisation.

Habermas and the Fate of the Nation State, Europe and Citizenship

Taking German reunification as the example, Habermas notes that the two dominant views on the meaning of reunification at the time correspond with two different conceptions of citizenship. On the one hand reunification was viewed as the restoring

---

1 R Hofmann, 'German Citizenship and European Citizenship' in M Le Torre, *European Citizenship: An Institutional Challenge*, Kluwer Law International: The Hague, 1998, pp 149–166.
2 L Fransman, *British Nationality Law*, Butterworths, London, 2001.
3 J Habermas, 'Citizenship and National Identity: Some Reflections on the Future of Europe' in R Beiner, *Theorising Citizenship*, SUNY, New York, 1995 pp 255–281.

of the unity of the nation state "torn apart for decades."[4] This image of the meaning of reunification corresponds to a nationalist perspective of citizenship. The domination of this vision of citizenship as an expression of the unity of an ethnicity is central to the development of German nationality law. The strength of this vision led to the admission of 400,000 Aussiedler[5] to Germany in the peak year 1990 and continuing at over 200,000 persons of ethnic German origin throughout the 1990s as members of the ethnicity who had been cut off from 'their land' returned 'home.'[6] This provides the framework for Habermas' definition of nationalism as "a form of collective consciousness which both presupposes a reflective appropriation of cultural traditions that have been filtered through historiography and which spread only via the channels of modern mass media."[7] In his view this vision of the nation, and the participant in the nation, designates a pre-political entity.

The transformation of the nation to a political entity he sees as based in the French Revolution and as giving rise to another concept of the citizen where identity does not derive from common ethnic or cultural properties "but rather from the *praxis* of citizens who actively exercise their civil rights."[8] As he puts it hereditary nationalism gave way to acquired nationalism and from there to a republican meaning of citizenship. From here it is only a short step to his position that "the political culture must serve as the common denominator for a constitutional patriotism."[9] On the basis of a voluntarist adoption of the praxis of citizenship Habermas considers that a European constitutional patriotism could grow out of the constitutional principles and traditions coming from the European level. He considers that the human rights component of citizenship will be intensified and strengthened through supranational rights "and especially through European Civil Rights . . ."[10]

Citizenship, Residence and "European Civil Rights"

What then are these European civil rights and how do they intersect with citizenship? As the example of the Aussiedler indicates, the heartland of citizenship rights is the

---

4   J Habermas, ibid p 256.
5   The descendants of German minorities in Central and Eastern Europe and the successor states of the USSR.
6   R Hofmann, 'German Citizenship and European Citizenship' in M Le Torre, *European Citizenship: An Institutional Challenge*, Kluwer Law International: The Hague, 1998, pp 149–166, P Martin, *Germany Reluctant Land of Migration*, American Institute for Contemporary German Studies, John Hopkins University, 1998 pp 24–26.
7   J Habermas, ibid p 257.
8   J Habermas, ibid p 258. For an interesting discussion of this see B Guiguet, 'Citizenship and Nationality: Tracing the French Roots of Distinction' in M Le Torre, *European Citizenship: An Institutional Challenge*, Kluwer Law International: The Hague, 1998, pp 95–111.
9   J Habermas, ibid p 264.
10 J Habermas, ibid p 273.

right to go to, live in and work on the territory of the state. These ethnic Germans did not wish to establish their German citizenship while continuing to live in Central and Eastern Europe and the former Soviet Union. What they wanted was the right to go to Germany and live there. This right they acquired from Article 116 German Constitution (or basic law). Although the provision requires that the individual had suffered persecution as a result of their heritage after WWII, there was a collective understanding that this was the case of ethnic Germans in the Eastern states and Soviet Union.[11] For those born after 1993 this understanding is no longer available. In the German tradition of citizenship, the vision of the nation as a pre-political entity meant that the exclusion of these Ausseidler from residence rights was politically highly risky. The meaning of citizenship as closely linked to ethnicity meant that the Ausseidlers' home was Germany.

A very different picture appears as regards another European state, the UK. When citizenship and ethnicity have failed to intersect, the result has been to exclude nationals from the right to move to and reside in the UK. The example of the East African Asians is instructive. Just as in the case of Aussiedler in Germany, the central organising principle around the treatment of a group of nationals is their ethnicity. In this case, however, the result is exclusion. The claim to entry and residence rights is eventually and only partially obtained at the European level. British nationality continued to be a single citizenship status for persons irrespective of whether their connection was through the UK and Islands or British colonies[12] until the 1981 British Nationality Act came into force. However, from 1962 one group of British nationals, those in the UK Parliament, began to create distinctions among this category of citizens in order to prevent another group, some of those who did not live in the UK, from coming to the UK.[13] In particular this division of residence rights from citizenship rights was aimed at excluding Asians from East Africa. British nationality was restructured in 1948 by the British Nationality Act 1948 primarily to permit colonies which were demanding independence to establish their own citizenship laws while their nationals retained a nominal British status. As de-colonisation gathered speed in the late 1950s and 1960s, a number of problems became manifest. Migration from British colonies in the Indian sub-continent to colonies in Africa had been encouraged by the colonial authorities. However, animosity between the Asian populations and the black African populations was particularly acute in East Africa before independence. As their states of residence ceased to be British colonies and became independent, on being given the choice, the majority of Asians resident in East Africa opted to remain British rather than become citizens of the newly independent states. As the Africanisation programmes began to gather speed in the newly

---

11 M Krajewski & H Rittstief, 'Germany' in B Nascimbene, *Nationality Laws in the European Union*, Butterworths/Guiffé, London/Milan, 1996 pp 365–366.
12 Citizens of the UK and colonies British Nationality Act 1948.
13 The Commonwealth Immigrants Act 1962.

independent countries of East Africa, the Asian population found itself increasingly in difficulties and began to seek to go to their state of citizenship – the UK. By 1968 a trickle became a substantial flow not least as the then ruler of Uganda, Idi Amin, threatened the collective expulsion of Asians from that country.

The British response in Parliament was to pass the Commonwealth Immigrants Act 1968 which permitted entry to the UK as of right only to those British nationals with an ancestral connection to the UK. The Asian British nationals from East Africa were, thereby, rather effectively excluded. The result was very substantial suffering for a not insignificant number of persons who found themselves suddenly with no state where they had a right of residence at a time when they were being expelled from the state where they had been living. The inverse process of the Aussiedler phenomenon was at work, though based on the same principle, Habermas' conjunction of ethnicity and state. Those British who lacked the right ethnicity, even though they had the right nationality were excluded from residence rights. The UK constitutional principle of sovereignty of Parliament meant that legal challenges in the UK failed. I will return below to the history of the legal measures taken by the UK in respect of the East African Asians in particular from Kenya and Uganda. Before doing so a number of comments on the challenge of citizenship, residence and ethnicity in Europe are warranted.

Habermas proposes, as an alternative to these ethnically oriented citizenship laws the concept of European Civil Rights. Taking as the point of departure the citizenship-territory-residence nexus, can one see the development of these European Civil Rights and if so where? There is, indeed, evidence of the development of supranational European Civil Rights in this sphere of national sovereignty. Their source is the ECHR, which, through its interpretation by the ECtHR transcends the constitutional limitations of national law and provides a threshold of European Civil Rights even in the field of citizenship. The central provisions by which this transformation is taking place are article 3 ECHR, the prohibition on torture, inhuman and degrading treatment, article 8 the right to respect for family life and Protocol 4. I will consider in some depth these provisions in chapter 7 below from the perspective of immigration and asylum. Here I will focus on the citizenship issues in so far as they may be seen as part of the development of European Civil Rights.

Citizenship, Degrading Treatment and European Civil Rights

Returning then to East Africa, the remaining venue for these Asian British nationals from there to seek a remedy was before the ECtHR. One difficulty in seeking such a remedy was the fact that the UK had not (and still has not) ratified the Fourth Protocol ECHR, the only part of the Convention which protects the right of the individual to enter his or her country of nationality. Thus the claims of the East African Asians had to be based on one of the substantive ECHR rights without that Protocol.

The claim was made on the basis that exclusion from a country of nationality, in particular when that country is the only one where the individual can claim a right of residence, is inhuman and degrading treatment contrary to Article 3 ECHR.

The cases of 25 East African Asians of British nationality came before the institutions of the ECtHR in 1973. Under the system in force at the time, a first consideration of a case was undertaken by the European Commission of Human Rights (ECmHR) in two steps, first a consideration of admissibility, then, if the case was found admissible, a reasoned decision on the complaints. The decision would, normally be transferred then to the Court of Human Rights for a second hearing and decision. However, between the two stages a case could be referred to the Council of Ministers (the political venue of the Council of Europe) where a compromise solution to the case might be arranged. In the East African Asians case, after admissibility, it was referred to the Council of Ministers and following an undertaking by the UK to open a quota system for the admission of these persons to the UK the action was determined as completed and did not proceed to the ECtHR. Thus the decision of the ECmHR stands as the authority in respect of the complaints.

While cases relating to immigration had come before the Strasbourg institutions before, this case predates the landmark decisions on the application of human right standards in the ECHR to the residence and expulsion of aliens.[14] Thus the ECmHR's first step was to consider the position of state sovereignty as regards the admission of persons to the territory and the nexus with the ECHR. It stated "the Commission has, nevertheless, found that the contracting parties agreed to restrict the free exercise of their powers under general international law, including the power to control the entry and exit of aliens, to the extent and within the limits of the obligations which they assumed under this treaty.[15] In certain exceptional circumstances, the deportation of a person may thus be contrary to the Convention and, in particularly, constitute 'inhuman treatment' within the meaning of Article 3 thereof.[16] ... The Commission finds that the above considerations concerning the position of aliens apply, *mutatis mutandis*, to the present application brought by citizens."[17]

Thus the ECmHR places the issue of the exclusion from the national territory of citizens into the framework of inhuman and degrading treatment. The next step for the Commission is the consideration of the meaning of degrading treatment. The UK government argued that degrading treatment must involve a physical act. The Commission did not agree. It found that degrading treatment is such that lowers the individual in rank, position, reputation or character, whether in his or her own eyes or in those of other people.[18] Further, the purpose of the provision in the

---

14 These cases start as regards family members with *Abdulaziz, Cabales and Balkandali* [1985] Ser A No 95; and *Berrehab* [1988] Ser A No 138; see chapter 7.

15 Application No 4314/69, 32 CD 96, 97.

16 Application No 1802/62 6 Yearbook 462, 480.

17 *East African Asians* [1973] 3 EHRR 76 paras 186–187.

18 Ibid para 189.

ECmHR's view is to "prevent interferences with the dignity of man of a particularly serious nature."[19] The interpretation thus brings into the centre of article 3 ECHR the concept of human dignity as a right protected in supranational law both for aliens and citizens.

The next issue to be addressed is that of discrimination on the basis of race. In the admissibility decision on one of the joined group of cases, the ECmHR had already found that discrimination on grounds of race could in certain circumstances amount to degrading treatment within article 3 ECHR. It confirmed this opinion. Considering the evidence before it on the Commonwealth Immigrants Act 1968, it found it established that the Act had racial motives and that it covered a racial group: "The main purpose of the Government's Bill was apparently to exclude that 'most of the 200,000 Asians in East Africa would continue to be free to come here at will.' "[20, 21] On this basis the ECmHR found that the UK Act, by subjecting to immigration control citizens of the United Kingdom and colonies in East Africa who were of Asian origin, discriminated against this group of people on grounds of their colour or race.

The ECmHR then comes to the crux of the matter as regards citizenship. When Uganda and Kenya become independent in 1962 and 1963, the British laws on independence of these states permitted the Asian population to retain their British nationality. The 1962 Commonwealth Immigrants Act expressly exempted from immigration control any person who had a UK passport and was a citizen of the UK and colonies. A UK White Paper in 1965 on *Immigration from the Commonwealth* did not propose any limitation of access to the territory of British nationals and made no reference to the East African Asians. The ECmHR concluded on the basis of the evidence before it that "these people had apparently not opted for local citizenship, but retained their status as citizens of the United Kingdom and Colonies, because they considered this status as a safeguard for their future position, in that it gave them rights of entry into, and residence in, the United Kingdom."[22] Their exclusion from this right, which had informed their decision to remain British nationals, on the basis of their race constituted, according to the ECmHR, inhuman and degrading treatment contrary to article 3 ECHR.[23]

The central issue which motivated the voluntary choice by the East African Asians of citizenship in this case was the right to reside in the UK. When Habermas discusses the voluntary nature of "republican" citizenship, his assumption is that the citizen makes the choice to retain or abandon citizenship. The possibility that

---

19 Ibid para 189.
20 Cf the statement made by Lord Stoneham, Minister of State at the Home Office, before the House of Lords on 29 February 1968.
21 Ibid para 199.
22 Ibid para 203.
23 A claim that the acts breached article 5 the right to liberty and security of the person in conjunction with article 14 (which prohibits discrimination in the application of the rights of the ECHR) failed.

the state should withdraw from the citizen not the title of citizenship but the element of greatest importance to the individual, the right to reside, does not enter the discussion.[24] The fact that in a state which is generally classified as one with a liberal 'republican' model of citizenship, the UK, such a reconfiguration of the meaning of citizenship could take place and constitutional guarantees regarding equality of treatment of citizens would be unable to protect the individuals deprived of the functional heart of citizenship does not enter his discussion. However, the categorisation by a supranational dispute resolution mechanism, the ECmHR, of the state's act as a breach of European Civil Rights in the form of the ECHR supports his demand for the creation of durable European rights which can transform citizenship at the European level.

The choice of the UK was to exclude some of its nationals in a reversion to an ethnic vision of the nation. In a dissenting opinion, one of the ECmHR members states "The respondent Government has explained convincingly that following the grant of independence of Kenya and Uganda the policy of 'Africanisation' adopted in those countries, the number of United Kingdom citizens of Asian origin who wanted to leave Africa to settle in the United Kingdom rose substantially to a point where it was not possible to absorb all who might wish to enter."[25] The use of the discourse of "absorption" in respect of citizens indicates a substantial debasement of the principle of citizenship. If citizens are subject to an absorption test, meaning a test on whether they should be permitted to live in their country of nationality, and this test can legitimately be carried out on the basis of race, i.e. persons of certain racial backgrounds will pass the test and others will not, there is no longer any essential equality before the law in the meaning of citizenship. The explicit differentiation which the member of the ECmHR intends in his dissenting opinion is even clearer a little further on: "Racial tensions exist beneath the surface in all the European States which have admitted a sufficiently large number of foreign workers. These tensions are obviously much to be regretted. They are nonetheless a reality and the passage of the applicants' memorandum which I have just cited shows that Great Britain has not been spared them. These foreigners mix very little with the native population ..."[26] The elision of citizens of some ethnic origins with foreigners by a person the equivalent of an international judge is remarkable. Fortunately, this racialisation of citizenship was rejected by the majority of the ECmHR. The UK was condemned. It is also worth noting as regards the "numbers" argument, the UK was facing a total

---

24 This paradox has become even more pronounced with the entry into force of section 40 Nationality, Immigration and Asylum Act 2002 which permits the UK authorities to withdraw citizenship from an individual on specified (security related) grounds. Of course, the UK's commitments under the UN Convention relating to the status of stateless persons 1954 prevents the removal of citizenship from any person who as a result would be made stateless. Thus it is in effect applicable only to dual nationals.

25 Dissenting Opinion of Mr F Welter.

26 Dissenting Opinion of Mr F Welter.

of 200,000 East African Asians arriving in the UK. When the Ausseidler began to go to Germany, this was the annual rate of admissions for almost a decade. The "absorption" argument which is intrinsically tied to the numbers argument is rather dependent on political will.

Citizenship, Residence and the European Union

The British nationals from East Africa excluded under the Commonwealth Immigrants Act 1968 did not disappear with the ECmHR decision finding the UK to have committed inhuman and degrading treatment by discriminating against them on the basis of race in excluding them from residence in the UK. On 1 January 1973 the UK acceded to the European Economic Community (as it then was) and deposited its Declaration regarding those persons who were to be British nationals for the purposes of Community law. This group excluded the British nationals who were in the category of East African Asians. In 1981 the UK changed its citizenship laws re-allocating persons depending on their link to the UK as different types of British national. The link was primarily dependent on whether a parent had been born in the UK and islands, thus indirectly it was based on an idea of ethnicity – only "real" Britons have parents born in the UK. The East African Asians were, by and large, re-categorised as British Overseas citizens.[27] A new UK declaration was lodged on the meaning of British national for Community law. British Overseas citizens were excluded.

In September 1994, a British Overseas citizen, Mrs Kaur, requested permission to remain in the UK where she was visiting. This was refused. She appealed *inter alia* on the basis that she wished to exercise rights of free movement in other EU Member States. The national court referred to the ECJ the question central to Mrs Kaur's residence – does citizenship of the Union confer a right to enter and remain in a Member State of which an individual is a national even where this right is denied under national law.

In a short judgment of only 29 paragraphs, the ECJ rejected the claim to a remedy of Mrs Kaur on the basis of citizenship of the Union. The ECJ, repeating previous jurisprudence stated that "under international law, it is for each Member State, having due regard to Community law, to lay down the conditions for the acquisition and loss of nationality."[28] The ECJ noted that UK national legislation reserved the right of residence for those citizens who had the closest connection with the state. When acceding to the EU, the UK signalled this decision and excluded all persons in Mrs Kaur's situation from the acquisition of any Community law rights.

---

27 British Nationality Act 1981.
28 C-192/99 *Kaur* 20 February 2001 para 19.

Therefore, the ECJ found "adoption of that declaration [in 1972] did not have the effect of depriving any person who did not satisfy the definition of a national of the United Kingdom of rights to which that person might be entitled under Community law. The consequence was rather that such rights never arose in the first place for such a person."[29]

Thus the ECJ upheld the UK declarations on British nationals and refused to interfere with the choice of a Member State in designating who are and are not entitled to residence rights on the basis of citizenship choices. As Shah puts it "The *Kaur* decision also means that the last possible international judicial remedy against the injustices suffered by British passport holders from East Africa consequent to the Commonwealth Immigrants Act 1968 has been ruled out."[30]

The hands off approach of the ECJ is in sharp contrast to that of the ECmHR. The fact that the ECJ decision was taken in full knowledge of the ECmHR opinion in the *East African Asians* case makes it all the more curious. While on the one hand the ECJ has gone out of its way since the early 1960s to proclaim its duty to protect fundamental rights including those in the ECHR,[31] when faced with a politically sensitive case but one where the ECmHR had already found a breach of article 3, inhuman and degrading treatment, instead of taking up the challenge of European Civil Rights, the ECJ backed off with the implicit argument of lack of jurisdiction. The criticisms which Weiler made in 1992 about the failure of the ECJ to take human rights seriously particularly when third country nationals are involved may justifiably be repeated ten years on.[32]

Following Citizenship in European Civil Rights

The right of residence does not recover its position as exclusively tied to citizenship after the East African Asians case in 1973. The fracture which takes place between the two principles begins to take shape in European human rights law in a form which may have surprised the dissenting member of the Commission in the earlier case. While the institutions of the ECHR were not again faced with the problem of a division between residence and citizenship rights, they are increasingly challenged in the 1990s by claims to rights of residence by citizens and their foreign national family members. The fact of the continuing diversity in citizenship acquisition laws in Europe results in the situation where different members of the same family may

---

29 Ibid para 25.
30 P Shah, *Case note on Kaur*, European Journal of Migration and Law, Vol 3 No 2 2001 pp 271–278.
31 E Guild & G Lesieur (eds), *The European Court of Justice on the European Convention on Human Rights: Who said what when*, Kluwer Law International, The Hague, 1997.
32 J H H Weiler, 'Thou Shalt Not Oppress a Stranger: On the Judicial Protection of the Human Rights of Non- EC Nationals,' 3 EJIL (1992) 65.

not enjoy the same citizenship. Parents may acquire one citizenship but the children do not, or the inverse. Husbands and wives may have different citizenships and little possibility of obtaining that of the other. For many, the acquisition of citizenship would be extremely difficult and subject to conditions which would be hard to fulfill. For instance, young people born in Europe of Moroccan parents are not able effectively to deprive themselves of Moroccan citizenship, as the authorities of their parents' state of nationality does not recognize renunciation of citizenship. Thus if divesting oneself of any previously held citizenship is a requirement for acquiring citizenship of the state of residence (as is the case in many European countries) these young people will not be able to acquire the citizenship of their state of birth and residence.

In a highly criticized judgment in 1996, the ECtHR considered whether the article 8 right to protection of private and family life had been breached with in respect of the expulsion of a child from the Netherlands to Morocco. The child of a first marriage came to visit his father, Salah Ahmut, in the Netherlands. The father had acquired Dutch citizenship and was working and living in the Netherlands. The child sought to remain with his father (and older sister who came with him and was eventually permitted to remain by the authorities) but his application was rejected and he was expelled to Morocco. The family appealed against the decision but failed to get relief in light of national law limiting family reunification. When domestic remedies had been exhausted, the family brought a petition to the ECHR. The ECtHR found that the link of citizenship of the father to the Netherlands did not entitle him to enjoy family life with his young son in that country. The ECtHR states "The fact of the applicants' living apart is the result of Salah Ahmut's conscious decision to settle in the Netherlands rather than remain in Morocco. In addition to having Netherlands nationality since February 1990, Salah Ahmut has retained his original Moroccan nationality ... Soufiane [the son] has Moroccan nationality only. It therefore appears that Salah Ahmut is not prevented from maintaining the degree of family life which he himself had opted for when moving to the Netherlands in the first place, nor is there any obstacle to his returning to Morocco. Indeed, Salah Ahmut and Souffiane have visited each other on numerous occasions since the latter's return to that country. It may well be that Salah Ahmut would prefer to maintain and intensify his family links with Souffiane in the Netherlands. However, ... Article 8 does not guarantee a right to choose the most suitable place to develop family life. The fact of the applicants' living apart is the result of Salah Ahmut's conscious decision to settle in the Netherlands rather than remain in Morocco."[33]

Of course the Court could just as easily have noted that the fact of the applicants' living apart was the result of the Dutch authorities refusal to permit Souffiane to continue to reside in the Netherlands. What is important regarding this discussion, however, is the Court's approach to citizenship. While the Dutch authorities have not directly sought to separate the right to reside from the right of citizenship, by refusing to allow

---

33   *Ahmut v Netherlands* 28 November 1996.

Salah Ahmut's young son to reside with him in the Netherlands it could be argued that the authorities have indirectly done exactly that. In order to fulfill his parental duties to his child, the father is required to abandon voluntarily his residence right in his country of citizenship, at least temporarily. The Court specifically refers to the fact that the father has a second nationality and that he can rely on the rights relating to that nationality if he wishes to enjoy family life with his child. The value of European citizenship is diminished by the retention (even where it is not possible to renounce the other citizenship) of another citizenship. The mechanism for the devaluation of the European citizenship is through residence rights and their indirect weakening.

A different approach has been taken by the Court in cases of expulsion of foreigners married to nationals whose citizenship is supplemented by strong cultural affiliation. The examples of *Boultif v Switzerland*[34] and *Amrollahi v Denmark* is instructive here. In the first case, an Algerian national was convicted of a serious crime against property and an individual. The Swiss authorities began expulsion proceedings against him. He appealed against those proceedings and when all national recourses had been exhausted he lodged a petition before the ECtHR on the basis that his expulsion would constitute a breach of article 8 as his wife, a Swiss national, could not be expected to go to Algeria to enjoy family life with him there. The ECtHR revealed itself rather susceptible to Ms Boultif's situation: "The Court has considered, first, whether the applicant and his wife could live together in Algeria. The applicant's wife is a Swiss national. It is true that the applicant's wife can speak French and has had contacts by telephone with her mother-in-law in Algeria. However, the applicant's wife has never lived in Algeria, she has no other ties with that country, and indeed, she does not speak Arabic. In these circumstances she cannot, in the Court's opinion, be expected to follow her husband, the applicant, to Algeria".

In the second case, an Iranian national living in Denmark was convicted of a serious criminal offence involving the importation of prohibited drugs. Denmark sought to expel him. He contested the decision on the basis of his right under article 8 to protection of his private and family life on the basis of his marriage to a Danish national and the existence of their children there. The Court held: "The applicant's wife, A, is a Danish national. She has never been to Iran, she does not know Farsi and she is not a Muslim. Besides being married to an Iranian man, she has no ties with the country. In these circumstances the Court accepts even if it is not impossible for the spouse and the applicant's children to live in Iran that it would, nevertheless, cause them obvious and serious difficulties. In addition, the Court recalls that A's daughter from a previous relationship, who has lived with A since her birth in 1989, refuses to move to Iran. Taking this fact into account as well, A cannot, in the Court's opinion, be expected to follow the applicant to Iran."[35]

The right of residence based on private and family life is related both to citizenship rights and ethnicity. In respect of Mr Ahmut dual citizenship provided

---

34 *Boultif v Switzerland* ECtHR 2 August 2001.
35 *Amrollahi v Denmark* ECtHR 11 July 2002.

a basis to diminish his right to private and family life in the state of citizenship in which he resided. The implicit assumption is that his ethnic origins in Morocco link his identity and thus his rights to that country to a greater extent than to the Netherlands. For Ms Boulltif and Amrollahi, their ethnicity in conjunction with their citizenship strengthens their right to have their husbands remain with them in Europe notwithstanding the threat which they are considered to pose to society. A Swiss or Danish national who has never visited Algeria or Iran, (and in the latter cases knows no Farsi) and who are not Muslims have a different quality of right to residence on European territory. There is no balance of their right to remain in Switzerland or Denmark against a right to live in Algeria or Iran as the wife of a national.

These cases indicate an ethnic element which the Court reads into the right of residence attached to citizenship. However, two other cases indicate a weakening of this ethnic element in European Civil Rights. In the case of *Yildiz v Austria*[36] a Turkish national who joined his family in Austria when he was 14 was subject to an expulsion order and ban on return to the country. The basis for the authorities action is a number of petty criminal convictions, including seven road traffic offences. He was considered a danger to public policy as a result. He was married to a Turkish national who had been born in Austria and lived there all her life. They had one child there. After exhausting all possible remedies in Austria without success, the man brought an action against Austria before the ECtHR under article 8. The Court states: "43. The Court will first examine the applicants' family situation and the length of their stay in Austria. It observes that the first applicant is not a second generation immigrant, i.e. a person who was born or has lived the main part of his life in the country from which he is going to be removed. He only came to Austria in 1989 at the age of fourteen and must therefore have links with his country of origin and in particular be able to speak Turkish. On the other hand, he was still an adolescent when he came to Austria, where his close family was and is still living. In December 1996, when the Administrative Court confirmed the residence ban against him, he had been living in Austria for seven years, he had been working there and had been co-habiting for a little less than three years with the second applicant, who is also a Turkish national but was born in Austria and has lived there all her life. Their daughter, the third applicant, was one year and four months old at the material time. In fact, the Austrian authorities issuing the residence ban acknowledged that the first applicant had reached a high degree of integration in Austria. Nevertheless, the Court considers that, as regards the possible effects of the residence ban on his family life, the authorities failed to establish whether the second applicant could be expected to follow him to Turkey, in particular whether she spoke Turkish and maintained any links, other than her nationality, with that country."[37]

The ECtHR distinguishes Mr Yildiz from second generation immigrants. Implicit in this differentiation is that second generation immigrants who are born on

---

36 31 October 2002.
37 *Yildiz v Austria* 31 October 2002.

the territory have a higher claim to residence rights even though they may lack formal citizenship than those who have arrived even as children to the territory. In effect, the ECtHR seems to be creating the concept of de facto citizenship which results from long residence and compensates, in the field of protected residence rights, for the lack of formal citizenship. This has most eloquently been expressed by Professor Schermers in his partly concurring, partly dissenting opinion in 1993: "I am not so sure, however, whether international law concerning the expulsion of aliens is not changing fundamentally as a result of growing concerns for human rights and of a perceived need for solidarity among States in the face of increasing interstate relations. By admitting aliens to their territories, States inevitably accept at least some measure of responsibility. This responsibility weights even more heavily in the case of children educated in their territory. For any society, individuals like the present applicant are a burden. Even independent of human rights considerations, I doubt whether modern international law permits a State which has educated children of admitted aliens to expel these children when they become a burden. Shifting this burden to the State of origin of the parent is no longer so clearly acceptable under modern international law. It is at least subject to doubt whether a host country has the right to return those immigrants who prove to be unsatisfactory."[38] I return to this point in chapter 7 when considering in depth the ECtHR's jurisprudence in the field.

Mrs Yildiz, who is one of these second generation immigrants, seems to be accorded the same degree of protection as regards her residence right on the basis of article 8 as Mrs Amrollahi. Unlike in the Ahmut case, the Court does not assume that the passport of Mrs Yildiz is definitive of her identity and thus of her claim to residence in Austria. Indeed her link of nationality with Turkey is treated by the Court as if it were incidental to her identity. Her husband's claim to remain in Austria succeeds because her residence right is sufficiently strong to support it.

The choice of the state not to grant citizenship to persons resident on the territory is related to the state's desire to be able to expel those individuals if they prove unsatisfactory. That decision is founded on the division between the residence right attached to citizenship and a residence right which is free standing and thus capable of rupture. The transformation of citizenship rights as regards residence which is apparent from the East African Asians decision is part of a reformulation of European Civil Rights as rights which are capable of application beyond formal citizenship.

Conclusions

In the transformation of the nexus of citizenship and residence, can one see the development of a new unifying principle which makes sense of citizenship in the

---

38 *Lamguindaz* Series A No 258-C 28 June 1993.

face of regionalisation and globalisation, as Habermas has sought to do? In the first two examples which I have considered here, the Aussiedler and the East African Asians, national constitutional settlements on citizenship have privileged an ethnically motivated definition of belonging. The 'real' citizens, those who have the right to reside on the territory are those whom national constitutional mythology classifies as inside the ethnos rather than outside. One of the difficulties which the German example exposed was that for many Germans, in fact the Turks who had been living next door for the last thirty years seemed much more familiar than the Aussiedler who had been living many generations in the farther reaches of the former USSR many of whom did not speak German. The East African Asians who managed to come to the UK have been singled out as the integration "stars" of the recent UK migratory experience.[39] Both conclusions raise questions about the adequacy of the national definitions of citizenship and residence rights in parts of Europe.

The challenge which the separation of residence rights from citizenship has posed to the European institutions has arisen only in respect of the UK case (at least so far). The consequences are still being felt. However, what is evident already is that the lack of respect for the undertakings of citizenship which the UK government showed caused the field to move beyond the control of the state and its constitutional settlements into the supranational European field. Here there are two rather different results. First in the field of European human rights, the ECmHR found that European human rights commitments could compensate for the member State's withdrawal of residence rights from citizenship where this constituted inhuman or degrading treatment. Secondly, the ECJ refused to intervene in the same domain, even where doing so would have strengthened its claim to legitimacy in the area of human rights and could have provided a useful mechanism to safeguard the content of citizenship of the Union.

Thus the supranational venue where European States have been most challenged has been the ECtHR on the basis of human rights which have an increasingly tenuous relationship with citizenship. The monopoly of the Member States over the definition of citizenship of the Union was upheld by the ECJ, even in a case where by so doing it acquiesces to an injustice already condemned by the ECmHR as discriminatory on the basis of race. The result appears to be that while Habermas' European Civil Rights are in the process of developing, they are increasing divorced from formal citizenship itself. The failure of the Member States and the ECJ to respond to the reality of belonging and exclusion in Europe has transformed the field into one of fundamental human rights in which formal citizenship may only have a secondary part to play. The redefinition of the meaning of citizenship is taking place in the human rights field responding to the pressures of regionalism and globalisation which the national constitutional settlements of at least some Member States have been unable to take on board.

---

39   See for instance the British Council's explanation of British society: http://www.britishcouncil.org/languageassistant/ess_uk_multiculturalukcv.html.

Chapter 5

From Immigrants to Citizens in the European Union: Expulsion and Exclusion

The rights of citizens of the Union have grown out of the rights of Community nationals to free movement as economic actors. The inclusion of the objective of free movement of persons in article 3 EC was turned into specific rights in Title III articles 39–49 EC/article III-133–150 EU Constitution, free movement of workers, the self-employed and service providers. The legislator extended this to include the right of free movement for service recipients.[1] Included in the original EEC Treaty which came into force in 1957 was the right of free movement of workers and others. The transitional period for the achievement of this right of free movement ended in 1968. From that moment the right of nationals of the Member States to be migrant workers in other Member States was assured. The rights of access to the territory, employment, family reunification and protection from expulsion were included in the secondary legislation in particular regulation 1612/68 for workers, directive 73/148 for the self-employed and service providers. Directive 68/360 sets out the practical matters regarding the issue of documents and directive 64/221 sets out the limitations on expulsion and exclusion from the territory. These four acts of secondary legislation regulate the position of movement of nationals of the Member States for economic purposes until replaced by a new citizens of the Union directive. A directive on citizens of the Union and their family members to move and reside freely within the territory of the Member States will consolidate rights contained in the four measures together with the three right of residence directives regarding the economically inactive though it is not intended to replace them completely.[2] As of February 2004, it has not yet been adopted or completed its legislative consideration.

---

1 Article 1 directive 73/148; an extension approved by the ECJ as implicit in the Treaty provision: 186/87 *Cowan* [1989] ECR 195.
2 COM (2001) 257 final, 23.05.01.

In this chapter I will first examine how migrant nationals of the Member States have acquired a right to migrate so substantial as to no longer merit the use of the term "migration" but instead to become known as free movement of persons. I will then examine the extent to which this right of free movement has become incorporated into the legal structure of citizenship. In doing so I will test the key characteristics of citizenship of the Union against the fundamental legal dividing line between immigrant and citizen: security of residence.

The Three Fundamental Interests of a Migrant

There are three fundamental interests of immigrants when they move to a new country: first are the conditions of entry onto the host territory and protection from expulsion; second is access to employment and the conditions of employment; the third is family reunification.[3] For the citizen these three interests are regulated by the principle of equality. Citizens have a right in international law to enter and reside on their state of nationality. There is no internationally recognized right for a state to expel its citizens. As regards employment, equality in access to employment and the conditions of employment is one of the central civil liberties of citizenship. The principle of equality between citizens in access to employment is so central that in much employment protection legislation it is implicit. The accepted grounds for employment discrimination among citizens are primarily qualification and ability. Discrimination in employment on grounds of foreign nationality, however, is linked centrally to immigration status. The limitation of immigrants' rights of employment is foremost in the conditions of their entry and residence in the state. Thus expressly permitted is discrimination in employment on the basis of nationality where this is linked with immigration status. Indeed, employers who fail to discriminate on this ground may be violating national law which sanctions employers which hire foreign nationals without the necessary permission to work. The exclusion of nationality as a prohibited ground for discrimination in employment in the directives on discrimination adopted under article 13 EC/article III-124 EU Constitution (prohibiting racial and other discrimination) indicates just how attached the Member States are to the principle of permitted discrimination in these fields on the basis of nationality. I will consider the issue of discrimination and citizenship in chapter 11.

For the majority of citizens, family reunification will take place with other nationals of the same state. The legal rules which regulate capacity to marry in EU

---

3 Or family formation; EC law on free movement of workers does not make a distinction between reunification of a family which is already in existence abroad when one member of the family migrates and family formation where the family is founded after the immigrant has moved to his or her host state and then travels abroad and forms a family.

states are primarily designed around protection of young persons – the age at which a person may marry, or to discourage bigamy and polygamy. Whether a family chooses to live as an extended family with numerous generations living under the same roof or apart is only tangentially a matter of concern for the state. State interference in family life between parents and children is an exception and justified only in respect of grave considerations of the interest of the child. For the migrant, however, family reunification can be a matter of extensive state control and scrutiny. Before the EU state permits even a foreign spouse or child to join an immigrant (specifically a third country national immigrant) numerous requirements will need to be fulfilled. I will consider in some depth the legal provisions on family reunification for migrant nationals of the Member States and third country nationals and compare them in the next chapter.

The fundamental mechanism for the immigrant to gain security in the three fields of most central interest to him or her is by becoming a citizen. I will focus here on the issue of security of residence and its transformation in EC law in the light of citizenship of the Union. Does the re-designation of migrant nationals of the Member States as citizens of the Union have the consequence of extending to them the security of residence which is inherent in citizenship?

The Migrant to Citizen – National Law Mechanisms

At the national level, the mechanism for transforming immigrants into citizens is to be found in the nationality laws of the Member States. There are two primary ways in which this takes place: first, through birth on the territory and/or to persons with a certain status there (either citizens themselves, or persons with a certain immigration status).[4] The vast majority of citizens acquire their status as such in this manner, automatically. The second mechanism for transforming immigrants into citizens is naturalization – an individual process by which citizenship is conferred on a non-citizen by the state. The transformation of a non-citizen into a citizen has consequences in all three areas of fundamental interest of immigrants. First, their right to entry and residence and their protection against expulsion is assured. As citizens these issues can no longer be called into question. Secondly, their right to access to employment and equal treatment in employment is no longer in issue. They can no longer be discriminated against on the basis of immigration status. Thirdly as regards family reunification, there are diverging approaches in the Member States as regards the admission of foreign family members. In some Member States such as Germany

---

4   Among the Member States only Ireland retains a system of pure ius soli where birth on the territory to a person with or without any legal status on the territory confers citizenship.

and Austria there are very different and more generous rules for family reunification of citizens in relation to immigrants.[5] In other Member States such as the UK and the Netherlands the same rules apply to both citizens and immigrants.

The means the EU has used to transform immigrants into citizens has been collective, through operation of law. There has been no question of using the tools of compulsory integration, acculturation or assimilation of the individual. Indeed, these words are not applied in the texts to individuals. Where they apply at all to individuals they relate to the duties on states to behave in certain ways, such as in the preamble of regulation 1612/68 which requires the best conditions of integration to be made available by the state to migrant workers from other Member States. Indeed, at the EU level, the dominant discussion is about diversity as a positive value in the Union. Even the question of language acquisition which Bauböck considers central to the lowest threshold, acculturation, cannot be required of EU migrant workers and cannot be raised as an issue regarding their citizenship of the Union.

Acquisition of Rights in EU Law and Citizenship

From the establishment of the European Economic Community with the entry into force of the EEC Treaty (as it then was) freedom of movement of persons was among the objectives.[6] I shall very briefly run through the economic free movement provisions of the Treaty which have already been referred to and outline in earlier chapters.[7] The object of abolition of obstacles to the free movement of persons, fleshed out in Part III Title III articles 39–49/article III-133–150 EU Constitution. Article 39 EC/article III-133 EU Constitution provides for the abolition of obstacles to free movement of workers among the Member States. It is subject to two main limitations: first, on the grounds of public policy, public security and public health (to which I shall return at some length below); secondly, Member States are permitted to restrict access to their civil services to own nationals. Both of these exclusions have been restrictively interpreted by the Court of Justice. Article 43/article III-137 EU Constitution provides for a right to non-discrimination for the self-employed – the right of establishment. This incorporates a right to move for the purpose of self-employment to another Member State and to reside there. The right is in terms of non-discrimination and abolition of obstacles to the exercise of economic activities

---

5   R Cholewinski, *The Conditions of Family Reunification in 8 Council of Europe member States*, Council of Europe, Strasbourg, 2001.
6   Article 3(c) EC – this is no longer reflected in the same way in the EU Constitution – see article 3.
7   For an examination in greater depth see E Guild, *Immigration Law in the European Community*, Kluwer Law International, The Hague, 2001.

as self-employed in different Member States. Among the main obstacles are differences in regulation of professions and trades. All Member States have complex systems of regulation operated by state authorities, quasi-state authorities and professional bodies. While most of the rules which excluded non-nationals directly on grounds of nationality have been abolished, indirect discrimination is still prevalent in the form of rules which fail to recognise skills and experience obtained in other Member States.[8] Finally, Article 49/article III-144 EU Constitution provides a right to provide services and through secondary legislation and the interpretation of the ECJ, it also incorporates a right for persons to move to receive services. This right is designed to recognise that of individuals to go to other Member States for economic purposes without the intention of setting up an infrastructure or staying a long period of time.

The transitional period for the achievement of the rights ended in 1968. At that point the free movement of persons for economic purposes was to have been achieved. It is worth noting that the right to move as included in the original EEC Treaty was designed for those exercising some sort of economic activity. Individuals are treated as economic actors only and have rights as such. The humanitarian reasons for permitting persons to move across borders which so occupy newspapers and European policy makers, asylum seekers, refugees and displaced persons, find no direct place in the Treaty as originally adopted. Provisions relating to them will only be inserted later with the Amsterdam Treaty. Rather it is the right to work which is central to a right to cross a border. The type of economic activity is wide – covering most situations, in particular as developed by the ECJ in its jurisprudence.

The space which is being created is one within which rights of entry, economic activity and residence are created for a class of persons defined on the basis of nationality. This is a substantial and important departure from the position in international law where only humanitarian grounds give rise to a duty on states to admit non-nationals (see chapter 7 on the European human rights norms as regards migration). To complete the rights of movement on the territory of the Union which accrue to nationals of the Member States, the 1990 Directives on the right of residence for pensioners (90/365), the economically inactive (90/364) and students (93/96) were adopted extending movement rights beyond economic capacities. In each case the individual must be able to support him or herself (to the level of the national social security or assistance benefits) and have health insurance. When the concept of citizenship of the Union was introduced into the EC Treaty in 1993 the rights and limitations of that citizenship as referred to are those above, which neither approach the Marshallian perspective of citizenship nor that of the ECHR (see chapter 3).

---

8   European Commission, *Communication Free Movement of workers – achieving the full benefits and potential*, COM (2002) 694 final, Brussels 11.12.2002.

The Power to Exclude and Expel

Integral to the right of free movement of persons in Community law is the right of the State to control that movement where there are concerns of national security. This is expressed in the public policy, security and health provisos contained in article 39(3) EC/article III-133(3) EU Constitution and mirrored in the rights of establishment and service provision. The longest remaining directive in this field covers this aspect of the right of movement in respect of the three economic capacities.[9] Directive 64/221 sets out the meaning and limitations on the rights of States to exclude or expel nationals of another State on grounds of security.[10] It applies to all Community nationals (and their family members) who move from their home State to another for an economic purpose or otherwise. It is these exclusions which are of foremost significance in the "limitations" referred to in article 18(1) EC/article 124 EU Constitution, citizenship of the Union. It applies to all measures of exclusion, including refusal of entry onto the territory; issue and renewal of residence permits and expulsion. The directive sets out the limitations on the right of states to control the movement of persons on the grounds set out in the provisos. Thus rather than setting out what states can do, it focuses on what states cannot do. This is important from the perspective of implementation at the national level. It is sometimes easier to indicate instructions to civil servants explaining exactly how they must act and what they are entitled to do rather than draft circulars and instructions on what they cannot do particularly when the limitations are subtle.

No case has come before the ECJ on the interpretation of the public health proviso. No doubt this is in part, at least, a consequence of the fact that the only illnesses on the basis of which a Community national can be refused entry to a state or expelled (before the issue of a first residence permit) are those contained in the annex to the directive and are very limited. Similarly the public security proviso has given rise to little jurisprudence as regards its meaning.[11] Instead, those few cases which have come before the ECJ have revolved around procedural remedies. The battleground of exclusion and expulsion has been the public policy proviso.

Public Policy, the Economy and the Individual

The first ground prohibited to the Member States regarding controls on movement is the service of economic ends (article 2(1) directive 64/221). When the directive was

---

9   The right of residence directives, 90/364 and 90/365 and the student directive 93/96 extend the scope of the 1964 directive to persons within the new remit.

10 See also N Fennelly, 'The European Union and Protection of Aliens from Expulsion' EJML 3 (1999) pp 313–328 where he reviews the rules relating to Community nationals before considering their potential application to third country nationals.

11 C-175/94 *Gallagher* [1995] ECR I-4253; C-65/95 & C-111/95 *Radiom and Shingara* [1997] ECR I-3343.

adopted in 1964 the emphasis was on labour shortages. After the oil shocks of 1973, unemployment became a substantial consideration. Employment authorities sought to create or reserve jobs for own nationals to whom a duty of employment was owed.[12] Foreign workers were encouraged to return home, not least Greek and Turkish workers from Germany and North Africans from France.[13] Measures to exclude Community national workers could not, however, be taken on these grounds because of the protection provided to them by the directive. The battle to protect migrant workers, nationals of other Member States, against expulsion took place within the courts and provided the framework for the assumption of control over the meaning of security by the ECJ. While on the one hand the Member States sought to retain the right to define the meaning of the security provisos which enabled them to exclude and expel nationals of other Member States, the ECJ rejected their claims providing ever stricter interpretations of their meaning.[14]

Secondly, a decision by a national authority to control or prevent movement for economic reasons must be based exclusively on the personal conduct of the individual (article 3(1) directive 64/221). Specifically, previous criminal convictions in themselves do not constitute sufficient grounds for expulsion. This means that general preventative measures cannot be taken against Community nationals. The most common ground for exclusion and expulsion of nationals of the Member States from one another's territory is criminal convictions. The majority of the cases which come before the ECJ under the heading of exclusion and expulsion revolve around this question. The ECJ has narrowly interpreted the power of the Member States to expel on this ground: it must show that there is a genuine and sufficiently serious threat to the requirements of public policy affecting one of the fundamental interests of society before exclusion will be consistent with Community law.[15] On this ground, an automatic ban on readmission to Greece as part of an expulsion order based on criminal conviction for drugs possession was held unlawful insofar as it was applied to an Italian national.[16] Nonetheless, the decision to expel the citizen of the Union from Greece was lawful according to the ECJ. It only considered the case under article 49 EC/article III-144 EU Constitution, in other words, Ms Calfa's right to enter and reside in Greece as a service recipient. It expressly declined to consider the consequences of her status as a citizen of the Union on the lawfulness of her expulsion.

12　E Guild, 'Labour Migration in Europe' in D Bigo and E Guild, *Controlling Frontiers: Free Movement into and within Europe*, Ashgate, Aldershot, 2004 forthcoming.

13　M Piore, *Birds of Passage: Migrant Labour and Industrial Societies*, CUP, Cambridge, 1979.

14　The starting point is 41/74 *Van Duyn* [1974] ECR 1337; see F Mancini 'The Free Movement of Workers in the Case Law of the European Court of Justice' in D Curtin, D O'Keeffe (eds), *Constitutional Adjudication in European Community and National Law: Essays in Honour of Mr Justice T. F. O'Higgins*, Butterworths, Dublin, 1992.

15　30/77 *Bouchereau* [1977] ECR 1999.

16　C-348/96 *Calfa* [1999] ECR I-7637.

Public Policy and Discrimination

Citizenship of the Union as a status is clearly still closely linked to immigration. The ECJ confirmed this, and its position in *Calfa*, stating "It should be noted that Article 8A [now Article 133][17] of the Treaty, which sets out generally the right of every citizen of the Union to move and reside freely within the territory of the Member States, find specific expression in Article 48 [now Article 151][18] of the Treaty in relation to the free movement of workers. Since the facts with which the main proceedings are concerned fall within the scope of the latter provision, it is not necessary to rule on the interpretation of Article 8A [now Article 133][19] of the Treaty."[20] In this case a Spanish national resident in France was convicted by a French court of conspiracy to disturb public order, a charge which was related to the kidnapping of an industrialist in Bilbao (Spain). As part of the sentence, the French court made an order restricting Mr Olazabal's place of residence, effectively prohibiting him from living in the Basque country. When the sentence had been completed, the French authorities through an administrative order extended the conditions of Mr Olazabal's residence in France. The administrative order was challenged on the ground that it constituted discrimination against a national of another Member State contrary to articles 18(1)/article I-10 EU Constitution, 39(2)/article III-133(2) EU Constitution and 12 EC/article III-123 EU Constitution. The parties were agreed that such an order restricting the place of residence of Mr Olazabal after completion of his criminal sentence could not have been made in respect of a French national. Thus Mr Olazabal argued that the place of residence order discriminated against him as a Spanish national exercising a free movement right in France as a worker and as a citizen of the Union.

In 1975 the ECJ had found such discrimination as regards an administrative order limiting the place of residence of a national of another Member State contrary to the Community law right of equal treatment. Again in that case the offending state was France though the nationality of the worker was Italian. In this earlier case, the ECJ held that measures restricting the right of residence which are limited to part only of the territory may not be imposed by a Member State on nationals of other Member States except in the cases or circumstances in which such measures may be applied to nationals of the state concerned.[21] Much emphasis was subsequently placed on that judgment by one of the leading judges of the ECJ, Mancini, in his analysis of free movement of workers, thus making a withdrawal from the position somewhat contentious.[22]

---

17 Article I-8 EU Constitution.
18 Article III-18 EU Constitution.
19 Article I-8 EU Constitution.
20 C-100/01 *Olazabal* [2002] ECR I-10981.
21 36/75 *Rutilli* [1975] ECR 1219.
22 G F Mancini, 'The Free Movement of Workers in the Case Law of the European Court of Justice in Constitutional Adjudication in European Community and National Law,' D Curtin, D O'Keeffe (Eds),

Nonetheless, in the 2002 case, the ECJ distinguished the earlier decision on the basis that the ECJ had many times confirmed that States are permitted to apply measures to nationals of other Member States which they cannot apply to their own nationals on the grounds of public policy insofar as only non-nationals can be expelled or denied access to the territory. These measures are specifically permitted under the Treaty as regards nationals of other Member States. Thus the ECJ went on to state: "where nationals of other Member States are liable to banishment or prohibition of residence, they are also capable of being subject to less severe measures consisting of partial restrictions on their residence, justified on grounds of public policy, without it being necessary that identical measures be capable of being applied by the Member State in question to its own nationals."[23]

The result of such a finding is to permit discrimination at the heart of citizenship of the Union on the basis of immigration status. Because an individual is a "foreigner," he or she is liable to expulsion or exclusion. Thus the state is permitted to take less severe measures against him or her within the state even though such measures are prohibited against own nationals. The only limitation which the ECJ placed on this unwelcome departure from its earlier jurisprudence was the requirement that the same activity by a national of the Member State in question must give rise to punitive measures or other genuine and effective measures against nationals of the state intended to combat that conduct. What has been lost, or has failed to be affirmed is the link to the right to occupy the territory on the basis of non-discrimination with nationals of the state for citizens of the Union.

The Treaty provisions themselves demand equal treatment and thus would appear to exclude this option for states. That the ECJ permits a state to use administrative measures against a citizen of the Union in circumstances where against a national of the state itself only criminal law is capable of providing the punishment is also indicative of the relationship of the two spheres of justice. The state's legitimate exercise of violence against its own nationals is ring fenced in the field of criminal law. If the state seeks to imprison or restrict the right of movement of its nationals it can only do so within the parameters of criminal law or for the persons own protection, for instance in mental health circumstances. The rights of the defense and procedural rules of criminal law are designed to find the balance between the citizen and the state exactly in this sensitive field of legitimate state violence.

Foreigners, however, can be the subject of state violence without the engagement of criminal law. For instance, the detention of aliens is widely used in administrative law regarding immigration and expulsion. The state is not required to justify detention of foreigners on the grounds of criminal law, which in most cases would not

---

(Cont.)

Constitutional Adjudication in European Community and National Law: Essays for the Hon. Mr Justice T.F. O'Higgins, Butts, Dublin, 1992.

23 C-100/01 *Olazabal* para 41.

otherwise be possible as the foreigner has not committed a crime for which he or she would be convicted or sentenced.[24]

The failure of the ECJ to protect this space of citizenship for citizens of the Union, instead permitting states to opt for administrative measures to limit their movement on the territory indicates the extent to which the concept of citizenship of the Union is still incomplete. The weak insistence of the ECJ that the state, in order to exercise its administrative powers to restrict movement on the territory of a national of another Member State, must take either punitive or "other genuine and effective measures" against their own nationals for the same conduct is highly unsatisfactory.

While there have been substantial moves towards a more complete form of citizenship of the Union in the field of social rights (see chapter 3), the same cannot be said of some of the other central fields of citizenship. It is worrying that the interpretation of citizenship seems to be coloured by normative considerations extraneous to the central issue of equality. In the *Olazabal* case, the fact that Mr Olazabal appears to have been engaged in Basque separatist activities in Spain seems to colour the case. The phantom of terrorism stalks through the judgment deforming the rights of citizens, extending the legality of the states use of exceptional powers beyond the scope of the constitutional settlements of the citizen and the state regarding the use of state violence.

The Public Service Exception

The other main exclusion permitted to Member States as regards workers is the public service. Article 39/article III-133 EU Constitution specifically states that Member States are entitled to refuse admission of nationals of other Member States into their public services. In times of low unemployment this may not be particularly important, but after 1973 when unemployment rose this became increasingly problematic. One of the tools used by many Member States in the 1970s and 1980s (though less so afterwards) to generate jobs was to create them in the public service. This strategy to reduce unemployment was in principle closed to nationals of other Member States even if they had been living and working in the host State for some time.[25] The first challenges to the width of the public service exception came after 1974. The case revolved around the strategy of Germany in the early 1970s to reduce costs in the public service by applying less generous working conditions to migrant workers than own nationals as happened in the post office.

---

24 See E Guild, 'Exceptionalism and Transnationalism: UK Judicial Control of the Detention of Foreign "International Terrorists"' Alternatives Vol 8 (2003) pp 491–515; N Blake and R Hussain, *Immigration, Asylum and Human Rights*, OUP, Oxford, 2003 pp 114–141.

25 M Esposito, 'Libera Cirolazione e pubblica amministraione prassi nationale e prospettive' in B Nascimbene, *Le Libera Circolazione dei lavoratori*, Guiffre, Milan, 1998.

An Italian worker in the post office appealed against the fact that he was entitled to a lower allowance in comparison with his German co-workers. The post office argued that this was a post in the public service and thus the right to non-discrimination in Community law did not apply. The Court disagreed stating that the exclusion cannot be used to justify discriminatory measures as regards remuneration or other conditions of employment against workers once they have been admitted to the public service.[26] By 1980 the Court went further in attacking the Member States reservation of the public service for its own nationals. Not only are nationals of other Member States entitled to equal treatment if employed in the public service but the Court found that they had to be admitted to most posts in the public service. The only posts which can be reserved for own nationals are those which "involve direct or indirect participation in the exercise of powers conferred by public law and duties designed to safeguard the general interests of the State or of other public authorities. Such posts in fact presume on the part of those occupying them the existence of a special relationship of allegiance to the State and reciprocity of rights and duties which form the foundation of the bond of nationality."[27]

Member States have been reluctant to open up their civil services to nationals of other Member States. The lack of subsidiary legislation at EU level to provide administrative guidelines for the Member States regarding the ECJ jurisprudence may be a consideration. Faced with a definition as difficult to apply as "reciprocity of rights and duties which form the foundations of the bond of nationality," one can well imagine a personnel manager in any government department scratching his or her head in wonderment. The complexity of the definition does not easily translate into the hierarchical gradations of Member States' civil services. The personnel officer cannot simply send out a circular advising that any posts below for example A3 must be open to nationals of all Member States while posts above can be limited to own nationals. Instead each post must be assessed individually as regards compliance with the ECJ's test.

Incomplete Citizenship

A number of questions arise from the incomplete nature of citizenship of the Union in this equation. First, if the nationals of other Member States are excluded from certain types of employment on the grounds that they fail to have a special relationship of allegiance and fail to enjoy the bond of nationality, what does this mean for the reality of citizenship of the Union? The relationship of allegiance is only to a part of the Union not to the whole of it though the citizenship applies to the whole of the

---

26   152/73 *Sotgui* [1974] ECR 152.
27   149/79 *Commission v Belgium* [1980] ECR 3881.

territory. If as the Court has stated "Union citizenship is destined to be the fundamental status of nationals of the Member States ..."[28] then this limitation must be
questioned. Secondly, the question of rights and duties as the test for participation in
the public service also becomes hard to justify when citizenship of the Union gives
nationals of one Member State the right to vote and stand for election in local and
European Parliament elections in their host State. At the moment it would appear
that representing the people in the European Parliament or the municipal legislature
requires a lower degree of allegiance to the state than to work in the higher echelons
of the public service. A foreign national can hold the elected post but must be
advised only by nationals of the state.

Enlarging Citizenship of the Union

The mechanism for enlarging citizenship of the Union, independent of the individual
choices of Member States to naturalise or permit the automatic acquisition of citizenship by foreigners, is through enlargement. When Austria, Finland and Sweden entered
the EU in 1993 the number of citizens of the Union expanded automatically to incorporate the nationals of the new Member States. The 2004 enlargement adds a further
ten countries[29] whose nationals will immediately become citizens of the Union though
their free movement rights will be delayed. In the negotiations on enlargement, the
question of the acculturation of nationals of the states joining the Union has not arisen.
Instead, the Copenhagen principles have provided the basis for the assessment of
necessary criteria for membership of the European Union. Respect for human rights,
democracy and liberal markets are the core values which are reflected in the principles.
This might be presented as a sort of collective acculturation or integration.

The gradual transformation of immigration status into citizenship is still not
complete in the EU. What is most noteworthy, however, is that none of the legal
questions and issues which have arisen in the process reflect any form of "pre-
scriptive list" regarding citizenship. The right to remain completely un-acculturated
or un-assimilated is so central to the process of EU citizenship that it becomes
transformed into a discourse of strength in diversity.

Conclusions

In Europe where a substantial rise in immigration was perceived in the mid-1990s,
social scientists sought to determine the rules by which liberal states should turn

---

28 *Grzelczyk* supra.
29 Cyprus, Czech Republic, Estonia, Hungary, Latvia, Lithuania, Malta, Poland, Slovakia and Slovenia.

immigrants into citizens. The treatment of the "others" among "us" was a matter of concern and the approach of the "other" among "us" led in the direction of theories about acculturation, assimilation and integration. What remains surprising is the failure in this literature to notice the most obvious transformation of migrant workers into citizens which was taking place around them – that of nationals of the Member States. The effect of the right of equal treatment which nationals of the Member States enjoyed as a result of the EC Treaty provisions on their immigration meant that they slipped out of sight. The position of the right of equal treatment in working conditions, as regards family, and deep protection against exclusion and expulsion diminished the difference of position between migrant workers, nationals of other Member States, and nationals of the host state itself. The fact of diminishing that difference in rights was the disappearance of the individuals as objects of integration, acculturation or assimilation projects. Because Member State nationals already had wide rights of equal treatment, they could not be required to assimilate before being deemed eligible for those rights.

Nonetheless, the protection of the most central right of the citizen, that to equal treatment fares worse in the field of a right to free movement on the territory than it has done in respect of social rights. Here the ECJ has permitted the Member States to retain their right to exclude and expel nationals of other Member States on the basis of public policy, expressly acknowledging that such powers are inimical to 'genuine' citizenship, in other words, Member States cannot take such measures against their own nationals. While permitting States this leeway may be justified on the ground that the Treaty itself preserves the right of the Member States to act in this way, the ECJ's extension of this power to include the limitation by administrative measure of the right of free movement on the territory of a national of another Member State on the grounds of public policy where no such measure could be taken against a national of the state is highly questionable.

Chapter 6

Family Migration in EU Law

In much academic discussion on family life in EU law, the rights of migrant Community nationals and those of third country nationals are treated separately.[1] This is justified on the ground that the legal basis for family reunification for Community nationals is found in Title III EC/Title III Chapter I EU Constitution while that for third country nationals is in Title IV EC/Title III Chapter IV EU Constitution. Further, the argument goes, family reunification for citizens of the Union is a necessary corollary of free movement of persons, a central part of the internal market. Thus it is a right. Family reunification for third country nationals is a power found in the part of the Treaty dedicated to developing the area of freedom, security and justice. Although the area is linked to the completion of the internal market it is not integral to it. Thus family reunification for third country nationals is not a right. Instead it is a power of the Community to extend to Europe's third country nationals or not as it chooses. For the migrant, the importance and centrality of family reunification to the quality of his or her life does not differ depending on whether he or she is a Union citizen or a third country national. For this reason I will treat the field as singular, and compare the treatment of family reunification from a consolidated perspective, the legal rules in respect of nationals of the Member States and in respect of third country nationals.

The right of a state to privilege some family life choices against others so as to place obstacles in the way of a marriage or relationship with a foreigner expresses a very strong concept of identity and approved identity behaviour. The recognition of the central role of family in the maintenance of traditions and values is found in the

---

1 G Barrett, 'Family matters: European Community law and third-country family members', CMLRev 40 (2): 369–421, Apr. 2003; N Reich and S Harbacevica, 'Citizenship and family on trial: A fairly optimistic overview of recent court practice with regard to free movement of persons' CMLRev 40 (3): 615–638, Jun. 2003.

Universal Declaration of Human Rights.[2] It is stated to be the fundamental group unit of society. Thus it is perhaps not surprising that marriages which involve two nationals of the state are generally to be privileged in law as there is no intersection with immigration law. The legal requirements for marriage between nationals are limited. State interference must be justified against a high threshold of individual rights. No family member is seeking to enjoy a residence right on the basis of the family relationship. Where citizens marry or otherwise acquire family members who are not nationals of the state, in all EU states national law sets out the conditions which apply to whether they will be able to live together in the state of nationality of the EU citizen.

In all cases, the interference of the state in the choice of the individuals is justified on the ground that there is an immigration benefit at issue. Thus the state may apply a more strict regulation of the private life of some citizens than others. For instance, Member States consider it their duty to make enquiries into the genuineness of the family relationship. This is, in effect, an assessment of whether the family members' behaviour corresponds to the state notion of the correct family relationship. The state may place a requirement that the citizen be able to support and accommodate the foreign family members without state assistance before the family will be permitted to join the principal. Thus the state places a different and higher economic threshold for family life where a foreigner is involved. Where the family is already in the state, extra benefits may be made available to assist the family to obtain state housing or a higher income to benefit. However, states frequently place a condition on admission of foreign family members that these benefits will not be requested without putting at risk the family members' residence permits. Thus the state makes family life with foreign family members contingent on the family members denying themselves the national economic social inclusion rights designed to strengthen and promote family cohesion within the state.

These are only some examples of the difference of treatment which separate some citizens from others as regard family life on the basis of the nationality of the family members. Where the person seeking family reunification with third country national family members is also a third country national, EU states have adopted two separate methods of regulation. In some cases, such as the Netherlands and the UK, the rules are the same both for own nationals and resident third country nationals to bring family members to the state to enjoy family life. In other cases such as Germany or Austria, different rules apply which are more advantageous for the citizen than for the resident third country national.

---

2   See for instance Article 16(3) UN Universal Declaration of Human Rights "The family is the natural and fundamental group unit of society and is entitled to protection by society and the State."

The EU has now adopted measures regulating family reunification both for citizens of the Union and third country nationals. In this chapter I will examine the two legal regimes in Community law and compare them:

1. Regulation 1612/68 as regards the right of family reunification for migrant nationals of the Member States (repeated in directive 73/148 for the self-employed and service providers and recipients and followed in the right of residence directives with some variations on which I shall comment as they arise);
2. Directive 2003/86 on family reunification for third country nationals.

I will analyse the two systems of family rights and highlight the differences between them.

Identity and Family Reunification

EU secondary legislation adopted in the 1960s and 1970s takes a generous approach towards the right of migrant Community nationals to live with their family members in a host Member State, even where the family members are third country nationals. These rights have been unrelated to the legal framework of citizenship of the Union.[3] While they appear in the proposal for a directive on the rights of citizens of the Union which would replace the earlier measures, the rights are reproduced from the earlier measures.[4] Where the citizen is residing at home, he or she cannot normally access family reunion rights which exist at EU level. The situation is considered wholly internal to the Member State and as such the Member State's national law applies exclusively.[5] Community law relating to citizens of the Union and their right to family reunification can only be accessed where the citizen is a migrant in another Member State, or has been such a migrant and returns to his or her home Member State[6] or is exercising a cross-border economic activity even though he or she remains resident at home.[7] As the ECJ has clarified, "Community legislation concerning freedom of movement for workers, freedom to provide services and freedom of establishment is not applicable to situations not presenting any link to the

---

3 C-60/00 *Carpenter* [2002] ECR I-6279.
4 Draft Directive on the right of citizens of the Union and their family members to move and reside freely within the territory of the Member States (COM (01) 257). As the UK House of Commons Select Committee on European Scrutiny stated in its 7th Report 2001 on the proposal "This new proposal aims to consolidate existing legislation and case law as well as extending the law in certain areas."
5 35 & 36/82 *Morson & Jhanjhan* [1982] ECR 3723.
6 C-370/90 *Singh* [1992] ECR I-4265.
7 C-60/00 *Carpenter* [2002] ECR I-6279.

situations envisaged by Community law. Consequently, that legislation cannot be applied to the situation of persons who have not exercised those freedoms."[8]

Thus EU family rights can only be unlocked through movement across EU borders (see chapters 4 and 5). As such, the mechanism through which EU rights formation takes place has been tied to economic migration rather than human rights. EU citizenship, human and cultural rights and constitutional principles will not normally provide the citizen of the Union at home with an EU right to live with his or her spouse and other family members. Only his or her capacity to exercise a free movement right can deliver the result. The right of family reunification originally applied only to workers, the self-employed and service providers and recipients who migrated within the Union. In 1990 it was extended to the economically inactive but on the basis of self-sufficiency. In the extension, some family reunification rights were not extended to the new group of beneficiaries. For instance, the economically inactive can only enjoy an EU family reunion right with children (of any age) who are dependent on them (unlike the economically active who can enjoy this right with independent children under the age of 21).[9] Further, students only get a right to family reunification with spouses and children. Relatives in the ascending line are not included.[10] I will return to the class of family members entitled to join a migrant Community national shortly.

The struggle regarding identity, then, takes place in two rather different fields: the national and the supranational. The national level embraces its citizens gripping them tightly to minimise foreign influence in private life. A normative value of family life is imposed: on the one hand fellow nationals are privileged as marriage partners. The importance of inclusion of the extended family is evidenced in, for instance, family photos of European monarchs. On the other hand, a very limited, truncated vision of the family is permitted entry and residence in the state where the members of the family are third country nationals.[11] At the EU level, citizenship of the Union gives no apparent family rights but the act of migration between Member States provides access to a very wide definition of family members for family life and a very limited array of restrictions. The mechanism, however, finds its roots not in citizenship and identity rights as such but economic activity – the fact of being part of the means of production and consumption. While in theory these two fields do not intersect, in practice they do, as will be discussed below. In these two different visions of identity and rights, the arbiter is no longer the state.

---

8   C-459/99 *MRAX* [2002] ECR I-6591.
9   Article 1 Directives 90/364 and 90/365.
10 Article 1 Directive 93/96.
11 For instance, in UK immigration law, children under 12 are considered to belong with their mothers, and children over 12 are only admissible if the family can show that they have had sole responsibility for the child's upbringing. This means that if another family member, for instance a grandparent, in the country of origin took decisions about the child's schooling before the family sought family reunion in the UK with the child, the chances are that the child would not be permitted to join the other family members in the UK. The recent judgment of the ECtHR in *Sen v Netherlands* 21 December 2001 revolves around a very similar provision of Dutch law which excluded a child.

A different picture emerges when Community law encounters third country nationals as principals. So long as third country nationals are the family members of migrant citizens of the Union, they enjoy wide rights to install themselves with their principal.[12] In practice even where the family member who is the Community national is economically inactive and it is the third country national spouse who seeks to work in the Union, the applications for residence permits will be based on the right of the Community national as the principal. The third country national is always cast as the dependant not the principal. However, when both parties to the marriage or relationship are third country nationals the rights discourse is more uncertain. The brave rhetoric of freedom and dignity as requiring wide family reunification rights which is to be found in the preamble of the regulation which deals with family reunification for Community national migrants (regulation 1612/68) is nowhere to be discerned in the directive on family reunification for third country nationals.[13] Instead the EU institutions appear to have had trouble finding a floor of fundamentally humane treatment below which the Union cannot fall in subjecting third country nationals to differential treatment as regards family reunification.[14] If there is to be found a floor it is not internal to the Union but rather comes from outside – the ECHR (to which I shall return in the next chapter).

There are four main concerns for the migrant in respect of family reunification: (1) which family members? (2) what documents must be produced? (3) what conditions must be fulfilled to enjoy family reunification? (4) what rights do the family members have in the host Member State? I will consider each of these interests for each group of migrants.

EC Law on Family Reunification – Citizens of the Union

In this first section I will consider only family reunification for migrant citizens of the Union. EU provisions permitting a right to family reunification were introduced in the first implementing regulations regarding the rights of workers.[15] In the current regulation, 1612/68, they are found at articles 10–12. Similar provisions are

---

12 It is worth noting the wording of article 10 Regulation 1612/68. It states that the right belongs to the family member, not the principal and the right is one to install him or her self with the principal. Thus on the face of the regulation at least, the right belongs to the family member not to the Community national.

13 Instead the preamble mentions fair treatment of third country nationals and that it helps create sociocultural stability facilitating the integration of third country nationals.

14 This has been revealed not least by intention to commence annulment proceedings in respect of the family reunification directive by the European Parliament on the basis that it does not satisfy the minimum requirements of the ECHR, see Note à l'attention de M. Jorge Salvador Hernández Mollar Président de la commission des libertés et des droits des citoyens de la justice et des affaires intérieures 21 October 2003 (SJ-0326/03).

15 Regulations 16/61 and 38/64, see E Guild, *Immigration Law in the European Community*, Kluwer Law International, The Hague, 2001.

also contained in the implementing directive regarding establishment and service provision (directive 73/148).

The Family Members

The family members who are entitled to join a Community national exercising a right of residence in the territory of a Member State other than that of his or her nationality are:[16]

1. Spouses: these are persons who are legally recognised as such under the national law of the state of origin (or residence). A spouse continues to be a spouse until such time as the marriage is ended in law. The fact that the spouses may not live together is not determinant. So long as the marriage is legally subsisting the spouse continues to be such for the purposes of Community law. On this basis they have a right of residence (and work – see below) on the territory of the host State.[17] The residence right of a spouse is only lost on divorce or when the principal leaves the territory of the host State permanently. The proposed directive on the rights of citizens of the Union will insert a right to an autonomous residence permit for EU migrant citizens and their family members after five years residence in the host State. Unmarried partners do not qualify as spouses. They only enjoy the right to non-discriminatory treatment in comparison with nationals of the Member State. Thus only if nationals of the host Member State are permitted to have their third country national unmarried partner join them in the state must the same right be extended to nationals of other Member States and their unmarried partners.[18]

2. Children: these are defined as the children of either or both parents, thus the concept includes adopted children and children of one of the spouses but not the other. Children of economically active Community nationals, which children are under 21 have a right to move to and reside in the same host State as their Community national parent. Children over 21 must be dependent on their parent(s). Irrespective of their age, the children of economically inactive Community nationals must be dependent on the principal or spouse. The right of the children continues after marriage breakdown and indeed as the children have a right to education in the host State[19] they also have a right to continue

---

16 Article 10 regulation 1612/68; article 1 directive 73/148 and the three right of residence directives. The nuts and bolts of application are found in directive 68/360.
17 267/83 *Diatta* [1985] ECR 1283.
18 59/85 *Reed* [1986] ECR 1283.
19 Article 12 regulation 1612/68.

to reside even after the departure of the Community national parent from the host State.[20]

3. Dependent relatives in the ascending (and descending) line: the parents, grandparents (and other relatives in the direct ascending line) of the principal or his or her spouse who are dependent on the principal have a right to join the family in the host State (under the students directive, 93/96, this category is excluded).

4. Other relatives: there is a duty to facilitate the admission of other family members not coming within the above definitions if they are dependent on the principal or living under his or her roof in the country whence he or she comes. The ECJ has neither clarified what the extent of the duty to facilitate is nor the level of dependency which is required for a presumption to be activated.

The nationality of the family members is irrelevant. The category of the family members entitled to join a migrant Community national principal is very wide. It is so wide that it appears to exceed the needs and wishes of Community nationals themselves for family reunification. The fact that no case has come before the ECJ even on adopted children or grandparents within these measures indicates that either the Member States implement them very generously (a position which is questionable in view of the number of cases on spouses which have come before the ECJ) or there is little demand to exercise the rights.

One conclusion is that by a very wide definition of the family the EU avoids the difficulty of Member States limiting family life of migrant nationals of the Member States to a greater extent than that of their own nationals (with family members who are citizens). Thus the potential for discriminatory state interference with family life is never realised.

Proving the Relationship

One of the issues which has been the subject of friction between residents seeking family reunification with third country national family members and Member States is the documentation or other evidence which the families must provide to establish to the satisfaction of the state their relationships. In the Netherlands, for instance, the obligation of families to have all documents legalised has resulted in very long delays in some countries. In the UK the possibility for a visa officer to accept nothing less that DNA results to prove the relationship of a parent and child for the purpose of family reunification is both time consuming, complicated when the family members are living in different countries and expensive. For migrant EU citizens,

---

20   389 & 390/87 *Echternach & Moritz* [1989] ECR 723.

the Member States are restricted regarding the documents can be demanded. While the Member State authorities are permitted to require a visa of third country national family members they must be provided every facility to obtain them (article 3(2) directive 68/360). I will return to this point below. To obtain a residence permit, third country national family members can only be required to produce the document on which they entered the state, a document issued by the competent authorities of the state of origin or the state whence they came proving their relationship. Where the family members' admission is based on their dependence on the principal then the Member State may require a document issued by the competent authorities of the state of origin or the state whence they came testifying that they are dependent on the worker or that they lived together under his or her roof in such country (article 4 directive 68/360). Member States must accept the genuineness of documents unless they have serious grounds for doubting them.[21]

Conditions: Support, Housing and Visas

As regards spouses and children under 21 there is no obligation for the economically active principal to be able to support them. Even where the principal is dependent on state benefits so long as he or she comes within the personal scope of Community law the right exists.[22] For other family members there is a condition that they are dependent on the principal and his or her spouse. The extent of dependency is unclear. For instance, must the family member be dependent financially, or would emotional dependency be relevant? The ECJ has rejected, however, that the concept of dependence may be defined by national law. Similarly it has excluded an assessment of the reasons for dependence: "It must be pointed out, secondly, that the status of dependent member of a worker's family does not presuppose the existence of a right to maintenance either. If that were the case, the composition of the family would depend on national legislation, which varies from one state to another, and that would lead to the application of Community law in a manner that is not uniform. Article 10(1) and (2) of Regulation No 1612/68 must be interpreted as meaning that the status of dependent member of a worker's family is the result of a factual situation. The person having that status is a member of the family who is supported by the worker and there is no need to determine the reasons for recourse to the worker's

---

21 C-336/94 *Dafeki* [1997] ECR I-6762.
22 In practice citizens of the Union encounter administrative obstacles in a number of Member States when they are unemployed and when they are seeking to effect family reunification with third country national family members. The European Commission, however, is vigilant is bringing to task Member States which fail to fulfil their obligations in this area, see European Commission *Communication Free Movement of workers – achieving the full benefits and potential* COM (2002) 694 final, Brussels 11.12.2002.

support or to raise the question whether the person concerned is able to support himself by taking up paid employment."[23]

Where the family members are subject to a dependency requirement for the purpose of admission, they are nonetheless entitled, like all family members to take employment.[24] If they do so they may then no longer be financially dependent on the principal in which case their right to family reunification under the regulation (and other measures) could be placed in doubt. The ECJ seems to have dismissed this possible consequence in a case of a daughter over 21 who had studied in her family's home Member State and then returned to the host Member State where her parents were resident. She applied for a social benefit which was only available to her in her personal capacity (in other words not as a member of her parents' family). The ECJ rejected the possibility that her right of residence might be questioned as a result of her receiving a benefit and thus no longer being dependent on her parents. This, according to the ECJ, would be contrary to the intention of the provisions.[25] There is no reference to sickness insurance as regards the economically active and their family members. The inactive but self-sufficient, however, are required to have health insurance for all risks.

A mechanism practiced by many Member States to control family reunification of third country nationals is to require such family members to obtain visas in their country of origin before coming to the Member State. The fees Member States charge for family reunification visas have risen dramatically over the past decade in some states such as the Netherlands and the UK. Should the family members already be in the Member State, particularly in a temporary capacity, they may be required to return to the country of origin to obtain such a visa. The selective allocation of resources to the examination of visa applications and their issue at consular posts in third countries means there are quite striking differences in processing times, ranging for instance, from a few days at the UK consulate in the USA to many months at consulates on the Indian subcontinent.[26] Directive 68/360 permits visas to be required of third country national family members (article 3(2)) but requires that they must be issued free of charge. Further family members must be given every facility to obtain them.

Some Member States became increasingly insistent, in national legislation, that all third country national family members obtain visas before taking up residence. Belgium was among this group. A Belgian non-governmental organisation, MRAX, challenged this requirement as regards migrant citizens of the Union on the basis of the right of Community nationals to enjoy family reunification. The matter was referred by the national court to the ECJ for an answer as to whether the strict application of the visa requirement in respect of third country national family

---

23   316/85 *Lebon* [1987] ECR 2811.
24   Article 12 regulation 1612/68.
25   316/85 *Lebon* [1987] ECR 2811.
26   E Guild "Entry into the UK: the changing nature of national borders," Immigration and Nationality Law and Practice, Vol 14 No 4, 2000 pp 227–238.

members of migrant Community nationals was consistent with Community law in three situations:[27]

1. Where the third country national family member arrives at the border without the required visa;
2. Where the third country national family member has entered and stayed in the Member State unlawfully and then marries a migrant Community national;
3. Where the third country national family member has entered lawfully but stayed beyond his or her permitted period and then seeks to remain on the basis of the family relationship with the migrant Community national.

Starting with the first and most difficult question, the ECJ noted that the Community legislature recognised the importance of ensuring protection for the family life of nationals of Member States in order to eliminate obstacles to the exercise of the fundamental freedoms guaranteed by the Treaty. While the ECJ recognised that the secondary legislation does not, on its face preclude sending such a person back at the border, it noted that the Member States are under a duty to facilitate the issue of visas. It found that Member States are under a duty to give full effect to this duty of facilitation even to the extent of issuing the visa at the border to such a family member. It added "it is in any event disproportionate, and, therefore, prohibited to send back a third country national married to a national of a Member State where he is able to prove his identity and the conjugal ties and there is no evidence that he represents a risk to the requirements of public policy, public security or public health."[28]

As regards the second question, the ECJ noted that it was established case law that the issue of a residence permit cannot be regarded as a measure which gives rise to rights but as a measure by a Member State which proves the position of the individual. While sanctions for failure to respect administrative requirements as regards residence permits of a Member State are permitted, an expulsion order on this basis alone would be manifestly disproportionate. Thus Member States are not permitted solely on this ground to refuse to issue a residence permit and to issue an expulsion order against a third country national who is able to furnish proof of identity and relationship with a migrant Community national.

The ECJ then came to the final issue: overstayers. It found that as Member States are obliged to grant a right of residence to workers who can produce either a valid identity card or passport regardless of the document on which they entered the territory so too must Member States issue residence permits to these family members. A Member State is precluded from making the issue of a residence permit in Community law conditional upon production of a valid visa. The underlying rationale of the judgment is the obligation on Member States to eliminate obstacles to the exercise of fundamental

---

27   C-459/99 *MRAX* [2002] ECR I-6591.
28   C-459/99 *MRAX* [2002] ECR I-6591.

freedoms in the Treaty. Of course, the right to family reunification can always be defeated by a successful claim by the state that the individual is a threat to public policy, public security or public health. These terms however, have been narrowly defined by the ECJ – an interpretation which applies equally to third country national family members as to the Community national principal (see Chapter 5).

The clarity of this judgment has been somewhat clouded by another decision, taken only a year later where a British national had moved to Ireland and taken employment there so that her Moroccan husband who had been expelled (twice) from the UK could join her. When the couple sought to return to the UK, the UK authorities refused to issue the husband with the necessary visa (or residence permit) not least as they considered that the couple had moved to Ireland solely in order to benefit from Community family reunification law in a circumstance where UK national law would not have permitted the husband to remain. The ECJ held that "Where a citizen of the Union, established in a Member State and married to a national of a non-Member State with a right to remain in that Member State, moves to another Member State in order to work there as an employed person, that move must not result in the loss of the opportunity lawfully to live together ... Conversely, where a citizen of the Union, established in a Member State and married to a national of a non-Member State without the right to remain in that Member State, moves to another Member State in order to work there as an employed person, the fact that that person's spouse has no right under Article 10 of Regulation No 1612/68 to install himself with that person in the other Member State cannot constitute less favourable treatment than that which they enjoyed before the citizen made use of the opportunities afforded by the Treaty as regards movement of persons. Accordingly, the absence of such a right is not such as to deter the citizen of the Union from exercising the rights in regard to freedom of movement conferred by Article 39 EC."[29] This finding creates a certain tension with earlier judgments, in particular *MRAX*, regarding the right of family reunification and the right to cross borders. While in the earlier judgment the ECJ relied on the importance of abolishing obstacles to free movement of Community nationals, in the later decision the rationale of equal treatment is applied and then extended to constitute an absence of an obstacle. It must be hoped that the logic of the later judgment will be confined to its facts.

The Rights of the Family Members

Family members are entitled work[30] and as mentioned above, they are entitled to access to education on a non-discriminatory basis with own nationals.[31] However,

---

29 C-109/01 *Akrich* judgment 23 September 2003.
30 Article 11 regulation 1612/68.
31 Article 12 regulation 1612/68.

the host State is entitled to apply a housing test, i.e., that the principal has housing available for the family which is normal for workers in the region. The housing test can only be applied once at the beginning of the principal's residence and cannot be reassessed every time there is a change in the composition of the family.[32] In any event, the principal is entitled to equality of treatment in social housing thus lack of funds for housing should not be a reason for refusing family reunification so long as there is a system of housing assistance available to own nationals.

As regards an independent right of residence for family members, however, Community law is very frugal. So long as the parties to the marriage have not finally divorced then the third country national spouse will continue to have a right to residence in the state.[33] However, by implication, once the divorce is final the third country national spouse will no longer have a basis for residence and work unless he or she has children of the Community principal. Here the children may have a right, as citizens of the Union in education or intended education under article 12 regulation 1612/68, to have their parent resident in the state with them.[34] If the principal leaves completely the host Member State then the right of residence of the spouse ceases though the children will have a continuing right through their right to education. If the presence of the third country national spouse is necessary so that the children can enjoy their right to education then the state is obliged to accept a right of residence for that person.[35] Otherwise family members only get a right of residence independent of the sponsor on his or her death under regulation 1251/71. The proposed directive on the right of residence of citizens of the Union will provide a continuing right of residence to family members on the event of divorce, annulment of marriage or termination of registered partnership. Further it will create a right of permanent residence for Community nationals and their family members after fulfilling the requirements (i.e. economic activity or self-sufficiency for the economically inactive) after a period of five years.[36]

Enjoying Family Life at Home: Challenging National Restrictions

Family reunification rights only come into existence when the principal exercises a right of free movement to live and exercise an economic activity in another Member State.[37] In principle they do not apply to nationals of the Member States within their

---

32   205/84 *Commission v Germany* [1986] ECR 3793.
33   267/83 *Diatta* [1985] ECR 567
34   C-413/99 *Baumbast* [2002] ECR I-7091.
35   C-413/99 *Baumbast* [2002] ECR I-7091.
36   Article 16 Common Position adopted by the Council on the draft directive on the right of citizens of the Union and their family members, Council Document 13263/03.
37   35 & 36/82 *Morson & Jhanjhan* [1982] ECR 3723.

own state (see above).[38] When the principal exercises a free movement right (more substantial than service receipt for a couple of days) he or she is entitled to enjoy family reunification in the host Member State. On return to his or her country of origin would the principal retain the right to family reunification under Community law or fall back into the embrace of his or her Member State of nationality and its national legislation? The case which raised and resolved this question was that of Mr and Mrs Singh.[39] Mrs Singh, a British national had moved to Germany to work. Her husband, a third country national, joined her there. Subsequently they decided to return to the UK where Mrs Singh opened a shop. The UK authorities sought to deport Mr Singh on the basis of national law when he stopped living with Mrs Singh. He argued that national law did not apply to him as he was the spouse of a Community worker (now self-employed). The ECJ held that the UK could not apply its national law to persons in this situation as this would constitute an obstacle to free movement of persons. Community nationals would be discouraged from exercising their free movement right if they feared they would not be able to return to their home state with their family members. Thus Mr Singh was entitled to remain in the UK so long as he continued to be married to Mrs Singh. A small question mark has arisen over the completeness of the right as a result of the *Akrich* case considered above. It may be that if the third country national family member was never lawfully present in the Union, his or her return to the country of nationality of the principal is not covered by Community law.[40]

Thus Community nationals normally retain the family reunification rights acquired under Community law by virtue of their exercise of a free movement right at least for a period of time after then return to their home Member State. So, while an EU state could make family reunification impossible for its nationals at home, it could not stop them going to another Member State to enjoy the right and then returning to the home Member State with those same family members. This, in fact, became quite common for UK nationals who on being refused permission to have their foreign spouses live with them in the UK went to work in another Member State, primarily Ireland. Following *Singh*, in practice the UK authorities accepted that 6 months of genuine economic activity in Ireland was sufficient for these naughty Britons to be allowed to come back to the UK with their foreign spouses. This informal banishment of the "identity offenders" could not, however, be applied to those lucky Britons who were dual nationals holding also the citizenship of another Member State (most commonly Ireland) as they were already entitled to rely on this other identity to enjoy family life under EU rules within the Member State without having to migrate.[41]

---

38 N Shuibhne, 'Free Movement of Persons and the Wholly Internal Rule: Time to Move On?' CMLRev 39 (4): 731–771, Aug. 2002.

39 C-370/90 *Singh* [1992] ECR I-4265.

40 C-109/01 *Akrich* judgment 23 September 2003.

41 The Commission proposed to extend EC family reunification rules to all Community nationals whether or not they exercised a free movement right. This was included in the proposal for a

However, not every national of a Member State who marries a third country national either has a second EU passport in his or her back pocket or is capable of moving to another Member State and living there for an extended period before moving back home with the spouse. This was the situation of a British national which came before the ECJ.

Mr Carpenter, from the account in the ECJ's judgment,[42] appears to have been quite an ordinary Englishman, living in the UK. He was a self-employed businessman selling advertising space in medical and scientific journals. He had responsibility for his young children by a previous marriage. Mr Carpenter married Mrs Carpenter, a Filipino national, who was irregularly in the UK having overstayed her permitted visit. The UK authorities refused, as is consistent with national law, to allow Mrs Carpenter to remain in the UK with her husband. In the face of the rejection of Mr Carpenter's choice to live in the UK with his Filipino wife, who was centrally engaged in the upbringing of his children by his previous marriage, Mr Carpenter sought to establish this right of residence as a citizenship right at the level of European Union law. The UK Government argued that since Mr Carpenter had not exercised his right of free movement by physically moving and residing in another Member State, his spouse could not rely on an entitlement to residence in EU law as the matter was wholly internal to the UK.

The ECJ found as a matter of fact that Mr Carpenter was self-employed selling advertising space, a significant proportion of which was to advertisers in other Member States. As a result, he came within the scope of article 49 EC/article III-144 EU Constitution as a service provider. Once within the scope of Community law, the ECJ considered whether his demand to live with his wife in the UK could come within the ambit of the implementing directive (73/148). It found it could not as that directive seeks only to regulate family reunification for service providers in Member States other than that of their nationality. Instead, the ECJ "borrowed" article 8 ECHR, the respect for family life, and applied it to the situation of Mr Carpenter who was now within the scope of Community law. The ECJ found that it was not compatible with article 8 as protected by Community law that Mrs Carpenter should be required to leave the UK. "A decision to deport Mrs Carpenter, taken in circumstances such as those in the main proceedings, does not strike a fair balance between the competing interests, that is, on the one hand, the right of Mr Carpenter to respect for his family life, and, on the other hand, the maintenance of public order and public safety. Although, in the main proceedings, Mr Carpenter's spouse has infringed the immigration laws of the United Kingdom by not leaving the country prior to the expiry of her leave to remain as a visitor, her conduct, since her arrival in the United

---

(Cont.)

directive on family reunification (COM (1999) 638 final 1.12.1999) but it was among the first provisions to be rejected by the Council.

42 C-60/00 *Carpenter* [2002] ECR I-6279.

Kingdom in September 1994, has not been the subject of any other complaint that could give cause to fear that she might in the future constitute a danger to public order or public safety. Moreover, it is clear that Mr and Mrs Carpenter's marriage, which was celebrated in the United Kingdom in 1996, is genuine and that Mrs Carpenter continues to lead a true family life there, in particular by looking after her husband's children from a previous marriage. In those circumstances, the decision to deport Mrs Carpenter constitutes an infringement which is not proportionate to the objective pursued."[43]

The whereabouts of Mr Carpenter's customers are central to his right to live with his wife in the UK. Had all his customers been in the UK he would not have succeeded according to the ECJ's reasoning. It is noteworthy that the ECJ avoided any mention of Mr Carpenter's capacity as a citizen of the Union. Instead it relied entirely on his identity as an economic actor. The ECJ allowed both the Singhs and Carpenters to escape the national law regime on the basis of their economic activities.

Third Country Nationals and Family Reunification

The Amsterdam Treaty introduced by articles 63(3) and (4) (article III-267(2)(a) EU Constitution) the power to adopt measures in respect of resident third country nationals including family reunification. Its objective is the development of an area of freedom, security and justice which itself is intended to contribute to the completion of the internal market.

The first proposal for a family reunification directive for third country nationals was presented by the Commission in 1999.[44] This was to be the first and most important piece of legislation to be adopted at EU level after the entry into force of the Amsterdam Treaty in respect of third country nationals and to establish a high threshold of rights for third country nationals.[45] The Commission noted in its explanatory memorandum the importance of family reunification not only as a quantitative issue but as "a necessary way of making a success of the integration of third-country nationals residing lawfully in the Member States."[46] The issue of integration would come back to haunt the directive later and indeed, the insertion of integration requirements would be the ground for an attack on the final version by the European Parliament before the ECJ. However, in the first draft, the Commission notes that the

---

43 The ECJ's reasoning on article 8 ECHR was quite generous in comparison with the ECtHR's own decision making.
44 COM (1999) 638 Final, Brussels, 1 December 1999.
45 G Brinkmann, 'Family Reunification' in E Guild & C Harlow, *Implementing Amsterdam: Immigration and Asylum Rights in EC Law*, Hart, Oxford, 2001 pp 241–266.
46 Para 2.2 Explanatory Memorandum COM (1999) 638 final.

Member States are already constrained as regards the rules they adopt for family reunification by their international commitments and the Commission lists the instruments, beginning with the Universal Declaration of Human Rights and finishing with the European Social Charter and the European Convention on the Legal Status of Migrant Workers. The Commission carefully highlights the various measures adopted at EU level before the transfer of competence to the First Pillar. Relying on the Council Conclusions in Tampere 1999, the Commission states "to ensure that [third country nationals] can look forward to being treated in the same way as Union citizens, the proposal for a directive is based on certain provisions of existing Community law as regards the family reunification of Union citizens who exercise their right to free movement."[47] Under the protocols in respect of Title IV regarding the position of Denmark, Ireland and the UK, all three opted out of the effect of the directive.

Following consultation with the Council, the Economic and Social Committee and the European Parliament, the Commission produced a second version of the proposal in October 2000.[48] While some changes were made to the proposal in the second version, the general approach remained in accordance with the Commission's initial proposal. However, following the Laeken Council meeting in December 2001 there was a substantial change in tone. The Council lamented, in its conclusions, the fact that in the field of immigration and asylum "progress has been slower and less substantial than expected."[49] It called on the Commission to submit by 30 April 2002 a further amended draft proposal on family reunification.[50] The Commission complied with the Council's request and presented a new, watered-down version on 2 May 2002.[51] Putting a brave face on the compromises required of it by the Council, the Commission, in the explanatory memorandum, states that it is adopting a new method regarding the outstanding issues: "the new method acknowledges that, to achieve harmonisation of national legislation on family reunification, there are several stages to be gone through. The amended proposal is only the first of these. It is inspired by a certain concern for flexibility on the basis of two main parameters: first, as regards substance, the use of a standstill clause. Second, as regards the time frame, a deadline for the next stage."[52] The end result was the subject of political agreement on 28 February 2003 and adoption on 22 September 2003.[53] It must be implemented by 3 October 2005 but on 17 December 2003 the European Parliament announced

---

47   Para 7.2 Explanatory Memorandum COM (1999) 638 final.
48   Amended Proposal for a Council Directive on the right to family reunification COM (2000) 624 final Brussels 10 October 2000.
49   Laeken Council Conclusions, 14 & 15 December 2001 para 38.
50   Laeken Council Conclusions para 41.
51   May 2002 (COM (2002) 225 final).
52   Para 2 COM (2002) 225 final.
53   Council text 6912/03.

that it was commenced annulment proceedings before the ECJ in respect of the directive.[54]

The progress of this measure through the institutions of the EU gives some important insights into the extension of Community competence regarding family reunification to third country nationals. I will analyse in some depth here the legislative history of the directive as it moved from its first 1999 form to that finally adopted in 2003. I will focus on the same four points which have been matters of particular concern in the development of family reunification rights for migrant Community nationals: (1) which family members? (2) what documentary evidence? (3) what conditions must be fulfilled before family reunification can be enjoyed? (4) what rights do family members have once in the State? On following these four main points in the drafting history one can see the increasing retention of control by the Member States away from a right of family life in Community law for third country nationals. However, just before commencing this analysis, I will look briefly at the changes which took place regarding the personal scope of the proposal.

The Personal Scope of the Family Reunification Directive

The personal scope of the original proposal included both third country nationals with a residence permit of more than one year, refugees, persons with subsidiary protection and citizens of the Union who had not exercised their free movement rights (if the applicant's family members are third country nationals, irrespective of their legal status).[55] 'Third country nationals' are defined in the directive as anyone who is not a citizen of the Union (article 2(a)). More favourable provisions of bilateral and multilateral agreements are preserved. Specific reference is made to the European Social Charters 1961 and 1987 and the European Convention on the Legal Status of Migrant Workers 1977. By the second proposal in 2000, persons with subsidiary protection were abandoned from the scope of the proposal.

Article 4 of the original proposal provided that third country national family members of citizens of the Union who have not exercised free movement rights will be governed by the same provisions as family reunification for citizens of the Union who *have* exercised free movement rights. In other words the messy legal situation caused by the application of the wholly internal rule to family rights of citizens of the Union would be tidied up. All citizens of the Union, whether they had exercised free movement rights or not would be entitled to the wide EU family reunification

---

54   Case C-540/03, Council document 5372/04.
55   Article 3 COM (1999) 638 final.

rights. This provision survived until the third draft in 2002 when the Commission finally relinquished it in the face of implacable opposition in the Council.

As Brinkmann notes, in the final version of the directive the scope was weakened again: "During the negotiations the Directive has been watered down and it sets lower standards than the second amended proposal of the Commission of 2002 which already had been watered down. The directive recognizes the right to family reunification for third country nationals holding a residence permit for one year or more who have "reasonable prospects" of obtaining "permanent residence"; these two terms were not defined at the time of adoption of the directive and therefore were left to the Member States' interpretation."[56] In addition, in the first two drafts, Member States are permitted to require the principals to have resided lawfully in a Member State for a period not exceeding one year (article 10 first draft; article 11 second draft). In the third draft this prior residence requirement has drifted up to two years of lawful residence. Further, there is a derogation for Member States which have, at the entry into force of the directive, national legislation on reception capacity. Where this is the case, for instance in Austria, the state may delay entry of family members for a maximum of three years. I will return to this provision later.

The directive creates a right to family reunification. Article 5(1) requires Member States to authorise the entry of some family members to their states and permits the admission of another larger group. However, a number of conditions were placed on the exercise of the right, such as housing, income and health insurance, which permitted a substantial margin of discretion to Member States.

Defining Family Members for Third Country Nationals

The definition of family members in the first draft of the directive included the following:

1. spouses including unmarried partners living in a durable relationship where such relationships are recognised for immigration purposes in the Member State. While the spouse had the right of admission, the admission of unmarried partners was only on the basis of non-discrimination with nationals of the Member State. Thus it would have brought the position of third country nationals into line with that of migrant citizens of the Union;
2. children who are below the age of majority set in the host Member State of either party to the relationship and including adopted children (where the adoption is recognised in the host state);

---

56 G Brinkmann 'An Area of Freedom Security and Justice: Five Years After its Creation: The Immigration and Asylum Agenda' ELJ 10:2 (2004).

3. children again under the age of majority of whom one of the parties has custody;
4. ascending relatives who are dependent on the applicant and who have "no other means of family support in the country of origin;"
5. children over the age of majority who are "objectively unable to satisfy their needs by reason of their state of health." (All children were required to be unmarried.)[57]
6. where the principal is a refugee the original text requires the Member States to facilitate reunification with other family members if they are dependent on the principal. Member States may provide for unaccompanied refugee minors to be joined by relatives in the ascending line or, if they cannot be traced, with other family members but these provisions on unaccompanied refugee minors are optional.

Already there is a substantial difference in comparison with the rights of migrant Community nationals. Children are not defined as under 21 irrespective of whether they are dependent as they are for migrant Community nationals. Dependent children over the age of majority must show "no other means of family support in the country of origin" unlike children of Community nationals. Adoption must be recognised in the host state; ascending family members not only have to be dependent (as in respect of Community nationals) but they also must "have no other means of family support in the country of origin".

In the second proposal, the rights of family members were reduced first by the exclusion, at Member State discretion, of relatives in the ascending line and children over the age of majority from a right to employment or vocational training (articles 5 and 6).

By the 2002 proposal, the right to family reunification only applies to spouses and children (articles 4 and 10). Children are still defined as minor children under the age of majority set by the Member State and must be unmarried. However, a derogation had slipped in: "where a child is aged over 12 years, the Member State may, before authorising entry and residence under this Directive, verify whether he or she meets a condition for integration provided for by its existing legislation on the date of adoption of the Directive."[58] I shall discuss in some detail the principles of integration requirements when considering the long term residents' directive in chapter 12, suffice it here to say that this requirement is problematic. It does not lead towards convergence of criteria or standards but rather in the opposite direction. Another substantial difficulty with the integration requirement is that it applies before the child is admitted to the Member State. Thus any child over 12 could be required to undertake integration courses in his or her country of origin before being

---

57 Article 5 COM (1999) 638 final.
58 Article 4(1)(c).

admitted to the Member State. This is clearly impractical if not impossible on the grounds of lack of availability of integration courses in countries of origin. It is also abhorrent as setting a condition on family life which fails to respect the right to an identity of the child and the family. The admission of relatives in the ascending line (and adult unmarried children where they are objectively unable to provide for their own needs on account of their state of health) and unmarried partners is left to the discretion of the Member States. Further, Member States are permitted to require an applicant and his or her spouse to be "of a minimum age and in any event the age of legal majority" before a spouse can join the individual.[59]

In the final version the definition of family members tightens up the wording in respect of adopted children so that only those adopted in procedures with automatic effect are included. Member States are given a discretion whether to admit children subject to shared custody arrangements.

In the adopted directive a right of family reunification applies only to spouses (though Member States may place a minimum age limit of 21 on their right of admission) and children who are unmarried and minors in national law. Adopted children are only entitled to admission under the directive where the decision was taken by the competent authority in the Member State concerned or by a decision which is automatically enforceable due to international obligations of the Member State or must be recognised in accordance with international obligations. Such obligations include the ECHR. Where the child is the offspring of only one of the parties to the marriage he or she must have custody of the child and the child must be dependent on him or her. For refugees the right is slightly greater. There is no need for the sponsor to have custody of the child or for the child to be dependent on him or her. Member States may permit unaccompanied minor refugees to be joined by first degree relatives in the direct ascending line (article 10(3)(a)). Member States may limit the family relationships eligible to those which predate the entry of the refugee in the host Member State (article 9(2)). To summarise, the discretionary powers of the Member States in the end cover:

1. minor children where custody is shared (article 4(1)(b) and (d));
2. children over 12 subject to an integration test (article 4 second indent);
3. first degree relatives in direct ascending line who are dependent on the sponsor and spouse and do not enjoy proper family support in the country of origin (article 492)(a));
4. adult unmarried children of the parties where they are objectively unable to provide for their own needs (article 4(2)(b));
5. unmarried partners in duly attested stable long term relationships or registered partnerships (article 4(3));

---

59   Article 4(5).

6. unmarried minor children including adopted children of unmarried partners (article 4(3));

7. unmarried adult children who are objectively unable to provide for their own needs on account of their state of health of unmarried partners (article 4(3));

8. in respect of refugees, Member States may also admit other family members who are dependent on the refugee (article 10(2)), the legal guardian or any other member of the family of an unaccompanied minor refugee where the refugee has no relatives in the direct ascending line or such relatives cannot be traced (article 10(3)(b)).

In the final version a further derogation was inserted at article 4(6) whereby Member States may request applications concerning family reunification of minor children to be submitted before the child reaches the age of 15 so long as such a requirement existed in national law at the time of the entry into force of the directive. If a Member State exercises this option and an application is made for a child over 15, the application cannot be considered under the family reunification rules. This provision, inserted at the last moment at the request of the German authorities, is included in the European Parliament's legal challenge to the directive.

Documentary Evidence

Already from the 1999 proposal the principle that the application for family reunification should be made while the family members are outside the host Member State was established (article 7(1)). The third country national principal is the applicant and makes the application to the authorities within the host Member State. In the first text, the application had to be determined by written notification within six months. Refusal of an application must carry reasons. The application must be accompanied by documentary evidence of the family relationship, that there is no question of a threat to public policy, domestic security or public health. The principal must also provide evidence of adequate accommodation, sickness insurance and stable and sufficient resources. For refugees and those enjoying subsidiary protection where documentary evidence of the family relationship is not available Member States are required to have regard to "other evidence" of the existence of the family relationship. Further in these cases only, a decision rejecting the application may not be based solely on the fact that documentary evidence is lacking (article 7(4)). While family members must obtain visas to enter the Member State they must be granted every facility to obtain them and they must be free of charge.

In the 2000 text, there is little change to these provisions other than the exclusion from the personal scope of the directive of persons enjoying subsidiary protection. The 2002 proposal, however, marks something of a transformation. First the place of application is no longer the authorities of the Member State within the State. It is left to the Member States to choose how and by whom the application is made (article 5(1)). In exchange the rule that the family members must be outside the territory of the Member State has been relaxed. A Member State is no longer required to justify considering an application from family members who are resident within the State on exceptional circumstances or on humanitarian grounds (as existed in the first text at article 7(2)) but now may do so in appropriate circumstances (article7(3)). In addition to the documentary evidence of the relationship, the family members must now also submit their travel documents with the application – in effect meaning that they are unable to travel over the period of processing of the application. In the same text, the period for consideration of an application is lengthened from six months to nine from the date of application with a let out clause where in exceptional circumstances the consideration of the application may take 12 months (article 5(4)). Further, documentary evidence is no longer the only evidence of the relationship for the purposes of the application. The text provides that "in order to obtain evidence that a family relationship exists, Member States may carry out interviews with the applicant and his/her family and conduct other investigations that are found necessary." The introduction of this provision indicates that at least in the view of some Member States there is an issue of abuse and fraud.[60] Special provision is made for unmarried partners, in particular that "evidence of the family relationship, factors such as a common child, previous cohabitation, registration of the partnership and any other reliable means of proof" will be sufficient here (article 5(2) third indent). Finally, Member States are no longer required to issue visas free of charge as they must do for the family members of community nationals. They are still obliged to provide every facility to family members to obtain their visas (article 13(1)).

In the adopted text a slight change is made to enable family members to travel while their applications are pending – they may submit certified copies of their travel documents (article 5(2)). While the application normally must be considered within nine months, the 12 month long stop was removed and instead the words "the time limit referred to in the first subparagraph may be extended" was inserted (article 5(4) second indent).

---

60 A salutary tale of the development of a culture of disbelief in family reunification law and practice is that of the UK's infamous primary purpose rule. Introduced in 1980 it required the principal and the spouse to prove that the primary purpose of their marriage was not for the spouse to enter the UK. This provision was in addition to a requirement that the marriage must be genuine. The result was that officials began interviewing spouses and their wider family members to discover whether the choice of partner might have been influenced by an immigration possibility. The rule became discredited and was withdrawn in 1997. S Sachdeva, *The Primary Purpose Rule in British Immigration Law*, Trentham Books, Stoke-on-Trent 1993.

The Conditions

The conditions which the Commission proposed initially for family reunification were:

1. A limitation on grounds of public policy, domestic security or public health;
2. Adequate accommodation being that normal for a comparable family living in the same region;
3. Sickness insurance which covers all risks in the Member State for the individual and family members;
4. Stable and sufficient resources defined as "no less than those below which welfare benefits may be given by that Member State" or a minimum pension and applied without discrimination both to nationals of the state and third country nationals seeking family reunification;[61]
5. A waiting period of one year was permitted before an immigrant could seek family reunification.[62]

Here there has been a substantial departure from the conditions which apply to migrant Community nationals. While the limitation on public policy and health are familiar, domestic security is unclear and introduces a very Member State specific consideration to an EU right. The accommodation requirement does not differ dramatically from that applicable to migrant Community nationals. The sickness insurance and stable resources requirements are imported from the right of residence directives for economically inactive Community migrants.[63] Among the difficulties of the sickness insurance requirement is the fact that it can vary substantially among Member States depending on the availability of insurance under state systems for the family or whether private insurance must be acquired. The income requirement constitutes a divergence from the rights of economically active citizens of the Union. However, the fact that the level is originally tied to that of social welfare benefits provides some degree of certainty for the third country national as regards the possibility of exercising the right of family reunification. Further if Member States apply the income requirement to foreigners they must also apply them to family reunification rules for their own nationals thus only migrant Community nationals who are economically active, under the original proposal, would be free of a resource requirement. (This aspect of equal treatment between third country nationals and own nationals as regards the resources requirement did not survive into the adopted directive.) The waiting period is new. Exactly why third country nationals

---

61 Article 9.
62 Article 10.
63 Directives 90/365; 90/366 and 93/96.

should have to wait one year before enjoying family reunification is inadequately justified.

In the second proposal, in all the key fields of the right of family reunification a very substantial discretionary control by the Member States is inserted. The field of eligible family members with a right of reunification has decreased while Member States have been given a discretion to extend family reunification to other groups of family members. The housing requirement was hardened to include the words "which meets general health and safety standards in force in the Member State;" the resources requirement was changed to require at least an equivalent to a minimum pension thus creating a lower limit but no upper one (articles 9 and 10). In the final adopted directive, the resources condition is now free from any objective reference to the state's assessment of support requirements for its own nationals. The Member States are in effect free to place the resources condition so high as to effectively prevent most if not all third country nationals from enjoying family reunification.

In addition to the pre-existing limitations, the 2002 text adds that resources are now to be "evaluated by reference to [their] nature and regularity."[64] Further, Member States are permitted to apply the test again on the first renewal of residence permits. However, if the applicant does not meet the resources condition, Member States are required to have regard to the household income. Further, the conditions on accommodation, sickness insurance and resources may only be applied to ensure that the family will not have recourse to public funds.

Member States are also permitted to apply a two-year waiting period before family reunification can be requested.[65] In addition, and again by way of derogation where national legislation has regard to the Member States "reception capacity" at the date of adoption of the directive, a Member State can require a waiting period of three years.[66] This distasteful "reception capacity" provision introduces a rather arbitrary condition, unrelated to the individual's position into the directive but rather to the level of xenophobia in the host Member State.

In the final text a new possibility to limit the admission of spouses was created for the Member States – they can require that the sponsor be at least 21 years of age in addition to the spouse being of a minimum age (not exceeding 21) (article 4(5)). Another new requirement is that the parties to a marriage neither marry another person nor enter into a stable long term relationship without placing at risk the spouse's residence permit, a sort of fidelity requirement (article 16(1)(c)). As regards the conditions, the resources condition has been made more difficult – regard will now be had to the number of family members as well as the regularity of the resources.[67]

---

64 Article 7(1)(c).
65 Article 8.
66 Article 8.
67 Article 7(1)(c).

All third country nationals may be required to comply with integration measures under national law with no restriction on changes to these laws.[68]

Member States are not permitted to apply these provisions to refugees (article 12(1)).

The Rights for Family Members

The rights which the family members would have had according to the Commission's first proposal were:

1.   Education on the basis of non-discrimination with own nationals;
2.   Employment and self-employment;
3.   Vocational training, initial and further training and retraining;
4.   After four years an autonomous residence permit.

The rights of education and employment are among the most important for migrants in the context of family reunification. Spouses will normally seek to work and children need to go to school. Thus the inclusion of (1), (2) and (3) reflects some key issues for the migrant. These provisions are also not so far from equality of treatment with migrant Community national under article 11 and 12 regulation 1612/68.

The fourth right, to an autonomous residence permit, is new. Family members of migrant Community nationals only enjoy such an autonomous right in the event that the principal dies after a sufficient period of work and residence in the host Member State (regulation 1251/71). The proposal for a directive on the right to move and residence for citizens of the Union includes such a right. The inclusion in both measures for Union citizens and third country nationals at the same time indicates a commitment to achieving equality between the two groups. In the first draft of the family reunification directive these autonomous permits must be issued for the spouse, unmarried partner and minors after four years residence in the host State in the category. For other family members there is a discretion to the Member States. However, in the event of widowhood, divorce, separation or death of the principal where the third country national family member has been resident for one year or more, he or she may apply for an autonomous residence permit. Member States are required to take into account special difficulties.[69]

In the 2000 text, the main change was to exclude relatives in the ascending line or children of full age from automatic access to employment and vocational training. This is now left to Member State discretion (article 12(2)). While the time limit of

---

68   Article 7(2).
69   Articles 12 and 13.

four years residence where after family members acquire an independent residence permit survived the 2000 changes they fell at the 2002 text. The time limit is raised to five years (article 15(1)) and is subject to the relationship with the principal continuing.[70] This period corresponds with the change which the Council inserted into the draft directive on the right to move and residence for citizens of the Union. A proposal by the Commission for a standstill clause on the re-evaluation of the resources requirement after the first residence permit was issued was short lived.[71]

In the adopted text, Member States are left free to exclude all family members from employment or self-employment for up to one year. After that they are permitted to continue to refuse to permit all family members except spouses and minor children from working or self-employment.[72] The provisions on autonomous residence permits for family members are made somewhat more onerous in particular as Member States are given more discretion on whether to grant such permits or not in the case of the break down of the relationship with the principal.[73] Further the conditions for granting and renewing the permits are specifically left to national law (article 15(4)).

Just before the final version was adopted a non-governmental organisation, the Meijers Committee of Experts on International Immigration, Refugee and Criminal Law, in a detailed letter to the Commission, requested the withdrawal of the proposal on the grounds that it no longer fulfilled the minimum requirement of respect for family life as contained in the ECHR and interpreted by the ECtHR. In March 2003 an inter-faith coalition of church groups criticised very heavily the proposal, and cast doubt on whether it fulfilled the Member States commitments under the ECHR.[74]

Early Challenge on Human Rights Grounds?

The directive was adopted on 22 September 2003 and published in the OJ on 3 October. Member States were given two years – until 3 October 2005 – to bring their national legislation into line with the directive. Three standstill provisions are included:

1. Article 4(1)(d) third indent: by way of derogation, where a child is aged over 12 years and arrives independently from the rest of his or her family, the

---

70 Article 15(1).
71 ILPA European Update December 2002.
72 Article 14(2) & (3).
73 Article 15.
74 "The New EU Directive on Family Reunification: Right for Families to Live Together or Right for EU Member States to Derogate from Human Rights?" Caritas Europa, CCME, Commission of the

Member State may before authorising entry and residence verify whether he or she meets a condition for integration on the date of implementation of the directive; this provision did not appear in the Commission's initial proposal and was the subject of intensive negotiation in the Council; the European Parliament proposed an amendment to weaken the provision as it considered it to be a grave derogation from the general principle which could give rise to unjustifiable variations among the Member States;

2. Article 4(6): Member States may request that applications concerning family reunification of minor children have to be submitted before the child reaches the age of 15, as provided for by its national legislation on the date of the implementation of the directive; this provision was introduced into the text after the final consultation of the European Parliament on 9 April 2003;

3. Article 8 second indent: by way of derogation, where the legislation of a Member State relating to family reunification in force on the date of adoption of the directive takes into account its reception capacity, the Member State may provide for a waiting period of no more than three years between submission of the application for family reunification and the issue of a residence permit to the family members.

As the implementation date is delayed until October 2005, this provides a substantial period of time for Member States to put in place legislation which could constitute a real obstacle to family reunification with children. On 14 October 2003 the European Parliament's Civil Liberties Committee requested an opinion from its legal service on whether the directive violates article 8 ECHR. The legal service provided a reasoned opinion dated 21 October 2003, considered the duty of the EU to respect article 8 ECHR, notwithstanding that the EU is not a signatory. It advised that the concept of the family in the directive although limited to the nuclear family permits the Member States to admit a wider group of family members. In this regard then it did not consider the directive in breach of article 8 ECHR.

The legal service, however, considered it doubtful that the standstill provision on integration as a criterion for admission of children over 12 contained in article 4(1)(d) was in conformity with Article 8 ECHR. The legal service stated that the fact that the directive permits national legislation to derogate from the right of family reunification with minor children on the basis of an integration requirement which is not subject to the limitations set out in article 8 ECHR may constitute in itself a breach of a fundamental right which is recognised in the legal order of the Union. To allow Member States to adopt or apply such a provision is in itself an unlawful constraint on the right to family life.

(Cont.)
Bishops' Conferences of the EC, International Catholic Migration Commission, Jesuit Refugee Service Europe, Quaker Council for European Affairs, March 2003.

The European Parliament notified that it was commencing legal proceedings for annulment of the directive before the ECJ on 17 December 2003. In the notice, the Parliament is attacking the directive for its failure to respect fundamental rights in particular those contained in article 8 ECHT as regards the three provisions: that in article 4 which permits Member States to apply an integration test to children over 12 years before admitting them; the rule that allows Member States to refuse reunification to children over 15 years in article 4(6); and the waiting period of two or even three years in article 8.[75]

Conclusions: Comparing Family Reunification

To insist on the centrality of family unity to identity is banal. In balancing the role of the state in private and public life, in Europe the most protected field is that of the family. Interference by the state in family life is prohibited by article 8 ECHR except on the grounds carefully enumerated. Perhaps because of the importance of family to identity, the approach of European states to the admission of foreign family members has become increasing harsh from the 1980s onwards.[76] By placing administrative obstacles in the way of own nationals seeking to marry a foreigner or acquire other foreign family members, the state privileges family life within the state. The equation of foreign with negative qualities is reinforced by the state's restrictive response to its citizens' relationships with foreigners. The implicit position of the state is that foreigners are dangerous and citizens should be discouraged from entering into family relations with them. The insistency of some member States that the family reunification directive include provisions requiring family members to undergo integration tests before they are permitted to join their family members in the host State evidences the seriousness with which some Member States view their need to control the family within their state.

The solution to this negative positioning of family reunification in Community law has been the adoption of measures on family reunification which, on the one hand accept the Member States' right to control family reunification in a way which is unacceptable where the family members are nationals of the same state, but on the other to create such a wide definition of qualifying family members, so few qualifying conditions and such wide rights for the family members that the control becomes barely visible. Community nationals are entitled to family reunification and while it is apparent from the cases before the ECJ that Member States still seek to impede family life, the robust approach of the ECJ has protected the identity choices of

---

75 Case C-540/03, Council document 5372/04.
76 J Bhabha, S Shutter et al, *Women's Movement, Women under Immigration, Nationality and Refugee Law*, Trentham Books, Stoke-on-Trent, 1994.

migrant Community nationals. Indeed, the protection of this group has been so successful, in particular against Member State's restrictive policies towards their own nationals, as to create an incentive for Community nationals to use their free movement rights in order to establish a right to family reunification with third country national family members. This then results in a temptation for citizens to value more highly their status as citizens of the Union rather than nationals of the Member States in light of the important identity benefits which derive from the one status which have been refused as a corollary of the other.

No such solution appears forthcoming for Europe's third country nationals. The family reunification directive (2003/86) places many obstacles of a variety of different types in the place of their family reunification. The definition of the family members is fraught with limitations and must be substantiated with many official documents; the conditions for enjoying family reunification are riddled with discretionary elements to be assessed by Member State authorities and in principle permit high financial barriers to family reunification to be created or maintained; the rights granted to family members are restricted. The barriers to family reunification created in the directive will not cause the line of control by the Member States to disappear as has happened in the case of Community nationals. Instead of satisfying the legitimate interests of the EU's third country national families to live together in the country of choice, it is likely to impede family life with all the disastrous consequences for social cohesion which so many national policies around families are designed to avoid. An EU law which appears to justify national practices preventing some spouses and children from living together (that is to say third country national ones) while privileging other spouses and children (that is to say migrant citizens of the Union and their third country national spouses and children) is unlikely to command the respect of those who suffer from its effects.

Perhaps most seriously, though, the odious concept of "integration" has crept in and with it the implied notion that there is a homogeneous community within a Member State to which the heterogeneous third country national must transform him or herself. At the heart of the concept of integration is a hatred of diversity: a refusal to acknowledge its existence within all European communities; the false suggestion that it comes from abroad; the association of negative values to it; the justification for crushing it. Identity is built on difference – how one individual is different from another. Through acknowledgement of difference similarity is apparent. To cut the individual off from his or her family members with the justification that if the family wishes to live together they should do so somewhere else is to deny a right to a personal identity. Identity politics based on integration are used to justify punishing third country nationals for having foreign family members. Implicit is the argument that they should abandon their foreign identities (and families) abroad and start again with nationals of the host state. The European Union is Janus faced in this discussion. On the one hand it protects migrant nationals of the Member States from any suggestion that they should be required to integrate in their chosen host Member State or indeed that their families should have to do so while on the other hand it plays the identity politics game as regards third country nationals and their family reunification. A more evenhanded approach would be more befitting of the Union. This opinion appears to be shared by the European Parliament.

Chapter 7

Identity Beyond Citizenship: the European Convention on Human Rights

So far I have considered the development of immigration and citizenship law in the European Union and the relationship between the two. The normative framework of rights for migrants and citizens in EU law is not uniform. The development of rights of family reunification for immigrants who are nationals of the member states took place over a period of years with a gradual widening of the understanding of the right through the interpretation given by the ECJ. While the development of EU family reunification law for third country nationals is only just beginning and there has been no clarification yet by the ECJ of the meaning of the terms, there is little convergence between the rights of migrant citizens of the Union and those of third country nationals. The declaration of principle made at the Tampere Council of 1999 to pursue a policy aimed at granting legally resident third country nationals in the Union rights and obligations comparable to those of EU citizens is not evidently reflected in the field of family reunification.

Where then is the floor of rights for third country nationals in Europe? The European Convention on Human Rights (ECHR) has come to occupy this space as the expression of the threshold of treatment of foreigners which cannot be breached by the signatory states. The ECHR as a foundational treaty of the Council of Europe has now been ratified by 45 member States.[1] All signatory states are require to accept the jurisdiction of the European Court of Human Rights (ECtHR) which receives petitions directly from individuals (the member States are also entitled to bring actions though this is rare in comparison with the overall number of cases) and is charged with determining whether member States are fulfilling their obligations to

---

1 The most recent signatory is Serbia. All EU Member States are signatories.

respect the rights contained in the ECHR. Before considering the relationship of the threshold of the ECHR on the rights of foreigners with that of EU law and examining what the threshold itself is, I shall consider briefly why states accept and comply with the ECHR even in such a sensitive area as identity rights. Before one begins to examine the decisions of the ECtHR in the field, particularly those which are controversial, it is valuable already to have considered what the mechanisms are which result in member State obedience.

Understanding State Obedience: Identity and the ECHR

There are a number of ways of considering the processes by which the ECHR becomes central to the development of identity rights in Europe. One starting place is to examine why the European human rights system is effective, or as O'Boyle claims, "without doubt the world's most successful regional treaty system for the protection of human rights."[2] Taking an institutional analysis approach, he singles out four main reasons for ECHR's success:

1. The ECtHR retained the confidence of the member States. At the heart of this argument is the question of deference or defiance of the judiciary towards the executive. In this case the executive is that of each of the member States while the judiciary is that of the supranational entity. O'Boyle considers central the ECtHR's characteristics of "reputation for fairness and intellectual rigour" while respecting "the principle of subsidiarity which recognizes the primary competence and duty of the state to protect effectively, within the domestic legal orders, the rights;"[3]
2. Constant development of the system; he sees as central to the success of the project the continuation of negotiations leading to new protocols developing the legal framework of human rights and creating the mechanisms for their legal recognition. Moreover, he insists on the importance of the consolidation of the institutions of the Strasbourg court as central to their effectiveness;
3. A system within which the members are "like minded and have a common heritage of political traditions, ideals, freedom and the rule of law."[4] O'Boyle states that the member States have (or until the enlargement of the 1990s had) a shared vision of the need for collective enforcement of human rights which, coupled with a high place accorded to the rule of law, has led to compliance even where states are hostile to the ECtHR judgments;

---

2   M O'Boyle, 'Reflections of the Effectiveness of the European System for the Protection of Human Rights' in A Bayefsky (ed), *The UN Human Rights Treaty System in the 21st Century*, Kluwer Law International, The Hague, 2000, p 169.
3   Ibid p 178.
4   Ibid p 178.

4. Popular support: O'Boyle also finds fundamental to the success of the project the "formation of a sensitized and informed public conscience"[5] on human rights as an issue which exceeds the control of the nation state. In his opinion, few governments would now take the political risk of denouncing the ECHR.[6] Implicit in O'Boyle's third ground is the role of the aggregation of individuals in the formulation of policy.

Caporaso provides some useful indications on the meaning of this effect. He highlights three points – first the centrality of microfoundations. "Individuals situated within their material and symbolic environments and these incentives, motivations, and beliefs are taken as important. Thus macrobehavior – whether aggregate trans-actions, political institutionalization, or decision-making – is rooted in the world of individuals."[7] Secondly he considers it central to re-think the relationship of transnational society and supranational institutions. Here he seeks to provide a tool to understand how as transnational activity increases governments are required to adjust their policies. They can seek to change the rules on the transactions but the costs are likely to be intolerable electorally.[8] He notes "agents in transnational society, in their attempts to solve problems, may go directly to supranational institutions."[9] This understanding provides a strong foundation for the development of identity rights through the ECHR – the refuge of individuals engaged in transnational activities, most centrally migration, in the supranational jurisdiction of ECtHR. Thirdly he develops the analytical tool of path-dependency building on the work of economists P David[10] and W B Arthur.[11] "If a process is path dependent, its present behavior is heavily constrained by the past. Path-dependent processes are strongly biased in one direction. Reverse movement is possible but there are strong forces working against it."[12] A field which is exceptionally path dependent is judicial consideration. Once a court of final instance, in particular, has decided on the correct interpretation of legislation, treaties or procedures, it will be extremely reluctant to reverse its finding.

---

5   Ibid p 178.
6   This view is supported by the rapidity with which the British government moved away from suggestions by the British Prime Minister on 26 January 2003 that the UK would need to resile from its obligation to protect asylum seekers from return to torture under article 3 ECHR, which in light of the fact that there is no provision to derogate from article 3 would mean a withdrawal from the ECHR as a whole.
7   J Caporaso, 'Integration Theory, Past and Future' in W Sandholtz and A Stone Sweet, *European Integration and Supranational Governance*, OUP, Oxford, 1998 p 349.
8   Ibid p 349.
9   Ibid p 350.
10 P David, "Clio and the Economics of QWERTY" (1985) American Economic Review 75:332–7.
11 W B Arthur, *Increasing Returns and Path Dependence in the Economy*, University of Michigan Press, Ann Arbor, 1994.
12 J Caporaso, ibid p 350.

For supranational courts this characteristic is critical. If these institutions at the top of the judicial food chain are to command the respect of the courts (and administrations) at the national level, they must maintain a very high degree of consistency. The slightest deviation from any previous interpretation of a provision is likely to give rise to great consternation at the national level and the opportunity for actors at the national level to seek to redefine positions.

All of these theoretical tools are important for understanding the development of identity rights as human rights in the ECHR. O'Boyle's four grounds for the strength of the ECHR system and Caporaso's development of three analytical tools for understanding the Europeanisation of the politics of identity help to explain and make comprehensible the development of supranational immigration and asylum rights through the mechanism of human rights. One of my students expressed substantial dismay at what seemed to him the interference of international judges in the fundamental question of belonging and identity which he considered a state prerogative. The development of the ECtHR jurisprudence providing extensive rights of residence and indeed admission for foreigners to the state as human rights seemed to him to be an unacceptable interference with sovereignty. In the light of this revulsion, we considered the meaning of the inclusion of all of the substantive rights of the ECHR in the EU Charter on Fundamental Freedoms. The Charter, the result of extensive consultation and deliberation in the form of a convention at EU level, was solemnly adopted in December 2000 by all of the main EU institutions. While it began its life as specifically not legally binding, it was rapidly incorporated into the ECJ's reasoning as an aid to interpretation.[13] The development of the EU constitution in 2003 has incorporated the Charter into the constitution permitting it to have legal effect.

This political decision regarding the inclusion of the ECHR rights into the Charter and via the Charter in the EU Constitution indicates that the political leaders of the EU were willing to include the identity rights for foreigners which the ECtHR had interpreted as part of the meaning of the rights. It would have been possible for the Charter to have excluded the application of the ECHR rights it incorporated from applying to situations of immigration, asylum or the residence rights of foreigners. This choice was not taken thus the inclusion of these rights must be taken as the acceptance of the 15 Member States of the ECtHR's jurisprudence. The judgments of the ECtHR on identity of foreigners cannot be attacked as usurping the sovereignty of the state if the state subsequently incorporates and expressly includes those rights in other treaties which bind it even more tightly.

---

13   A Ward and S Peers, *The European Charter of Fundamental Rights*, Hart, Oxford, 2004.

Human Rights and Foreigners

The ECHR consists of the convention with 14 substantial rights followed by the administrative and institutional rules amended by 11 Protocols which build on the rights or deal with procedural transformations (such as Protocol 11 which merged the former European Commission on Human Rights and the ECtHR) or have never come into force. The ECHR was opened for signature in 1950 and entered into force in 1953. In article 1 comes the inclusion of foreigners in the personal scope of the ECHR: the member States "shall secure to everyone within their jurisdiction the rights and freedoms" of the ECHR. The use of the word "everyone" includes foreigners and immigrants, whether lawfully or unlawfully on the territory of the state.[14]

Jurisdiction for the purposes of the ECHR rights is primarily territorial according to the ECtHR. It recognised that in public international law, extra-territorial jurisdiction has specific bases premised on the inviolability of the borders of judicial territory between sovereign states.[15] But it also engages responsibilities in its activities outside its territory. The conditions for responsibility are when the Member State has:

1. Effective control of the relevant territory and its inhabitants abroad as a result of:
2. Military occupation (the situation regarding Turkey and Cyprus); consent, invitation or acquiescence of the state concerned; and
3. Exercises all or some of the public powers normally exercised by that Government.[16]

Thus the starting place for the application of the ECHR is a definition of sovereignty which few states would have come up with on their own. The result is suspiciously like a legal formulation of Weber's definition of the state as a bureaucracy which claims a monopoly over the legitimate use of violence within a territory.[17]

---

14 *Conka v Belgium* ECtHR 5 February 2002.
15 The exceptions to which the Court refers are nationality, flag, diplomatic and consular relations, effect, protection, passive personality and universality, which in fact cover a rather large territory of jurisdiction. One could even begin to argue that the exceptions have overtaken the rule and thus replaced it – the lack of extraterritorial effect now being the exception. However, this would be contrary to juridical orthodoxy.
16 *Banković v Belgium* ECtHR 19 December 2001 (admissibility).
17 M Weber, *Economy and Society*, vol 1, Ed Roth G & C Wittich, University of California Press, Berkeley, 1978.

Human Rights and Immigrants

The intersection of human rights and immigration for the ECHR starts with article 8, the right to respect for private and family life.[18] The treatment of asylum seekers and others with humanitarian claims to remain on the territory also engage human rights obligations of states through the application of article 3 ECHR, the prohibition on torture. I have outlined briefly in chapter 4 the development of citizenship rights as human rights, I will here follow immigration rights as such. First I will deal with the issues in respect of article 8 and family life, then in respect of article 3 and asylum seekers and others with humanitarian claims to remain on the territory. I will not specifically cover the right to liberty (article 5), procedural guarantees (article 13) or Protocol 4, which has not been ratified by all EU Member States.[19] What is important to note is that the claims which come before the ECtHR are in respect of foreigners whom the state has rejected and required to leave or prohibited from entering. When the authorities exercise their powers to refuse to permit a foreigner access to the territory or the possibility to remain they are acting within the scope of sovereign powers. The authorities' decision may be challenged within the state through the courts according to national rules and the national courts must obey the definitions of human rights obligations which the authorities and superior courts have determined.

Thus in principle the system of protection of human rights remains within the ambit of the nation state. However, in the European context it escapes national control through the intercession of the institutions of the Council of Europe designed to oversee the implementation of the ECHR. Most importantly this includes the ECtHR which has the power to adjudicate a claim of a breach of the ECHR after the individual has exhausted national remedies. Thus if an individual is still aggrieved after the national system has determined that he or she has no claim, then the individual is entitled to submit a petition to the Strasbourg Court which may decide that all the decisions of the administrations and the courts within the Member State and in the exercise of sovereign powers to exclude foreigners are wrong and do not conform to the ECtHR's interpretation of the meaning of the state's human rights obligations under the convention. In effect, the ECtHR is entitled to tell national authorities and courts who they must permit to remain on their territory. In this sense the right of identity, which in law is so closely linked with the right to remain on a particular territory, no longer resides at the national level. Not only has much of the competence already been passed to the level of the European Union but a further part of this sovereign right has been ceded to the field of human rights adjudicated by a supranational court.

---

18 P van Dijk, 'Protection of "Integrated" Aliens Against Expulsion under the European convention on Human Rights' EJML 1999 Vol 1 No 3 pp 293–312.

19 For an excellent analysis of these provisions in immigration and asylum law see N Blake QC and R Husain, *Immigration, Asylum and Human Rights*, OUP, Oxford, 2003.

Before looking at the ECtHR's interpretation of immigrants' rights as human rights, I shall take a moment to consider how the ECHR and EU relate to one another.

The Relationship Between the EU and the ECHR

The relationship between the ECHR and EU law has a rather fragmented history. No reference was made to the ECHR in the original treaties of the EU. The predecessor treaties of the EU were intended to create a system of economic integration among the Member States. The ECHR was intended to create a foundation of human rights standards across the Council of Europe's member States. That the two should overlap was not anticipated by many. However, as both systems developed and their scope enlarged, they began to intersect. Both systems include supranational dispute resolution mechanisms, the ECtHR for the ECHR and the ECJ for the EU, charged with the interpretation of their respective treaties. While the rules of procedure, scope and effect of the two courts are very different, they share a number of particularly important characteristics: they are both supranational thus beyond the immediate control of any one signatory state; they both adjudicate in respect of natural persons, in other words their scope is not limited to legal persons such as states or international organizations; they both share the principle of supremacy over national courts' decisions and neither is subject to appeal.[20] They are both monuments to a European conviction in the success of dispute resolution through judicial decision (rather than, for instance, negotiation or armed struggle).

The first point of intersection came before the ECJ where an individual argued the ECHR right to private property against a decision by one of the EU institutions.[21] The ECJ chose to incorporate into its legal legitimacy human rights, stating: "... fundamental rights form an integral part of the general principles of law which [this Court] enforces", a position which would in due course be introduced into the Treaty on European Union and eventually into the EU Charter on Fundamental Rights. The amount of academic interest which has been paid to the way in which the ECJ has dealt with the ECHR and the decisions of the ECtHR far outweighs the interest which has been expressed in the other direction – the ECtHR's interpretation of the EU.[22] The ECJ has made an increasing number of references to the ECHR starting

---

20 In the EU system there is a two-tier court where, depending on the subject matter and the nature of the case it may be brought before a Court of First Instance with the possibility of an appeal to the ECJ.

21 C-4/73 *Nold v Commission* [1974] ECR 491.

22 Two very eminent examples suffice – F Matscher and H Pertzold, *Protecting Human Rights: The European Dimension – Studies in honour of Gérard J Wiarda*, Carl Heymanns Verlag KG, Cologne, 1990 where all the important academics and judges in the field contributed and spend much time considering the ECJ and EC's view of the ECHR; secondly, P Alston, *The EU and Human Rights*,

seriously in the mid 1980s. It has held that the rights and indeed the ECHR itself must be upheld within the scope of Community law.

A small number of cases came before the ECHR judicial institutions where the applicant pleaded a failure of the EC to respect the ECHR starting from 1978.[23] In the first case the ECmHR found that it was not competent to consider acts of the EC, ratio personae, as the EC is not a party to the ECHR.[24] Subsequent cases were also rejected by the former European Commission of Human Rights (ECmHR) with an implicit or explicit recognition of the special nature of the EC which deserved respect from the Strasbourg institutions. In 1990 the ECmHR had to consider the case of a German limited partnership which had been fined by the European Commission for a concerted practice (i.e. anti trust action) against which penalty the business had sought a remedy unsuccessfully before the ECJ, and a substantial number of German national courts including the constitutional court. Its claim was finally renewed before the Strasbourg institutions on the basis of articles 1 (jurisdiction of the ECHR) and 6 (procedural safeguards).

In this case, the ECmHR commenced a line of argument which would inform its decision-making in the future. It found: "It has next to be observed that the Convention does not prohibit a member State from transferring powers to international organisations ... The Commission considers that a transfer of powers does not necessarily exclude a State's responsibility under the Convention with regard to the exercise of the transferred powers. Otherwise the guarantees of their Convention could wantonly be limited or excluded and thus deprived of their peremptory character."[25] However, the ECmHR found no violation in light of the ECJ's care that there had been a fair trial and indeed that the right to a fair hearing was a fundamental principle of Community law. It considered that "it would be contrary to the very idea of transferring powers to an international organisation to hold the member States responsible for examining in each individual case, before issuing a writ of execution for a judgment of the European Court of Justice, whether Article 6 of the Convention was respected in the underlying proceedings." Thus the ECmHR accepted in principle a claim to human rights legitimacy by the ECJ.[26]

(Cont.)
OUP, Oxford, 1999 – nine years later another extremely authoritative and large collection of essays on the subject fails to consider even once the perspective from Strasbourg towards Luxembourg and Brussels. The extensive bibliographies in the two books also reflect the same tendency. Somewhat more balanced is F Jacobs, 'European Community Law and the European Convention on Human Rights' in D Curtin and T Henkels, *Institutional Dynamics of European Essays in Honour of H G Schermers*, Vol II, Martinus Nijhoff, Dordrecht, 1992.

23 *CFDT v European Communities* Dec. 10 July 1978, DR 13 p 231.
24 See also *Dufay v European Communities* Dec. 19 January 1989.
25 *M & Co v Germany (FRG)* ECmHR 9 February 1990.
26 See also F Jacobs, 'European Community Law and the European Convention on Human Rights' in D Curtin & T Henkels, *Institutional Dynamics of European Integration: Essays in Honour of H G Schermers*, Vol II, Martinus Nihjoff, Dordrecht, 1992.

A further examination of the possibility of conflict became unavoidable in Strasbourg in 1995 when Ms Piermont, a German national and member of the European Parliament, was expelled from French Polynesia and New Caledonia where she sought to speak in her official capacity about French nuclear testing. She pleaded a number of breaches of ECHR rights, under Protocol 4 the representation rights, under article 10 the right of expression and article 14 discrimination.[27] The ECtHR held that there had been a breach of article 10, no breach of the Protocol rights and no need to consider the discrimination issue. However, in order to reach this decision the ECtHR had to determine to what extent article 16 ECHR which provides that "nothing in Article 10 [ ] shall be regarded as preventing the High Contracting Parties from imposing restrictions on the political activity of aliens" was relevant. If Ms Piermont is an alien for the purposes of article 16 when she is seeking to express her views in French Polynesia and New Caledonia then the French authorities are not bound by article 10 and the duty to respect her right to free speech. If Ms Piermont is not an alien for the purposes of article 16 then what is she?

The ECtHR was first presented with an argument on the basis of citizenship of the Union which it easily rejected as the Maastricht Treaty had not been ratified at the time the events took place and thus the citizenship did not exist at the relevant time. It went on to confirm the special position of the Union and thus the duty of the French authorities to apply article 10 to Ms Piermont as follows "Nevertheless, [the ECtHR] considers that Mrs Piermont's possession of the nationality of a Member State of the European Union and, in addition to that, her status as a member of the European Parliament do not allow article 16 of the Convention to be raised against her, especially as the people of the [Overseas Territories] take part in the European Parliament elections."[28] Thus the ECtHR acknowledged the special nature of the EU through the limitation of the defences available to the Member States as regards the treatment of nationals of other Member States as aliens.

The field of the Piermont dispute, the effectiveness of political representation in the European Parliament, was also the subject of the second substantive decision of the ECtHR on the EU. Here a British national resident in Gibraltar, Ms Matthews, sought to register to vote in the European Parliament elections of 1994. According to the terms of the UK's accession to the EU Gibraltar is excluded from various parts of the Treaty provisions, including the suffrage rights to the European Parliament. Ms Matthews pleaded article 3 Protocol 1, the right to free elections and article 14 in conjunction with article 3 Protocol 1 – that the right to free elections must be carried out without discrimination. The ECtHR had to consider "whether, notwithstanding the nature of the elections to the European Parliament as an organ of the EC, the United Kingdom can be held responsible under Article 1 of the Convention for the absence of elections to the European Parliament in Gibraltar, that is, whether

---

27 *Piermont v France* ECtHR 20 March 1995.
28 *Piermont v France* ECtHR 20 March 1995, para 64.

the United Kingdom is required to 'secure' elections to the European Parliament notwithstanding the Community character of those elections."[29]

The ECtHR confirmed that acts of the EU (including the EC) cannot be challenged before it as the EU/EC is not a party. However, it found that the UK (and the other parties to the EU Treaties) is responsible under article 1 ECHR for the consequences of the EU Treaties. Restating its constant jurisprudence that the ECHR is intended to guarantee rights that are not theoretical or illusory but practical and effective, it noted that Gibraltar is affected by EU legislation in the same way as by legislation which is passed through its own assembly. Thus according to the ECtHR the UK is responsible under article 1 ECHR to secure the rights in article 3 Protocol 1 in Gibraltar. The ECtHR was careful to insist on the entry into force of the Maastricht Treaty in order to overcome the UK government's argument that the relationship in time between the EC Treaty and the Protocol meant that the latter came after the commitments and thus could not vary them. A dissenting opinion by two ECtHR judges, Freeland and Jungwiert, is noteworthy: they were against the finding of a breach of the Protocol on the grounds that the European Parliament is not a legislature for the purposes of article 3.

The ECtHR through these two judgments made it clear that it would treat the acts of the EU as acts of the Member States for the purposes of review according to the ECHR. It thus reserved to itself the final interpretation of the human rights compliance of the EU at least in so far as the ECHR is concerned.

The next decision of the ECtHR relevant to this consideration falls directly into one of the fields of concern in this book – asylum. In 1990 the EU Member States entered into an agreement tied to but outside the EU Treaties, that they would pool their responsibilities for asylum seekers within the common territory and on the basis of the principle of mutual negative recognition, permit asylum seekers only one chance to have their asylum application considered within the EU.[30] The Dublin Convention came into force on 1 September 1997 and was replaced by an EC regulation 343/2003 (commonly called Dublin II) in 2003 which repeats all the major provisions of the Dublin Convention.[31] Because the Convention was based on the idea that only one Member State would consider an asylum application and if rejected, any further application in another Member State would be automatically inadmissible/rejected, without a harmonization of the key elements of the determining who is a refugee, trouble was bound to follow. At the heart of the case which rapidly came before the Strasbourg judges, was the fact that some Member States, France

---

29 *Matthews v UK* ECtHR 18 February 1999 para 31.
30 For a detailed critique of the Dublin Convention see E Guild, 'Between Persecution and Protection – Refugees and the New European Asylum Policy' in *The Cambridge Yearbook of European Legal Studies Vol 3 2000*, A Dashwood, J Spencer, A Ward C Hillion, Hart, Oxford, 2001 pp 169–199; E Guild, 'The Case Law of the Dublin Convention in the UK' in the *Dublin Convention on Asylum: Between Reality and Aspirations*, C Faria (ed), European Institute of Public Administration, Maastricht, 2001, pp 149–172.
31 OJ 2003 L 50/1.

and Germany, for example, do not recognize (or did not at that time) as refugees persons whose fear of persecution comes from non-state agents. Other Member States, such as the Netherlands and the UK do recognize non-state agents of persecution as giving rise to a sustainable claim for protection.[32]

I will return shortly below to the ECtHR's jurisprudence regarding the duty of states not to return persons to countries where there is a substantial risk that they will be subjected to torture (the interpretation of article 3 ECHR). Suffice it here to note that this brought the question of the Dublin Convention within the territory of the ECHR. An asylum seeker whose application for protection had been rejected in Germany, inter alia on the ground that he feared persecution from non-state agents, went to the UK and applied again for protection there. The UK authorities rejected his application, consistent with the Dublin Convention, on the ground that he had already made an application in Germany which had been rejected. The applicant argued that his application in Germany was rejected on grounds which would not be the reason for his protection claim to be rejected in the UK: that he feared persecution by non-state agents. Thus in fairness and in compliance with its duties under article 3 ECHR the UK must consider his claim.

When the issue came to the ECtHR in an admissibility hearing the ECtHR confirmed its case law that "the existence of the obligation [not to commit torture] is not dependent on whether the source of the risk of the treatment stems from factors which involve the responsibility, direct or indirect, of the authorities of the receiving country."[33] (This might be interpreted as the ECtHR criticizing the German position on agent of persecution as incompatible with its duties under article 3). Nonetheless, it had to determine whether the UK's obligations under article 3 were engaged if the UK sent the applicant back to Germany without considering his application for protection. The ECtHR held "the indirect removal in this case to an intermediary country, which is also a Contracting State, does not affect the responsibility of the United Kingdom to ensure that the applicant is not, as a result of its decision to expel, exposed to treatment contrary to Article 3 of the Convention. Nor can the United Kingdom rely automatically in that context on the arrangements made in the Dublin Convention concerning the attribution of responsibility between European countries for deciding asylum claims. Where States establish international organizations or *mutatis mutandis* international agreements, to pursue co-operation in certain fields of activities, there may be implications for the protection of fundamental rights. It would be incompatible with the purpose and object of the Convention if Contracting States were thereby absolved from their responsibility under the Convention in relation to the field of activity covered by such attribution."[34]

---

32   U Brandl, 'Distribution of Asylum Seekers in Europe? Dublin II Regulation determining the responsibility for examining an asylum application' in C Dias Urbano de Souza, *The Emergence of an European Asylum Policy*, Bruylant 2004 (forthcoming).

33   *TI v UK* ECtHR 7 March 2000 (admissibility) p 14.

34   *TI v UK* ECtHR 7 March 2000 (admissibility) p 15.

The ECtHR went on to find, relying on information provided by the German government, that the claim was inadmissible as, if the applicant were returned to Germany, his application would be reconsidered.

The final ECtHR admissibility decision I shall consider here is *SEGI & others v Germany and others*.[35] The applicant was a Basque youth organization whose application was joined with that of a Basque human rights association. Both associations were subject to the arrest of their directors and the suspension of their activities on the basis of two EU measures against terrorism.[36] Both associations brought petitions to the ECtHR against the anti-terrorism measures adopted under the Common Foreign and Security Policy of the EU (commonly known as the Second Pillar of the EU). The applicants argued that they were the subject of breaches of articles 6, 8, 10, 11, 13 ECHR and article 1 Protocol 1 (some of the applicants also argued breaches of other ECHR provisions). They noted that under the Treaty on European Union (TEU), the jurisdiction of the ECJ is excluded thus there is no judicial dispute mechanism available at the EU level to which they could bring their complaint.[37] The ECtHR found the cases inadmissible on the basis that the applicants were not victims within the meaning of article 34 ECHR as regards the operation of the Common Positions (notwithstanding the fact that the two main applicants were listed as groups or entities implicated in acts of terrorism in the Position) as the Positions do no more than require Member States to act together and do not enlarge the powers which are already being exercised. In so finding, the ECtHR considered in detail the content of the two EU measures and the possibility of recourse against the Member States individually in respect of their effects. By so doing it has shown itself willing to engage in the substance of EU measures and claims the right to investigate them where they are alleged to breach fundamental rights.

Thus the ECtHR has developed a position on the EU and human rights claims which holds the Member States individually responsible for any human rights violations which result from their application of common agreements including EC law. It has refused the argument of collective responsibility of human rights compliance (or breach) where this would place the issue itself beyond the scope of the ECtHR. This protection of jurisdictional space may be of substantial importance as the EU adopts legislation on third country nationals.

It is now time to consider how migrants' rights have become human rights within the ambit of the ECHR.

---

35   6422/02, ECtHR 23 May 2002.
36   Common Positions 2001/930 and 2001/931/CFSP.
37   The EC Court of First Instance had already rejected an application for annulment of the Common Positions T-177/01 *Jégo-Quére* [2002] ECR II-2365.

Article 8: Losing Control Over Family Members

The intersection of immigration and human rights has had important consequences for the idea of the nation state and the meaning of state sovereignty over which persons have a right to reside on the territory. Article 8 is the starting place.[38] There are four steps which must be considered when looking at the protection of family life as required by the ECHR:

1. Is there family life: it is for the applicant to establish that he or she in fact has family life in the state concerned;
2. Has there been an interference with that family life: this is usually agreed – an attempt to expel, or indeed even the refusal of a residence permit which will have the effect that the individual will become irregularly present and subject to expulsion measures will constitute an interference;[39]
3. Is the interference in accordance with the law: this requirement enforces the rule of law. If the national measures are insufficiently clear and public so as to qualify as law, then the interference will never be lawful as it will lack an essential element of legality – the absence of the arbitrary;[40]
4. Is the interference necessary in a democratic society: in determining this fourth step, it is for the state to establish the justification on the six grounds which are permitted: national security, public safety, the economic well being of the country, for the prevention of disorder or crime or for the protection of the rights and freedoms of others.

Each step is considered in turn by the ECtHR. Only when all four questions are answered affirmatively will the state's action be consistent with article 8.

There are three groups of immigrants for whom Article 8 has been relevant for immigration purposes: (1) foreign parents seeking to remain with children resident in a state; (2) young foreign adults who have spent their formative years in a state other than that of their nationality; (3) foreign children seeking to join other family members in the host state. In each case the dividing line between the individual

---

38 *Article 8:* "(1) Everyone has the right to respect for his private and family life, his home and his correspondence. (2) There shall be no interference by a public authority with the exercise of this right except such as is in accordance with the law and is necessary in a democratic society in the interests of national security, public safety or the economic well-being of the country, for the prevention of disorder or crime, for the protection of health or morals, or for the protection of the rights and freedoms of others."

39 *Amrollahi v Denmark* ECtHR 11 July 2002.

40 *Dougoz v Greece* ECtHR 6 June 2001 is a good example where the detention of an alien by the Greek authorities was held unlawful as the legal basis on which it took place did not fulfil the requirements of rule of law as developed by the ECtHR.

as a foreigner and the state has been the subject of an increasing number of judgments of the ECtHR and through them protection of the foreigner.[41]

Family Life Between Parents and Children

As regards the concept of family life, here the ECtHR has held that it always exists between parents and children irrespective of whether they live together. When the Netherlands sought to expel foreign men after the breakdown of their marriages to women resident in the state the ECtHR held that as the men had children still resident in the Netherlands and with which children the men had real relationships notwithstanding the fact that they did not live with the children, there was family life within the meaning of Article 8. The interference, in the form of expulsion of the man, although in accordance with the law, was not necessary in a democratic society.[42]

Clearly the Dutch government was not pleased with the first decision in 1988. It would appear, however, that it managed to keep its actions in respect of divorced foreigners with children in the Netherlands within the scope of the ECtHR judgment until 2002 when a further case on very similar facts came before the ECtHR. The ECtHR followed its previous jurisprudence. All three of Caporaso's analytical tools are at work here – first the working of the micro level – the individual seeks to achieve at the European level the benefit which he is refused at the national level – the right of residence in the state. Secondly, the interaction of transnational and supranational actors and the constraints which they place on the nation state. Mr Ciliz is a transnational actor – an immigrant whose presence is no longer permitted by the Dutch government. He engages a supranational actor, the ECtHR to achieve his objective to prevent the Dutch government from expelling him, the basis being his human right to family life with his child (of which his wife has custody and thus will remain in the Netherlands should he be expelled). Finally, path dependent behaviour, on the one hand, the Dutch government appears to have shown some degree of obedience to the ECtHR between 1988 and 2002 – the first and second judgments on the same issue of expulsion of fathers of Dutch resident children. The ECtHR has demonstrated a very strong degree of path dependent behaviour – its two judgments follow one another both in their reasoning and effect.

---

41 K Groenendijk, E Guild and H Dogan, *Security of Residence of Long Term Migrants: A comparative study of law and practice in European countries*, Council of Europe (English and French) Strasbourg, 1998.
42 *Berrehab v the Netherlands* [1988] Ser. A 138; *Ciliz v Netherlands* ECtHR 11 July 2000, Reports 2000-VIII.

The Unsatisfactory Young Men

The second group of foreigners who sought to engage article 8 to prevent the state from expelling them are young adults in France and Belgium who do not hold the nationality of the state and have been engaged in criminal activities. The first cases, *Moustaquim v Belgium*[43] and *Beldjoudi v France*[44] involved the same type of issue – young men, the children of immigrants who had come to the host state when young and during their youth became involved in various criminal activities. In the early cases the young men all had parents and siblings resident in the host state, and in the case of Beldjoudi, a wife as well. In each case the state argued first that there was no family life. As in the cases of parents and minor children, the ECtHR found that there is always family life between parents and children irrespective of whether those children are adult or minor and equally without regard to whether they live together. Thus these young men who were over the age of majority and no longer living with their parents were nonetheless included in the ambit of article 8.

The host states argued that the interference with family life of the proposed expulsion of these men was justified on the grounds of the prevention of disorder or crime. The ECtHR weighed the interests of the individual and those of the state: the individual's claim to his family life is protected in the ECHR and the state's right to interference is an exception to the right. It came up with a rather flexible list of criteria which it would take into account in weighing the interests of the parties including the nature and seriousness of the offence, the length of the applicant's residence in the country, the time elapsed between the offence and the expulsion and the individual's conduct during that period, the nationalities of various persons involved (i.e. family members), the applicant's family situation and length of marriage (if married), other factors expressing the effectiveness of family life, whether the individual has children in the host state and if so their ages, the difficulties a spouse or child might have in the country of origin, links with the country of origin, ability to speak the language and schooling. The consistency of the ECtHR's application of the criteria has been reviewed elsewhere.[45] However, what has become central to the ECtHR's approach has been the principle that people who have been born on the territory or who have spent most of their formative years in a state cannot be liable to expulsion except in very exceptional cases. In 2003 the ECtHR again confirmed its jurisprudence that very weighty reasons had to be put forward to justify the expulsion of a young person (16 years old), alone, to a country which had recently experienced a period of armed conflict and when there was no evidence that he or she had close relatives living there.[46]

---

43   ECtHR 18 February 1991 Ser A 193.
44   ECtHR 26 March 1992 Ser A-234-A.
45   R Cholewinki, 'Strasbourg's Hidden Agenda? The Protection of Second generation Migrants from Expulsion under Article 8 of the European Convention on Human Rights' Netherlands Quarterly of Human Rights (1994) 298–301.
46   *Jakupovic v Austria* ECtHR 6 February 2003.

The development by that Court of the concept of integrated aliens against who expulsion can only be justified on very substantial grounds has been resisted by a number of Council of Europe countries as evidenced by the continuing stream of cases pending before the ECtHR. The possibility that the Court might have been moving towards a position of prohibition of expulsion of long resident foreigners as promoted by Professor Schermers in his concurring opinion in *Lamguindaz*[47] seems to be receding, though the position of enhanced protection remains. The balancing of the interests of the individual and the state even in the light of substantial criminal activity by the foreigner does not necessarily come down in favour of the state security interest.

The 'bad' children category gave rise to substantial jurisprudence from the ECtHR through the 1990s in particular from Belgium and France. Young integrated foreigners who got caught up in criminal activity were subject to expulsion decisions which in turn were challenged on grounds of article 8, integration and close family in the state. Only after the turn of the millennium did the number of cases from these two countries drop.[48] Now it would appear that Germany and Austria are the most . common defendant states in article 8 cases.

The Wives

The next group of cases where article 8 has changed the relationship of the foreigner and the state is in respect of marriage choices. The cases are all in respect of unsatisfactory young men, as in the previous category, but who have wives resident in the host state. In these cases often the unsatisfactory young men have not lived a substantial part of their lives in the host state and their residence right has been premised on their marriage to a national of the state. *Boultif v Switzerland*[49] and *Amrollahi v Denmark*[50] are very representative of this line of cases. I have considered

---

47 "I am not so sure, however, whether international law concerning the expulsion of aliens is not changing fundamentally as a result of growing concerns for human rights and of a perceived need for solidarity among States in the face of increasing interstate relations. By admitting aliens to their territories, States inevitably accept at least some measure of responsibility. This responsibility weighs even more heavily in the case of children educated in their territory. For any society, individuals like the present applicant are a burden. Even independent of human rights considerations, I doubt whether modern international law permits a State which has educated children of admitted aliens to expel these children when they become a burden. Shifting this burden to the State of origin of the parent is no longer so clearly acceptable under modern international law. It is at least subject to doubt whether a host country has the right to return those immigrants who prove to be unsatisfactory." [1993] Ser A 258-C.

48 E Guild & P Minderhoud (eds), *Security of Residence and Expulsion: Protection of Aliens in Europe*, Kluwer Law International, The Hague, 2001.

49 ECtHR 2 August 2001.

50 ECtHR 11 July 2002.

these cases in chapter 4 in the light of citizenship and equality. Both cases revolved around a decision of the state to expel the husband of a national, Mr Boultif to Algeria and Mr Amrollahi to Iran. The men had lived varying periods of time in their host state and neither of them had been born in the state or arrived there at a young age. They had both been convicted of criminal acts, in one case robbery with violence and the other serious drugs importation. The states had in both cases sought to expel the men from the state irrespective of their wives (and children). In both cases the wives were unwilling to go to their husbands' country of nationality not least as they had never even visited there, did not speak the language and had no intention of seeking to integrate into their husbands' culture of origin. In both cases (and others in this line) the ECtHR considered the wives' interest in their husbands' continued residence in the host state and found that this outweighed the states' interest in expelling the men.

Two aspects of this line of cases are worth noting. First, European states are willing to punish, effectively with expulsion, their nationals who choose to marry foreigners whom the state considers unsatisfactory. The plight of an average Swiss or Danish woman faced with either following her husband to Algeria or Iran or being separated permanently from him is not inconsiderable. The woman is punished for her husband's failure to respect the criminal law and her loyalty to her husband. She is encouraged, by the stark choice which the state presents her with, either to abandon her husband and stay (presumably with the children) in her home country or abandon her home country (and the relatives she has there) and join her husband abroad. Such a punishment is, of course, not possible where women chose to marry fellow nationals no matter what crimes they commit. In such cases the choice to remain with the husband or to separate from him is left to the private domain of the family. Where the husband is a foreigner this decision is taken into the public domain.

Secondly, the integration of the wife and her interest in living in her state of citizenship compensates for her husband's vulnerability to expulsion. Concern about whether a racial tinge is slipping into the jurisdrudence has been somewhat allayed by a further decision, Yildiz. In *Yildiz*, Austria sought to expel a Turkish national on the basis of what it considered an excessive number of traffic violations. The situation of Mr Yildiz's wife was important to the decision that his expulsion would be contrary to article 8: "In December 1996, when the Administrative Court confirmed the residence ban against him, he had been living in Austria for seven years, he had been working there and had been co-habiting for a little less than three years with Ms Yildiz, a Turkish national, who was born in Austria and had lived there all her life. Their daughter, the third applicant, was one year and four months old at the time. In fact, the Austrian authorities issuing the residence ban acknowledged that Mr Yildiz had reached a high degree of integration in Austria. Nevertheless, the Court considered that, regarding the possible effects of the residence ban on his family life, the authorities failed to establish whether Ms Yildiz could be expected to follow her husband to Turkey, in particular whether she spoke Turkish and maintained any links, other than her nationality, with that country."[51] The ECtHR implicitly criticized the national court for assuming that a Turkish national could speak Turkish without assessing the facts. However the criticism is mild in comparison with the *Boultif* and *Amrollahi* line of cases. In this same light, a woman who married an unsatisfactory foreigner after he has been convicted of a criminal offence gets very little sympathy from the ECtHR.[52] Her interests in continued residence are not taken into account. Thus even the ECtHR accepts the punishment of women who knowingly marry foreigners with criminal records.

The Children Left Abroad

Until 1999, the ECtHR had taken a rather strict view of family reunion where a family had migrated to a host state leaving one or more children behind in the state of origin. Two cases have been criticized as regards this approach. In *Gül v Switzerland*[53] the family sought asylum in Switzerland having left a child behind in Turkey. The family were accorded a residence status in Switzerland, though not recognized as refugees. They sought to be reunited with their child left behind in Turkey. This application was rejected at the national level, and the ECtHR found that article 8 would not help them – it was open to them if they wished to live with the children left behind to go back to Turkey. In a second case, *Ahmut v Netherlands*[54] a father who had become a Dutch citizen and was resident in the Netherlands sought to be reunited with his two children left behind in Morocco. This application was rejected at the national level and when it came before the ECtHR, that Court found that article 8 would not help him. The child could live in a boarding school in Morocco and the father could go and visit him there.

The ECtHR's decisions on the exclusion of children were justified as reflecting the state's right to decide on who can and cannot enter its territory. One can differentiate between protecting a right of residence already countenanced by the state – i.e. where the state has already permitted the entry and residence of the foreigner on its territory and then subsequently seeks to get rid of him or her, from the situation where the state has never admitted the individual at all. In the former case the state has voluntarily modified its claim to sovereignty over admission, in the later it is still intact. Of course legal niceties like this do not provide much solace to the divided family.

In something of a departure from its previous jurisprudence the ECtHR held in 2001 that there are circumstances where it will require a state to permit the entry of a child left behind in a state of origin when other members of the family are resident

---

51 *Yildiz v Austria* ECtHR 31 October 2002.
52 *Boultif v Switzerland* supra.
53 ECtHR 19 February 1996, Reports 1996/1.
54 ECtHR 28 November 1996 Reports 1996-VI.

in the host state.[55] The Sen parents moved to the Netherlands in the 1970s leaving behind with close family members their first child. When the child was nine and they had settled in to their new country they began to seek to bring her to join them in the Netherlands. The Dutch government, however, considered that the child has ceased to be part of the Sen family and had become part of her host family in Turkey. The Sens had two further children born in the Netherlands after their arrival there and who lived with them. In considering whether the Dutch authorities were required by article 8 to admit the child left behind, the ECtHR considered in some depth the nature of the family relationship. It found that a breach of article 8, *inter alia*, on the grounds that the children born in the Netherlands had a right to remain there and were integrated into Dutch society. They were entitled, however, to have family life with their sister left behind in Turkey. Thus the presence of the other children in the host state, who had no control over their choice of country, was central to the right of the child left behind to be admitted to the state.

It is important to note that this is the first time the ECtHR has effectively required a state to permit an individual who has never lived in a state to enter and reside there. The argument that the sovereignty of borders remains intact in the face of immigration rights as human rights must now be reassessed. From the perspective of Caporaso's theory, this is an excellent example of limits of path dependency theory. When the result becomes seen as no longer consistent with the developing principles of human rights, even sovereignty over admission to the state can be lost to the supranational level.

The Asylum Seekers

Article 3 ECHR has had a substantial effect on states' sovereign right to exclude and expel foreigners, in particular asylum seekers. The history begins in 1989 when the ECtHR found that the extradition of a German national from the UK to stand trial in a US state where the application of the death penalty resulted in a long period on death row with harrowing consequences for the individual, to be contrary to the state's duty not to torture, or expose an individual to inhuman or degrading treatment.[56] While the connection between article 3 ECHR and return to torture had been pleaded in previous cases, the *Soering* judgment was the first time the ECtHR dealt with the issue head on. The extension of the obligation under article 3 ECHR in 1989 to return to torture should not have been particularly surprising to any observer of the human rights field and least of all to the member States. In early 1980s a number of member States had participated in the drafting of the UN Convention Against Torture which was opened for signature in 1985. It has now been

---

55   *Sen v Netherlands* ECtHR 21 December 2001.
56   *Soering v UK* ECtHR 7 July 1989.

signed and ratified by all EU Member States. Article 3(1) CAT specifically states "No state party shall expel, return ("refouler") or extradite a person to another State where there are substantial grounds for believing that he would be in danger of being subjected to torture." Thus the meaning of the prohibition on torture had already been accepted by European states as including this ban on expulsion by the time the ECtHR reached the *Soering* decision.

Under CAT, a dispute resolution mechanism has an optional the power to receive complaints and give opinions on state actions' compatibility with the Convention. 14 current Member States have accepted this jurisdiction: Austria, Belgium, Denmark, Finland, France, Germany, Greece, Ireland, Italy, Netherlands, Portugal, Spain, and Sweden.[57] Among the 2004 accession states Cyprus, the Czech Republic, Hungary, Malta, Poland, Slovakia and Slovenia have done so.[58] A not insignificant percentage of the cases which come before the CAT are from asylum seekers in European states challenging the state's decision to expel them on the ground of return to torture.[59] In the light of these developments which began in the mid 1980s it is not surprising that the ECtHR's interpretation of Article 3 ECHR would follow suit.

Thus in 1990 the ECtHR was faced with the case of an asylum seeker from Chile who had sought protection in Sweden which had been refused. While the ECtHR rejected the case on the merits it confirmed that article 3 ECHR also prohibits the return of an individual to a country where there is a serious risk that he or she would be subjected to torture.[60] In the following year a further case came before the ECtHR of Sri Lankans who feared persecution and torture in their country of origin and sought, unsuccessfully, asylum in the UK.[61] The ECtHR again affirmed the interpretation of article 3 but as the serious risk of torture must be on the basis of the individual being singled out and not just generalized violence, the claim failed. Two notable cases led to the ECtHR finding in favour of the individual, both against the UK.[62] First, in *Chahal*, an Indian national faced expulsion to his country of origin on grounds of national security. According to the UK and Indian authorities he had been implicated in various terrorist activities in India and the UK government claimed that he was also a threat to the national security of the UK through his terrorist activities abroad. He presented substantial evidence to substantiate his fear of torture if he were returned to India on the basis of the inability of the Indian authorities to control the region, the wide spread abuse of power by the police. The ECtHR held that article 3 ECHR is absolute. There is no exception to the prohibition

---

57　In other words, all Member States except the UK.
58　Only the three Baltic states have not done so.
59　L Holmström, *Conclusions and Recommendations of the UN Committee against Torture*, Martinus Nijhoff, The Hague, 2000.
60　*Cruz Varas v Sweden* [1991] Ser A201.
61　*Vilvarajah v UK* ECtHR [1991] Ser A215.
62　Not all cases went in favour of the individual over this period, for instance, *Bensaid v UK* ECtHR 6 February 2001, Reports 2001–1.

on torture on the basis of national security. Further, the fact that the government of the individual's country of nationality confirmed it would not torture the individual if he were returned there was not sufficient. Where the government did not have sufficient control to ensure this, the fact that torture would be carried out by non-state agents, or state agents without the authority of the state, did not alter the obligation of the Member State not to return to person there.

The politicization of asylum determination systems has also caused concerns in the ECtHR where this appears to interfere with an unbiased assessment of the claim for protection. A Tanzanian from Zanzibar sought asylum in the UK on the basis of his fear of persecution and torture for his political activities if returned there. Although he had a consideration of his case, and an appeal against the negative decision, he claimed that the procedure was flawed as there was a reluctance by the state (the UK) to consider fairly the evidence he adduced in support of his fear. Here the ECtHR found he was justified. Not only the administration but the UK adjudicator and Tribunal had refused through the draconian application of procedural rules and a general disbelief of him and his evidence, to grant him the protection he sought. Considering the evidence before it the ECtHR agreed with him, obliquely criticising not only the UK government but the judicial instances for their failure to accept the validity of the evidence.[63]

The Terminally Ill

Another group of foreigners, the terminally ill, may also claim a right of residence based on article 3 and the consequences of their return to their country of origin.[64] D, a national of the Carribean island of St Kitts, arrived in the UK with a substantial quantity of prohibited drugs. He was apprehended at the airport, tried and sentenced to a six-year prison term. By the time he came to the end of his prison term, he was

---

63 "62. The Government have urged the Court to be cautious in taking a different view of the applicant's claims than the Special Adjudicator who heard him give evidence and found him lacking in credibility. The Court notes however that the Special Adjudicator's decision relied, *inter alia*, on a lack of substantiating evidence. Since that decision, the applicant has produced further documentation. Furthermore, while this material was looked at by the Secretary of State and by the courts in the judicial review proceedings, they did not reach any findings of fact in that regard but arrived at their decisions on a different basis – namely, that even if the allegations were true, the applicant could live safely in mainland Tanzania, the "internal flight" solution.
63. The Court has examined the materials provided by the applicant and the assessment of them by the various domestic authorities. It finds no basis to reject them as forged or fabricated. The applicant has provided an opinion from the Professor of Social Anthropology at All Souls College, Oxford, that they are genuine. Though the Government have expressed doubts on the authenticity of the medical report, they have not provided any evidence to substantiate these doubts or to contradict the opinion provided by the applicant. Nor did they provide an opportunity for the report and the way in which the applicant obtained it to be tested in a procedure before the Special Adjudicator." *Hilal v UK* 6 March 2001 Reports 2001-II.
64 *D v UK* ECtHR 2 May 1997 Reports 1997-III.

suffering from advanced AIDS which at the time had no cure and treatment with anti-retroviral drugs was still in the experimental stages. The UK authorities issued a decision to expel him back to his country of origin. He unsuccessfully appealed against the decision and eventually brought a petition to the ECtHR. He claimed that in light of the state of medical care available in his home country in comparison with that in the UK, his links with the UK (mainly through friendships he had established while in prison) and the isolation he would suffer in St Kitts, it would constitute torture, inhuman and degrading treatment to send him back there.

The ECtHR agreed, "The Court notes that the applicant is in the advanced stages of a terminal and incurable illness. At the date of the hearing, it was observed that there had been a marked decline in his condition and he had to be transferred to a hospital. His condition was giving rise to concern (see paragraph 21 above). The limited quality of life he now enjoys results from the availability of sophisticated treatment and medication in the United Kingdom and the care and kindness administered by a charitable organisation. He has been counselled on how to approach death and has formed bonds with his carers ... The abrupt withdrawal of these facilities will entail the most dramatic consequences for him. It is not disputed that his removal will hasten his death. There is a serious danger that the conditions of adversity which await him in St Kitts will further reduce his already limited life expectancy and subject him to acute mental and physical suffering ... In view of these exceptional circumstances and bearing in mind the critical stage now reached in the applicant's fatal illness, the implementation of the decision to remove him to St Kitts would amount to inhuman treatment by the respondent State in violation of Article 3."

This case raised serious concerns in a number of member States about the possibility of health tourism by the terminally ill. The extent to which these may be realized in practice seems rather limited.

Conclusions

The development of identity rights for foreigners through human rights in Europe is still quite a recent event. However, the mechanisms at work bear out both the theses of O'Boyle and Caporaso. Starting with the first, the confidence of the Member States, the ECtHR by maintaining the role of ECHR as one of providing human rights protection for the individual, permits the member States to hope that "next time" the case will go their way. The importance of the individual facts can justify a variety of competing answers, so much so as to create a certain degree of inconsistency in the treatment of the unsatisfactory young men. Secondly, the interpretation of the system as one which is developing, has permitted the ECtHR to respond to pressure for increasingly high standards of human rights protection, through cross-fertilization with other treaties. The obvious cross-referencing between UNCAT and ECHR, though unacknowledged in the jurisprudence, was clearly necessary to maintain the loyalty of those working for the upgrading of human rights standards internationally. Thirdly, the like-minded common heritage argument has swept aside many arguments heard in the early 1990s that the enlargement of the ECtHR to include a majority of judges from places with no immediate past history of high standards of rule of law would lead the system into disrepute. The judges from the Soviet Union's successor states were seen as a high risk to the belief in a common heritage. The refusal of the institutions themselves to give any credence to these fears and the will to continue to believe in the system from numerous sources, within governments, in NGOs, among individuals seeking remedies, held the system together and indeed strengthened it. Finally, the popular support for the system has withstood the bad press which the ECtHR gets every time it challenges the sovereign choice of a state to exclude a foreigner. The popular thirst for supranational judicialisation of rights has proven greater than some state's efforts in selling xenophobia against those 'foreign judges.'

Caporaso provides a deepening of our understanding of compliance. Returning always to the individual situated in his or her environment and struggling for various advantages is the starting place. As is apparent from a consideration of the cases, the complaints to the ECtHR are legal formulations of the hopes and fears of individuals seeking desperately (and a great personal cost) to establish their right of identity. These individuals fill a certain space between transnational society and supranational institutions. As foreigners seeking identity recognition in a foreign state they are a central part of transnational society. Their only chance in the end of this recognition which is denied them at the national level is via the supranational institutions. Finally, both the national and supranational institutions are fine examples of path dependent actors. They follow the procedures, systems and precedents they have established and only change when directly challenged. The states gradually adjust to the idea of partial loss of sovereignty over the identity of foreigners as regards their right of entry and residence. From time to time, as in respect of the Netherlands and divorced foreigners with Dutch children, they forget their new path and fall back into the previous behaviour, at which point the path dependency of the ECtHR catches them short. Yet when pressure between differing path dependent behaviours becomes too great, the ECtHR can loosen the rules on the basis of the individual facts of the case and permit the member State authorities a chance to adjust their thinking to the new requirements.

The insertion of the ECHR system into the EU framework becomes increasingly complex as both supranational systems take on responsibilities for identity struggles at the national level. In the previous chapter, I noted on the one hand that the ECJ has interpreted article 8 more widely than the ECtHR as regards citizens of the Union and their family members and on the other hand that already some NGOs and a coalition of church groups have challenged the legitimacy of the EU directive on family reunification on the ground that it does not satisfy the minimum standards of article 8 ECHR. These two facts may be indicative of the gathering pressures on the two systems, and the difficulties which may arise in their articulation. In chapter 9 I will consider the insertion of general immigration and asylum competences into the EC. At this point, the intersection between the two supranational systems becomes particularly sensitive.

Chapter 8

EU Identity? The Third Country Agreements

The development of EU identity rights which I have considered here has so far been based directly on the provisions of the EC Treaty itself. However, there is another source of rights which foreigners can claim from EU law which trump national law to the contrary. These rights are based in the power of the Community to enter into agreements with third countries (article 310 EC; constitution article III-303). In this chapter I will review migration rights in this context and consider their meaning for the purposes of national control over third country nationals.

Supranational Immigration Law and Sovereignty

What is the role of supranational law in immigration from third countries? So far I have plotted the course of EU law as regards migration and citizens of the Union and the ECHR's engagement. Both have proven substantial, gaining momentum in 1980s and 1990s. Yet at the same time in academic literature there has been a resurgence of the theory that immigration is a heartland of sovereignty, a place of national interest. Collinson represents well this line of thinking, "Control over the admission of aliens has historically been viewed as inherent in the very nature of sovereignty."[1] If migration is thus a site of key interest of national sovereignty, it should be subject to the rules applicable to such key areas. Koskenniemi explains that "a conventional understanding, widely accepted in the corridors of foreign ministries, regards the conduct of statesmen or diplomats in key areas of national sovereignty and defence as inherently resistant to the application of legal rules ... If law should play a role in it, it is only as an instrument for the expression and

---

1   S Collinson, *Beyond Borders: Western European Migration Policy Towards the 21st Century*, Royal Institute of International Affairs/Wyndam Place Trust, London, 1993, p 3.

realisation of those wills and interests, a handmaid of the diplomat or the politician, providing a language and institutional arrangements that sometimes facilitate the attainment of consensus, a coordinative regulation of inter-sovereign relations. But in the realm of vital interests, national security, peace and war, rules cannot constrain."[2]

Three issues thus are raised by the juxtaposition of these ideas. First, if migration is an aspect of key national interest to what extent does it remain within the national domain when posed against the centrifugal force of the EU's internal market? As is apparent from the development of the concept of citizenship of the Union, one of the mechanisms which has been used to deal with the creation of a legal right of migration within the EU has been to dress it in the clothing of citizenship and thus make natural the creation of rights of movement in the guise of citizenship rights. The resistance to extending the full clothing of citizenship of nationals of other Member States is apparent in the fierce retention of the right of exclusion, expulsion and administrative internal exile discussed in Chapter 5. Secondly, in Koskenniemi's words, law plays a role in vital fields as the handmaid of the diplomat and politician. It does not constrain them. In the field of immigration, as this relates to individuals who need to know the rules by which their admission, residence, work and expulsion are regulated, a degree of law must, in the end, come into the equation. The diplomat may remain in political control but the language of law is inevitable. How, then, can the national diplomat and the politician be constrained by law in key national security fields beyond the border? The third issue is the extent to which the diplomat and the politician at the national level no longer control the law around the regulation of a field of national interest where it passes to a supranational level. The creation of a set of rights through EU law for third country nationals expresses the limitations of the traditional thinking about national security and supranational law making.

The event which is taking place in this development of supranational law in the field of migration is the reconfiguration of identity. While on the one hand individuals, foreign nationals, are claiming rights of identity through international law agreements, on the other hand the move outwards in the development of relations with third countries is also central to EU identity. Koskenniemi expresses this as follows: "Identity is formed in relationships. We are what communal ties we hold and not how we imagine ourselves. These relationships can be managed either through *ad hoc* manipulative arrangements, as responses to contingencies. Or they can be managed through law. There is much to be said for an increased coherence of European foreign policy. But even more important is that focus shifts away from internal relationships – divisions of powers – between the Union members and institutions to

---

2 M Koskenniemi, 'International Law Aspects of the Common Foreign and Security Policy' in M Koskenniemi, *International Law Aspects of the European Union*, Kluwer Law International, The Hague, 1998 pp 27–28.

the world at large. It is that larger set of relationships that defines European identity."[3] Thus as the EU adopts and develops law through agreements with third countries which touch on the treatment of nationals of those third countries it also forms its own identity as regards its citizens. The identity of nationals of the Member States is also extended by the interpretation of the rights of foreigners through these agreements.[4]

The EU Mechanism for Creating Supranational Immigration Law

The EC agreements with third countries date back to the commencement of the EEC. Provision was made in the original Treaty for such agreements to be entered into, the list of countries to be so privileged were the independent former colonies of the original Member States. The other countries which were offered association agreements from an early stage were Greece and Turkey in 1960 and 1961. The assumption was that they would become Member States in the fairly near future. A certain degree of difficulty in retaining democratic governments resulted in substantial delays for both. In the meantime a number of other countries stole the march on these two in joining the EU starting with Denmark, Ireland and the UK in 1973. Greece then managed to recapture independent, democratic institutions and the offer of membership became a reality in 1981. Spain and Portugal joined in 1986, after they had formed democratic governments. The entry of these three southern European countries was premised on the argument of needing to strengthen democracy in the region and ensuring that they did not slide back into dictatorships.

Enlargement to the Nordic states took place rather quietly in 1995. At that time much of the consideration about the direction of the Union was focused to the east on Central and Eastern Europe. The decision to enlarge to the east was contested, some Member States argued for deepening of the Union rather than widening. The interests of other Member States however, in particular pressure from Germany and the UK, led to a decision to move towards enlargement with all of the CEECs (Central and Eastern European countries), the Baltic states, Slovenia and the two Mediterranean island states.[5]

---

3 Koskenniemi, 'International Law Aspects of the Common Foreign and Security Policy' in M Koskenniemi, *International Law Aspects of the European Union*, Kluwer Law International, The Hague, 1998 pp 44.
4 For example the right of citizens of the Union who have become voluntarily unemployed has been forged from the ECJ judgments of Turkish nationals (see for instance C-171/95 *Tetik* [1997] ECR I-329). Similarly, the right to expel a citizen on the basis of public policy has been changed by the interpretation of the protection of Turkish nationals – C-340/97 *Nazli* [2000] ECR I-957.
5 J Zielonka, *Europe Unbound Enlarging and Reshaping the Boundaries of the European Union*, Routledge, London 2002.

Each enlargement means, for the nationals of the state being incorporated into the Union, a new status of identity and belonging. The force of Article 12 EC, the right to non-discrimination on the basis of nationality, suddenly applies to them. It is the 'open sesame' which guarantees equal access to social benefits, education, health care etc. (see chapter 3). All the rights of the national at home are suddenly also available to these foreigners who have become citizens. Those who continue to be third country nationals are outside this charmed circle unless through a third country agreement their state has protected their interests.

Non-Discrimination and the Key to Identity

For the individual the test of identity acquisition is his or her treatment in comparison with nationals of the state. So long as the foreigner can be treated differently, that difference justified on the basis of his or her nationality (i.e. he or she is a foreigner), then the claim to an.identity is diminished. The fewer the fields of activity within which the foreigner can be excluded on the basis of his or her nationality, the greater his or her claim to participation in the dominant identity. However, the power to enforce a right to non-discrimination depends on security of residence. If a foreigner can be expelled easily, his or her willingness to pursue an equality claim is diminished. Where the right to non-discrimination comes from a different source from that of residence this contrast will be particularly marked.

The main EU third country agreements which contain provisions prohibiting discrimination on the basis of nationality for nationals of the third country with nationals of a Member State fall into five categories:

1. The European Economic Area Agreement with Norway, Iceland and Liechtenstein which extends almost completely the free movement of persons rules applicable to nationals of the Member States;[6] and the agreement with Switzerland which has a similar consequence for Swiss nationals;[7]
2. The agreement which together with its protocol and implementing legislation contains express provisions on non-discrimination in respect of workers, working conditions, remuneration, dismissal and social security – the EEC Turkey Association Agreement;[8]
3. The agreements with ten Central and Eastern European countries which provide for a right of entry, residence and self-employment as well as non-discrimination

---

6   OJ 1994 L 1/1.
7   OJ 2002 L 114.
8   12 September 1963 OJ 1973 C 113.

in working conditions, dismissal and social security.[9] Stabilisation and Association Agreements which are broadly similar to the CEEC agreements have been concluded and are being ratified with Croatia[10] and Macedonia.[11] Identical agreements are planned for Albania, Bosnia-Herzegovina and Serbia/Montenegro. These stabilisation and association agreements differ from the CEEC agreements in that the entry into force of the provisions on the right of self-employment (see below) is delayed for five years from ratification and will be subject to further rules;

4. The agreements which contain provisions protecting workers of the states against discrimination on grounds of nationality in wages, working conditions including dismissal and social security (including for their family members resident in the Union): EC-Algeria,[12] EC-Morocco,[13] EC-Tunisia[14] cover working conditions, remuneration, dismissal and social security. The ACP-EC Agreement only protects workers of the African, Caribbean and Pacific states parties from discrimination as regards working conditions, remuneration and dismissal.[15] There are agreements with some successor states of the USSR – Armenia,[16] Azerbaijan,[17] Georgia,[18] Kazahkstan,[19] Kyrgyz Republic,[20] Moldova,[21] Russia,[22] Ukraine,[23] and Uzbekistan.[24] Agreements with the other successor states have run into political difficulties or been otherwise delayed. These agreements provide for non-discrimination in working conditions, remuneration and dismissal for workers;

5. The Chile-EC Association Agreement[25] which includes provisions on free trade in services including admission of employees of service providers and the establishment of businesses.

The first three groups of agreements are of particular importance as they touch on one of the essences of identity – the right to be present on the territory and to work.

---

9   All these countries with the exception of Bulgaria and Romania became Member States on 1 May 2004. The Bulgaria Agreement: OJ 1994 L 358; the Romania Agreement: OJ 1994 L 357.
10 COM (2001) 371.
11 COM (2001) 90.
12 This agreement has not yet been ratified by all Member States: COM (2002) 157.
13 OJ 2000 L 70.
14 OJ 1998 L 97/17.
15 Article 13(3) OJ 2003 L 83.
16 OJ 1999 L 239.
17 OJ 1999 L 246.
18 OJ 1999 L 205.
19 OJ 1999 L 196.
20 OJ 1999 L 196.
21 OJ 1998 L 181.
22 OJ 1997 L 327.
23 OJ 1998 L 49.
24 OJ 1999 L 229.
25 OJ 2002 L 352/1.

The struggle of the foreigner to secure his or her residence and access to the labour market lies no longer exclusively with the Member State and its determination of the right of identity. A supranational authority in the form of the EU has taken over this aspect of control of identity for the group of persons on the basis of their nationality, a fact determined by the third country. The fifth type of agreement will potentially also regulate access to the territory and economic activities for individuals but only where this is sanctioned by a business.

The fourth group of agreements ensures non-discrimination in a more restricted field, that of working conditions, remuneration, dismissal and social security. However, the Member States have so far succeeded in excluding from the ambit of these agreements any right connected with residence on the territory.[26] The value of such a right of non-discrimination on the basis of nationality for a foreigner is questionable. If there is a dispute between the state and the individual over, for instance, equal treatment in working conditions, if the individual seeks to exercise his or her right in supranational law in circumstances where the state controls the right of residence, the option will be available to the state to expel the foreigner. This is the same problem which arises in most dramatic form at the national level as regards the enforcement of working conditions legislation for workers who are not documented. When they seek to enjoy their labour rights they are at high risk of expulsion from the state. Thus the rights tend to be illusory. While the rights both at national and supranational level appear important elements of equality and part of the acquisition of identity by the individual foreigner, in practice without protection of residence they can be easily circumvented by the state.

Protecting Residence: Migrant Workers and the EC Turkey Association Agreement

The most extensive of the third country agreements is the EEC Turkey Agreement under which secondary legislation in the form of Association Council Decisions have been adopted. Currently as regards workers, Decision 1/80 is in force.[27] As the ECJ has insisted on many occasions, although the Agreement, through its Additional Protocol provides that freedom of movement for workers between the Member States and Turkey is to be secured by progressive stages in accordance with the principles set out in the Agreement,[28] it does not in fact provide for the admission of Turkish workers into the EU. This remains within the power of the Member States.

---

26 C-416/96 *El Yassini* [1999] ECR I-1209.
27 For the history of Decision 1/80, the Decision which preceded it and the draft Decision which was almost adopted to replace it see E Guild, *Immigration Law in the European Community*, Kluwer Law International, The Hague, 2001.
28 Article 12 Agreement, Article 36 Additional Protocol.

However, once a worker is lawfully in a Member State and admitted to the labour force, no matter whether the Member State placed other conditions on his or her admission (for instance made it dependent on the continuation of marriage[29] or limited the length of residence a work to a short period[30]) the Decision takes priority over national law limiting the right of residence. Thus a cook whose work permit was limited to not more than three years in the Member State could successfully rely on the Decision to demand an extension of his work and residence permit.[31]

Article 6 Decision 1/80 provides for a gradual acquisition of rights by the individual worker. After one year of continuous employment (duly registered as belonging to the labour force) he or she is entitled to an extension of the work and residence permit for the same employer and the same job. After three years the individual is entitled to change jobs within the sector and after four years he or she is entitled to free access to the labour market.[32] Where authorised to join a Turkish worker, family members who have remained in a Member State for at least three years are entitled to respond to offers of employment. They are entitled to free access to the labour market after five years residence. Alternatively, if a parent has worked for three or more years in the Member State and the child has completed vocational training there (whether or not authorised to live with the parent) the child is entitled to free access to the labour market.[33]

The acquisition of rights by Turkish nationals under the Agreement is dependent on the state having admitted the individual lawfully to the territory. Thus the control of the Member State takes place at the beginning, in the decision whether or not to admit an individual. The ECJ has interpreted the rights under article 6 (the article 7 rights are dependent first on the principal having a secure status as a worker) as having two limbs. First the individual must be a worker and here it has transposed its jurisprudence on the meaning of employment from the EC Treaty directly. A worker is a person who for a period of time provides services under the direction of another in return for which he or she received remuneration.[34] The additional requirement that a Turkish worker must be duly registered as belonging to the labour force depends first on whether the legal relationship of employment can be located within the territory of the Member State or retains a sufficiently close link with that territory "taking account in particular of the place where the Turkish national was hired, the territory on or from which the paid activity is pursued and the applicable national legislation in the field of labour and social security law."[35]

---

29   C-237/91 *Kus* [1992] ECR I-6781.
30   C-98/96 *Ertanir* [1997] ECR I-5179.
31   C-36/96 *Gunaydin* [1997] ECR I-5143.
32   Article 6 Decision 1/80.
33   Article 7 Decision 1/80. The individual does not have to have been admitted to the state for the purpose of family reunification to enjoy the benefit of the provision C-355/93 *Eroglu* [1994] ECR I-5113.
34   For a fuller discussion of the meaning of the term 'worker' under Article 39 EC see E Guild, *Immigration Law of the European Community*, Kluwer Law International, The Hague, 2001.
35   C-188/00 *Kurz* ECJ 19 November 2002.

The requirement of duly registered as belonging to the labour force adds an additional hurdle which provides the Member State's key to retention of control over the third country national. It has been interpreted as including only those workers "who have complied with the conditions laid down by national law and regulation in the host Member State governing entry into its territory and employment and are thus entitled to pursue an occupation in that State."[36] However, the ECJ has limited the space of control of the state first by finding that it cannot be interpreted as applying to the labour market in general as opposed to a restricted market with a specific objective.[37] Secondly, the fact that the ground on which the Member State admitted the individual to the labour force was for a purely temporary and specific purpose, for instance an apprenticeship, does not exclude the individual from the acquisition of protected residence and employment rights under the Decision.[38]

When a state seeks to expel a Turkish worker or a family member of such a person, article 14 of the Decision requires that this be justified on the grounds of public policy, public security or public health. The ECJ has held that these three terms are to be interpreted in the same manner as those in Article 39 EC relating to nationals of the Member States.[39] These rights are central to security of residence of foreigners and their continuing access to employment.

The rights, contained in an agreement between the EU and a third country and its subsidiary legislation, can have direct effect where they are clear, precise and unconditional, in which case they take priority over national laws to the contrary.[40] The resistance to the loss of control over residence, employment and expulsion of Turkish workers has been noticeable particularly in Germany and Austria where the most substantial numbers of workers of this nationality live.[41] The insistence of the ECJ to re-enforce its jurisprudence notwithstanding the resistance indicates the degree of loss of power of the national authorities. Member States and their courts are required to implement them.

The status of the rules as internationally recognised law has had support from another venue: the ECtHR. Article 8 ECHR requires that the decision of the state, which is challenged as breaching the right to family life, be in accordance with the law. As Decision 1/80 has direct effect in the Member States, it is also law for the purposes of article 8. If a Member State applies its national law which is contrary to

---

36 C-340/97 *Nazli* [2000] ECR I-957.
37 This was the case in C-1/97 *Birden* [1998] ECR I-7747 where the Turkish worker was employed in a make work programme for the unemployed. The State argued that he could not be considered as duly registered as belonging to the labour market, which argument was rejected by the ECJ.
38 C-188/00 *Kurz* ECJ 19 November 2002.
39 C-340/97 *Nazli* [2000] ECR I-957.
40 This interpretation begins with the ECJ decision in C-192/89 *Sevince* [1990] ECR I-3461 and is reviewed in C-188/00 *Kurz* [2002] ECR I-10691.
41 See for instance the rather grudging acknowledgement of the acquisition of rights by Turkish workers of the formost German academic jurist: K Hailbronner, *Immigration and Asylum Law and Policy of the European Union*, Kluwer Law International, The Hague, 2000.

the rights contained in Decision 1/80 it is arguable that its decision to interfere with the family life of the Turkish worker is not in accordance with the law and thus breaches article 8 even without a consideration of whether the breach is justified in a democratic society (see chapter 7). This argument was put to the ECtHR in *Yildiz v Germany*[42] to which the ECtHR replied "The Court observes that the residence ban against the first applicant had a basis in domestic law, namely section 18(1) and (2) of the 1992 Aliens Act. However, the applicants' argument is that these provisions were overruled by decree no 1/80 of the Association Council established under the Association Agreement between the European Union and Turkey. The Court notes that the Administrative Court dealt with the issue in detail but found that the first applicant had failed to show that he fulfilled the conditions for the application of these provisions. Thus, the Court is satisfied that the interference complained of was 'in accordance with the law'". The deceptive tautology (i.e. because the Administrative Court said so it is so) may be a prelude to a more substantial finding by the ECtHR in the future which links more directly legality at the national and supranational level.

Protecting Entry and Residence: The Europe Agreements

The right to move and reside for the purpose of self-employment was first introduced into third country agreements with the Central and Eastern European countries (CEECs). Following the fall of the Berlin wall and the restructuring of Europe, the EU was determined to act quickly to provide support for the transition of the CEECs from command economies to market-led ones and towards democratic governance. The legal mechanism for this activity was the Europe Agreements – a series of agreements with ten countries between 1991 and 1996 (the CEECs, Baltics states and Slovenia).[43] Further agreements were settled with the successor states of the Soviet Union but none of them contains a clear right to establishment[44] for natural persons. The right of movement, including access to the territory, for nationals of the ten countries seeking to be self-employed was ring-fenced with limitations, though the gradual interpretation of the right by the ECJ has restricted the limitations.[45] The nationals of all but two of these countries become citizens of the Union on 1 May 2004 though a right of free movement for employment or service provision and receipt is delayed for between 2 and 7 years under the provisions of the

---

42 31 October 2002 ECtHR (no. 37295/97).
43 A Ott & K Inglis, *Handbook on European Enlargement: A Commentary on the Enlargement Process*, TMC Asser Press, The Hague, 2002.
44 Which includes self-employment.
45 See A Böcker & E Guild, *Implementation of the European Agreements in France, Germany, the Netherlands and the UK: Movement of Persons*, Platinum, London 2002.

accession agreement. Romania and Bulgaria are candidate countries but have not yet begun negotiations on accession.

Although each of the Europe Agreements commences its Title IV Chapter 1 "Movement of Workers ..." there is in fact no provision for free movement of workers. The only provisions on movement of workers are included in the articles relating to the rights of establishment and service provision for companies. The agreements do not expressly include protection of residence and continuing access to the labour market for workers already present and working within the territory of the parties. Thus as regards security of continued employment and residence, the Europe Agreements are less favourable than the secondary legislation of the EEC-Turkey Agreement.[46]

From entry into force (the last to enter into force was the Slovenia Agreement in March 1999) the Agreements require each Member State to grant a treatment no less favourable than that accorded to its own companies and nationals for the establishment of companies and nationals of the other party. Establishment is defined "as regards nationals, the right to take up and pursue economic activities as self-employed persons and to set up and manage undertakings ..."[47] The meaning of this duty on the Member States became an important question for a substantial number of Central and Eastern European nationals living and working in EU states between 1994 and 2004. The adequacy of implementing rules, where adopted at national level were disputed in the courts of all the Member States where some trans-position had taken place (and indeed even in the courts of countries which have not transposed the provisions, such as France). Some Member States relied on a let out provision in the Agreements (the proviso) which states that "for the purpose of [this Title] nothing in the Agreement shall prevent the Parties from applying their laws and regulations regarding entry and stay, work, labour conditions and establishment of natural persons and supply of services, provided that, in so doing, they do not apply them in a manner so as to nullify or impair the benefit accruing to any Party under the terms of a specific provision of the Agreement."[48]

Three references were made in rapid succession in 2001 and the judgments handed down from the ECJ with only one month's difference in 2001. The first case, *Gloszczuk*,[49] involved a Polish national who entered the UK as a tourist lawfully in 1989 and was joined in due course by his wife. They did not leave at the end of their permitted stay but instead entered into self-employment in the building industry. They did not seek to extend their permission to reside or to work. They applied to remain on the basis of the right of establishment in the Poland Agreement in January

---

46 See N Rogers, *A Practitioners' Guide to the EC-Turkey Association Agreement*, Kluwer Law International, The Hague, 2000.
47 See Article 44(3) and (4) Poland-EC Agreement.
48 Article 59 Poland Agreement.
49 C-63/99 *Glozsczuk* [2001] ECR I-6369.

1996. In the second case, *Kondova*,[50] the applicant, a Bulgarian national, obtained a short stay visa for seasonal work and went to the UK in 1993. She applied for asylum and when interviewed said that she had lied to get the visa and to enter the country as she always intended to apply for asylum (which application was rejected). She was considered under national law to be irregular. However, she established herself as self-employed in general household care services and sought to stay relying on the Bulgaria Agreement. In the third case, *Barkoci & Malik*,[51] the Czech applicants arrived at the UK border and sought asylum in 1997. Before they were admitted or refused admission to the UK they applied to enter the UK as self-employed persons, Barkoci as a gardener and Malik as a provider of domestic and commercial cleaning services. While in all three cases the UK government was the defendant, other Member States intervened in all the cases. In the first, *Gloszczuk*, seven other Member States intervened,[52] all more or less supporting the position of the UK. In the second, *Kondova* six other Member States came in to help the UK.[53] By the third case only five other Member States got involved: Spain refrained from intervening. Thus the cases are politically very important. The importance of the control of access to the territory and work is evidenced, as in the case of *Gloszczuk*, by the fact that more than half the Member States are involved and all of them are arguing against the applicant.

A fourth reference from a Dutch court *Jany*,[54] related to a number of prostitutes from Poland and the Czech Republic who established themselves in the Netherlands between 1993 and 1996. They applied for residence permits on the basis of the Europe Agreements which were refused on the basis that they were not genuinely self-employed but in employment. Further, the Dutch government argued that prostitution is an exception and cannot be treated as an economic activity.

Direct Effect

First the ECJ held that the right of establishment has direct effect within the legal order of the Community and can be relied upon directly by individuals. "This rule of equal treatment lays down a precise obligation to produce a specific result and, by its nature can be relied on by an individual before a national court to request it to set aside the discriminatory provisions of a Member State's legislation making the establishment of a [Europe Agreement national] subject to a condition which is not imposed on that Member State's own nationals, without any further implementing

---

50 C-235/99 *Kondova* [2002] ECR I-6427.
51 C-257/99 *Barkoci & Malik* [2002] ECR I-6557.
52 These were Belgium, Germany, Spain, France, Ireland, Italy and the Netherlands.
53 Belgium, Germany, Spain, France, Ireland and the Netherlands.
54 C-268/99 *Jany* [2001] ECR I-8625.

measures being required for that purpose."[55] The Court went on to confirm that the purpose and nature of the agreements confirms this finding and makes specific reference to the intention to facilitate accession of the CEECs to the European Community. Thus the Court found that the proviso permitting Member States to apply their national rules does not have the effect of depriving the establishment right of direct effect. In this first finding the Court is not far from a number of the intervening Governments which agreed that the provision should have direct effect, however, the consequences of that direct effect were much disputed.

A Right to Enter and Reside

The fact that the establishment right has direct effect presupposes a right to enter and reside in the host Member State. The ECJ stated in *Kondova*, "The right of a Bulgarian national to take up and pursue economic activities not coming within the labour market presupposes that that person has a right to enter and remain in the host Member State." Regarding the proviso, it found that the rights of entry and residence conferred on CEEC nationals as corollaries of the right of establishment are not absolute privileges "inasmuch as their exercise may, where appropriate, be limited by the rules of the host Member State concerning entry, stay and establishment of [Europe Agreement] nationals."[56] In this context, the ECJ held that a system of prior control, in other words a visa / entry clearance requirement, does have a legitimate aim in so far as it makes it possible to restrict the exercise of the rights of entry and stay to those persons who are establishing themselves. *Barkoci & Malik* added an important element to the right of establishment which makes the visa / entry clearance system much more vulnerable. The ECJ here considered the refusal of admission to the territory and residence permits for two Czech nationals who had arrived at the UK border without visas. Because the applicants had not been refused or admitted to the UK at the time when they made their applications on the basis of the Europe Agreements they were considered in UK law to be making applications for admission to the UK.

The ECJ accepted that the state is permitted to verify that the individual genuinely intends to take up an activity as self-employed without entering into employment at the same time and that "he possesses, from the outset, sufficient financial resources and has reasonable chances of success." However, the ECJ found that where the application was made at the border before a decision had been made to admit or refuse to admit the individual it had to be considered by the state authorities so long as the person's application clearly and manifestly satisfies the same substantive

---

55   C-235/99 *Kondova* para 34 (and repeated in the other two judgments).
56   C-235/99 *Kondova* para 54.

requirements as those which would have been applied had he or she sought a visa before entry.

Finally, in the Dutch reference the ECJ determined the definition of self-employment as consistent in EC law whether under the third country agreements or the EC Treaty. The definition is that work is carried out:

1. outside a relationship of subordination concerning the choice of activity, working conditions and conditions of remuneration;
2. under that person's own responsibility; and
3. in return for remuneration paid to that person directly and in full.

Provided that a CEEC national fulfils these criteria he or she will be self-employed and enjoy rights of entry and residence under the Europe Agreements. However, the ECJ insisted on the fact that the Member States are entitled to check whether the individual has from the outset sufficient financial resources to carry on the activity in question in a self-employed capacity.

The Dutch government argued that prostitution is not an economic activity. This led to rather rude suggestions about what it might be – for instance a charitable or religious activity? The ECJ held that "prostitution can be regarded as a commercial activity, it is sufficient to hold that prostitution is an activity by which the provider satisfies a request by the beneficiary in return for consideration without producing or transferring material goods." As the Netherlands permits the carrying out of activities as a prostitute by its own nationals and as there is no indication that there is a genuine and sufficiently serious threat affecting one of the fundamental interests of society in the carrying out of activities as a prostitute in the Netherlands the ECJ held that CEEC nationals could not be excluded from exercising this form of self-employment. The argument of the Dutch government that this is a particularly difficult sector to monitor as regards working conditions was not considered persuasive enough to change the ECJ's finding. What is key to the ECJ's assessment is whether the elements of self-employment are fulfilled not the sector in which the activities are undertaken.

Non-Discrimination on the Basis of Nationality Without Residence Protection

The right to non-discrimination on the basis of nationality is both theoretically and practically one of the most important rights contained in the third country agreements. It can be found in all of the agreements dealing with natural persons. In practice, it has come before the ECJ in respect of all the groups of agreements where individuals have claimed that their right to non-discrimination has been breached. In theory, it is particularly revealing as it is the dividing line of identity – nationality is a permitted ground of discrimination in international law. The exclusion of non-nationals from the territory, from employment, from equality of working conditions, political participation and otherwise is a common feature of national law. Thus the prohibition of discrimination on the basis of nationality has a particular importance in understanding identity. If foreigners must be treated the same way as nationals where is the difference between the two? The central point of differentiation falls away. The right to nationality based non-discrimination in working conditions and social security first appears in an EU third country agreement in the 1970 Additional Protocol of the EEC Turkey Agreement (article 36) then in 1976 it is inserted into the agreements with Algeria, Morocco and Tunisia on their renewal. A non-discrimination provision in working conditions is included in those agreements which include a chapter on workers – the Turkey, Euro-Mediterranean and CEEC agreements, some of the agreements with the successor states of the USSR and the ACP agreement (though no non-discrimination provision as regards social security exists in the CEEC, successor states of the USSR or ACP agreements).

However, if the right to non-discrimination in respect of foreigners fails to include protection of residence then the interest of the foreigner to continuing residence may well be more important on the personal level than his or her right to non-discrimination in working conditions or access to a social benefit. The docility of a foreign labour force as regards working conditions is likely to be linked to the security of their residence.

In this light then, the case law of the ECJ on the right to non-discrimination in working conditions and access to social security in third country agreements reveals also the degree to which the individuals who insist on their right to non-discrimination either do not care about their residence rights or those rights are protected at the national level. The first case, *Kziber*[57] relates to the child of a Moroccan worker already retired in the host State. The child's residence status was the strongest possible under the national legislation. Her parents had worked for many years in the host State and thus the possibility of challenging the state on access to a social security benefit did not involve a substantial risk of expulsion. Similarly, Mr Yousfi, the second claimant before the ECJ, sought his right to equal treatment in social security under the Morocco Agreement, when he was incapacitated as a result of an accident at work in Belgium.[58] He had been born and lived all his life in the country thus had the highest degree of protection against expulsion possible under national law.[59]

Mrs Krid sought to establish her right to equal treatment for a social security benefit as the widow of an Algerian migrant worker who had worked his whole life

---

57   C-18/90 [1991] ECR I-199.
58   C-58/93 *Yousfi* [1994] ECR I-1353.
59   K Groenendijk & E Guild, 'Converging Criteria: Creating an Area of Security of Residence for Europe's Third Country Nationals' in EJML Vol 3 No 1 2001 pp 37–59; K Groenendijk, E Guild and R Barzilay, *The Legal Status of third-country nationals who are long-term residents in a Member State of the European Union*, European Commission, Luxembourg, 2001.

in France,[60] as did Mrs Hallouzi-Choho another widow, this time of a Moroccan worker who had worked his whole life in the Netherlands. She sought her entitlement to equal treatment in social security only at a time when their residence status was the most secure possible in national law.[61] In Babaheneni, the applicant was the spouse of a retired Algerian worker in Belgium. Her husband received a retirement pension from the state and she sought a disability allowance.[62] Another married woman, Mrs Djabali sought to exercise her right to equal treatment as regards a disabled adult's allowance in France. However, she was married to an Algerian national who was a worker and long resident in France. Her residence status was secured by that of her husband.[63] Mr Fahmi, a Moroccan national, had already returned to Morocco at the end of his working life when he sought to rely on his right to equal treatment in social security under the EC-Morocco Agreement against his former host state, the Netherlands, so that he could continue to receive an allowance for his son who was still in full-time education.[64]

When the Mesbah family sought equal treatment in social security benefits for their elderly mother of Moroccan nationality, they had already naturalised as Belgian citizens.[65] Because they were already Belgian nationals, the ECJ rejected their claim to non-discrimination on the grounds of nationality in the provision of a social security benefit under the EC-Morocco. However, as nationals of the state they were also excluded from EU law guaranteeing equality of treatment in social security on the principle that the matter was wholly internal to Belgium. Thus too much security of residence (i.e. citizenship) can be injurious to a claim of equal treatment by migrant workers while too little can result in the threat of expulsion.

Finally, in a curious decision in February 2003, the ECJ considered the matter of a Moroccan national, Mr Alami, and his claim to a seniority supplement to his unemployment benefit in Belgium.[66] This supplement is only payable where the worker has twenty years occupational experience as an employee. It appears that Mr Alami only fulfilled this requirement if his work experience in France was taken into account (which the Belgian authorities refused to do). The ECJ, by order, found in favour of Mr Alami. How long Mr Alami worked in France is not clear, nor is the immigration history that took him from Morocco to France and then to Belgium. However, with twenty years working experience between the last two states it is likely that Mr Alami would have acquired a rather secure residence status in both countries.[67]

---

60 C-103/94 *Krid* [1995] ECR I-719.
61 C-126/95 *Hallouzi-Choho* [1996] ECR I-4807.
62 C-113/97 [1998] ECR I-183.
63 C-314/96 [1998] ECR I-1149.
64 C-33/99 *Fahmi and Cerdeiro-Pinedo Amado* [2001] ECR I-2415.
65 C-179/98 *Mesbah* [1999] ECR I-7955.
66 C-23/02 *Alami* 12 February 2003.
67 K Groenendijk, E Guild and H Dogan, *Security of Residence of Long Term Migrants: A comparative study of law and practice in 18 European countries*, Council of Europe (English and French) Strasbourg, 1998.

When a migrant worker tried to use the right to equal treatment in working conditions under the Morocco Agreement to protect his right of residence, the ECJ rejected his claim stating, "it follows from the substantial differences between not only the wording but also the object and purpose of the rules governing the EEC-Turkey association and the EEC Morocco Agreement that the Court's case law on the governing of the EEC Turkey association cannot be applied by analogy to the EEC Morocco Agreement. In those circumstances, it must be concluded that, as Community law stands at present, a Member State is not in principle prohibited from refusing to extend the residence permit of a Moroccan national whom it has previously authorised to enter its territory and to take up gainful employment there, where the initial reason for the granting of his leave to stay no longer exists by the time that his residence permit expires. The fact that the adoption of such a measure by the competent authorities will oblige the person concerned to terminate his employment relationship in the host Member State before the contractual term agreed with his employer comes to an end will not, as a general rule, affect that conclusion."[68] Thus the security of residence for the foreigner must come from a national law source; the ECJ will not protect the individual (but see chapter 12). As a result only those whose residence right is extremely secure (for instance the second generation immigrant who is protected by the ECtHR) or those who do not mind being expelled, as may be the case with elderly retired persons for whom a social security benefit (which will be exportable to their country of origin) is more important than the residence right in the host state, will dare to enforce their non-discrimination right.

Non-Discrimination on the Basis of Nationality with Residence Protection

Where foreigners have a right to non-discrimination on the basis of nationality which is coupled with a right of residence from the same source of law, i.e. EU, a very different picture emerges. Mr Sürül was a Turkish worker in Germany, although his work is complimentary to his studies. He and his wife, however, eventually benefited from the ECJ jurisprudence on Decision 1/80 and enjoyed a right to extension of their work and residence permits under article 6. They were the first foreign workers with contingent residence rights in national law who challenged discrimination against them on the basis of nationality in social security benefits.[69] The ECJ found that discrimination against them on the basis of their nationality in the provision of a child rearing allowance was contrary to their rights under the subsidiary legislation of the Turkey Agreement.[70] Similarly, five Turkish workers in Austria who fulfilled

---

68 C-416/96 *El Yassini* [1999] ECR I-1209.
69 C-262/96 *Sürül* [1999] ECR I-2685.
70 Article 3(1) Decision 3/80.

the conditions of Article 6(1) Decision 1/80 third indent were willing to challenge Austrian legislation excluding them from election as representatives in chambers of workers on the grounds of their nationality. Again the ECJ found that the exclusion was contrary to their right of non-discrimination in working conditions under Article 10(1) Decision 1/80.[71]

However, Turkish nationals were only willing to seek to establish their rights to equality in working conditions after the ECJ had clarified their rights of residence. The first case of *Sürül* did not come before the ECJ until after a substantial jurisprudence had been developed protecting the residence rights of Turkish workers in EU law. The second case came to the ECJ quickly thereafter. Between the inclusion of the right of non-discrimination for Turkish workers in law in 1970 and the first and second cases in 1999 and 2003 a significant lapse of time occurs.

When foreigners have a right of residence and a right of entry for economic purposes in EU law as well as a right of non-discrimination on the basis of nationality in working conditions, there appears to be even more willingness to challenge national law excluding them from benefits. Mrs Pokrezptowicz-Meyer, a Polish language teacher in Germany challenged national legislation which permitted her, as a foreigner, to be granted a temporary contract of employment in circumstances where a German national must be granted a permanent contract. The ECJ found that her right to non-discrimination on the basis of nationality in working conditions under the EC-Poland Agreement made this difference of treatment unlawful.[72] A second case on the non-discrimination right in the Europe Agreements was decided in 2003 – a Slovak handball player working in Germany challenged his categorisation as a foreign player for the purposes of certain matches as contrary to his right regarding working conditions. The ECJ found in his favour, applying its jurisprudence relating to Community national professional sportspersons.[73]

Conclusions

Just as the rule of law at the supranational level began to have real consequences in the 1990s, a theoretical battle began regarding immigration from third countries as a core part of national sovereignty. The challenge of EU law entering this field through specific arrangements based on nationality in the arena of international relations changed the dynamic between the Member States and individual foreigners on their territory. The insertion of EU law as a fixed element in the relations between the state and the individual is very different from the type of law which regulates migration at the national level. At national level this law is characterised by a suppleness and

---

71 C-171/01 *Zajedno/Birlikte* [2003] ECR I-4301.
72 C-162/00 *Pokrzeptowicz-Meyer* [2002] ECR I-1049.
73 C-438/00 *Kolpak* [2003] ECR I-4135.

flexibility which does not give rise to a hard right of residence except after a sub-stantial period of time in the state. The nature of law in this field as Koskenniemi's handmaid of the diplomat or politician remains in essence true. The behaviour of foreigners reflects this rather blunt reality, foreigners are not eager to challenge the state as regards rights they may have in the field of non-discrimination in working conditions or social security unless they are really secure.

The change takes place only once foreigners have a right of residence which derives from a source outside the state itself and which lacks a high degree of responsiveness to national sovereignty issues (including changes of legislation premised on the need to react to support for far right/anti-immigrant political parties). However, once foreigners have a secure residence right from a non-supranational source, they are able to seek to diminish the differences between their status and that of nationals of the state. What had been symbolic law on non-discrimination becomes real law with consequences for allocation of resources, access to job security, protection from disability etc.. The claims to identity are no longer differentiated in practice around the issue of belonging as contained in the passport and liability to expulsion. If identity is formed in relationship, as Koskenniemi claims, the transformation of these relationships by the insertion of rights through third country agreements also transforms European identity.

Chapter 9

Bringing Immigration and Asylum into the EC Treaty

· The fields of immigration and asylum became a battleground of sovereignty from 1985 until 1999 and the entry into force of the Amsterdam Treaty. 1985 saw the signature of the first Schengen Agreement with the intention of the abolition of controls on movement of persons among the five original partners, Belgium, France, Germany, Luxembourg and the Netherlands and secondly the European Commission's White Paper on completion of the internal market which called for the abolition of border controls among the twelve Member States, the principle of which was incorporated via the Single European Act into the EC Treaty. It also was also the year that the Commission dared to adopt a Decision on a consultation procedure whereby the Member States would be required to notify it of proposals for amendment to their immigration laws.[1] Five Member States attacked the Decision (three of them where Schengen signatories – France, Germany and the Netherlands; the other two were Denmark and the UK) as beyond the competence of the EC (as it then was).[2]

Three points are central to these events: first, the original Member States (except for Italy) chose to regulate the abolition of border controls on persons and the creation of a common external border control amongst themselves outside the framework of Community law, in the Schengen institutions. Secondly, although the big Member States (with the exception of Italy and the UK) all wanted to move ahead on common border controls for persons and the concomitant harmonisation of immigration and asylum law, they fought the Commission as a group and with a certain desperation against the Commission's effort to assist the process. Thirdly, that the ECJ found almost entirely in favour of the Commission's competence in the field

---

1 OJ 1985 L 217/25.
2 281/85 *Germany & Ors v Commission* [1987] ECR 3203.

may well have convinced the Justice and Home Affairs (JHA) ministries that more drastic measures needed to be taken to keep immigration, asylum and borders away from Community control. How are these competing and contradictory moves to be understood?

Agamben describes the relationship between the state and the exception as follows: "Law is made of nothing but what it manages to capture inside itself through the inclusive exception of the *exceptio*: it nourishes itself on this exception and is a dead letter without it."[3] Further "the violence exercised in the state of exception clearly neither preserves nor simply posits law, but rather conserves it in suspending it and posits it in excepting itself from it ... As long as the state of exception is distinguished from the normal case, the dialectic between the violence that posits law and the violence that preserves it is not truly broken, and the sovereign decision even appears simply as the medium in which the passage from one to the other takes place."[4] But is the state sovereign in its exercise of sovereignty? Agamben considers that "In the system of the nation-state, the so-called sacred and inalienable rights of man show themselves to lack every protection and reality at the moment in which they can no longer take the form of rights belonging to citizens of a state"[5] and thus the state reveals the full power of the exception towards the individual outside the reference of the state and allegiance, i.e. the foreigner.

It is this power over the exception at the heart of sovereignty which structured the struggle on powers in immigration, asylum and borders in the EU over the 1985–2004 period. The gradual shift of powers from the 1985 position of absolute rejection of a supranational incursion into the heartland of sovereignty, as encapsulated in the right to treat foreigners as the state chooses, took place in three main steps. First there was the creation of a venue for the JHA ministries to exchange views and adopt declaratory documents in immigration and asylum: the Ad Hoc Group Immigration. This operated without any treaty or legislative basis from 1985 until 1993. The second step was the incorporation of the working of the Group into a very loose treaty framework through the creation of the Treaty of European Union which accommodated the EC Treaty as the First Pillar, the Common Foreign and Security Policy as a Second Pillar subject to an extremely light common control, and the Third Pillar, Justice and Home Affairs which was responsible for immigration, asylum and borders (as well as policing and judicial cooperation) but not subject to the strict rules of the EC Treaty.[6] In order words the Commission and the Parliament were loosely associated with the inter-governmental work of the Third Pillar but the ECJ, punished for its lack of sensitivity to the security needs of the JHA ministries,

---

3   G Agamben, *Homo Sacer: Sovereign Power and Bare Life*, Stanford University Press, Stanford, 1998, p 27.

4   Ibid p 64.

5   Ibid p 126.

6   For a good account of this rather complex period see I Boccardi, *Europe and Refugees – Towards an EU Asylum Policy*, Kluwer Law International, The Hague, 2003.

was excluded altogether.[7] The third step takes place with the 1997 Amsterdam Treaty which integrated the immigration and asylum fields of the Third Pillar and the Schengen acquis into the EC treaty (with some notable exceptions). A new Title IV EC was created into which these fields were inserted with a new objective: the creation of an area of freedom, security and justice. The Nice Treaty 2000 made no significant changes in the field. However, the constitution brought the field of immigration and asylum into the normal procedural rules of the Union. It is no longer a field of exceptionalism but a full Union competence (EU Constitution: articles III-257 to 268).

In this chapter I shall examine the development of the EC treaty provisions on immigration and asylum in the light of Agamben's claims regarding the state's sovereignty as regards the application of exceptionalism in particular to foreigners. What Agamben does not anticipate is exactly this shift in the meaning of sovereignty. The pressure of the rights of man for the citizen has already been breached through the equality of citizens and migrant nationals of the Member States in EU law. Thus the nature of the nation state's sovereignty in the EU can no longer be based on the citizen/foreigner divide. The degree of contention over the control of rights of third country nationals in the EU, however, evidences the difficult transition from nation state to supranational control.

Transferring Powers to the European Community in Immigration and Asylum

An area of Freedom, Security and Justice is the objective of Title IV EC, visas, asylum, immigration and other policies related to free movement of persons. Inserted by the Amsterdam Treaty in 1999, a five-year period was established for the adoption of the main legislative tools to provide a Community legal basis to finalise the abolition of border controls (which, for persons, took place in practice in the Schengen intergovernmental venue) and flanking measures as regards their management and the key areas of asylum and immigration.[8] Powers are set out in Articles 61–69 EC for measures to be adopted. The powers, while tied to the creation of the area, are also related in law to the achievement of the internal market and the objective of abolition of border controls among the Member States on the movement of persons (Article 14 EC introduced into the Treaty by the Single European Act in 1987). The general structure created by the Amsterdam Treaty in this field is retained in the EU Constitution.

---

7   E Guild, *Immigration Law in the European Community*, Kluwer Law International, The Hague, 2001 Chapter 7.

8   Denmark, Ireland and the UK negotiated protocols which permit them to remain outside the legal effect of Title IV EC. Ireland and the UK have the possibility to opt into any measure and have done so particularly in the field of asylum.

The meaning of the concept of an area of freedom, security and justice has been the subject of substantial discussion. Boeles finds it an option for the insertion of justice in the form of rule of law into a field characterised by a large degree of state exceptionalism but surrounded by opposing perspectives which seek to reinforce the separation of the field from the rule of law.[9] In order to provide clarification and impetus to the new area, in October 1999 at the Tampere Council Meeting the European Council set out its objectives for the new area in the field of immigration as well as asylum and security. The immigration agenda at that time focussed substantially on achieving a high degree of equality for third country nationals in the European Union in comparison with nationals of the Member States:

"4. The aim is an open and secure European Union, fully committed to the obligations of the Geneva Refugee Convention and other relevant human rights instruments, and able to respond to humanitarian needs on the basis of solidarity. A common approach must also be developed to ensure the integration into our societies of those third country nationals who are lawfully resident in the Union ...

18. The European Union must ensure fair treatment of third country nationals who reside legally on the territory of its Member States. A more vigorous integration policy should aim at granting them rights and obligations comparable to those of EU citizens. It should also enhance non-discrimination in economic, social and cultural life and develop measures against racism and xenophobia."

An ambitious programme of legislation and tightened deadlines for its adoption was set out, which for all the major pieces of legislation which are not security/control oriented has slipped substantially (the original deadline for the adoption of much of the Title IV legislation was 1 May 2004). Following the Tampere Council meeting, the Commission presented proposals for directives and regulations in virtually all areas of immigration and asylum covered by the powers. The Commission established a scoreboard procedure to set objectives and deadlines to track the efficient progress towards the adoption of the prescribed measures under Title IV EC.[10] These scoreboards have been updated on a six-month basis since the Tampere conclusions. In general they indicate that the Commission has been efficient at proposing legislation, the Parliament has been fairly efficient at review and commenting but the Council has been somewhat slower in adopting legislation.[11] In any event, by the

---

9   P Boeles, 'An Area of Freedom, Security and Justice' in E Guild and C Harlow, *Implementing Amsterdam Immigration and Asylum Rights in EC Law*, Hart Publishing Oxford, 2001.
10   See also comment on the Scoreboard in chapter 6.
11   See also the Council's Road Map from Seville 5 February 2003 6023/01/03 Rev 1 which indicates just how much slippage was taking place by February 2003 even in fields where there was largely political agreement.

time of the Seville Council meeting in June 2002 the temperature of the times had changed substantially.[12] In just over two years, the reality of a Community policy on immigration began to conflict with the very different national legislation. Important divergences among the Member States about the position of third country nationals in their communities were inexorably revealed. Major immigration legislation was introduced at the national level in many Member States: in Italy in 1998,[13] the UK in 1999,[14] the Netherlands in 2000,[15] Germany in 2000 which on account of constitutional challenges was delayed, as well as twice in Spain in 2000.[16] The UK again changed its legislation in 2001[17] and 2002[18] when new acts were passed. Greece and Portugal also joined the crowded field of changing immigration legislation after the signing of the Amsterdam Treaty.[19] This rush of national legislative activity might be considered somewhat surprising when the Member States had just agreed to Communitarise the field and to adopt binding common EU measures instead of national ones. The fundamentals of immigration at Member State level were sufficiently different, not least as a result of the legislative bonanza which the Member States had engaged in, that agreement would prove elusive. The addition of the post-11 September 2001 security issues as "immigration related" provided an opportunity for some JHA ministries to put a brake on progress towards the objective of equality at the EU level in favour of exclusion and discrimination in the name of national security.[20]

Efficiency in Immigration and Asylum

By April 2003 six legislative measures had been adopted in the area of asylum, eleven in the field of borders and visas and six regarding irregular migration. For legal migration three measures have been adopted, a regulation on residence permit formats, the family reunification directive (see chapter 6) and the long term resident third country nationals directive (see chapter 12). I will start each of the next sections with a table of the measures adopted so far followed by some commentary on them.

---

12 See D Bigo and E Guild (eds) 'De Tampere à Seville: bilan de la sécurité européenne' Cultures et Conflits, l'Harmattan, Paris, 2002 (1 & 2).
13 A di Pascale 'The New Regulations on Immigration and the Status of Foreigners in Italy' EJML Vol 4: 1 (2002) pp 71–77.
14 Immigration and Asylum Act 1999.
15 WV 2000.
16 C Gortazar, 'Spain: Two Immigration Acts at the End of the Millennium' EJML Vol 4: 1 (2002) pp 1–21.
17 Anti-Terrorism, Crime and Security Act 2001.
18 Nationality, Immigration and Asylum Act 2002.
19 C Urbano de Sousa, 'The New Portuguese Immigration Act' EJML Vol 4: 1 (2002) pp 49–69; A Skordas 'The New Immigration Law in Greece: Modernization on the Wrong Track' EJML Vol 4: 1 (2002) pp 23–48.
20 E Brouwer, P Catz & E Guild, *Immigration, Asylum and Terrorism: A Changing Dynamic in European Law*, Recht & Samenleving, Nijmegen, 2003; E Guild, 'Immigration, Asylum, Borders and

Asylum Measures Adopted[21]

Measure	Description	Number	OJ reference
European Refugee Fund (Decision)	Provision of funds for projects for asylum-seekers and refugees.	200/596	2000 L 252/12
Eurodac (Regulation)	The creation of a data base for comparison of finger prints of asylum-seekers and irregular migrants.	2725/2000	2000 L 316/1
Temporary Protection (Directive)	Common rules on provision of protection to persons fleeing their country of origin in humanitarian situations.	2001/55	2001 L 212/12
Implementing Eurodac (Regulation)	Provision for making the database system of mandatory finger printing of asylum-seekers and irregular migrants operational.	407/2002	2002 L 62/1
Reception conditions (Directive)	Common minimum standard for the conditions which states must make available to asylum-seekers.	2003/9	2003 L 31/18
Dublin II (Regulation)	System for allocation of asylum-seekers among the Member States based on the Dublin Convention 1990.	343/2003	2003 L 50/1
Dublin II implementation (Regulation)	Implementing the Dublin II Regulation.	1560/2003	2003 L 222/3

(Cont.)
Terrorism: the Unexpected Victims' in B Gökay and R B J Walker, *11 September 2001: War Terror and Judgement* Cass, London 2003 pp 146–194.

21 Many thanks to Professor Steve Peers of Essex University and Statewatch of their invaluable assistance in providing the information for these tables.

Of the seven measures, three relate directly to the inheritance which Community law received from the intergovernmental process of coordination in asylum which dominated the European field from 1985 until 1993, and the Third Pillar TEU procedure which gave a treaty base to the intergovernmental process and was the modus operandi from 1993 until 1999.[22] The remnants of the previous regime are found particularly in the Dublin II regulation and the two Eurodac measures. Dublin II got its name from the Dublin Convention determining the state responsible for examining an application for asylum lodged in one of the Member States of the European Communities 1990 (the Dublin Convention).[23] The Convention is based on two principles: first that the Member States are entitled to pool their responsibility for asylum-seekers; secondly, even though each Member State is separately a signatory to the Geneva Convention a decision on an asylum application by one of them absolves all the others from any duty to consider an asylum application by the same individual.[24] This is a negative mutual recognition duty only. Positive decisions by Member States on recognition of individuals as refugees do not trigger the mutual recognition requirement.[25]

This Convention is intended to regulate responsibility for asylum-seekers among the Member States. It is based on a hierarchy of principles of responsibility all relating to the actions of the Member States vis-à-vis the asylum-seeker. First, a state is responsible for an asylum-seeker if it recognised as a refugee a first degree family member of the individual.[26] Secondly, if the state issued a valid visa to the person, then it is responsible for the person in the capacity of asylum-seeker. Thirdly, and with many clarifications, the Member State through which the asylum-seeker gained access to the territory of the Union is responsible. In other words, the act of the Member State of failing to guard its borders against asylum-seekers is a ground for responsibility. The regulation adopted all of the main provisions of the Convention, notwithstanding the fact that the Commission itself had severely criticised the Convention both on legitimacy and efficiency grounds in 2000. [27]

---

22 E Guild, *Immigration Law in the European Community*, Kluwer Law International, The Hague, 2001.
23 Dublin Convention OJ 1997 C 254/1.
24 Article 3(2) Dublin Convention OJ 1997 C 254/1.
25 There is a growing literature on the validity of the Dublin system and the problems encountered by the Member States: A Hurwitz 'The 1990 Dublin Convention: A Comprehensive Assessment' IJRL 1999 Vol 11, pp 646–677; U Brandl, 'Distribution of Asylum-seekers in Europe? Dublin II Regulation determining the responsibility for examining an asylum application' in P de Bruycker & C de Souza, *European Immigration and Asylum Law*, Bruylant 2003 (forthcoming).
26 Article 4 Dublin Convention.
27 Articles 5–6 Dublin Convention. "The Dublin Convention establishes a link between the performance of controls on entry to the territory of the Member States and responsibility for subsequent applications for asylum. ... The criteria set out in Articles 5–7 of the Dublin Convention are based on the premise that the Member State which is responsible for controlling a person's entry onto the territory of the Member States should also be responsible for considering any subsequent asylum application. The questions which arise are first whether this is an appropriate basis for allocating responsibility and second whether it can be achieved effectively." European Commission Staff Working Paper: *Revising the Dublin Convention*, SEC (2000) 522 paras 24–25.

Eurodac was designed in the mid-1990s as a measure to supplement the Dublin Convention. It was to have been a separate convention attached or related to the Dublin Convention. In view of the changes which the Amsterdam Treaty would make to the field, the Member States agreed not to complete the Eurodac proposal as a protocol but rather to wait until the new provisions of Title IV EC were in place. Eurodac is a rather simplistic attempt to deal with one of the inadvertent consequences of the Member States measures to deter asylum-seekers – the arrival of asylum-seekers in the EU territory without documents.[28] Elsewhere I have considered the policy measures, including visas, carrier sanctions etc. which the Member States put into place which have the effect, and unfortunately all too often the intention as well of making it increasingly difficult for asylum-seekers to get to the EU territory to seek asylum.[29] Eurodac requires all Member States to take the fingerprints of asylum-seekers and persons suspected of having irregularly crossed the border and to send them to a central database. The Member States can then search the database every time they have an asylum applicant (or encounter an irregularly present third country national whom they suspect of having applied for asylum in another Member State) to see whether he or she had applied for asylum in another Member State prior to arrival. If a positive 'hit' is discovered, the theory is that the individual can be returned to the initial Member State immediately under the Dublin II regulation. As the Commission itself pointed out in its working document, in fact very few asylum-seekers (less than 2%) are subject to effective Dublin procedures.[30]

The new measures, which do not find clear precedents in the intergovernmental period are the Refugee Fund and the Directives on temporary protection and reception conditions. The objective of the Refugee Fund is to promote solidarity among the Member States as regards the reception of asylum-seekers and refugees. The fund covers a four-year period (01/01/00–31/12/04) and was given EURO 216 million. The projects to be funded must come within three categories: (a) conditions of reception (see below on the directive on this subject) (b) integration and (c) repatriation. Much of the money has been made available to governments for projects within this ambit. A substantial disagreement not only among the Member States but within the Commission has developed on the extent to which the Fund may be used for expulsion purposes particularly when this includes forced expulsion (see footnote 32).

---

28 It also constitutes a temptation to the Member States regarding the use of data, see E Brouwer, 'Eurodac: Its Limitations and Temptations' EJML 2002 Vol 4 No 2 p 231–245.

29 E Guild "Between Persecution and Protection – Refugees and the New European Asylum Policy" in *The Cambridge Yearbook of European Legal Studies Vol 3 2000*, A Dashwood, J Spencer, A Ward C Hillion, Hart: Oxford: 2001 pp 169–199; E Guild "The impetus to harmonise: asylum policy in the European Union", *Refugee Rights and Realities, Evolving International Concepts and Regimes*, Frances Nicholson and Patrick Twomey (editors), Cambridge University Press, Cambridge, 1999, pp 313–335.

30 European Commission Staff Working Paper: *Revising the Dublin Convention*, SEC (2000) 522.

The first directive is an effort to deal with mass influxes of persons fleeing humanitarian disasters and in need of protection. The directive sets out the minimum standards of treatment, including access to benefits, housing and health case, family reunification and labour market access.[31] The standards are fairly acceptable; an NGO which assessed the proposal on the basis of a human rights legitimacy score-board found it almost passed.[32] The power to open a temporary protection scheme for persons fleeing disasters rests with the Council. The directive was not used either in respect of the Afghanistan bombing in 2002 or the Iraq campaign of 2003. Instead of concerns about the protection of fleeing Afghan and Iraq nationals to the EU being expressed, the Member States expressed much greater concern to keep these persons in the region and to return them from the Member States as quickly as possible.[33] The second measure, the reception conditions directive, sets in place the minimum conditions which Member States must apply to asylum-seekers in their territory. It is a substantial step forward in so far as it places a limit on what has been termed the race to the bottom on reception conditions which some government officials see as a "pull factor" for asylum-seekers to their state. The concern was particularly acute during the negotiations when there was delay after delay in announcing an agreed text as one or other Member State came up with new demands for a reduction of obligations in some field.[34] In its press release on the adoption of the directive, the main EU umbrella NGO in the field stated "The European Council on Refugees and Exiles (ECRE) is concerned however that the negotiations by the Council had been reopened in provisions that had already found political agreement in April 2002, with the result of further watering down the standards originally proposed by the Commission."[35]

---

31 K Kerber, 'The Temporary Protection Directive' EJML 2002 Vol 4 No 2 pp 193–214.
32 Immigration Law Practitioners Association, *Alternative Scoreboard on The Temporary Protection Directive* 2000.
33 "Agreement on plan for return of Afghan refugees and on action plan for European return policy – insistence on financing problem" 28/11/2002 (Agence Europe) – The Internal Ministers Council finally approved, on Thursday, a plan for the return of Afghan refugees and the action plan for a European policy on the return of foreigners in an unlawful situation to their homeland, although the Commission has still not presented a report on Community funding of actions contained in this plan. The adoption of the plan for Afghanistan was approved but not that relating to the action plan, as several countries had told the Council that they refused to approve it if no financing indications were given. Although the Council criticised the lack of communication on financing, expected for October, the ministers gave their support to Commissioner Vitorino faced with internal divide within the Commission, Council sources say. Antonio Vitorino is preparing this document in collaboration with Commissioners Patten and Nielson, the latter being opposed to using allocations from the European Refugee Fund (EDF) for financing expulsions.
34 See E Guild, 'Seeking Asylum: Storm Clouds between International Commitments and EU Legislative Measures' EL Rev 2004 forthcoming.
35 ECRE Press Release, 19 December 2002.

Borders and Visa Measures Adopted

The Visa Country List (Regulation)	List of countries whose nationals must have visas for short stay entries to the EU (except Ireland and UK).	539/2001	2001 L 81/1
Amending the Common Consular Manual (Regulation)	The common consular manual sets out the instructions to visa officers on how to issue the common short stay visa. This provides power to amend the rules without participation by the Commission or Parliament.	789/2001	2001 L 116/2
Amending the border manual (Regulation)	Same as above but in respect of the external borders manual. Both measures have been challenged before the ECJ by the Commission C-257/01.	790/2001	2001 L 116/5
Freedom of travel for foreigners (Regulation)	Specifies which EU long resident third country nationals have a right to move freely for a period of three months in the Union.	1091/2001	2001 L 150/4
Removing Romania from visa list (Regulation)	Romania was the last accession state to be removed from the mandatory short stay visa list.	2414/2001	2001 L 327/1
Funding SIS II (Regulation)	The Schengen Information System contains data on all foreigners to be refused admission or a visa to the EU. It is to be expanded. Both a Regulation and a Decision were needed as SIS is mixed First/Third Pillar competence.	2424/2001	2001 L 328/4
More funding SIS II (Decision)	More powers for the funding of the SIS II system.	2001/886	2001 L 328/1
Visa stickers (Regulation)	The agreed sticker for short stay visas.	333/2002	2002 L 53/4
Common visa format (Regulation)	For the common short stay visa.	334/2002	2002 L 53/7

(Continued)

175

Rules on issuing visas at the border (Regulation)	Seamen can be issued visas at the border in certain specified circumstances.	415/2003	2003 L 64/1
Visa List amendments (Regulation)	The decision to add Ecuador to the list of visa national countries can be found here.	453/2003	2003 L 69/10
Facilitated Transit Document/ Rail Transit Document (Regulation)	Measure to provide for movement from the Russian enclave of Kaliningrad to the Russia mainland.	693/2003	2003 L 99/8
Format for TFDs (Regulation)	More for the not-called – "visa" visas for Russians in Kaliningrad.	694/2003	2003 L 99/15
Special visa rules	These are specific for the Olympic games in Athens 2004.	1295/2003	2003 L 183/1

More than 16 further measures of delegated legislation have also been adopted in the field in accordance with decisions 2 and 3 above. Clearly, the adoption of measures on the common border and its crossing is in practice the area where the largest number of measures have been adopted. This is not surprising as much of the legislative activity in fact only repeats measures which the participating Member States had already adopted in the context of the Schengen acquis.

The Schengen Protocol to the Amsterdam Treaty provides for the insertion of the Schengen acquis as defined in the protocol into the EC and EU Treaties. For the measures on visas, border controls and exclusion (with the exception of the Schengen Information System) Article 62 EC was the target legal base. Through a rather convoluted mechanism called ventilation and Council decisions, much of the Schengen acquis was allocated its legal bases.[36] By May 1999, the Council allocated a legal base within the new EC Treaty as amended by the Amsterdam Treaty for the Schengen acquis as identified in its decision.[37] Accordingly, the European Union has inherited the Schengen acquis which has been transferred in a somewhat less than systematic manner into new Title IV EC though the tidying up of the field through the constitution has helped greatly.

---

36 For a fuller history see K Groenendijk, E Guild and P Minderhoud, *In Search of Europe's Borders*, Kluwer Law International, The Hague, 2003.

37 Council Decision concerning the definition of the Schengen acquis for the purpose of determining, in conformity with the relevant provisions of the Treaty establishing the European Community and the Treaty on European Union, the legal base for each of the provisions or decisions which constitute the Schengen acquis, 8056/99 and 8054/99 Brussels, 12 May 1999.

As regards movement of persons, the Schengen system is based on three principles which are achieved through the deployment of four tools:

1. No third country national should gain access to the territory of the Schengen states (with or without a short stay visa) if he or she might constitute a security risk for any one of the states;
2. An assumption (not as high as a presumption in law) that a short stay visa issued by any participating state will be recognised for entry to the common territory for the purpose of admission (there are explicit exceptions justifying refusal specifically on security grounds);
3. Once within the common territory, the person is entitled (subject again to security exceptions) to move within the whole of the territory for three months out of every six without a further control at the internal borders of the participating states.

To achieve these objectives four tools were created:

1. The Schengen Information System which contains a database of names of third country nationals whose admission to the EU is prohibited (except in highly circumscribed circumstances);
2. A common list of countries whose nationals require visas to come to the common territory for short stays (visits of up to three months) and a common list of those excluded from the requirement;
3. A common format, rules on issue and meaning for a short stay visas;
4. Carrier sanctions.

The focus of the system is to ensure that persons who are not wanted by any participating state are not permitted into the territory. Thus the rules focus on who must be excluded and provide little guidance on who should be admitted. Because the underlying principle of the system is cross recognition of national decisions rather than harmonisation, finding legal mechanisms to achieve this has unexpected implications. The lifting of border controls between the states means that positive decisions on admission of persons are likely to be respected by default – the parties have fewer identity checks on the crossing of borders.[38] The cross recognition of negative decisions requires more specific measures. When the concept of internal security, the primary reason for refusal of admission of an individual into the combined territory, is not harmonised any examination of the grounds for refusal of an individual by another state needs to be avoided.

---

38 But see K Groenendijk 'New Borders Behind Old Ones: Post Schengen Controls Behind the Internal Borders and Inside Netherlands and Germany' in K Groenendijk, E Guild and P Minderhoud, *In Search of Europe's Borders*, Kluwer Law International, The Hague, 2003 pp 131–146.

The first step is clearly to identify persons who are individually known as a danger to national security. This is the role of the Schengen Information System (SIS). It is here that the divergent conceptions of what constitutes a risk and what is security in the Member States becomes central. What is perceived as a security risk in one state is not necessarily the same in another. This difference of perception of risk as it relates to an individual's activities has been the territory where national courts questioned the legitimacy of the system.[39] The capacity of the SIS is being expanded dramatically to adjust to the increasing numbers of Member States and to permit new functions. The second step is to identify persons who have not yet been identified as an individual risk to any state but who might be one. The intention is to identify groups of persons more likely than others to include persons who might constitute a risk. This group then is the subject of an additional level of control over their potential access to the territory of the Union. The tool here is the visa list which, on the basis of nationality, categorises persons as more or less likely to be a risk. For those persons who, on the basis of their nationality are considered a potential security risk, a special control in the form of a visa requirement is imposed. This has the effect of moving the effective border for these persons to their own state. The system of justification reverses the relationship of the individual and the state. It is no longer the EU's relationship with the state which determines the treatment of its nationals. Rather it is the assessment of the individual which determines the state's characterisation. The enforcement mechanism is via the transport sector as carriers are subject to fines and other sanctions for carrying persons who need visas but do not have them. The Member States distance themselves from the mechanisms of control abroad by devolving it to the private sector.[40]

Then the problem arises as to identifying who, within the *prima facie* suspect group should get visas. A comparison may be made between the policing technique of profiling: anticipating who is likely to be a criminal (or become a criminal). The purpose of the mechanisms is to anticipate through a profile of risk, who is likely, if he or she were given a visa to come to the EU territory, to be a risk (which of course raises the important question of the definition of risk and of security). In interviews with officials both at national and Community level,[41] it became apparent that a number of aids are provided to consular staff in consulates of the Member States abroad. First is the formalisation of a system of consular cooperation facilitates the regular meeting of visa officers of the EU states (including Ireland and the UK) in

---

39 H Staples, 'Adjudicating the Schengen External Border' in K Groenendijk, E Guild and P Minderhoud, *In Search of Europe's Borders*, Kluwer Law International, The Hague, 2003 pp 215–250.

40 V Guiraudon 'Logiques et practiques de l'Etat délégateur: les companies de transport dans le contröle migratoire à distance' Cultures et Conflits, l'Harmattan, Paris, 2002 (2) pp 51–79.

41 Interviews with French Foreign Affairs ministry officials carried out in the context of research on Schengen visas for the Institut des Hautes Etudes de Sécurité Intérieure, March 2001; with Community officials June 2000 and February 2001.

capitals around the world.[42] Meetings take place normally at least once during each 6-month presidency of the Union. Within this context of cooperation, information is exchanged on persons who are considered "bona fides." This is reflected in the Common Consular Instructions which provide, "In order to assess the applicant's good faith, the mission or post shall check whether the applicant is recognised as a person of good faith within the framework of consular cooperation . . ."[43] It appears that in addition to the bona fides information exchanged, mala fides persons are also identified. As regards the identification of risk categories, the Common Consular Instructions provides, "it is necessary to be particularly vigilant when dealing with 'risk categories' in other words unemployed persons, and those with no regular income etc."[44] Thus the most precise categorisation of mala fides persons who are profiled as a risk are the poor. These are the persons who will always menace the Member States' security.[45]

This system of identification and exchange of "risk analysis" in common found expression in the Seville Council Conclusions of June 2002. As a result nine Member States with Finland as the chair began a project on the Common Integrated Risk Analysis Model (CIRAM). The objective was described as follows: "The CIRAM was designed as a tool to be used mainly at strategic level, which enables the collection, analysis and distribution of border security related information to meet the needs of SCIFA+. The CIRAM, based on a six-field matrix, brings together the aspects of crime intelligence (threat assessment) and risk assessment, the latter focusing on the weaknesses of border management systems at the external borders of the European Union."[46]

Two of the adopted measures in this field do not relate to the transformation of the Schengen acquis: the two Kaliningrad measures. The accession of the Baltic states to the Union has the effect of cutting off the Kaliningrad enclave, part of Russia, from the rest of that country. The requirement that the accession states implement the EU visa list from accession (though they will not be admitted to the border control-free area until a date as yet unspecified) means that from 1 May 2004

---

42 The Council's Recommendation made in the Third Pillar on local consular co-operation regarding visas promotes 'local co-operation on visas, involving an exchange of information on the criteria for issuing visas and an exchange of information on risks to national security and public order or the risk of clandestine immigration' (Article 1 OJ 1996 C 80/1). Controls on the propriety of information are not included even though the Recommendation continues, 'their consular services should exchange information to help determine the good faith of visa applicants and their reputation, it being understood that the fact that the applicant has obtained a visa for another Member State does not exempt the authorities from examining individually the visa application and performing the verification required for the purposes of security, public order and clandestine immigration control' (Article 6). The concepts of public order and clandestine immigration control are not defined.

43 OJ 2000 L 238/332 point 1.5.

44 OJ 2000 L 238/329 point V.

45 D Bigo and E Guild 'Controller à distance et tenir à l'écart: le Visa Schengen' Cultures et Conflits, l'Harmattan, Paris, 2002 (4).

46 Council Document 6522/03 of 23 January 2003.

Russian nationals travelling by land from Kaliningrad to the rest of Russia will require common format visas to pass through the Baltic states (notably Lithuania). Long and troublesome negotiations between the Commission and Russia led to the rather unsatisfactory solution of the Facilitated Transit Document – a document which Russians seeking to pass from one part of their country to the other must obtain. For all the insistence that the word "visa" not appear, in fact this is no more than a visa by another name. The EU's insistence on a requirement that Russian nationals must obtain a document from a foreign authority to travel from one part of their country to another is perhaps the clearest manifestation of the symbolic investment the EU has made into the idea of efficient border controls.[47]

Irregular Migration

Mutual recognition of expulsion (Directive)	Member States agree to recognise expulsion decisions of the other without reconsideration of the third country national's case.	2001/40	2001 L 149/34
Carrier Sanctions (Directive)	Common levels of sanctions on transporters for carrying to the EU third country nationals without adequate documents.	2001/51	2001 L 187/45
Trafficking in persons (Framework decision)	Third Pillar measure on sanctions on persons designated as traffickers in human beings.	2002/629	2002 L 203/1
Facilitating illegal entry (Directive and Framework decision)	First and Third Pillar measure on punishing persons assisting foreigners to enter illegally.	2002/946	2002 L 328
Assistance for expulsion by air (Directive)	Measure providing for cooperation among the Member States in expulsion by air.	2003/110	2003 L 321/36

There are five "successes" in the field of illegal migration, though there is some discussion about the quality of the measures adopted on asylum in particular.[48] Carrier sanctions are part of the Schengen acquis. Their development, as part of the

---

47 O Potemkina, 'Some Ramifications of Enlargement on the EU-Russia Relations and the Schengen Regime' EJML 2003 Vol 1 No 1.

48 See D Bigo, E Guild (eds) De Tampere à Seville: bilan de la sécurité européenne ultures et Conflits No 45 et 46, l'Harmattan 2002.

attempt to engage the private sector in the policing of the EU border regime and in particular the visa requirements, has included increasingly severe obligations on the staff of carriers to check the passports, visas and other documents of potential passengers and to make an assessment as to whether they are likely to be admitted to the destination state.

Mutual recognition of expulsion decisions as a concept and a practice among the Member States raises rather complex problems. Article 3 of the directive provides that mutual recognition applies to expulsion decisions taken on the basis that the individual is a serious and present threat to public order, national security or safety (defined as a conviction and sentence to one year or more imprisonment or serious grounds for believing the individual has committed such an offence) or on the basis of a failure to comply with entry and residence requirements in the Member State. I will return to this measure in chapter 12 when I consider it in the light of the directive on long term resident third country nationals.

The final two measures were adopted either wholly or in part in the Third Pillar as they relate to criminal law. They come within the category of measures which bring criminal law into the field of immigration. The interaction of these two fields even at the national level is complex. The introduction of EU legislation is likely to further complicate the field. The policies of illegality and expulsion in the management of the common border are increasingly designed to be complimentary,[49]

Legal Migration

Residence Permit format (Regulation)	Common format for long stay residence permits for foreigners.	1030/2002	2002 L 157/1
Extension of social security system to third country nationals (Regulation)	The EU system of coordination of social security under regulation 1408/71 is extended to third country nationals on certain conditions see chapter 13.	859/2003	2003 L 124
Family Reunification (Directive)	See chapter 6.	2003/86	2003 L 251/22
Long Term Resident third country nationals (Directive)	See chapter 12.	2003/109	2004 L 16/44

49 For a full discussion of this see C Bogusz, R Cholewinski, R Cygan and E Szyszczak, *Irregular Migration and Human Rights*, Kluwer Law International, The Hague, 2004.

The EU agreed four measures in the field of legal migration: the common visa format, the extension of the EU regulation 1408/71 on coordination of social security to third country nationals (I will not expand further on this measure which better belongs in the field of EU social policy than immigration), the family reunification directive and the long term resident third country nationals directive.

So far, then, an area of freedom security and justice as regards immigration looks rather like an area of border construction and exclusion with a small number of other points. Justice, in the form of the European Court of Justice, has not yet entered the stage. No reference has been made for clarification yet to the ECJ. In terms of efficiency, it appears that exclusionary measures are able to achieve agreement more readily than measures which harmonise the protection of refugees and the rights of residence of immigrants.

The ECJ and the Area of Freedom Security and Justice

Title IV EC modified the powers of the ECJ as regards the area of freedom security and justice in comparison with all other parts of the EC Treaty. Article 68 EC provided that only a court or a tribunal of a Member State against whose decisions there is no judicial remedy under national law could request the Court of Justice to give a ruling. I will return to this provision shortly.

The provision also included an exclusion of the ECJ from consideration of any matter arising from the crossing of the internal borders and a right for some institutions to seek clarification on the meaning of Title IV. In light of the sensitive nature of the field and the fact that all the institutions and the Member States have been heavily involved in brokering compromises in the implementing measures, exactly what interests the institutions will have in bringing actions is unclear. If one considers arguments raised on the ECHR before the ECJ, the great majority are in respect of references from national courts; very few are in respect of actions brought by the Commission (or other institutions).[50]

The most serious limitation on the ECJ's jurisdiction was the prohibition of all lower courts and tribunals to ask preliminary questions of it. In many cases, the most important issues to the clarification of the fundamental elements of EC law have come before the ECJ as preliminary questions from courts of first instance. Superior courts have had a tendency to rule on issues of Community law more readily themselves and thus on the one hand to guard their interpretative power, but on the other to increase the risk of divergent national interpretation of Community law. The *Köbler* case indicates how sensitive national supreme courts can be about loss of interpretative powers. Mr Köbler was employed as an ordinary university professor in Austria. He applied for

---

50 E Guild and G Lesieur, *The European Court of Justice on the European Convention on Human Rights: Who said what when*, Kluwer Law International, The Hague, 1997.

a special length-of-service increment for university professors on the basis of completion of 15 years' service as an ordinary professor at universities in various Member States. His application was rejected on the ground that national legislation required that he complete the required service exclusively at Austrian universities. Mr Köbler thus appealed against that decision to the Austrian supreme administrative court on the grounds of discrimination contrary to the EC Treaty. The supreme administrative court referred the question to the ECJ for a preliminary ruling on the point.

When the case was registered in Luxembourg, the ECJ noted that it was very similar to a case it had just dealt with. It inquired of the Austrian court whether it wished to withdraw the reference in view of its recent jurisprudence (since at first sight the legal issue had been resolved by a ruling in a sense favourable to Mr Köbler's claim). The national court took the opportunity to withdraw its request for a preliminary ruling, and then dismissed Mr Köbler's application on the ground that the special length-of-service increment is a loyalty bonus which objectively justifies a derogation from the Community law provisions on freedom of movement for workers. As Mr Köbler was now excluded from further appeal, he brought a claim for damages against the Austrian state for his loss through the misinterpretation by the Austrian supreme administrative court of Community law.[51]

The difficult question politically, though perhaps not so complex legally, is whether the state is liable for damages to Mr Köbler for the clear and flagrant misapplication of Community law by the Austrian court. In Title IV the ECJ only had the courts of final instance to work with as all other courts are prohibited from making references in the Title. The arrogance shown by the Austrian supreme court in *Köbler* is not exclusive to Austria but is perhaps rather more structural about the nature of the judicial profession and how judges arrive at supreme courts. However, in the field of immigration and asylum another feature at the national level must also be taken into account. The emphasis in the large Member States on speeding up the process of determining immigration and asylum claims and in particular to force the courts to deal quickly with any appeals against the states' decisions has meant that appeal possibilities have been severely curtailed. Thus in an increasing number of Member States the court of first instance which hears an asylum appeal is also the court of final instance and thus has the possibility of making a reference to the ECJ.

In the EU constitution agreed in December 2003, the heterogeneous provisions of Title IV jurisdiction of the ECJ were removed. The exceptional exclusion of the ECJ's competence in the area of freedom, security and justice was retained only regarding "the validity or proportionality of operations carried out by the police or other law enforcement services of a Member State or the exercise of the responsibilities incumbent upon Member States with regard to the maintenance of law and order and the safeguarding of internal security, where such action is a matter of national law." (Constitution: article III-377)

---

51   C-224/01 Opinion 8 April 2003.

Conclusions

Agamben's field of sovereignty as revealed in the exception as regards the foreigner provides an interesting perspective on the developments in this field at EU level. On the one hand the entry of the supranational level as the determiner of the rules indicates a different pattern regarding sovereignty. Kostakopoulou coins the term floating sovereignty to describe this effect.[52] It is no longer national sovereignty embedded in the Member State, but capable of travelling and escaping from the nation state itself. However, the JHA ministries clearly are seeking to limit the damage to their understanding of sovereignty and the treatment of third country nationals. The insertion at every level of national discretion to claw back the sovereignty which is in the process of slipping away is perhaps the most consistent of themes in this history.

The concept of sovereignty is perhaps no longer clearly applicable. The relationship of the rule and the exception structured around the citizen and the state does not explain the transformation of law-making powers and their exercise in the field of EU immigration and asylum. Most symbolically important is, of course, the transformation of the meaning of borders and their control for persons in the EU. By applying a supranational law-making power to the definition of the border of the territory and with it a redefinition of the border from that of the nation state to the supranational entity which is not a state, the definition of the nation state itself crumbles. The relationship of the citizen to the state is transformed in that the citizen is no longer the measure of the repository of the law. The citizen and the state of exception are no longer bound together in opposition (see chapter 5). Similarly, the foreigner is no longer the foremost subject of the exception. Instead the antagonism of Community law (expressed most frequently by the ECJ) to measures which allow a different interpretation in different Member States sets up an alternative approach to the exception. The exception in Community law is not a field of sovereignty to be protected against judicial encroachment but, in principle, a threat to the integrity of the Community law system itself.

The struggle for control of the exception in the field of immigration and asylum will be played out at the EU level over the next 15 years. The role of the ECJ will be decisive in determining whether the EU in fact has a consistent immigration and asylum law which provides the same results across the Union or whether nation state sovereignty in the form of exceptionalism in the treatment of foreigners will manage to survive as the rule itself.

---

52 D Kostakopoulou, 'Floating Sovereignty: A Pathology or a Necessary Means of State Evolution?' Oxford Journal of Legal Studies Vol 22, No 1 (2002) pp 135–156.

Chapter 10

Identity in the EU Neighbourhood[1]

Political theory about the European Union has been dominated by intergovernmentalists, such as Moravcsik,[2] who have seen off the neofunctionalists or witnessed their transformation.[3] Recently, however, new competitive theories of the Union have been developing. Sandholtz and Stone Sweet have sought to develop a new way of looking at EU integration considering the interaction of three causal factors: exchange, organisation and rules.[4] The premise is that "transnational exchange provokes supranational organizations to make rules designed to facilitate and to regulate the development of transnational society."[5] While the Member State governments are important actors, they are themselves embedded in the process, the connections among the factors are inherently expansionary, in one way or another or both (i.e. vertically or horizontally). The process of integration creates its own dynamic which sparks new political arenas and thus qualitatively changes the nature of politics. Accordingly, they state: "we expect supranational bodies to work to enhance their own autonomy and influence within the European polity, so as to promote the interests of transnational society and the construction of supranational governance."[6] The processes

---

1 In this chapter I have relied heavily on the paper I presented at the ECSA World Conference 2002: Brussels 5 & 6 December 2002.
2 A Moravcsik, 'Negotiating the Single European Act: National Interests and Conventional Statecraft in the European Community' International Organisation (1991) 45: 19–56; 'Preferences and Power in the European Community: A Liberal Intergovernmentalist Approach' Journal of Common Market Studies (1993) 31: 473–524.
3 W Sandholtz 'Choosing Union: Monetary Politics and Maastricht' International Organisations (1993) 47: 1–39.
4 W Sandholtz and A Stone Sweet, *European Integration and Supranational Governance*, OUP, Oxford, 1998.
5 Ibid p 25.
6 Ibid p 26.

of European integration and enlargement have been seen as competing principles expressing different theoretical positions about the Union. The issue of immigration is rarely, if ever, examined from these perspectives on the nature of the Union. Either it is left to the intergovernmentalists as a field which is deeply protected by the JHA ministries from supranational rule making, or it is passed by in silence. People are central, however, to the debate.

The events of April 2003 in Cyprus are paradigmatic.[7] The Green Line which has divided the country since 1974 into Turkish and Greek sections each claiming statehood but only one succeeding internationally (the Greek side as rump state of the independent state) was breached by the mass movement of persons back and forth from one side to the other. The admission of the Greek state of Cyprus into the Union from 1 May 2004 to the exclusion of the Turkish side (as political negotiations broke down yet again) was central to the decision of the population to vote with their feet – forcing open the border. Most of the people who have been crossing the border do so on both sides out of curiosity, to see what has happened to on the other side of the Line and check where they used to live. Further, the option available to a large part of the Turkish population to obtain passports from the state of Cyprus which is joining the Union is transforming the nature of governance on the island. Can one really still speak of intergovernmentalism when the government of one part of the island is no longer actually in control of its population, which although it may still live on the territory, has transferred its allegiance, in the form of the most important identity document, the passport, to another state? This effect is part of the interaction between exchange, organization and rules but as a field it is so contested that academics tend to tiptoe around it.

What should the EU be? At the heart of the debate about the size and composition of the EU is the question of intergovernmentalism and integration. The size of the Union is considered institutionally as critical to its contents. Too many Member States will paralyse the institutions, the argument goes, and leaving states outside will create instability. Any answer other than deep ambiguity requires the EU to have a policy towards its neighbours either as potential candidates or in some other capacity. The neighbours question engages migration. Enlargement means, in terms of migration, that the citizens of the new Member States are entitled to free movement rights with only the very limited exceptions which I have discussed in chapter 5. A neighbourhood policy which does not engage enlargement must define how it will treat nationals of the neighbours. So far the Union has developed two very different policies, some neighbours like Switzerland and Norway enjoy for their nationals full free movement rights with citizens of the Union. Other neighbours such as Ukraine or Moldova have the most restrictive migration rules possible at EU level applicable to their nationals and are at the top of the EU list for the

---

7 'Cypriots wary of future as green line opens' Guardian Weekly, May 8–14 2002 p 5.

negotiation of readmission agreements to make expulsion from the EU of their nationals easier.

The enlargement process of the European Union which admitted, on 1 May 2004, 10 countries in Central and Eastern Europe, the Baltic states and two islands in the Mediterranean has brought an urgency to the neighbourhood question. The adjustment after 1989 to a new neighbourhood with states in transition on the EU eastern borders and states in development to the south and east is, at least in part, over. The treatment of the 10, both to the east and the south, changes the relationship of the EU with all of the others. The other "old" neighbours want better treatment. Turkey has managed to move into the category of serious candidate state, joining Bulgaria and Romania as regards entry into the club in the near future. Some other "old" neighbours which ceased to be neighbours after 1989 have again become neighbours, such as Ukraine, Belarus and Russia. The position of the Member States is ambiguous about these neighbours. Some Member States such as the UK are championing further enlargement quickly to include Bulgaria, Romania and Turkey. In May 2003, the Italian President was reported to have suggested that the EU will not be in a position to take an equal place in international affairs along side the USA until it has enlarged to include countries such as Belarus and the Ukraine.[8] Those in favour of rapid enlargement are suspected, however, of seeking to water down the EU to the point where it can no longer operate and thus sovereignty, which is perceived as having slipped to the EU, can be recovered. The map of Europe on the Euro notes is perhaps one of the clearest expressions of the territorial uncertainty of the EU. It does not end at the borders of the current or potential EU but rather gently fades into the distance and off the edge of the paper without ever seeming to define its end.[9]

One of the four freedoms which form the core of the EU's internal market is free movement of persons. The high status which this part of policy enjoys must find its reflection in external policy. In this chapter I shall look at the development of EU identity in its neighbourhood through the choices which it is making in respect of migration law and policy. In doing so I shall examine the extent to which Sandholz and Sweet Stone's theory that the supranational bodies seek to enhance and promote the interests of transnational society explains the developments. If their position is correct, then in the development of migration policy in the context of EU foreign affairs a rather different picture should emerge from that which I considered in the last chapter. As opposed to a supranational institution which shows substantial deference towards national JHA ministry concerns about sovereignty over foreigners, one should be able to discern a supranational institution promoting transnational society even beyond EU frontiers.

---

8   Financial Times, 13 May 2004 p 4.
9   M Anderson and E Bort, *Boundaries and Identities: The Eastern Frontiers of the EU*, University of Edinburgh Press, Edinburgh, 1998.

Policy on the Hoof: Migration and the Neighbours

Two competing perspectives clash in the field of migration. On the one hand there is the foreign affairs perspective of management of relations with other sovereign states. Among the tools which traditionally have been used in this area are privileges and sanctions for nationals of other states. Imposing visa restrictions on or indeed prohibitions of admission to the state for nationals of countries with which a state has bad relations has been part of the foreign affairs arsenal. When states are at war a restriction more or less substantial on the admission of nationals of the enemy (unless they are fleeing in the capacity of refugees) has been normal. Elsewhere I have plotted the move away from the foreign affairs use of migration restrictions or privileges to an aggregation of prospective individual behaviour perspective.[10] The development of an EU mandatory visa list was accompanied by an explanation of the reasons for putting some countries on the list and leaving others off which is rooted in JHA ministry thinking about individuals as risks of illegal immigration or criminal behaviour and only as an afterthought as a tool of international relations.[11] The political importance of submitting to or lifting obligatory visa requirements can be very important at the national level of the state concerned. Jileva plots very clearly how the lifting of EU obligatory visas became a central issue in Bulgaria in 2000 tied with the sense of injustice people felt when confronted with the bureaucracy of the Schengen visas system and the fact that their neighbours were immediate candidate states for admission to the EU.[12]

In the EU context, the international relations use of migration has not, however been excluded. For example, during the Kosovo bombing campaign by NATO troops in 1999 the Common Foreign and Security Policy adopted a number of common positions listing individuals who were prohibited from admission to the EU. The first measure began with a prohibition on the issue of a visa by an EU state to Slobodan Milosevic (a prohibition on entry which did not impede his delivery to the International Tribunal for the Former Yugoslavia in the Hague for trial).[13] It remains unclear whether the Common Position was consistent with the EU's constitutional arrangements at the time. Can the crossing of an external EU border by an individual for a short stay still be regulated by CFSP or must this be dealt with in JHA chapter which has exclusive competence over the crossing of the external border and the issue of short stay visas? Article 1 TEU requires measures adopted in the Second and Third Pillars to be without prejudice to the EC Pillar.[14] The constitution has clarified

---

10 E Guild, *Moving the Borders of Europe*, University of Nijmegen 2001.
11 See Explanatory Memorandum, Regulation 539/2001 OJ 2001 L 81/1.
12 E Jileva, 'Insiders and Outsiders in the Enlargement of the EU borders: Bulgaria' in K Groenendijk, E Guild, P Minderhoud, *In Search of Europe's Borders*, Kluwer Law International, The Hague, 2003 pp 273–288.
13 Common Position 1999/318/CFSP.
14 "The Union shall be founded on the European Communities, supplemented by the policies and forms of cooperation established by this Treaty."

the relationship of the field of activity of the Union into one somewhat more coherent whole. This is a rather extreme example of the intersection of the fields, but for that reason is interesting.

Immigration and Enlargement

The prime task of the European Community: the completion of the internal market through the abolition of controls on the free movement of persons incorporates a model of immigration. This is one where the control of movement of persons itself is prima facie inadmissible. The state must justify any control on movement of persons as an exception to the principle. This model is the one which is inherent in enlargement of the Union. Unlike the principles of the common European migration policy which is being developed in the framework of Justice and Home Affairs, it applies on the basis of agreements among states on movement of their nationals rather loosely based on reciprocity. Enlargement of the Union has been the main mechanism for increasing the numbers of persons enjoying rights under the system (and reducing the numbers of persons who could be categorised as illegally present in the Union). The EEC Treaty (1958) established a foundation for immigration based on three principles: nationality, economic activity and the right of the individual to choose to move or not. The right of the state to control immigration among the class of qualifying persons was highly limited (see chapter 5).

The mechanism of free movement of persons as the basis of migration law in Europe was fully operational by the end of the transitional period in 1968. Most labour migration at that time was moving from Italy towards the more northern Member States. In 1973 the Community enlarged to include Denmark, Ireland and the UK. The immigration law of the Community was extended immediately to nationals of these states notwithstanding public concerns in France and the Netherlands in particular about the risk of high levels of immigration which might result from the UK (in particular) destabilising their countries' labour markets.[15] In 1981 Greece joined the European Community thus including another immigrant sending state though transitional limitations on free movement of workers were not lifted for Greek nationals until 1 January 1988. Two more traditional migrant sending countries joined in 1986, Portugal and Spain but again their nationals were not permitted to exercise free movement rights as workers until 1 January 1992 (the delay was reduced by one year as fears of mass movement from those two states receded in the existing Member States). In 1994 Austria, Finland and Sweden joined the EU with immediate free movement rights for their nationals.

---

15   W R Böhning, *The Migration of Workers in the United Kingdom and Western Europe*, OUP, Oxford, 1972.

On 1 May 2004 Cyprus, the Czech Republic, Estonia, Hungary, Latvia, Lithuania, Malta, Poland, Slovakia and Slovenia join the EU and their nationals become citizens of the Union. Free movement of some economically active persons – the self-employed – takes place immediately, though nationals of all of the CEEC countries already enjoy a right of free movement for self-employment under the Europe Agreements (see chapter 8).[16] After the date of accession to the European Union, all accession state nationals will be covered immediately by the EC rules on social security (see chapter 3). According to the accession agreement, national immigration law (except in the field of self-employment) in the existing Member States will continue to regulate access to the territory and employment for nationals of the accession countries for a minimum of two years. By paragraph 2 of the accession treaty this can be extended to five years. In exceptional circumstances after the five years and only if a Member State considers that there will be a serious disturbance of its labour market or threat thereof, the Member State can add on an extra two years to delay free movement of workers and movement of service providers and recipients from the accession states. A number of Member States, the UK included, have indicated that they will not apply any transitional period for free movement of workers for nationals of the accession states.[17] The transitional arrangements to delay free movement of workers, service providers and recipients do not apply to nationals of Cyprus and Malta.[18]

There has been much discussion about the risk of substantial labour migration from these countries to the EU territory. At one point some trade unions in Austria called for a delay on free movement of workers from the CEECs for 20 years. However, the fears of destabilisation of labour markets by workers from the CEECs has gradually diminished.[19] The Commission has taken substantial steps in all of its publications on enlargement to reduce fears of mass migration from the candidate states. "The differences in the level of prosperity across Europe have generated concerns in some Member States of large-scale immigration from new members,

---

16 A Bocker and E Guild, *Implementation of the European Agreements in France, Germany, the Netherlands and the UK: Movement of Persons*, Platinum, London, 2002.

17 Ireland has indicated it will not apply transitional restrictions on free movement of workers; the Netherlands has also announced it will only place a maximum quota of 22,600 annually on new Member State workers access to their labour market. The UK has moved from a position in January 2002 where the government announced that no restrictions would apply to one where a registration system will apply to new Member State workers.

18 In theory then, Turkish Cypriots who are entitled to Cypriot passports issued by the Greek authorities (which under the constitution includes all of the original Turkish inhabitants of the island at the time of partition) are entitled to move as migrant workers anywhere in the Union and to live there. Thus they would be entitled to move en mass to say London or Frankfurt and desert their state altogether. The chances of this happening are very slight but are dependent on the degree of security and stability which the population feels in Northern Cyprus. The greater the risk of military action or annexation by Turkey, for example, the more likely it would be that people might consider their option of emigration.

19 C Boswell, *European Migration Policies in Flux: Changing Patterns of Inclusions and Exclusion*, Royal Institute of International Affairs, London, 2003.

with related anxieties about cheap labour threatening jobs or depressing wages, and about increased demands on health and social services, or even fears that racial tensions could jeopardise social stability. On closer analysis, these concerns appear exaggerated. When Spain and Portugal became Member States in 1986, there were anxieties that richer countries close by would be the target for mass immigration. But the opposite has happened: Spanish and Portuguese workers in France decreased ... Mass migration is a result of instability – and the EU enlargement is a factor for increased stability. It will reduce, not boost, the tendency to large scale population movements."[20]

The disassociation of the enlargement of the EU from the issue of migration was central to preventing the most important policies of the EU being sidetracked by JHA ministry concerns. The intergovernmentalist approach which one might expect to find expression in a heightening of immigration as a political issue in the enlargement negotiations in fact disappears as the actors most interested in the subject, the JHA ministries, fail to find a voice at the supranational level which is sufficiently strong to impose their perspective. Instead the voice of intergovernmentalism is expressed at the national level but because of competing interests in enlargement is not capable of pushing the item up the political agenda there either.

For example, at the national level in the UK, the Foreign Secretary announced on 10 December 2002: "Citizens of the new EU Member States will gain the same full rights to work in the UK as enjoyed by existing EU citizens from the date of their planned accession on 1 May 2004 rather than having to wait for two to seven years."[21] However, when the Secretary of State for the Home Department was asked whether in light of this at least the mandatory visa requirement of Slovak nationals which the UK had imposed would be lifted the interior minister answered: "Visa regimes are maintained only where they contribute to effective immigration control. The visa regime has proved effective in reducing the numbers of inadmissible passengers travelling to the UK from Slovakia. Following Slovakia's accession to the EU in 2004, all categories of Slovak nationals will enjoy rights of free movement and will not require a visa to come to the UK. In the meantime, the visa regime on Slovak nationals, as with all visa regimes, will be kept under review and will be lifted when we consider that the threat to our immigration control is at an acceptable level." This reveals a very different approach to movement of persons from that of the Foreign Ministry.

Enlargement has been the most important means by which (former) third country nationals have acquired full free movement, work and residence rights in the EU. It has also been an effective way to diminish illegal immigration as it redefines individuals who were in an illegal situation before accession into legal residents afterwards. Where accession has not been desirable or possible, the Union has entered into

---

20 European Commission, *The European Union: Still Enlarging*, Luxembourg 2001 pp 18–19.
21 Press Release, Foreign and Commonwealth Office, UK, 10 December 2002.

agreements with third countries to apply free movement of persons rules to their nationals. This is the approach the Union adopts when it wishes to avoid nationals of certain countries from finding themselves in an illegal situation in the Union. The European Economic Area Agreement 1991 extended full immigration rights to nationals of, Finland, Iceland, Liechtenstein, Norway and Sweden. The EC Swiss Agreement which came into force in June 2002 provides free movement for these nationals. The EC Turkey Agreement 1963 and its subordinate legislation provides for security of work and residence for Turkish workers in the Union and a standstill on access to the EU territory for self-employment.[22] The EC Agreements with the North African countries provide for protection of workers of those nationalities within the EU (see chapter 8).[23]

The key feature of these mechanisms of controlling immigration is that they are nationality-based establishing close cooperation between the countries involved and are regionally focussed. The right to move or not is given to the individual against whose choice the state must justify an interference. Even where free movement rights are not provided but only protection of work and residence, the foundation is that the individual is entitled to renewal of work and residence permits against which legal presumption the state must prove to a high threshold that the individual is a serious and continuing risk to public policy, security or health.[24]

The result of this model of immigration based on nationality and economic activity providing the individual the choice is surprising: less than 2% of the population of the EU Member States is made up of nationals of other Member States. The perspective of migration as part of a natural process of market integration has managed to make it a normal part of political decision-making in the commercial sector. Once the concerns of JHA ministries about security have been limited to the very small percent of cases where there is even a potential risk, the vast majority can exercise rights of movement, residence and economic activity without the obstacles and hindrances which have been at the heart of the Schengen system (see chapter 9). The Schengen paradox is that the abolition of border controls on persons moving within the territory of the Member States (other than the two opted out) has resulted in a reinforced external frontier based on the principle of exclusion unless the individual can justify admission. The starting point that all individuals are suspect and they only lose that characteristic when they prove themselves individually not to be a threat, leads to blocked borders, affront and offence to individuals, the frustration of good trading and cultural relations and a placing at risk of asylum seekers and refugees.[25]

---

22 R Gutmann, Die Assoziationsfreizügigkeit türkisher Staatsangehöriger, Ihre Entdeckung und ihr Inhalt, 2 Auflage, Nomos Verlag, Baden-Baden, 1999.
23 D Martin, 'Association Agreements with Mediterranean and with Eastern Countries: Similarities and Differences,' in Antalovsky, K Konig, B Perchinig, H Vana, *Assoziierungsabkommen de EU mit Drittstaaten*, 1998.
24 C-340/97 *Nazli* [2000] ECR I-957.
25 D Bigo and E Guild 'Controller à distance et tenir à l'écart: le Visa Schengen' Cultures et Conflits, l'Harmattan, Paris, 2002 (4).

Immigration, the Close Neighbours and Beyond

The alternative model of movement of persons as part of the normal relations among states and a necessary part of commercial activity is at the heart of the European Union's policies with the rest of the world. The Commission's Communication on the Wider Europe[26] sets out a new vision of the EU in its larger context. The Communication recognises that enlargement of the Union will end in the not too distant future.[27] However, the Commission recognises that it has been the prospect of membership of the Union which has provided the incentive for reform towards stable institutions guaranteeing democracy, rule of law, human rights and respect for the protection of minorities, functioning market economies and capacity to cope with competitive pressure and market forces[28] in many of the countries which are now in the accession process and led to economic development, the stabilisation of democratic institutions and the strengthening of the rule of law in the region. The completion of EU enlargement is seen by the Commission as providing impetus to draw closer to "the 385 million inhabitants of the countries who will find themselves on the external land and sea border, namely Russia, the Western NIS [Ukraine, Moldova and Belarus] and the Southern Mediterranean [Algeria, Egypt. Israel, Jordan, Libya, Morocco, Palestinian Authority, Syria and Tunisia] ... Over the coming decade the Union's capacity to provide security, stability and sustainable development to its citizens will no longer be distinguishable from its interest in closer cooperation with the neighbours."[29] A vision of the relationship between the EU and the neighbours is one which engages the individuals resident in the region around the Union and not just the governments of the countries on the EU's borders.

The Commission states that "the aim of the new Neighbourhood Policy is therefore to provide a framework for the development of a new relationship which would not, in the medium term, include a perspective of membership or a role in the Union's institutions."[30] The new vision is for an open and integrated market functioning on the basis of compatible or harmonised rules and further liberalisation. The Commission considers that it would bring significant economic and other benefits to both the EU and the neighbourhood. In terms of specific actions the Commission proposes that "all neighbouring countries should be offered the prospect of a stake in the EU's Internal Market and further integration and liberalisation to promote the free movement of – persons, goods, services and capital (four freedoms)."

The positive tone of the Communication towards the inclusion of free movement of persons as part of the policy towards the neighbourhood becomes somewhat

---

26   COM (2003) 104 final.
27   It would appear that Turkey and the Western Balkan states are likely to be the end point of enlargement.
28   The so-called Copenhagen criteria set out at the Copenhagen European Summit 1993.
29   Commission ibid p 3.
30   Commission ibid p 5.

less warm when the specifics are developed. In the section: Perspectives for Lawful Migration and Movement of Persons there is still the recognition that all parties have a stake in ensuring that the new external borders are not a barrier to trade, social and cultural interchange or regional cooperation. Taking into account some of the most pressing concerns in the social sphere in the Union, the ageing of the EU population, the demographic decline and the need for skills exchange the Commission states that "free movement of people and labour remains the long-term objective."[31] The establishment of free movement of persons in the region as an objective, albeit a long term one, is of considerable importance. The vision of what the EU will become and the role of movement of persons as a key feature towards stability and security in the region (and world) is vital. The Commission does not, at least in its objective, equate the exclusion of movement of persons with increased security but rather the reverse – inclusion is the way forward. The Communication proceeds to set out 8 measures towards the new regime:

1. A long stay visa policy to facilitate cultural and technical interchange;
2. An efficient and user friendly system for small border traffic;
3. Facilitating movement of citizens of neighbouring countries to participate in EU programmes and activities;
4. Visa-free access to holders of diplomatic and service passports;
5. A wider application of visa-free regimes;
6. A common approach to integration of third country nationals with special emphasis on nationals of neighbouring countries;
7. Assisting neighbouring countries efforts to combat illegal migration and returns policies;
8. Concluding readmission agreements with all the neighbours as an essential element in joint efforts to curb illegal migration.

There is an obvious incoherence at the centre of the list. The first five elements are designed to improve access for individuals to move between the neighbours and the EU. Item two deserves attention as it is based on article 3(1) Schengen Implementing Agreement which envisages the adoption of exceptions and arrangements on local border traffic. Under the "Schengen" years, no measure was adopted under this provision which had no doubt been inserted to authorise existing arrangements which a number of Member States have with neighbouring countries. The Commission picked up the point and is developing it as a supplementary mechanism to the Schengen border for the 'neighbourhood'. In a Commission Staff Working Paper, it develops the arguments for the establishment of a separate and parallel regime for local border traffic (which can be variously defined).[32] It puts forward a number

---

31 Communication ibid p 11.
32 SEC (2002) 947 Brussels 9 September 2002.

of options including a liberalised regime of cross-border movement for non-visa nationals on a facilitated travel document issued by their own authorities. For visa nationals facilitated travel documents would be issued by Member States. This option has now been chosen for the proposal for a regulation.[33] The proposal also makes provision for facilitating border crossing for nationals of the new Member States and their neighbours.

Item 6 is somewhat ambiguous, if economic integration is intended then this is coherent with the previous elements (see chapter 12). If some concept of cultural integration is intended, it is unclear how this could be common across a Union of 25 Member States most with their own languages and all with different social and cultural traditions. The 7th and 8th elements are clearly in contradiction with the earlier ones on any understanding of the objective. If providing a stake in the internal market including the free movement of persons is central to building stability and security in the region, then surely it is also a key for the neighbouring states in their policies towards their non-EU neighbours as well. The final point is readmission agreements.

The practice of readmission agreements relates to the desire of states to expel third country nationals in simplified procedures. If an agreement is negotiated whereby the relevant states undertake to take back their own nationals without question, or, in the view of the Member States, better still, any third country national who has passed through the state on the way to the Member State, expulsion is facilitated. The state seeking to expel an individual, in theory at least does not need to enter into negotiations with the destination state regarding each individual case. The first collective readmission agreement among the Member States with a third country was between the Schengen states and Poland in 1991. The example of a collective agreement was not repeated with the Schengen states.[34] Instead they entered into bilateral agreements with the surrounding states. The incentive to states surrounding the EU to enter into readmission agreements was primarily the promise that they would only be taken off the mandatory visa list if they did so.[35] The incentive was effective, the accession states signed almost without exception readmission agreements with those Member States which demanded them.[36] The power to adopt readmission agreements passed to the EU with the entry into force of the Amsterdam Treaty in May 1999. Since then, it has become a priority in JHA as an important way to attack illegal immigration. Agreements have been negotiated with Hong Kong,[37] Macao[38]

---

33   COM (2003) 502 Final.
34   A common format readmission agreement was designed and adopted within the Third Pillar in 1995 see E Guild and J Niessen, *The Developing Immigration and Asylum Policy of the European Union*, Kluwer Law International, The Hague, 1996.
35   E Guild, *Moving the Borders of Europe*, University of Nijmegen, Nijmegen 2001.
36   Not all Member States wanted to follow the route of readmission agreements. The UK for instance considered they might be an obstacle to expulsion as limiting the right of the authorities to expel a person by creating an expectation that the terms of an agreement would be respected.
37   November 2001 Council Document 8518/02, 2.5.02.
38   October 2002 COM (2003) 151, 31.3.03.

and Sri Lanka.[39] Negotiations are proceeding rapidly with Russia, Morocco, Ukraine, Algeria, Turkey, China and Albania.[40] In the constitution this power has been retained at article III-168(3).

According to Peers who has analysed the existing and proposed agreements, they place the following obligations on the states:

1. "The contracting parties have to take back their own nationals (or, in the case of Hong Kong and Macao, permanent residents) who have entered or stayed illegally in the other party.

2. The parties must also readmit nationals of non-contracting parties or stateless persons who have illegally entered or stayed on their territory, subject to certain conditions.

3. The parties must permit transit of persons back to a non-contracting party if necessary.

4. There are detailed rules on the procedure for handing back persons, including the types of documents which constitute proof or evidence that a person is a national or was on the territory.

5. The parties must either issue their own travel documents or use the EC's standard travel document.

6. There are detailed provisions on data protection, although these do not require the non-EC parties to apply basic principles concerning the effective collective or individual enforcement of data protection rules (such as the obligation to set up an independent data protection supervisor or the right of data subjects to apply to the courts for correction, blocking or erasure of data).

7. Article 16 of each agreement provides that the agreement is 'without prejudice to the rights, obligations and responsibilities' of the parties arising from 'International Law', but there is no specific reference to human rights or refugee law.

8. Member States can draw up special implementing protocols with the non-EC party, but each agreement takes precedence over any incompatible bilateral agreement between a Member State and the non-EC party.

9. All three treaties can be denounced, but there is no procedure for settling disputes that might arise."[41]

The insistence on readmission agreements and the choice of countries with which to negotiate on their settlement indicates how the EU wishes to deal with some of the neighbours. Clearly, only those states that are far from the EU are happy to enter into

---

39   May 2002 Council Document 7831/1/03, 9.4.03.
40   M Schieffer, "Community readmission agreements with third-countries – objectives, substance and current state of negotiations" EJML, 3(2003) forthcoming.
41   S Peers, 'Readmission Agreements' in S Peers and N Rogers, *Immigration and Asylum in EU Law after Amsterdam*, Kluwer Law International, the Hague, forthcoming.

these agreements (without the *quid pro quo* incentive of removal from the mandatory visa list). The difficulty and expense of an EU Member State using a readmission agreement with Hong Kong or Sri Lanka to get rid of unwanted third country nationals makes it not a particularly risky option for governments of those countries to enter into these agreements. The neighbours, however, seem much less keen to enter into these agreements as the temptation for the EU Member States to use them as dumping grounds for unwanted third country nationals is clearly substantial.[42] Measures as regards the control of the common border appear to be linked specifically with the perspective of illegal immigration and the control of third country nationals in light of this threat.

The assumption that free movement of persons is among the elements which foster political stability, economic development and the reduction of poverty has proven correct in the EU's enlargements. Thus turning individuals into illegal migrants, expelling them and encouraging neighbouring states to exclude them economically, socially and politically will not necessarily be contributing factors to the objective. Further the neighbours will have relationships with their neighbours which also need to be respected and developed unless there is to be a field of insecurity and instability at the edges of the neighbourhood.

As is clear from the EU's own enlargement, the most effective way to deal with illegal immigration is to provide those individuals who might become illegal immigrants in search of their personal or family needs with the possibilities in law to be legal migrants. As the ECJ has established in its case law on the movement of self-employed persons from the CEECs under the Europe Agreements before accession of these countries to the EU, Member States were free to reject an application to remain in the host state where the self-employed CEEC national was residing illegally within its territory.[43] However, where the individual leaves the Member State and seeks to return as self-employed, the fresh application must be considered on its merits and irrespective of any previous period of illegal residence in the Member State (see chapter 8).[44] The widening of the legal content of the term illegal migration only has the effect of pushing more people into that category. The narrowing of the category has the opposite effect. Emphasising a large scope for the concept of illegal migrant is de-stabilising for legal migrants who fear they may suddenly find themselves re-categorised as illegal. Promoting and encouraging expulsion of individuals as illegal migrants is humiliating for the citizens and their home states. These are not policies which lead to stability and security in any region.

---

42 This is also apparent in the proposal by the UK Government in May 2002 to move asylum seekers from the UK to camps in countries neighbouring the EU for processing of their asylum claims.
43 C-63/99 *Gloszczuk* [2001] ECR I-6369.
44 C-257/99 *Barkoci & Malik* [2001] ECR I-6557.

Migration Beyond the Neighbourhood in EU Trade Policy

The Commission's wide perspective on the benefits of movement of persons as a means of creating good relations with neighbouring countries, improving trade and cultural exchanges and enhancing security in a wider sense is central to the EU's position in international commercial affairs. The World Trade Organisation Agreement is made up of a series of agreements one of which is the General Agreement on Trade in Services (GATS). In 2000, the Doha Round of negotiations on GATS began with the objective of progressive liberalisation of trade in services. Within GATS it has been accepted that movement of persons is necessary to a substantial number of provisions and receipts of services. Thus movement of persons is an important aspect of the new negotiations. Liberalisation of rules on movement of persons as service providers has been an important objective of GATS and the Doha round. The European Commission, negotiating for the EU has consulted widely with the business world and civil society on the proposals which the EU should put on the table. The latest offer of the EU to the negotiations[45] specifically targets the interests of developing countries for access of their nationals to the EU for service provision. Temporary entry of foreign nationals (which can extend over a number of years under the GATS rules – and in combination with national rules frequently leads to permanent residence) is made simpler, in particular to facilitate movement of personnel of companies overseas to the EU. Individuals as service suppliers providing or seeking to provide services in the EU are included.

Conclusions

The theory and practice of the EU internal market regarding the importance of the movement of persons for economic purposes finds expression in many central fields of EU policy but is subject to resistance from JHA ministries. In the development of a stability and security policy for the EU with its neighbours the objective of free movement of persons is one of the four central planks. The policy of the EU in negotiations on liberalisation of trade in services with the rest of the world is to decrease restrictions on movement of persons for economic purposes related to service provision. In both cases, the driving force is the European Commission, promoting a vision of expanding transnational governance directed by a core, the EU in the form of institutions with Member State participation, over the neighbourhood which will

---

45 Brussels 29 April 2003 *WTO Services – EU proposes to improve trading opportunities giving developing countries a better deal.*

accept this form of governance without representation if enough incentives through internal market access are provided.

The approach of the JHA ministries in immigration negotiations at the EU level contrasts with that in other more EU-central policy fields. The JHA Council, which is limited to strictly immigration and asylum competences, emphases harder border controls to hamper the movement of persons from outside the Union. Even where the Commission proposes legislation which would enhance the position of third country nationals lawfully in the Union, the negotiations in the Council result in a lowering of standards which is then justified on the ground that these are just minimum standards thus maintaining the space for higher standards at the national level (see chapters 5 and 12). The fields in which the JHA Council is able to reach agreement are those which risk increasing the incidence of illegality among third country nationals in the Union by widening the category and limiting the protections. Thus the form is much more intergovernmental where the results of negotiations can be sold at home as national measures or requirements of the EU depending on the choices regarding national political concerns which JHA ministries make. This corresponds to an intergovernmental approach to rule making.

The JHA Council's insistence on expulsion and readmission agreements has knock-on effects on policy fields dominated by an integrationalist vision of the EU. In the neighbourhood policy it undermines objectives of expanding integration by indicating to surrounding countries that they are not really part of the project. Instead, they are responsible for illegal immigration, rather than on the way to free movement of persons. It is only with some neighbours, such as Russia, Morocco and Ukraine, that the JHA Council is demanding readmission agreements to simplify expulsion of their nationals (and others) from the EU. Other neighbours, such as Norway or Switzerland, are offered free movement of persons instead so that their nationals will not become illegally present in the Union.

The struggle in respect of competing theoretical principles at work in the EU is demonstrated with substantial clarity in the field of persons. Persons are part of a policy of stability, security and economic development in the form of widening integration in some areas of EU policy-making where the main actors are EU institutions and ministries other than JHA at the national level. In policy fields which are still struggling with a legacy of strong intergovernmental approaches, such as JHA, the incoherence is problematic. The alignment of the development of the area of freedom, security and justice with the wider objectives of the Union is already clearly moving towards the integrationist principle. Persons, instead of being seen as a threat, are acknowledged as the means by which prosperity and security can be achieved not only in the region but beyond and they must be treated accordingly.

Thus Sandholz and Stone Sweet are both right and wrong at the same time. They are right in that a number of the EU initiatives are designed to promote transnational society. But they are wrong in so far as other parts of the institutions are pulling in the opposite direction. By failing to disaggregate the institutions by their structural and functional purposes, Sandholz and Stone Sweet reach a general conclusion which can only be partially justified. Just as at the national level the interests of different ministries must be disaggregated to understand policy development so too at the supranational level the different mechanisms which regulate the construction of interests within the institutions must be taken into account.

Chapter 11

Racial Discrimination and EU Identity

'The Idea of Europe' has a long and dubious history. Mikkeli characterises it as an identity which is structured around the difference of the other, be it skin colour, religion, culture or whatever.[1] Picking up the same differentiation, Amin states starkly: "non-white residents and citizens of the European Union (EU) have no role to play in the 'Idea of Europe', which remains an ideal of unity drawing on a Christian-Enlightenment heritage to bridge the diversity of European national cultures."[2] In the EC Treaty as originally drafted, discrimination was only prohibited on two grounds. First nationality discrimination is unlawful, the prohibition applying equally to natural persons, tins of beans and television programmes.[3] But nationality discrimination only applies to nationality of the Member States and within the scope of the Treaty. Thus it only prohibits differential treatment attendant on a right to free movement, for instance, between a Belgian and a German in Germany not the differential and disadvantageous treatment of a Nigerian and a Belgian in Belgium.[4] The second prohibited form of discrimination is on the basis of sex in pay and working conditions (now much expanded by the Amsterdam Treaty amendments).[5]

Thus the Idea of Europe which found expression in the EC Treaty as an equality right is one which acknowledged only discrimination against women at work and nationality discrimination of a very limited kind as its business. Amin's claim that the Idea is one of a white, Christian Europe is supported by the treaty provisions as originally enacted as it is only these two forms of discrimination which are relevant.

---

1 H Mikkeli, *Europe as an Idea and Identity*, Macmillan, London, 1998.
2 A Amin, 'Immigrants, Cosmopolitans and the Idea of Europe' in H Wallace, *Interlocking Dimensions of European Integration*, Palgrave, Basingstoke, 2001, pp 280–301.
3 The key provision is article 12 EC/article 4(2) EU Constitution which finds specific expression in many other provisions of the EC Treaty.
4 C-230/97 *Awoyemi* [1998] ECR I-6781.
5 Article 141 EC/Article III-181(1) EU Constitution.

Diversity beyond national cultures of the Member States would take the thinking of the EU outside the scope of the Idea.

The architects of the Council of Europe, on the other hand had a rather different vision of the Europe they were seeking to achieve. Instead of economic integration, the main principle of the EU, their concern was human rights which they set out in the European Convention on Human Rights. For them the idea of prohibited discrimination covered a wide range of issues leaving aside that of nationality.[6] The Idea of Europe for the ECHR is complementary to that of the EU but quite separate in scope.

Nationality discrimination is at the heart of immigration control. Treating persons differently on the basis of their nationality is what immigration control is all about. Own nationals are permitted to enter the state as of right; nationals of other EU states have wide rights of entry, residence and protection from expulsion; nationals of third countries are subject to a variety of different regimes sanctioned at various levels of EU law. As regards citizens of the Union the ECJ has clarified that notwithstanding the citizenship provisions of EU law, it "permits Member States to adopt, with respect to nationals of other Member States, and in particular on the grounds of public policy, measures which they cannot apply to their own nationals, inasmuch as they have no authority to expel the latter from the territory or to deny them access thereto"[7] (see chapter 5).

As regards third country nationals, EU recognises substantial differences of treatment on the basis of nationality, for example, the requirement to obtain a short stay visa or not.[8] Thus US nationals are not required to obtain a short stay visa to come to any EU Member State while nationals of any African country will require a visa. Because this kind of nationality discrimination is not expressly prohibited by the Treaty, there is no need to justify it. Similarly, there is no obligation to have clear and precise criteria on the basis of which decisions must be made as regards the visa list as there is no legal sanction for arbitrary decision-making. The addition or removal of a country from the visa list is not necessarily accompanied by any substantive explanation as to why the change is being made. The result is sometimes surprising. After the 11 September 2001 terrorist attacks in the USA, the Council requested the Commission review the visa list as regards terrorist security concerns. This request was reinforced both at the Laeken and Seville Council meetings respectively in December 2001 and June 2002. When the review was completed, the Commission proposed the addition of Ecuador to the obligatory visa list. No substantive explanation was given for the action, notwithstanding substantial public

---

6 Article 14 ECHR: "The enjoyment of the rights and freedoms set forth in this Convention shall be secured without discrimination on any ground such as sex, race, colour, language, religion, political or other opinion, national or social origin, association with a national minority, property, birth or other status."

7 C-348/96 *Calfa* [1999] ECR I-11.

8 Regulation 539/2001.

outcry in Spain and Latin America. Thus the central question, how if at all, the addition of Ecuador to the visa list related to the objective of security was not specified or clarified.[9]

The degree to which immigration control as a form of permissible nationality discrimination may also be a form of prohibited racial discrimination is a highly contested issue. I shall look at some of the approaches to this question in this chapter. It is not considered polite to suggest that immigration laws discriminate on the basis of race. However, it is quite unavoidable. As the UK Home Secretary discovered on the entry into force of the Human Rights Act 1998, to continue to operate immigration controls as he wished he had to give himself the power to derogate from article 14 ECHR. He provided himself with a licence to discriminate including on the basis of race and issued a series of such licences in respect of different aspects of immigration controls.[10] So far the UK courts have been rather tame in accepting the validity and discriminatory effect of the Home Secretary's authorisations to himself to discriminate on the basis of race.[11] The legal venue where discrimination on the basis of nationality between and among nationals of third countries is most marked and accessible is in respect of visa requirements. It is at this junction of law and international relations that the justification of discrimination is particularly vulnerable. If one takes as an example the EU short stay mandatory visa list and expresses it as a map the effect is striking.[12] Every country in Africa and the Middle East is on the black list with the exception of Israel. Most of Asia is on the black list while North America and Australia are on the white list. The map of the countries whose nationals are required to have a short stay visa before coming to the EU indicates race and religion as unmistakeably central common characteristics. This does not prevent expressions of outrage from officials at every level and in every Member State when this reality of the Emperor's new clothes is noted.

Race, Citizenship and Migration

The international treaty negotiations on race and discrimination have had to deal with a number of essentially problematic issues. The first is the definition of race, how can the legislator define the impermissible practices without falling into the trap of inherent racial difference. In seeking to challenge and condemn doctrines of racial superiority as for example in the International Convention on the Elimination of all Forms of Racial Discrimination (ICERD), the use of the term and concept of race is

---

9 Regulation 453/2003, OJ 2003 L 69/10.
10 S19D Race Relations Act 1976 and the Authorisations made under it.
11 *R v Secretary of State for the Home Department ex p Tamil Information Centre*, QBD 18 October 2002.
12 D Bigo and E Guild 'Controller à distance et tenir à l'écart: le Visa Schengen' Cultures et Conflits, l'Harmattan, Paris, 2002 (4).

omnipresent.[13] Secondly, among the justified distinctions of ICERD are distinctions made between citizens and non-citizens.[14] Article 1(3) states "Due regard must also be given to state sovereignty in matters of citizenship, nationality, and naturalisation." Thus when discrimination against groups of persons is expressed in law in the form of citizenship, international human rights law steps back and permits the state a wide margin of appreciation.[15] For those states which take seriously their human rights obligations, if they want to discriminate lawfully against a group of persons, the differentiation between citizen and foreigner is crucial. Only under this heading will discrimination be permissible for instance in access to employment, secure residence status, limitations on movement, entitlement to social benefits. This is then the area in which states guard carefully their right to manoeuvre – in human rights legislation the exception of citizenship and the treatment of foreigners is universal.

One of the challenges of the international human rights treaty system in respect of racial discrimination rests here. The perception of international treaties prohibiting race discrimination as foreign policy instruments rather than measures for domestic implementation has plagued the application of ICERD.[16] Among the groups which suffer great discrimination but are least protected *inter alia* because they fail to see themselves as an identity group are immigrants, asylum seekers and refugees. As Van Boven eloquently expressed the problem: "Similarly immigrants, refugees, and asylum seekers – as temporary or permanent residents – encounter hostile sentiments and practices of racism, xenophobia, and intolerance. Some national and local communities have made better efforts than other communities, but the fact remains that virtually no society or community can rightfully claim to be free from racism and racial discrimination in dealing with newcomers from different cultures, religions, and lands ... The situation of undocumented migrants, the *sans papiers*, is even more dramatic. They usually belong to ethnic groups different from the 'host' community and they are excluded and discriminated against not only because of their undocumented status but also because of their ethnicity. And so they are called 'illegal aliens' they are often denied their fundamental human rights and freedoms, including access to education and basic health and social services."[17]

Fredman notes "migrant workers, refugees and asylum seekers are the subjects of not just exploitation, but also of racial hatred, denial of fundamental human rights, and exclusion due to their ethnicity from education, health, and other services."[18] For this reason, Chalmers' observation that "in the institutional history of the EC,

---

13 M Banton, *International Action Against Racial Discrimination*, Clarendon, Cambridge, 1996 p 52.

14 Article 1(2) ICERD.

15 K Boyle and A Baldaccini, 'International Human Rights Approaches to Racism' in S Fredman (ed), *Discrimination and Human Rights: The Case of Racism*, OUP, Oxford 2001 pp 135–191.

16 M Banton, *International Action Against Racial Discrimination*, Clarendon, Cambridge 1996.

17 T Van Boven 'Discrimination and Human Rights Law' in S Fredman (ed), *Discrimination and Human Rights: The Case of Racism*, OUP, Oxford 2001 pp 120–121.

18 S Fredman (ed), *Discrimination and Human Rights: The Case of Racism*, OUP, Oxford 2001 p 4.

it is probably correct to see Article 13 EC emerging as a concrete manifestation of the more general prohibition on non-discrimination"[19] is so surprising. In EU law, discrimination was only prohibited on two grounds – nationality and sex (in working conditions). As noted above, the individual and the tin of beans are similarly protected against discrimination on the basis of nationality. This means "rather bizarrely, the principle of safeguarding women's maternity rights were in some way taken to be comparable to those prohibiting certain forms of national labelling."[20] There is nothing normal or natural about this development. The strenuous efforts of EU Member States to separate the field of nationality discrimination from that of racial discrimination makes it rather extraordinary that the development of EU law in the field can be interpreted as coming from the same source. The treatment of discrimination in the commercial field of the EU, as in Chalmers example of national labelling, is categorised as based on nationality and prohibited. But it is only rarely related to or combined with any discussion of discrimination on the basis of nationality as a human rights challenge.

In the field of human rights, nationality discrimination has until recently been permitted, whilst only other less easily identifiable forms of discrimination are prohibited.[21] The hermetically sealed containers of nationality and race were challenged by the ECtHR in 1996 when it found that article 14 ECHR also prohibits discrimination on the basis of nationality. The Austrian social benefits legislation limited to Austrian nationals is a benefit which continues to provide support to an individual after the exhaustion of a contributory unemployment benefit. A Turkish national, Mr Gaygusuz, who had been resident in Austria for many years and had a stable residence status, became unemployed. He came to the end of the period of benefits to which he was entitled under his contributions to the system and he applied for the continuation benefit. This was refused on the basis of his nationality. The ECtHR considered his claim that there had been a breach of article 1 Protocol 1 (the enjoyment of property) and article 14 discrimination.

First, the ECtHR found that the benefit comes within the meaning of property in the Protocol, (a result not widely welcomed by EU social security funds but a logical result of its jurisprudence on property rights).[22] More surprisingly the ECtHR

---

19 D Chalmers, 'The Mistakes of the Good European' in S Fredman (ed), *Discrimination and Human Rights: The Case of Racism*, OUP, Oxford 2001 pp 202–203.

20 Ibid p 203.

21 The discussion of multiculturalism as a form of "self referential racism" is most interestingly developed by S Žižek, *The Ticklish Subject: The Absent Centre of Political Ontology*, Verso, London, 2000.

22 "Entitlement to this social benefit is therefore linked to the payment of contributions to the unemployment insurance fund, which is a precondition for the payment of unemployment benefit … The Court considers that the right to emergency assistance – in so far as provided for in the applicable legislation – is a pecuniary right for the purposes of Article 1 of protocol 1. The provision is therefore applicable without it being necessary to rely solely on the link between entitlement to emergency assistance and the obligation to pay 'taxes or other contributions' " *Gaygusuz v Austria* [1996] Reports 1996-IV para 39 and 41.

developed substantially its jurisprudence on article 14. The grounds of prohibited discrimination in article 14 are ambiguous. There are twelve specified grounds: sex, race, colour, language, religion, political or other opinion, national or social origin, association with a national minority, property, birth – but then at the very end of the list is added "other status". It is unlikely that the drafters of the ECHR intended this to cover also nationality or citizenship as a ground, not least because that ground is so assiduously avoided in the human rights field of prohibited discrimination. However, the ECtHR found that "other status" as a prohibited ground had to be given a wide interpretation. Thus "according to the court's case-law, a difference of treatment is discriminatory, for the purposes of Article 14, if it has 'no objective and reasonable justification', that is if it does not pursue a 'legitimate aim' or if there is not a 'reasonable relationship of proportionality between the means employed and the aim sought to be realised'. Moreover the Contracting States enjoy a certain margin of appreciation in assessing whether and to what extent differences in otherwise similar situations justify a different treatment. However, very weighty reasons would have to be put forward before the Court could regard a difference of treatment based exclusively on the ground of nationality as compatible with the Convention."[23]

This finding of the ECtHR may be the opening shot of a new effort to restrain the use by member States of citizenship as a justified criteria on which to exclude third country nationals from benefits and to subject them to discriminatory practices which, if based, for instance, on race or ethnic origin, would be prohibited both at national and international level.[24] Certainly the judgment, which was handed down during the intergovernmental conference which led to the Amsterdam Treaty and the insertion of a provision on race discrimination into the EC Treaty, extended the definition of prohibited discrimination through the interpretation of the concept of other status. This option would not be included in the wording of the EC prohibition.

The EU's Charter on Fundamental Freedoms adopted in 2000 and inserted into the EU constitution in 2004, however, re-introduces the possibility of widening the meaning of discrimination. Article II-81 has the unhappy task of trying to incorporate into one provision both the prohibition of racial discrimination and that of nationality discrimination. The result is not necessarily mutually exclusive: "(1) Any discrimination based on any ground such as sex, race, colour, ethnic or social origin, genetic features, language, religion or belief, political or any other opinion, membership of a national minority, property, birth disability, age or sexual orientation shall be prohibited. (2) Within the scope of application of the Treaty establishing the European Community and of the Treaty on European Union, and without prejudice to the special provisions of those Treaties, any discrimination on grounds of

---

23 *Gaygusüz v Austria* [1996] Reports 1996-IV para 42.
24 The UK government has expressly recognised this by providing itself with and using a power to discriminate on the basis of race in the effecting of immigration controls (see footnote 10 supra). The ECtHR has confirmed its interpretation of article 14 in *Koua Poirrez v France* ECtHR 28 September 2003.

nationality shall be prohibited." The argument in favour of exclusivity is that article 81(1) provides the general prohibition and 81(2) the specific one on nationality. The principle of *lex specialis* excludes 81(1) applying to situations envisaged in 81(2). However, the ambiguity of the provision and the lack of drafting consistency between the two parts raises doubts about this interpretation.

Engaging with Race Discrimination: Creating an EU Power

Until 1999, EU law expressed rather well, if inadvertently, the Idea of Europe as white and Christian. In the traditional thinking of the Union as an economic venue, the Member States had not perceived any need to include provisions prohibiting discrimination on the basis of race as this was not the objective of the EU. Race discrimination was a human rights issue and the venue for such a consideration was the Council of Europe. A perspective of the EU as a club with a very specific perspective on its membership and duties began to be challenged in the early 1990s. The history of the discussions and the treatment of fields of discrimination have been admirably described and analysed by Bell.[25] I shall focus on only a small number of issues which I consider significant to understanding identity in the European Union. The first is that the EU institutions, in particular the Council, rejected the premise that the Community had competence to adopt any legislation in respect of racial discrimination. The only solution, according to that institution, was to amend the EC Treaty to provide a competence for this. Thus in the 1996 intergovernmental conference, a provision was duly inserted providing the EU with such a competence.[26]

It is worth pausing a moment, however, at the insistence of the Council that the EC did not have a competence in this field. In effect what the Council was reinforcing was that the EU is the embodiment of the Idea of Europe. As a white, Christian club it is not the business of the Union if Black or Muslim citizens of the Union suffer discrimination because they do not fit the Idea. Even an acknowledgement of competence along the same design as that in article 14 ECHR, strictly limited to a breach of substantive rights in the treaties, was rejected. Thus even where a citizen of the Union from one Member State travelled to another Member State to receive services and was subject to, for example, racial abuse at the border, the Council considered this to be no responsibility of EU law. This was for national law or the ECHR. This lack of concern for race discrimination is somewhat surprising in light of the vigilance the EU exercises in respect of nationality discrimination. For instance, the ECJ found a breach of the right to provide services without discrimination on the basis of nationality among Member State nationals in the case of one

---

25 M Bell, *Anti-Discrimination Law and the European Union*, OUP, Oxford, 2002.
26 For the history of the struggle in particular between the European Parliament and the Council see M Bell, *Anti-Discrimination Law and the European Union*, OUP, Oxford, 2002 pp 54–63.

Member State's insistence on a certain spelling of the name of a national of another Member State.[27]

The suggestion which has been made by more than one academic that the inclusion in the Amsterdam Treaty of a power to take measures against racial discrimination indicates an acceptance of social Europe is disputable.[28] However, Bell notes that there was very little resistance in the Council for the amendment of the EC treaty to include the power.[29] The sheer unacceptability of the EU's position and the significance of a lack of power to act in the field are overwhelming. The ethics which are embedded in the political practices at the EU level do, occasionally, find legal expression.[30] The substantial investment which the Member States have made in anti-discrimination treaties and anti-racism programmes at the international level may have encouraged them to take a more positive position regarding inserting a competence in the EC Treaty in the field.[31]

The power which is inserted into the EC Treaty contains a number of interesting characteristics. First, it is without prejudice to other provisions of the treaty. Exactly what this means has been the subject of some speculation, not least by myself.[32] It would appear that these words in fact only restrict the application of the provision to the competences of the EC Treaty. Secondly, it provides only a power to adopt legislation without setting a deadline within which such legislation must be adopted. Finally, it sets out the grounds on which measures may be taken: sex (notwithstanding article 141 EC/article III-214 EU Constitution), racial or ethnic origin, religion or belief, disability, age or sexual orientation. These are a rather *sui generis* group of grounds which entail very different responses. For example, racial discrimination requires legislation which may provide at least some way of identifying the group to be protected; disability discrimination engages substantial financial consequences, for instance, access to public buildings for the disabled will require ramps; discrimination against persons on the basis of age raises a large number of questions about welfare state benefits and access to them. Sexual orientation discrimination requires not only robust legislative action in contested fields of social law but also a reconsideration of the correct comparator for the purpose of identifying discrimination (as opposed to lawful distinction) as Wintemute and Andenas

---

27 C-168/91 *Konstantinidis* [1993] ECR I-1191.
28 See for instance C Barnard, 'Article 13: Through the Looking Glass of Union Citizenship' in D O'Keeffe and P Twomey (eds), *Legal Issues of the Amsterdam Treaty*, OUP, Oxford, 1999. J Shaw provides a more balanced approach noting the challenge of the area of freedom, security and justice as a way of excluding third country nationals 'The many pasts and futures of citizenship of the Union' ELRev (1997) 22: 554–564.
29 Bell ibid p 63.
30 M Frost, *Ethics in International Relations: A Constitutive Theory*, CUP, Cambridge, 1996.
31 S Fredman, 'Combating Racism with Human Rights: The Right to Equality' in S Fredman (ed), *Discrimination and Human Rights*, OUP, Oxford, 2001 pp 9–44.
32 E Guild, 'Equality as an EC Right' in G Moon (ed), *Race Discrimination: Developing and Using a New Legal Framework*, Hart, Oxford, 2000 pp 65–80.

have clearly investigated.[33] Clearly, different types of approaches would be needed to deal with different grounds of discrimination which article 13 EC/article III-124(1) EU Constitution requires the institutions to take appropriate action to combat.

The mechanism adopted by the Commission was to divide the grounds of discrimination into two groups, racial and ethnic origin on the one hand and all the others on the other and to propose two different directives with somewhat different scope.[34] The highest priority was placed on moving forward on race discrimination, the adoption of legislation in respect of other grounds in article 13/article III-124(1) EU Constitution was considered less critical. As my interest is in the consequences for migration and both directives treat the subject in the same way, I shall only consider the first in detail.

Implementing the EU Non-Discrimination Power

The first directive adopted implements the principle of equal treatment between persons irrespective of racial or ethnic origin.[35] It was adopted at the end of June 2000, not least as a result of the success in Austria of J Haider's Freedom Party, considered far right. The strong reaction of the EU institutions towards the coalition government in Austria which included Mr Haider led also to a momentum for the adoption of the directive. Tyson, who participated in the negotiations on the part of the Commission, has provided an excellent discussion of the negotiating history of the directive and the rationale for the form various provisions have taken.[36] That the directive is extremely wide is not in doubt. Indeed, Chalmers considers it "the most wide-sweeping equal opportunities legislation in the Community's history".[37] However, the issue which interests me is the intersection of race discrimination and nationality, the one prohibited, the other permitted and developed into the acceptable face of discrimination on the basis of difference. In this field the directive reinforces the suspicion that the EU remains grounded in the Idea of Europe which hides its unacceptable practices of exclusion in the category of (permissible) nationality discrimination.

The Commission's original proposal for a directive expressly stated in the recitals that it was not intended to prevent differences of treatment based on nationality.[38]

---

33 R Wintemute & M Andenas, *Legal Recognition of Same Sex Partnerships: A Study of National, European and International Law*, Hart, Oxford, 2001.
34 See M Bell ibid, chapters 3 and 4 on the two directives and the differences between them.
35 2000/43 OJ 2000 L 180/22.
36 A Tyson 'The Negotiation of the European Community Directive on Racial Discrimination' EJML Vol 3 No 2 2001 pp 199–229.
37 D Chalmers, 'The Mistakes of the Good European' in S Fredman (ed), *Discrimination and Human Rights: The Case of Racism*, OUP, Oxford 2001 p 193.
38 A Tyson, 'The Negotiation of the European Community Directive on Racial Discrimination' EJML Vol 3 No 2 2001 pp 199–229.

Member States were reassured about the exclusion of nationality discrimination not only by the limitation of article 12 EC/article III-123 EU Constitution to Member State nationals but also by the omission of nationality as a prohibited ground of discrimination in article 13 EC/article III-124 EU Constitution. According to Tyson, one of the main reasons for which the Member States were keen to protect their power to discriminate on the basis of nationality against third country nationals was in order to maintain differences in treatment of immigrants in their social protection systems.[39] This links the directive's exclusion very closely with the ECtHR's judgment in *Gaygusuz* (supra). A further ground, according to Tyson, was that some Member States felt that it was not sufficient to preserve certain aspects of their systems, in particular, those dealing with immigration and asylum. Those countries argued, for example, that it was an essential part of the asylum system to draw differences based on ethnic origin where asylum seekers were persecuted in their country of origin precisely on the basis of their ethnic origin. The Commission apparently assured these Member States that in any event admission policies were outside the scope of the directive.

The Member States sought a belt and braces approach to ensuring that nationality discrimination could not creep back into the scope of the directive. Accompanied by a reinforced recital: article 3(2) was inserted stating: "This directive does not cover differences of treatment based on nationality and is without prejudice to provisions and conditions relating to the entry into and residence of third country nationals and stateless persons on the territory of Member States, and to any treatment which arises from the legal status of the third-country nationals and stateless persons concerned."[40] The same provision was repeated in the second directive which covers the other prohibited grounds in article 13/article III-124 EU Constitution.

Once the issue of third country nationals has been dealt with, the EU is able to be generous in the scope, fields of application and remedies in the directive. As regards the scope, it covers all aspects of employment, including professional hierarchy, pay etc; vocational training and guidance; participation in workers and employers associations;[41] social protection (including social security and healthcare); social advantages; education; and access to and supply of goods and services. Positive action is safeguarded in article 5 and the burden of proof for the victim is relaxed somewhat in article 8. Victimisation is also prohibited and bodies to promote

---

39 Ibid pp 199–229.
40 The recital which was added states: "This prohibition of discrimination should also apply to nationals of third countries, but does not cover differences of treatment based on nationality and is without prejudice to provisions governing the entry and residence of third country nationals and their access to employment and to occupation."
41 But see for instance the ECJ decisions in C-171/01 *Zajedno/Birlikte* [2003] ECR 08/05/2003 (not yet reported) where the Turkish workers were excluded from election to the works council in Austria not, of course, because of their ethnic origin, but because of their nationality; chapter 8 supra.

equal treatment must be established to assist in monitoring and assisting individuals. Member States were required to implement the directive by 19 July 2003.

Engaging with Race Discrimination: Protocol 12 ECHR

Two days before the EC Council adopted directive 2000/43, the Council of Europe's Committee of Ministers adopted the text of Protocol 12 ECHR establishing a free-standing non-discrimination right. The result of long discussions within the Council of Europe, the protocol seeks to remedy one of the main criticisms of article 14 ECHR that its application is dependent on a breach of a substantive ECHR right, by creating a right to non-discrimination on the specified grounds applicable to all law. As Mr Gaygusuz found, in order to complain of discrimination contrary to the ECHR, he had not only to be treated differently in law from nationals of the states but also to be treated differently in such a way as to bring into question another substantive right contained in the ECHR. In his case a wide interpretation of the right to property meant that his claim to discrimination was upheld because the social benefit was classified as a property right. However, had his claim been in relation to, for example, a benefit which could not be classified as an ECHR right, discrimination on the grounds set out in the article 14 ECHR list might be occurring, but the ECtHR would be unable to consider the matter as a substantive right under ECHR.

In order to remedy this shortcoming of the ECHR, the Council of Europe adopted the protocol which provides for a wide non-discrimination provision which does not depend on any other provision of the ECHR being breached. "Article 1 – General prohibition of discrimination: (1) The enjoyment of any right set forth by law shall be secured without discrimination on any ground such as sex, race, colour, language, religion, political or other opinion, national or social origin, association with a national minority, property, birth or other status. (2) No one shall be discriminated against by any public authority on any ground such as those mentioned in paragraph 1." This is the only substantive provision of the protocol which then goes on to specify the nuts and bolts of application and operation.

The first observation to make about the protocol is that the scope of the non-discrimination prohibition is the same as in article 14 notwithstanding the wide interpretation given to the latter by the ECtHR. Thus clearly the protocol is building on article 14 and its jurisprudence, not seeking to limit the definition of what is prohibited discrimination while widening the field within which the prohibition operates. The protocol accepts the ECtHR's 1996 jurisprudence and indeed extends its application. The second observation is that the prohibition on discrimination is only freestanding in so far as it no longer depends on an ECHR right being in question. However, it remains embedded in the field of law. Instead of the relevant law in which it is attached being an international human rights convention, it is national law. Thus the width (or narrowness) of national law determines also the scope of the discrimination prohibition. Activities which come within the scope of the prohibition in one country will not necessarily do so in another if those activities are not regulated by law in the second. Van Boven points out the risks which current trends in thinking about the role of the state present for the prohibition on discrimination: "Privatisation goes even so far as to cover areas which traditionally belonged to the public domain, such as the running of prison institutions, upholding public order and security, law enforcement, and even national defence. The Welfare State is in the process of being dismantled. Health care, education, housing and employment – areas of crucial importance to the racially marginalised and disadvantaged – are increasingly withdrawn from the public domain and transferred to private institutions and corporations which operate for financial gain and economic profit."[42] If the state diminishes its responsibility for what have been core activities the scope of the protocol is also potentially limited. If a field is not (or no longer) regulated by law then it falls outside the scope of the protocol.

The core of Van Boven's concerns are the consequences of the transformation of the state on the state's duties in international human rights law. The controversial moves by the ECtHR to find states liable for failure to control the private sector or to provide a regulatory regime within which the state obligations find expression in the private sector are one part of the answer to these concerns.[43] Unlike the EU law provision, the protocol applies only to public authorities. Direct horizontal effect so as to cover the activities of private parties among themselves has not been a characteristic of ECHR rights though there is much discussion on this point.

A third observation takes me back to the central issue of this chapter – the relationship between discrimination on the basis of race and immigration. The protocol does not deal with this question directly (unlike the directive). Instead in the explanatory memorandum of the Council of Europe it states: "Since not every distinction or difference of treatment amounts to discrimination, and because of the general character of the principle of non-discrimination, it was not considered necessary or appropriate to include a restriction clause in the present Protocol. For example, the law of most if not all member States of the Council of Europe provides for certain distinctions based on nationality concerning certain rights or entitlements to benefits. The situations where such distinctions are acceptable are sufficiently safeguarded by the very meaning of the notion "discrimination" ... since distinctions for which an objective and reasonable justification exists do not constitute discrimination. In addition, it should be recalled that under the case-law of the European Court of Human Rights a certain margin of appreciation is allowed to national authorities in assessing whether and to what extent differences in otherwise similar situations justify a different treatment in law. The scope of the margin of appreciation will vary

---

42 T Van Boven, 'Discrimination and Human Rights Law' in S Fredman (ed), *Discrimination and Human Rights: The Case of Racism*, OUP, Oxford 2001 pp 122–123.

43 A full discussion of this jurisprudence is beyond the scope of this book. See C Ovey & R White, *Jacobs & White: The European Convention on Human Rights*, 3rd Ed, OUP, Oxford, 2002.

according to the circumstances, the subject-matter and its background ..." This is an extremely delicate way for the Council of Europe to reassure the member States that their laws on immigration and asylum will normally be outside the scope of the protocol. In effect by doing so the ECHR accepted that differential and disadvantageous treatment between couples where both are citizens of the state and those where one party is not a citizen is not prohibited discrimination.

The explanatory memorandum makes specific reference to the ECtHR judgment in *ACB*[44] where the ECtHR was confronted with discriminatory treatment in family reunification for men and women in the UK. The ECtHR found a breach of article 14 in conjunction with article 8 only as regards sex discrimination in that men and women were treated differently under national law. The state's justifications as regards delaying or preventing family immigration on grounds of public policy were accepted by the ECtHR. The Parliamentary Assembly of the Council of Europe did not mention the vexing issue of immigration and asylum at all in its report on the protocol.[45] It is worth noting though, that the explanatory memorandum carefully placed the difference between prohibited discrimination and permitted distinction in the arena of objective and reasonable justification. It is exactly this issue of justification which is lacking at the EU level in discrimination on the basis of third country nationality. In the example of the addition of Ecuador to the obligatory visa list, it is exactly this lack of clear and precise criteria for subjecting a country's nationals to the visa obligation and the concomitant lack of objective and reasonable justification which characterise the process as arbitrary.

State reaction to the protocol has been widely positive. Twenty-eight member States of the Council of Europe have signed the protocol. Among the pre-May 2004 EU Member States, only five had failed to sign it by June 2003 (Denmark, France, Spain, Sweden and the UK). Among the acceding Member States only three of the ten had not yet signed up (Lithuania, Malta and Poland). As regards ratification, only Cyprus had done so by June 2003. In a period of approximately three years this is not a bad record for a protocol. However, what remains evident is that there is only a wide consensus to work towards the reduction or elimination of racial discrimination where this does not engage the issue of the treatment of third country nationals.

Conclusions

There has been an impressive amount of legislative activity in the field of discrimination on prohibited grounds including race and ethnic origin in Europe at the turn of the millennium. Both at the EU and Council of Europe levels there have been

---

44   *Abdulaziz, Cabales and Balkandali v. UK* ECtHR 28 May 1985.
45   Doc. 8614, 14 January 2000, Report Committee on Legal Affairs and Human Rights, Parliamentary Assembly, Council of Europe.

serious efforts to enhance the protection of individuals against unjustified discrimination. The good faith of the individuals and states which have been central to this push cannot be doubted. The creation of new legal rights is at the core of the issue. However, what has been less apparent has been a willingness of EU Member States to give up their practices of arbitrary decision making which, justified on the basis of immigration and asylum laws, in effect discriminate on the basis of race, ethnic origin or religion hiding behind the justification of nationality. As the Council of Europe indicated in its memorandum on the new protocol against discrimination, only objective and reasonable justification can turn apparently prohibited discrimination into permitted distinction. In the field of EU immigration and asylum measures, objective and reasonable justification for distinctions are thin on the ground.

For the EU, Member State transposition of the new anti-discrimination legislation must have been completed by July 2003. It is now up to the Member States to implement it and the courts to give effect to the spirit and letter of the law. As the International Council on Human Rights Policy has stated: "Adequate laws, access to courts, a willingness to interpret the law broadly and effectively, and a determination on the part of the courts to enforce the law are all essential prerequisites for the eradication of racism".[46] The courts both at national and supranational level will be required to interpret the scope of the non-discrimination provisions. What is at stake cannot be underestimated in a Europe where extreme right-wing parties have fed on anti-immigrant, anti-asylum seeker discourse (too often promoted by governments in power), managing to increase their proportion of the popular vote in too many countries. The relationship between law and populism must be clearly delineated. The rule of law, particularly in the form of protection of minorities and enforcement of non-discrimination, is the institutional counterweight to inappropriate state behaviour. However, that law must not accept as a field of exceptionalism beyond its reach discrimination which has as an essential element differential treatment on grounds race or religion merely because it has been formally categorised as nationality discrimination. Attempts by Member States to legitimise race discrimination in migration and asylum law and remove the field from judicial supervision can only be detrimental to social cohesion both in the short and long term.

---

46 International Council on Human Rights Policy, *The Persistence and Mutation of Racism*, 2000.

Chapter 12

Integration and Identity: Long-Resident Third Country Nationals

In the previous chapter I considered the meaning of prohibiting race discrimination in the context of the development of an EU identity. In the adoption of wide measures making racial discrimination illegal throughout the Union, the field which was carefully excluded was immigration and asylum. Discrimination on grounds of race and ethnic origin are permitted in EU law so long as they take place in the legal arena of provisions and conditions relating to "the entry into and residence of third country nationals and stateless persons on the territory of Member States and to any treatment which arises from the legal status of the third country nationals and stateless persons concerned."

The relationship between race discrimination and the protection of third country nationals has been both explicit and implicit. It is explicit because the history of 'the idea of Europe' has ethnic and religious affiliations as discussed in the previous chapter. However, as generation after generation of migrants acquire citizenship in the Member States the reality has changed. It is implicit in so far as the 'idea of the migrant' is racialised – the negative connotations of the term arise from the social construction of the migrant as ethnically and religiously 'different'. Migrants perceived as belonging to specific racial and religious groups are not categorized as such.[1] The Starting Line campaign of European non-governmental organisations which began in 1990, coordinated by the Churches Commission for Migrants in Europe and subsequently the Migrant Policy Group, began by demanding the adoption of EU legislation prohibiting race discrimination. It began a second campaign demanding free movement rights and security of work and residence for third country nationals legally resident in the Union.[2]

---

1 The most extreme example is that of Germany and the Aussiedler discussed in chapter 4.
2 I Chopin & J Niessen, *Proposal for Legislative Measures to Combat Racism and to Promote Equal Rights in the European Union*, Commission for Racial Equality, London 1998.

At the political and institutional level, however, extending free movement rights to legally resident third country nationals and creating a secure residence status for them met with substantially more resistance than the demands for legislation against discrimination on grounds of race, ethnicity and other prohibited grounds. The power to adopt legislation in both fields was introduced into the treaty in 1999. Legislation prohibiting race discrimination was rapidly adopted while its counterpart on the extension of movement, residence and work rights for legally resident third country nationals has progressed much more slowly, preceded by legislation facilitating the expulsion of third country nationals. These measures are the subject of this chapter.

Žižek provides a challenging point of departure to understanding the context in which the EU approaches third country nationals: "On today's market we find a whole series of products deprived of their malignant properties: coffee without caffeine, cream without fat, beer without alcohol . . . And the list goes on: what about virtual sex as sex without sex, the Colin Powell doctrine of warfare without casualties (on our side, of course), the contemporary redefinition of politics as the art of expert administration, that is, as politics without politics, up to today's tolerant liberal multiculturalism as an experience of the Other deprived of its Otherness (the idealized Other who dances fascinating dances and has an ecologically sound holistic approach to reality, while practices like wife beating remain out of sight)?"[3] Žižek is examining the meaning of what he describes as the twentieth century's passion for the Real. He explains how this passion is a fake passion "whose ruthless pursuit of the Real behind appearances was *the ultimate stratagem to avoid confronting the Real*".[4] This ruthless pursuit of the Real which must be perceived as nightmarish leads to a categorization of third country nationals within the Union as necessarily Other. The Real Other which they represent is by definition, then, nightmarish or at least potentially nightmarish.

How does the legal position of the Other become expressed in EU law when he or she is already present lawfully within the Union? I shall consider two ways in which the danger of Otherness is implicitly and explicitly reflected in EU legislation both relating to the central concerns of migrants – security of work, residence and protection from expulsion. In the first case, the adoption of a Directive on mutual recognition of expulsion decisions implicitly reinforces the dangerousness of the Other embodied in the migrant by refusing any common standard against which to assess that dangerousness. Thus national preoccupations with Otherness as danger are extended territorially to other Member States. The assessment by one Member State that an individual is a dangerous Other, though not necessarily or exclusively on the basis of criminal activity, is intended to result in that person being hunted down across the Member States and expelled. Secondly, the Directive on the status

---

3 S Žižek, *Welcome to the Desert of the Real*, Verso, London, 2002 pp 10–11.
4 S Žižek ibid p 24.

of third country nationals who are long-term residents reveals another aspect of the nightmare of Otherness. The Member States are permitted to apply an integration obligation to be tested at the national level to a third country national before acknowledging his or her status as an EU long-term resident. In Žižek's language what this means is that before the third country national can enjoy security of residence from EU law (and a right to move and engage in economic activities in other Member States) he or she must prove to the Member State that he or she is no longer the dangerous Other.

At the Tampere European Council meeting in October 1999, an inclusive approach to third country nationals resident in the Union was announced. Less than a year later, in August 2000, France proposed the measure on mutual recognition of expulsion decision. While the 11 September 2001 attacks in the USA were still unimaginable, the vision of foreigners who live among "us" in the EU was already framed by exclusion. Only in March 2001 did the European Commission table its proposal for a directive on the status of long-resident third country nationals in the Union.[5]

EU Law and Third Country Nationals

One of the first difficulties in trying to express the Other in law is just how complex the EU's relationship with third country nationals is. For example, there are the third country nationals who are not really considered to be Other at all but just slightly "failed" EU citizens. These are the nationals of Norway, Iceland, Liechtenstein and Switzerland. These are states where referenda for accession to the EU have been rejected by the population (or not held in the knowledge that they could not succeed). The EU entered into agreements with these states which provide nationals of the contracting parties almost identical rights of free movement, residence and economic activity as migrant nationals of the Member States. Then there are the third country nationals who must be treated in the same way as nationals of another Member State because of their relationship with such nationals. Family members of migrant Community nationals are one such group which I have discussed in depth in chapter 6. Another such group are third country national employees sent by their employer to carry out service provision in another Member State. These persons are covered by the right of the employer and are thus a separate category of Others. The third country agreements such as those with Turkey or the Central and Eastern European countries also create categories of third country nationals who cannot be treated as the undifferentiated Other. The agreements between their countries and the

---

5 Commission proposal for Directive on the status of long-term resident third-country nationals (COM (2001) 127, 13 March 2001).

EU provide for substantial rights of residence, economic integration and protection from expulsion (see chapter 8). The Other then, is defined in reverse. The persons who can be treated as the other are those who do not come within one of the other categories which enjoy higher protection.

Third Country Nationals and Expulsion

The power to adopt measures in respect of these Others is found in article 63(3) EC/article III-267(2) EU Constitution. The first measure adopted by the Council under this power was a directive on the mutual recognition of decisions on the expulsion of third country nationals in May 2001.[6] This directive was an initiative of France under the transitional provisions of the Amsterdam Treaty which permitted the Member States to introduce legislative proposals in Title IV during the first five years after entry into force. The proposal was published in the Official Journal in August 2000,[7] seven months before the Commission would make a proposal for a directive protecting the residence rights of long-resident third country nationals in the Union. The directive permits the recognition among the Member States of an expulsion decision against a third country national taken by any one of them subject to certain conditions which will be considered below. While the directive does not require a Member State other than the one which took the expulsion decision to effect the expulsion, it does provide for compensation of the Member State which chooses to do so (article 7). I shall return to this after examining the provisions of the Directive in a little more detail.

The rationale of the directive is worth considering before looking at the content. The preamble states that "the Council is to adopt measures on immigration policy within areas comprising conditions of entry and residence as well as illegal immigration and illegal residence." It then goes on to state "The Tampere European Council on 15 and 16 October 1999 reaffirmed its resolve to create an area of freedom, security and justice. For that purpose, a common European policy on asylum and migration should aim both at fair treatment of third country nationals and better management of migration flows." The reader might expect, at this point, a measure on the fair treatment of foreigners but the preamble continues "the need to ensure greater effectiveness in enforcing expulsion decisions and better cooperation between Member States entails mutual recognition of expulsion decisions." The relationship of the Treaty power, the Tampere Council conclusions and the measure is most unfortunately expressed.

---

6 Directive 2001/40 OL 2001 L 149/34.
7 OJ 2000 C 243/1.

Contrary to the protection of wide groups of third country nationals under other provisions of EC law, the directive only excludes one group of third country nationals from its ambit – family members of citizens of the Union who have exercised their free movement rights. This may cause substantial difficulties with the protection of a number of groups, not least Turkish workers in the Union. Their protection under the subsidiary legislation of the EC Turkey Association Agreement has been expressly interpreted by the ECJ as providing the same degree of protection from expulsion on grounds of public policy as is guaranteed to nationals of the Member States.[8] The directive is based on the principle of mutual recognition. An expulsion decision is defined as "any decision which orders an expulsion taken by a competent administrative authority of an issuing Member State." The types of expulsion decisions covered by the directive are those based on the state's assessment that the individual constitutes a serious and present threat to public order or to national security and safety (article 1(a)). It is worth noting that this definition of "a serious and present threat" is different from the concept in respect of expulsion of citizens of the Union where the words used are "public policy, public security and public health" as spelt out in Directive 64/221 and narrowly interpreted by the ECJ. There is thus potentially a wider definition of the grounds for expulsion of third country nationals than of citizens of the Union.

The definition is then given slightly more precision. First, cases involving the conviction of a third country national for an offence punishable by a penalty involving deprivation of liberty of at least one year are covered. This includes a very different group of offences depending on the Member State. Offences relating to prohibited drugs use is the most common example where the standard of punishment varies greatly. Thus a third country national could be the object of an assessment of threat in one Member State on the basis of possession of a small amount of cannabis which resulted in a conviction which could carry a penalty of one year's imprisonment though the individual was actually given a suspended sentence.

Secondly, the directive defines a serious and present threat to public order or to national security and safety for the purposes of mutual recognition of expulsion decisions as including a situation in which the authorities determine "the existence of serious grounds for believing that a third country national has committed serious criminal offences or the existence of solid evidence of his intention to commit such offences within the territory of a Member State." The difficulty of determining a common standard for the assessment of "serious grounds" or "solid evidence" are considerable. However, there is a more fundamental criticism of this ground. It removes the necessity of a court decision on criminal liability before an expulsion decision is recognized for the purpose of execution by the Member States. The state is no longer required to satisfy the standard of criminal procedural law necessary to

---

8   C-340/97 *Nazli* [2000] ECR I-957.

achieve a criminal conviction before the individual is subject to a penalty, which may be more punitive, depending on the circumstances, than imprisonment.

Finally, the directive permits the mutual recognition of expulsion decisions "based on failure to comply with national rules on the entry or residence of aliens." This is an extremely wide category of options. There are many situations where a Member State has the power to make an expulsion decision on the basis of failure to comply with national rules but does not. For example, where a foreigner is late in submitting his or her application for renewal of a residence permit, under national law of many Member States he or she is irregularly present and as a result eligible for expulsion. The period of residence between the expiry of the previous residence permit and the application for an extension may be classified in national law as a period of irregular residence capable of justifying an expulsion decision. However, in many cases the state authorities will proceed with the application without taking issue. Equally, where an individual applies for asylum but leaves the state before a (negative) decision is taken without notifying the authorities, in some Member States notably Germany, the authorities are entitled to determine that the individual has remained in breach of national rules on entry and residence and take an expulsion decision.[9] Thus a decision of expulsion by one Member State on this ground can be one taken on very different grounds for another Member State.[10]

The directive specifically states that the Member States shall apply the directive with due respect for human rights and fundamental freedoms. How an adequate assessment of a claim to article 8 ECHR respect for family life in the Union can be assessed by the state other than that where the foreigner has been living is difficult to imagine. The protection of personal data and data security is also regulated – in accordance with the EC data protection directive 95/46. On the one hand this provides some security to the individual about the use of data about him or her, on the other it may be a reason for the full situation of the individual and the article 8 ECHR grounds for suspending the expulsion decisions never to become available to the Member State which is carrying out the expulsion decision. The directive had to be transposed into national law by 2 December 2002.

It is difficult, however, to imagine under what circumstances a Member State would have the incentive to expel a third country national to his or her home state rather than return him or her to the Member State which had taken the expulsion decision. The latter course is likely to much cheaper (the exceptions would be rare, for instance a Turk ordered expelled by Germany who holidays in Greece, a Russian ordered expelled by Ireland who goes on a business trip to Finland) while the former will result in substantial expense. The key to this question is found in article 7: "Member States shall compensate each other for any financial imbalances which

---

9 C Saas, 'Les refus de deliverance de visas fondés sur une inscription sur le Système Information Schengen' Cultures et Conflits 2002(4), l'Harmattan, Paris.

10 For a fuller discussion on the grounds of expulsion see B Nascimbene (ed), *Expulsion and Detention of Aliens in the European Union Countries*, Guiffre Editore, Milan, 2001.

may result from application of this Directive where expulsion cannot be effected at the expense of the national(s) of the third country concerned." In February 2003 the Commission presented a proposal for a Council Decision setting out the criteria and practical arrangements for the compensation of the financial imbalances resulting from the application of the directive.[11] As the Commission outlines in the Explanatory Memorandum, "the core principle of this Decision is that the issuing Member State should reimburse the enforcing Member State on the basis of actual costs." The Memorandum then goes on to explain that there are three types of costs which may be incurred "transport costs, administrative costs and accommodation costs." The Commission states that "a ceiling would need to be established for each category to ensure that any costs are at all times kept reasonable, comparable and balanced." Already it is clear that the implementing measures needed for the directive do not relate to the fairness of the enforcement measure against the foreigner, nor, indeed the compatibility of the expulsion decision with fundamental rights of the individual but rather whether immigration officers of one Member State can take holidays at the expense of another Member State on the basis of carrying out the second Member State's expulsion decision.

Viewed from the perspective of those who carry out expulsion decisions, the immigration officials, exotic destinations and accommodation costs which do not have to be justified to the direct superior because they will be passed on to another Member State might be attractive. It is the immigration officials who make the decision as to who will be expelled when and where. As there are very substantial delays in expulsion in all Member States, the hierarchy of who is expelled when (or at all), falls on those charged with carrying them out. The power, then, of the immigration officials charged with this task is substantial. Presented with overwhelming numbers of persons who ought to be expelled immediately, limited resources, and targets to achieve, they are required to make the best of an impossible task. The first group to be expelled is, of course, those who obey orders. These persons require the least amount of effort. Often they will be family members, aged parents and the like, who have family with residence permits in the state and who are fearful of placing in jeopardy the residence of their family members should they resist expulsion. Those foreigners who are violent and resist at great length their expulsion tend to be the most difficult to expel and accordingly, there is a natural reluctance to tackle them. However, the directive changes the balance of interest in expulsion somewhat. If the foreigner is a difficult expulsion case then he or she will have to be accompanied. The decision limits to two the number of escorts for whom the expelling state can recover costs. Thus there are two immigration officials who may travel together providing one another with company on the trip for the purpose of expelling a foreigner. The cost does not have to be justified to their national authorities. Under the decision one can see the economic and social interest in expulsion developing.

---

11 COM (2003) 49 final.

Article 2 of the decision provides specifically as minimum recoverable costs on the basis of actual costs in respect of "the returnee and two escorts per returnee" "flight tickets up to the amount of the official IATA tariff ... the actual costs for land transport by car or train can be claimed on the basis of a second class train ticket ... administration costs; this includes the costs for visa fees and the fees for issuing of return travel documents; accommodation costs: this includes the actual costs for the returnee's stay in a detention facility for a duration of no more than three months. During enforcement, accommodation costs for the returnee and the escorts are covered in a transit area of a third country and for the unavoidable short stay of the escorts in the country of origin."

The economic interests of expulsion are revealed by this passage. The concern of the Member States is that immigration officials of one Member State are taking "expulsion" holidays at their expense. Their specific interest is to detail clearly and carefully what are reimbursable costs so that there is no possibility that one Member State is paying for the upkeep of otherwise partially empty detention centres in another Member State and the holiday plans of officials there. When one considers these interests in the light of the killing of foreigners in the course of forced expulsions, such as that of the Nigerian, Semira Adamu, who died at the hands of Belgian immigration officers in the course of her expulsion,[12] it is difficult not to be concerned. EU law on expulsion seems to deny the humanity of the individual subject of expulsion who is no longer a rights holder but in Agamben's expression homo sacer – the individual so deprived of his or her humanity that he or she is no longer even capable of being sacrificed.[13] The preoccupation of the legislation appears not to be with the moral/ethical or indeed even legal questions of expulsion but with the practical costs and holidays of immigration officials.

The Third Country Nationals Directive

The history of the EU seeking to incorporate (or not) third country nationals who have been long-resident in the Union has been well plotted by Kostakopoulou. The tentative moves in the 1990s in the Third Pillar were intensified when campaigns by NGOs for an equalisation of rights gained strength in the late 1990s.[14] Finally, in 1997, as the Amsterdam Treaty negotiations finished, the Commission made a proposal for a convention under the pre-Amsterdam Third Pillar for a status

---

12 Human Rights Watch, 'Asylum Policy in Western Europe', *World Report 1999*; the responsible officers were convicted of unlawful killing in Belgium.
13 G Agamben, *Homo Sacer: Sovereign Power and Bare Life*, Stanford University Press, Stanford, 1998.
14 Resolution on the status of third country nationals residing on a long-term basis in the territory of the Member States OJ 1996 C 808/2.

and free movement rights for third country nationals long-resident in the Union. The Commission was well aware that this proposal was doomed as the decision had already been taken to move the field of immigration into the new Title IV.[15] However, it did have symbolic importance and provided a foundation for the Commission's subsequent proposal for a directive under the new arrangements. In August 2001 the European Commission proposed a directive concerning the status of third country nationals who are long-term residents.[16] The directive was adopted on 25 November 2003.[17] It seeks to fulfil the declaration of the European Council in Tampere October 1999 to bring the rights of legally resident third country nationals closer to those of citizens of the Union and in particular to provide for free movement rights for long-term resident third country nationals within the whole of the Union for economic and study purposes. I shall consider the initial proposal and the subsequent result from the perspective of the migrant and his or her interest. First, what is the scope of the directive, which migrants get to benefit and which do not; secondly what is the migration right – on what basis can a third country national move freely for work or self-employment within the Union and subject to what limitations; thirdly, family reunification – can the individual have his or her family members come to the host Member State; and fourthly what protection is there against expulsion.

Scope

First, then, who is covered by the proposed directive and who is included in the final version? The Commission's initial proposal would have covered all third country nationals without prejudice to greater rights from other sources of EC law. As explained in the Commission's accompanying memorandum: "It applies to all third-country nationals residing legally in a Member State, irrespective of the grounds on which they were originally admitted. The scope thus includes third-country nationals admitted for purposes of employment or work in a self-employed capacity, family reunification, the exercise of non-gainful activities, and persons admitted without any active status. The proposal also covers third-country nationals born in the territory of a Member State and residing there without having acquired its

---

15 T Kostakopoulou, " 'Integrating' Non-EU Migrants in the European Union: Ambivalent Legacies and Mutating Paradigms" Columbia Journal of European Law, Vol 8 No 2 Spring 2002 pp 181–201.

16 OJ 2001 C 240; COM (2001) 127 Final. As the intergovernmental conference which led to the Amsterdam Treaty closed in 1997 the Commission took the opportunity to make a proposal for a Decision of establishing a Convention on Rules for the Admission of Third Country Nationals to the Member States of the European Union OJ 1997 C 337-9. Though it was clear the proposal would not survive the new treaty, it provided the Commission to set out its initial draft of free movement for third country nationals.

17 Directive 2003/109, OJ 2004 L 16/44.

nationality. Refugees recognised on the basis of the Geneva Convention are also covered ...".[18] Students were covered only as regards advanced studies and their continuous residence only counted for half that of others. The first group to be excluded in the Council negotiations were students. Thereafter refugees were removed from the scope of the directive. Persons with temporary or subsidiary protection are also excluded along with anyone with a protection application pending.

A new exclusion inserted by the Council negotiations is anyone whose residence is "solely on temporary grounds such as *au pair* or seasonal worker or as workers posted by a service provider for the purposes of cross-border provision of services, or as cross-border providers of services or in cases where their residence permit has not been formally limited". The addition of the final words – where their residence permit has not been formally limited – seems to be an attempt to transform the scope of the directive. The intention of the original draft was to ensure that the Member States could not exclude people from the scope of the directive on the basis of national law. Thus the central criterion for acquisition of the status by a third country national was not whether or not he or she had fulfilled national law requirements to have a residence permit of unlimited duration and resided for five years. Instead there was an objective criterion was established, five years lawful residence, after which the individual would have a right to the EU status irrespective of whether the Member State had granted him or her a long-residence permit.

When Member States admit a third country national under national law, he or she rarely gets, immediately, an unlimited residence permit. Thus all new migrants get residence permits which are formally limited, either in time or economic activity or both. Member States do not lift the formal limits until they are really convinced that the individual is one whom they wish to permit to reside permanently. Depending on the political climate of the state at any given time fewer or greater numbers of third country nationals are admitted to the magic circle of those who no longer have a formal limit on their residence permits. Some groups such as domestic workers may never get a residence permit which has not been formally limited. The qualification of five years residence would be meaningless if the Member States can nonetheless and after the five-year period exclude a third country national who has resided lawfully on the territory for five years, for instance as a domestic worker, on the basis that he or more likely she only has a limited residence permit and thus is excluded from the scope of the directive.

How did this qualification come into the directive? At the discussions of the Working Group on Migration and Expulsion of 6–7 January 2003 this addition had not yet been made.[19] In that reconsideration of Articles 1–11 of the proposal, discussion focussed on periods of permitted absence and other issues. No question

---

18 OJ 2001 C 240.
19 Council Document 6424/03 (18.02.03).

appears to have been raised about the inclusion of all third country nationals fulfilling the five-year requirement and not excluded on specific grounds.

On 18 February 2003 the Strategic Committee on Immigration, Frontiers and Asylum, the intermediary body between the working group and the JHA Council, considered the proposed draft. It was concerned about the application of the directive to refugees and for the first time proposed the inclusion of a requirement for third country nationals to fulfil integration requirements (I shall return to this point below).[20] The Presidency proposal to the delegations of 6 May 2003 reports that following the meeting of the Permanent Representatives Committee on 30 April 2003 a new draft was ready for presentation to the JHA Council in two days. In the draft the addition of the new limitation was present for the first time.[21] There is no explanation or comment regarding it, unlike many other changes to the proposal. At the JHA Council meeting on 8 May 2003 the matter was discussed. According to the press release, the Council agreed to exclude refugees altogether from the scope of the directive on the agreement that the Commission, would, within one year of adoption of the proposal table an amendment extending the scope of the Directive to refugees and persons benefiting from subsidiary protection. This, in effect, would give the EU a chance to adopt pending legislation on qualification as a refugee and subsidiary protection before extending the scope of the long-term residents directive to these groups. The press release also notes that there was discussion about the conditions for mobility of long-resident third country nationals. It specifically states that "the new status is not intended to replace the existing national long-term resident status". However, there is no indication that the significant qualification of the scope of the proposal had already been agreed and inserted into the text.[22]

The addition of these nine words qualifying the scope of the directive may mean, in effect, that the Member State retains control over access to the status. It would appear that only if the Member State has granted a residence permit of unlimited duration does the individual enter into the scope. In all other circumstances, the Member State could be argued to have "formally limited" the duration of the residence permit and so the individual is excluded from the scope. It must be hoped that this interpretation of the directive's scope is avoided as it makes a mockery of the intention of the Tampere Council Meeting's statement of intention. It is unfortunate that such a fundamental uncertainty has been inserted into the directive which will have to be resolved by the judicial instances and finally by the ECJ.

A second exclusion in the scope of the directive is also worrying. Service providers and their employees are excluded from the scope of the directive. When the EU, in the Doha round of WTO negotiations, is pressing for wide rights of movement for service providers and their employees, the exclusion of these persons

---

20 Council Document 7393/03 (14.03.03).
21 Council Document 9025/03 (06.05.03).
22 JHA Council 8 May 2003 Press Release 8278/03 Press III.

from a long-residence status is particularly cynical (see chapter 10). In effect the result of the two positions, on the one hand demanding wide movement rights internationally and then excluding the individuals from acquisition of independent residence rights after five years in a Member State is to trap the employees of service providers in indefinite servitude to their employers. Under the GATS rules the individual employee of a service provider may move to another WTO state only in his or her capacity as an employee. As soon as the individual changes job he or she loses the right to be on the territory under the GATS rules. If the EU expressly denies the possibility for such persons to obtain long-term residence status and thus independence from his or her employer under the directive, then the EU, in effect, strengthens hugely the hand of the employer against the employee. If residence on the territory is important to the individual then he or she can be coerced into abandoning any claim to social and employment protection rights.

One of the particularly refreshing aspects of the original proposal by the Commission was that it created a right for the individual which did not depend on the absolute control of the Member State. This is no longer so clear from the final version. However, a wide interpretation of the scope of the directive coupled with substantial limitations on the Member States' power to exclude individuals would be well justified on the basis of the purpose of the directive as set out in its preamble.

Acquisition of the Right

The central provisions of the Commission's proposed directive are found in chapter II. This deals with three areas: the conditions that third country nationals have to fulfil to obtain the status, including the length of residence in a Member State and means by which this status can be acquired and withdrawn; the rights and benefits that flow from the status; and the protection afforded third country nationals holding such status from expulsion.

In the original proposal, the key for third country nationals residing in the EU to qualify for long-term resident status is five years of legal and continuous residence in the territory of a Member State (article 5(1)). In justifying this choice of period, the Commission noted that five years is the qualifying period for access to security of residence under ILO Convention No. 97, the Council of Europe Convention on Establishment, and the recent Council of Europe Committee of Ministers Recommendation (2000) 15 concerning the security of residence of long-term migrants.[23] During the negotiations, a number of Member States sought to extend the

---

23 This was much criticised by one NGO, the Immigration Law Practitioners Association who had proposed a period of three years. See The ILPA Alternative Scoreboard on the Long Term Resident's Directive, June 2001.

period before an individual could qualify. At the end of the negotiations only Italy was still holding out for a six-year period and in the end gave in.[24]

In the original proposal absences from the Member State concerned for a period of less than six consecutive months or for certain 'important or serious reasons' or absences by family members of EU citizens, who have resided for at least two years in the Member State concerned and who move to a third state for up to three years, do not interrupt the continuous and legal residence necessary to obtain long-term resident status. By the end of the negotiations, the period had been limited to six months at a time and no more than 10 months over the five-year period. There is, however a possibility for Member States to permit longer absences under national law.[25]

In the original proposal the other conditions to be meet by third country nationals (with the exception of recognised refugees and second-generation migrants), were evidence that they have, both for themselves and dependent family members, stable resources and sickness insurance covering all risks in the Member State concerned. According to the Commission's explanatory memorandum, the criteria for assessing evidence of whether third-country nationals applying for long-term status are likely to become a burden on a Member State's social assistance scheme 'are determined very strictly to avoid rendering eligibility of the status nugatory and to harmonise the conditions in all the Member States.' To this end article 6(1)(a) provided that stable resources cannot be higher than the minimum income guaranteed by that Member State in the form of social assistance or, where no such social assistance is provided, the level of the minimum social security (retirement) pension paid by the Member State concerned. This requirement provided a measure against which to assess resources, even if that measure would have varied from Member State to Member State depending on the threshold for state benefits.

In the final version the resources provision has been supplemented. The individual must show that not only are they stable but that they are regular. The question must arise, if the resources are stable but they are not regular can the Member State refuse to acknowledge the right to the status? The relationship between the resources and social assistance system has become less direct. The resources must be sufficient so that the individual and his or her family can maintain themselves without recourse to social assistance but is not limited to the threshold for social assistance. Nonetheless, when this provision comes to be clarified by the ECJ it can be expected that a direct causal relationship between the two must be recognised. Further, in the final version it is for the Member States to evaluate the resources by reference to the nature and regularity and taking into account the level of minimum wages and pensions. This complicates the issue somewhat. If, as in some Member States the level of social assistance is lower than the level of minimum wages, how is the

---

24   See Council Press Release 6 June 2003.
25   Article 4.

assessment to take place? The margin of manoeuvre of the Member States will need to be interpreted narrowly if arbitrary decision-making is to be avoided.

The sickness requirement remained in the final version of the directive. However, this requirement has been softened by the passage of Regulation 859/2003 which extends the scope of Regulations 1408/71 and 574/72 on coordination of social security for persons moving within the Union to third country nationals. As third country nationals who have been resident and exercising economic activities in one Member State will belong to the social security system of that Member State, when they move to another Member State they should be covered by sickness insurance for all risks until such time as they become assumed into the social security system of their new host Member State.

In the original proposal, the individual must not be a risk to public policy or security. If the host Member State wishes to invoke this ground to refuse the status to a third country national who otherwise fulfils the conditions it must consider the severity or type of offence against public policy or security or the danger that "emanates" from the person. The only limitation is that the exclusion from the status cannot be founded on economic grounds. Although the Commission's Explanatory Memorandum noted that this provision as originally worded was based on Directive 64/221 by the time the Council had finished negotiations it no longer resembled the directive on migrant citizens of the Union at all. While a strict limitation on the meaning of public policy or public security is present in Directive 64/221 it will require a vigilant interpretation by the ECJ to apply the same criteria to the third country nationals directive. For citizens of the Union a uniform and standard level of protection arises from the moment when they seek to enter the territory of another Member State. Under this directive there is to be a sliding scale: the Member State is to have regard to "the duration of residence and to the existence of links with the country of residence".

The Commission's proposal for a duty on Member States to examine an application within six months of being lodged was removed before the final draft. However, provided the conditions are met, the Member State is under an obligation to grant him or her long-term resident status. This is, effectively, still a right to permanent residence. A permit valid for five years and automatically renewable (though in the Commission's proposal the document would have been valid for ten years) must be issued. The expiry of the permit does not mean the withdrawal of the status. A limitation on the fees chargeable for the document was removed by the Council in negotiation.

A worrying requirement inserted in the Council negotiations is contained in article 5(2) "Member States may require third country nationals to comply with integration conditions, in accordance with national law."[26] Thus before a long-resident

---

26 See also chapter 6 on family reunification. The two provisions on integration in that directive have been the subject of a challenge by the European Parliament against the Council before the ECJ on the grounds of a breach of the right to family life contained in article 8 ECHR and guaranteed by the EU Case C-540/03.

third country national can enjoy a protected status in EU law he or she must abandon attributes of being a third country national. Here is Žižek's Real. The foreigner who is a Real foreigner has nightmarish qualities. Kostakopoulou challenges the integration discourse regarding third country nationals at the EU level. She notes that "the vocabulary of integration seems ... inappropriate to a polity in which there is: i) a plurality of cultures and sub-cultures; ii) no shared definition of the terms of a common life; and iii) multiple definitions belonging to political and communal 'homes' formed at national, subnational and supranational levels of governance."[27]

At one point in the negotiations of the directive the Austrian delegation proposed that there should be the possibility to apply a double integration test both in the Member State where the individual acquires the long-residence status and in the state where he or she seeks to take up residence (the second test to be applied before the individual takes up residence). This proposal went too far even for the other Member States and it was rejected before the end of the negotiations.

Loss of Status

There are three aspects to loss of status. The first is on what basis the Member State can refuse to recognise to a third country national the status of long-resident third country national in EU law. The second is after acknowledgement of the status, where the Member State seeks to remove the status. The third aspect relates to the situation where the individual has acquired the status and moved to another Member State to exercise a residence right there. What are the grounds on which the newly acquired status in the new host Member State can be lost? In the first case, the circumstances under which long-term resident status is lost has become less favourable to the foreigner: absence from the territory for a period of two consecutive years was proposed by the Commission, the final version limits absence to 12 months (but with a possible derogation on the basis of national law); adoption of an expulsion measure or the fraudulent acquisition of long-term resident status. While the original proposal stated that withdrawal of a permit is not synonymous with expulsion, the final version permits withdrawal on the basis of an expulsion decision and on the basis of constituting a threat to public policy which does not constitute a reason for expulsion. A right of remedy survived the Council negotiations but in a somewhat more limited form, as a "legal challenge" rather than as originally proposed as a right to legal remedies.

In the second case the original proposal of the Commission afforded third country nationals with long-term resident status protection against expulsion.

---

27   D Kostakopoulou " 'Integrating' Non-EU Migrants in the European Union: Ambivalent Legacies and Mutating Paradigms" Columbia Journal of European Law Spring 2002 Vol 8 No 2 pp 181–201.

The Explanatory Memorandum states: "Long-term residents must enjoy enhanced protection against expulsion; the proposal is inspired by existing Community law on free movement of citizens of the Union." Enhanced protection is not the same as equal treatment with EU citizens but even this did not survive the discussions in the Council. In the final version, expulsion may be ordered where the individual constitutes an actual and sufficiently serious threat to public policy or public security, though it still prohibits expulsion on economic grounds. Where a Member State seeks to withdraw the status which it has granted to a third country national it is obliged to have regard to the duration of residence in their territory; the age of the person concerned; the consequences for the person concerned and family members; and the links with the country of residence or the absence of links with the country of origin. While these are clearly the considerations arising from the ECHR jurisprudence no direct reference is made. While the individual is entitled to "judicial redress procedures" (article 12(4)) there is no longer any reference to suspensive effect which the Commission had proposed.

The rules which apply to withdrawal of a residence permit in a "new" host Member State are slightly differently from those which apply as regards the "original" host Member State. Article 22 provides for the withdrawal of a residence permit and an obligation (on the first host Member State) to readmit the foreigner. These grounds are: first, public policy or public security within the same definition as for expulsion; secondly, if the individual is no longer exercising the activity which permitted him or her to have the residence right or fails to be able to support him or her self and any family members without recourse to public assistance or ceases to be a permitted family member; or thirdly if the individual is not lawfully residing in the state. This third requirement is somewhat worrying as it presupposes that the individual can fall into illegality while still fulfilling the other conditions for the exercise of the free movement right and even though the failure to renew a residence permit does not trigger the end of the right.

The Rights

In principle long-term residents are entitled to equal treatment with nationals, principally in the economic and social fields. Enumerated in article 11 are access to employment and self-employment (with a public service exception), education and vocational training, recognition of professional diplomas and certifications (in accordance with national procedures) and social security, social assistance and social protection as defined by national law. In the Commission's proposal these rights were clearly specified as ones to which non-discrimination must apply but in the form adopted limitations were inserted. At the last minute the Member States allowed restrictions on equal treatment in particular as regards study grants (now 'in accordance with national law', and with a clause in the preamble distinguishing grants from social assistance) and social benefits (Member States may restrict these to 'core benefits' which are undefined). However, a German reservation to restrict equal treatment in education to cases of prior employment of the student or parent was dropped. A right to equal treatment also applies to tax benefits, access to goods and services and their supply, freedom of association and affiliation and membership of trades unions and free access to the entire territory of the Member States subject to the limits of national law for reasons of security.

A territorial limitation has been placed on study grants and education, social benefits, tax, goods and services and trades union membership. A language limitation may be placed on access to education and training. Social benefits may be limited to "core benefits" which are not defined though a preamble was added that "core benefits cover at least minimum income support, assistance in case of illness, pregnancy, parental assistance and long term care. The modalities for granting such benefits will be determined by national law."[28]

Free Movement

Once a third country national has acquired the recognition of the status in one Member State he or she is entitled to exercise a right of residence and economic activity in any other Member State. The conditions for the exercise of free movement are that the individual is exercising an economic activity (employed or self-employed); is pursuing studies or vocational training; pursuing other purposes, for instance retirement or economically inactive residence. A number of limitations apply. First if the individual is economically active, the Member State may apply its rules for filling vacancies. In the final version, a qualification was added which creates some uncertainty around the right of access of the third country national to the labour market of other Member States. Article 14(3) contains the words: "Member States may examine the situation of their labour markets and apply their national procedures regarding the requirements for, respectively, filling a vacancy, or for exercising such activities." It would be contrary to the meaning of the directive if this provision were to be interpreted as meaning that States are entitled to continue to apply their national requirements on work permits as this would render pointless the "right" of free movement for paid employment which the directive purports to grant qualifying third country nationals. It seems that the right of Member States is

---

28   Directive 2003/109, OJ 2004 L 16/44.

to apply their existing procedures regarding access to the labour market but not their requirements. The only requirements which can be applied under the directive as regards labour market access for qualifying third country nationals are those set out in the directive itself. Such an interpretation of this provisions would also be consistent with the ECJ's interpretation of article 6(3) Decision 1/80 of the EEC Turkey Association Agreement which permits Member States to apply their national procedures regarding the continued employment of Turkish workers. It was argued that this meant that the right to continued employment could not be directly effective as it was mediated by national procedures. The ECJ held: "That conclusion cannot be invalidated by the consideration that under Article 6(3) of Decision No 1/80 the procedures for applying paragraph (1) are to be established under national rules. As the Court has already observed in its judgment in Sevince (paragraph 22), Article 6(3) of Decision No 1/80 merely clarifies the obligation incumbent on the Member States to take such administrative measures as may be necessary for the implementation of that provision, without empowering them to make conditional or restrict the application of the precise and unconditional right which the provision grants to Turkish workers."[29] Further, Member States are permitted to give preferences to Community nationals and third country nationals receiving unemployment benefits in the Member State concerned. In the final negotiations on the directive the Council accepted an amendment sought by the Austrians that national legislation existing at the time of adoption of the directive on quotas of third country nationals for employment may be preserved. In addition to the power to apply quotas, the final version of the directive permits Member States to restrict the right of long-resident third country nationals from changing jobs or self-employed activities for the first 12 months of their residence in the second host Member State. Further for the self-employed, the Member States are permitted to apply all their national legislation limiting and restricting the activity.

The mechanism for the exercise of the right requires the third country national to submit an application to the host Member State within three months of arrival, or while still in the first host Member State, for a residence permit. With the application they must provide evidence that they have stable and secure resources sufficient to maintain themselves and their family members without recourse to social assistance. The definitions are the same as regards the acquisition of the right in the first instance. The Member State can require evidence of accommodation. Additionally the individual will have to prove sickness insurance. If the third country national was not required to comply with integration conditions in the first Member State he or she may be required to submit to them in the second. In addition the individual may be required to attend language courses. It would seem that language training may be additional to integration conditions.

---

29   C-237/91 Kus [1992] ECR I-6781.

Family Members

For long-resident third country nationals in their first host Member State, the directive on Family Reunification determines the rules which apply to the admission of their family members to the Union (see chapter 6). For those long-resident third country nationals who move to another Member State to exercise free movement rights under this directive and have already been joined in the first Member State by family members, those family members "may be authorised to accompany or join" the principal. The documents to be produced are set out in the directive. The possible width of the family was the subject of substantial discussion in the negotiations. According to Peers, the final trade off was that Austria would withdraw its demand for a quota on family members and the Dutch would withdraw their demand for a wider group of family members than in the Family Reunification Directive.[30] While a public policy and public security proviso as discussed above is found here, there is also the possibility of exclusion on grounds of public health.

Conclusions

The two measures I have considered here are intrinsically related. An objectification of third country nationals follows from categorising them as potential or actual objects of an expulsion decision in one Member State. The individual becomes the object of a transnational "hunt" with the objective of expulsion. Into the framework of the "hunt" are placed a series of economic incentives for the officials of the Member States to carry out expulsion decisions for other Member States. The supra-national mechanism which releases the individual from becoming potentially the object of such a search is the acquisition of an EU status of protected third country national. The willingness, or rather lack thereof, among the Member States to create a full and inclusive protected status for third country nationals has the consequence of leaving larger numbers of third country nationals in the limbo of potential objects of the "hunt".

When a comparison is made between the first proposal of the Commission for a directive on long-resident third country nationals and the final directive as adopted it is difficult to avoid the conclusion that the Member States consider third country nationals even after five years stable and lawful residence in the Union an intrinsically suspect category. Asylum seekers, refugees and persons granted subsidiary protection must be excluded entirely from any access to the free movement rights which are at the heart of the internal market. For them the borders remain as solidly as if the

---

30   S Peers, ILPA Update June 2003.

objective of the original Treaty had been to achieve free movement of persons with the exception of any one in need of protection against persecution. Article 14 EC/article II-74 EU Constitution, the abolition of intra-Member State borders controls on persons, might just as well not exist for the JHA Council where the concept of borders is restrictive fences between the Member States which keep out the unwanted and potentially dangerous Other.

The determination of the Member States to maintain their stranglehold over the marginalization of third country nationals is astonishing. In the end the justification appears to be the tacit agreement among the Member States that third country nationals are potentially dangerous Others. Before they can be permitted to move in the Union and reside they must be subject to "integration", a concept abhorrent to the Member States when considering activities among themselves. Article 151(4) EC/article III-280(4) EU Constitution proudly states "The Community shall take cultural aspects into account in its action under other provisions of this Treaty, in particular in order to respect and to promote the diversity of its cultures." Cultural diversity, it would appear, is only an asset when it is compatible with Žižek's world of the false Real which excludes the Other. The cultures of Europe which deserve respect and promotion in their diversity do not appear to include those of long-term resident third country nationals. Exactly what they do include is somewhat more ambiguous.

Instead, for this group, integration is the key to the acquisition of rights. Because the foreigner is potentially a nightmare he or she must abandon being a foreigner before acquiring rights. It is for each Member State to determine what integration is and what integration conditions the individual must fulfil. The idea of integration in itself presupposes that diversity is a bad thing. Diversity within the host society must be denied if one is to require foreigners to integrate. If diversity within the society were accepted how could one ever design programmes for third country nationals on integration? When the perfectly lawful life style of travellers and gypsies or dissipate aristocrats must be factored into the equation the idea of integration crumbles. Those who promote integration tests do not mean integration into communal gay households. The concept of integration as a requirement to "civilise" the foreigner (though this discourse is usually couched in the argument of making life easier for the foreigner, helping him or her) becomes the means by which a specific vision of society seeks to dominate other definitions of a society. The construction of the society into which the integration of foreigners is to take place is intended to be undertaken by those conservatives who best "understand" the society. This construction itself gains legitimacy through the process of expression and the fact that it is transmitted to foreigners.

Conclusions

What are the Legal Elements of European Identity?

In this book I have examined how the legal issue of identity and the right to define it has become diffuse in Europe including the national level, the European Union and the Council of Europe. The result for the individual has been a multiplication of legal identities. Some legal elements of identity overlap but others find their source exclusively at one level or another. To understand this multiplication of legal identities, I have taken as a starting point the twin concepts of citizenship and nationality. The most fundamental status of an individual in the nation state is that of belonging or not, expressed in law as nationality. The content of belonging, in particular the principle of equality (which has become inherent in the European idea of nationality) is often expressed as citizenship. The categorisation of the individual as inside or outside the concept of citizenship/nationality is the foremost legal mechanism for placing boundaries on the individual's right to entry, residence, work, family life and protection from expulsion. Beyond the category of citizenship/nationality, there are a vast number of separate statuses which an individual can have which reflect the different levels of legal protection which he or she has as regards participation in the society. Thus a long-term legally resident third country national in a European country will have a higher degree of protection in all spheres than an asylum seeker whose application has been rejected. They will both be excluded from the golden circle of rights expressed as citizenship/nationality rights but thereafter their positions as regards partial access to rights is entirely different. The long-term resident third country national will usually have substantial protection against expulsion, including a right of appeal with suspensive effect against any decision by the state to end his or her right of residence. The asylum seeker whose application has been rejected will often have no appeal against expulsion and indeed will be awaiting that expulsion. The expression in law, encompassing three different levels of governance, of this right of identity has been the subject of this investigation.

Over the past ten years, the highly political nature of the subject matter has been reflected, both at the national, EU and Council of Europe levels, by very substantial amounts of legislative and judicial activity. As an area of law, this one has been subjected to great scrutiny by social scientists in related fields. This body of research is so rich and central to understanding the political debates which have determined the legal measures that it can only be ignored at peril. Thus I have sought to examine the legal elements of EU identity in light of the theoretical analyses relating to immigration and citizenship which experts in political science and international relations have put at our disposal.

There are three main themes which I have pursued through the chapters:

1.　Whose identity: what are the issues which surround the legal definition of an individual as a citizen, a resident, an (im)migrant, an alien/foreigner or simply a person/individual? How does the categorisation change the rights and entitlements of the individual and his or her relationship with the territory and the persons who live in the neighbourhood? The focus of this book has been first and foremost on the individual rather than the state or supranational governance. It is the individual, the object of legislative and judicial action, which has taken the centre stage. In so doing the individual has appeared as an actor in an increasing number of domains as he or she seeks to establish rights to identity. In the political, social and judicial spheres, the individual's claim to identity rights of participation, security of residence, work, protection from expulsion, family life, protection from arbitrary state action and exclusion on the basis of nationality, religion or race (or the combination of the three) has resulted in the appearance of the individual as an actor in every area.

2.　Which authority determines identity: three main actors have sought to determine the content of the identity of the individual within Europe. The first has been the nation state. There is no question that until the 1970s, the main status which an individual enjoyed as citizen or foreigner awaiting expulsion and any category between the two was determined by the nation state through national law and administration. The struggle for rights took place at the national level. However, a second actor who entered the stage in 1957 began playing a substantial role from 1968 onwards. This is, of course, the European Union (under its various guises as the European Economic Community, the European Community and the European Union). Free movement of persons across the Member States was an objective of the Union from 1957, included in the original article 3(c), with a transitional period ending in 1968. Since then, the increasing communitarisation of the field has led the EU to play a pivotal role in the definition of the individual's identity. The EU Member States have, in consequence, lost exclusive control over the definition of identity of the individual in those (increasing) spheres where the EU has been granted competence. The third actor which moves onto the stage from about 1985 is the European Convention on Human Rights. As the ECtHR gradually interprets the provisions of the convention as having consequences for the identity status of the individual in immigration and asylum, so the nation state in Europe, party to the ECHR, has been constrained as to its right to define the identity status of the individual.

3.   The venues of the struggle of the individual for an identity status within a territory: as there has been a diversification of the arenas and bodies participating in the definition of the legal identity of the individual, so the individual has sought to achieve a particular result through different institutions and in different contexts. As I noted above, in Europe, the struggle regarding legal elements of identity takes place in three venues – the nation state, the EU and the Council of Europe. But within those venues there are political, administrative and judicial arenas within which identity struggles occur. Thus the individual who has been declared by the nation state authorities to be irregularly present and subject to expulsion has sought and received relief from that determination via EU law as interpreted by the ECJ (see, for instance, chapter 5) and from the ECtHR (see chapter 7). The individual has become visible throughout Europe and within its institutions as a potential or actual rights holder. He or she is no longer defined as visible or invisible in law by the nation state alone. The veil of statehood no longer hides the individual within its jurisdictional rules.

Taking my bearings from these three main themes, I have examined, in 12 chapters, the way in which law in Europe defines the status of the individual and his or her entitlements as regards identity. The result is a multilayered identity for the individual based on a variety of sources of rights and limitations. The challenges which this complex system presents for the individual are considerable – for instance, as I examine in chapter 6, if the individual will only gain a right to family reunification if he or she moves within the European Union for a considerable period of time, he or she will have to weigh the importance of living with his or her family members against the disruption to work and social life of making such a move. The challenges for the nation state are dramatic: if the loyalty of the citizen depends on the state providing him or her with protection, where does the loyalty of the citizen forced to migrate in order to enjoy family life lie? In the remainder of these conclusions, I will take the reader through the conclusions of each of the chapters, which highlight the three issues set out above.

Borders and Citizenship

Citizenship and the right to move across borders are both intrinsically connected and oppositional in the EU. The categorization of individuals into citizens and non-citizens is central to state formation: the fixing of the borders and the people. In accordance with Torpey's analysis, the relationship of the border and the citizen derives legitimacy from the principle that the state has responsibility for "its" people as regards extracting resources and providing protection.[1] The success of both these operations depends on the identification of the citizens and the control of movement across borders both territorial and of legal orders. Citizenship of the Union presents a series of challenges to traditional thinking about the control of borders and their significance. The documentation on the basis of which the control of territorial borders is carried out, identity documents and passports, have taken on new characteristics. They are no longer systematically checked at the intra-Member State territorial borders (with notable exceptions) but they are central to the borders of the legal order – for instance checks within the territory, access to benefits. The Member States are no longer entitled to refuse to issue identity documents or passports to their citizens who wish to cross the borders (except on the basis of public policy, public security or public health) nor are they necessarily entitled to determine the identity of their citizens, for instance in the form of their names. The nature of the border in Europe has been changed as regards its centrality to the relationship between the individual and the state. The state's right to "fix" as its own certain people and exclude others using the border and identity documents as the tools of differentiation has been modified by EU law on free movement.

Citizenship of the Union

When citizenship of the Union was established in 1993, a very limited number of rights were attached to it: (1) the right to move and reside subject to the conditions set out in the treaty; (2) the right to vote and stand as a candidate in municipal and European Parliament elections in a Member State other than that of his or her nationality if he or she resides there; (3) the right to seek help from the consular authorities of another Member State when in a third country; (4) the right to petition the European Parliament and Ombudsman (though this right is also given to third country nationals and so cannot truly be considered a citizenship right). What is striking about all of these rights is that they only apply to immigrants. When a person is in his or her home state, the rights have no effect – the result of the wholly internal rule. Thus the meaning of citizenship of the Union when considered from the perspective of fundamental freedoms is as a citizenship which only gives rights to persons outside their state of nationality (or on their return from migration). The only exception is the right to petition the ombudsman but in reality that is a right given to third country nationals as well. The EU constitution does not extend or develop these rights substantially.

This reflects the fact that citizenship of the Union has not been a building block of legitimacy of the Union until very recently. It has not been a central element of

---

1 J Torpey, *The Invention of the Passport*, Cambridge University Press, Cambridge, 2000.

the constitution in which it appears. The EC and EU Treaties form the central elements of the constitution of the Union. However, the process of constitutionalisation of the EU is one which has been cautiously developed primarily in fields far from citizenship.[2] Commercial adventures have been much more pertinent to the development of the central constitutional principles of the Union, such as direct effect and supremacy of EU law.[3] From the start of the project in 1957 until the transformation in 1993, individuals enjoyed rights primarily as a result of their exercise of economic activities – as workers, self-employed or service providers or recipients. Further, the rights which individuals gained through the treaty from work were only available to them if they were immigrants in another Member State. Thus, for example, the right to family reunification in EU law only comes into existence when the individual carries on his or her economic activities in another Member State.[4] The right to emigrate to any other Member State which the treaty provides to nationals of the Member States was and continues to be central. But the rights of the individual in EU law still depend largely on the individual having exercised that migration right.[5]

Equality and Citizenship

While the legislator has been reluctant to attach substantial rights to the concept of citizen of the Union, the ECJ has been much more receptive to an expansive understanding of the concept. The language of the ECJ on citizenship of the Union is that of equality before the law,[6] the principle which T.H. Marshall found as central to the acquisition of other rights.[7] The right which the ECJ has most focused on is a social one, access to social benefits, Marshall's latest and most contested of the citizenship rights.

Marshall's premise that citizenship must be expanded to include social rights is borne out in the development so far of citizenship of the Union. As Member States are obliged to grant social benefits to citizens of the Union from other Member States (or their own citizens on their return) the social content of citizenship is

---

2   The key theorist on this subject is Joseph Weiler whose book *The Constitution of Europe* is central to any discussion of this kind: J H H Weiler, *The Constitution of Europe* (Cambridge University Press: Cambridge: 1999).
3   These principles were enunciated by the European Court of Justice in 6/62 *Van Gend en Loos* [1962] ECR 1; 6/64 *Costa v ENEL* [1964] ECR 585.
4   Article 10 Regulation 1612/68 – there can be continuing effects if the family return to the home Member State C-370/90 *Singh* [1992] ECR I-4265; very recently there has been a further extension C-60/00 *Carpenter* [2002] ECR I-6279.
5   These comments are in respect of rights which attach to citizenship rather than those which are generally available to anyone living in the Union – such as health and safety rules or consumer protection.
6   C-184/99 *Grzelczyk* [2001] ECR I-6193; C-224/98 *D'Hoop* [2002] ECR I-6191.
7   T H Marshall, *Citizenship and Social Class*, CUP, Cambridge, 1950.

enlarged. It is curious to note that of the three important cases on citizenship of the Union and social benefits, two relate to students. Marshall's argument that social citizenship is closely linked with the development of universal education which is a prerequisite for the extension of the franchise finds an echo here. It is in paying for the education of the citizen that Member State resistance to social citizenship has arisen before the ECJ.

There is, however, another perspective to the development of European social citizenship. Gellner's argument on the rise of nationalism depends on the transformation of political boundaries into a new configuration of the homogeneity of culture.[8] The acquisition of citizenship rights and in particular social rights is central to the legal definition of individuals as within or outside a homogeneous culture. The role of high literacy and education-linked culture as key to the social transformation of societies towards a citizenship-based concept of solidarity is the second element to the emergence of nationalism. If Gellner's position is correct, and the two features which he sees as central to the rise of nationalism are appearing in EU citizenship law, the question must be examined whether this is also laying a foundation for the development of negative aspects of nationalism at the EU level.

The Residence/Citizenship Nexus

In the transformation of the nexus of citizenship and residence, can one see the development of a new unifying principle which makes sense of citizenship in the face of regionalisation and globalisation, as Habermas has sought to do?[9] According to Habermas, a European constitutional patriotism needs to be located. He considers that it could grow out of the constitutional principles and traditions coming from the European level with the human rights component of citizenship intensified and strengthened through supranational rights "and especially through European Civil Rights ..."[10] Two EU examples indicate how differently in national law the nexus of citizenship and residence are treated: the Aussiedler (persons living in the former Eastern Block countries but considered to be ethnically German and thus German citizens or entitled to citizenship) and the East African Asians (who remained British nationals after independence of their states of residence in East Africa but in respect of whom the UK took measures to prevent admission to the UK in the 1960s when they were being expelled from some East African states).

Both these groups of "contested" identity have had consequences for the EU definition of citizenship. In both cases, the 'real' citizens, those who have the right

---

8   Gellner, E, *Nationalism*, Phoenix, London 1997.
9   J Habermas, 'Citizenship and National Identity: Some Reflections on the Future of Europe' in R Beiner, *Theorising Citizenship*, SUNY, New York, 1995 pp 255–281.
10 J Habermas, ibid p 273.

to reside on the territory are those whom national constitutional mythology classifies as inside the ethnos rather than outside. One of the difficulties which the German example exposed was that for many Germans, in fact the Turks who had been living next door for the last thirty years seemed much more familiar than the Aussiedler who had been living many generations in the farther reaches of the former USSR many of whom did not speak German. The East African Asians who managed to come to the UK, in the face of great state opposition, have subsequently been singled out as the integration "stars" of the recent UK migratory experience.[11] Both conclusions raise questions about the adequacy of the national definitions of citizenship and residence rights in parts of Europe.

The challenge which the separation of residence rights from citizenship has posed to the European institutions has arisen only in respect of the UK case (at least so far). What is evident already is that the lack of respect for the undertakings of citizenship which the UK government showed caused the field to move beyond the control of the state and its constitutional settlements into the supranational European field. Here there are two rather different results. First in the field of European human rights, the ECmHR found that European human rights commitments could compensate for the Member State's withdrawal of residence rights from citizenship where this constituted inhuman or degrading treatment.[12] Secondly, the ECJ refused to intervene in the same domain, even where doing so would have strengthened its claim to legitimacy in the area of human rights and could have provided a useful mechanism to safeguard the content of citizenship of the Union.[13]

Thus the supranational venue where European states have been most challenged has been the ECtHR on the basis of human rights which have an increasingly tenuous relationship with citizenship. The monopoly of the Member States over the definition of citizenship of the Union was upheld by the ECJ, even in a case where by so doing it acquiesces to an injustice already condemned by the ECmHR as discriminatory on the basis of race. The result appears to be that while Habermas' European Civil Rights are in the process of developing, they are increasing divorced from formal citizenship itself. The failure of the Member States and the ECJ to respond to the reality of belonging and exclusion in Europe has transformed the field into one of fundamental human rights in which formal citizenship may only have a secondary part to play. The redefinition of the meaning of citizenship is taking place in the human rights field responding to the pressures of regionalism and globalisation which the national constitutional settlements of at least some Member States have been unable to take on board.

---

11 See for instance the British Council's explanation of British society: http://www.britishcouncil.org/languageassistant/ess_uk_multiculturalukcv.html.
12 *East African Asians* [1973] 3 EHRR 76.
13 C-192/99 *Kaur* [2001] ECR I-1237.

From Immigrants to Citizens in the European Union:
Expulsion and Exclusion

In Europe where a substantial rise in immigration was perceived in the mid-1990s, social scientists sought to determine the rules by which liberal states should turn immigrants into citizens. The treatment of the "others" among "us" was a matter of concern and the approach of the "other" among "us" led in the direction of theories about acculturation, assimilation and integration.[14] What remains surprising is the failure in this literature to notice the most obvious transformation of migrant workers into citizens which was taking place around them – that of nationals of the Member States. The effect of the right of equal treatment which nationals of the Member States enjoyed as a result of the EC Treaty provisions on their immigration meant that they slipped out of sight. Having a right of equal treatment in working conditions, as regards family, and extensive protection against exclusion and expulsion diminished the difference of position between migrant workers, nationals of other Member States, and nationals of the host state itself. As the difference in rights became narrower, the individual disappeared as an object of integration, acculturation or assimilation projects. Because Member State nationals already had wide rights of equal treatment, they could not be required to assimilate before being deemed eligible for those rights.

Nonetheless, the protection of the most central right of the citizen, that to equal treatment fares worse in the field of residence on the territory than it has done in respect of social rights. Here the ECJ has permitted the Member States to retain their right to exclude and expel nationals of other Member States on the basis of public policy, expressly acknowledging that such powers are inimical to 'genuine' citizenship, in other words, Member States cannot take such measures against their own nationals.

Family Migration in EU Law

To insist on the centrality of family unity to identity is banal. In balancing the role of the state in private and public life, in Europe the most protected field is that of the family. Interference by the state in family life is prohibited by article 8 ECHR except on the grounds carefully enumerated. Perhaps because of the importance of family to identity, the approach of European states to the admission of foreign family members has become increasingly harsh from the 1980s onwards.[15] By placing

---

14 R Bauböck, 'The Crossing and Blurring of Boundaries in International Migration. Challenges for Social and Political Theory' in R Bauböck & J Rundell, *Blurred Boundaries: Migration, Ethnicity, Citizenship*, Averbury, Aldershot, 1998.

15 J Bhabha, S Shutter et al, *Women's Movement, Women under Immigration, Nationality and Refugee Law*, Trentham Books, Stoke-on-Trent, 1994.

administrative obstacles in the way of own nationals seeking to marry foreigners or acquire other foreign family members, the state privileges family life within the state. The equation of foreign with negative qualities is reinforced by the state's restrictive response to its citizens' relationships with foreigners. The implicit position of the state is that foreigners are dangerous and citizens should be discouraged from entering into family relations with them. The insistence of some Member States that foreign family members undergo integration tests before they are permitted to join their family members in the host State evidences the seriousness with which some Member States view their need to control the family within their state.[16]

The solution to this negative positioning of family reunification in EU law has been the adoption of measures on family reunification which, on the one hand accept the Member States' right to control family reunification in a way which is unacceptable where the family members are nationals of the same state, but on the other create such a wide definition of qualifying family members, so few qualifying conditions and such wide rights for the family members that the control becomes barely visible. Community nationals are entitled to family reunification and while it is apparent from the cases which have come before the ECJ that Member States still seek to impede family life, the robust approach of the ECJ has protected the identity choices of migrant Community nationals. Indeed, the protection of this group has been so successful, in particular against Member State's restrictive policies towards their own nationals, as to create an incentive for Community nationals to use their free movement rights in order to establish a right to family reunification with third country national family members.[17] This then results in a temptation for citizens to value more highly their status as citizens of the Union rather than nationals of the Member States in light of the important identity benefits which derive from the one status which have been refused as a corollary of the other.

No such solution appears forthcoming for Europe's third country nationals. The family reunification directive for third country nationals (2003/86) places many obstacles of a variety of different types in the place of their family reunification. The definition of the family members is fraught with limitations and must be substantiated with many official documents; the conditions for enjoying family reunification are riddled with discretionary elements to be assessed by Member State authorities and in principle permit high financial barriers to family reunification to be created or maintained; the rights granted to family members are restricted. The barriers to family reunification created in the directive will not cause the line of control by the Member States to disappear as has happened in the case of Community nationals. Instead of satisfying the legitimate interests of the EU's third country national

16   This is the case, for instance, in the Netherlands and Austria. The issue was much discussed in the Council in the negotiations of the family reunification directive, 2003/86.
17   R Gutmann, "Discrimination against own nationals: a brief look at European and German immigration law," Immigration and Nationality Law and Practice, Vol 9 No 3 1995.

families to live together in the country of choice, it is likely to impede family life with all the disastrous consequences for social cohesion which so many national policies around families are designed to avoid. An EU law which appears to justify national practices preventing some spouses and children from living together (that is to say third country national ones) while privileging other spouses and children (that is to say migrant citizens of the Union and their third country national spouses and children) is unlikely to command the respect of those who suffer from its effects.

Perhaps most seriously, though, the dubious concept of "integration" (disaggregated from economic integration) has crept in and with it the implied notion that there is a homogeneous community within a Member State to which the heterogeneous third country national must transform him or herself. At the heart of this concept of integration is an intolerance of diversity: a refusal to acknowledge its existence within all European communities; the false suggestion that it comes from abroad; the association of negative values to it; the justification for crushing it. Identity is built on difference – how one individual is different from another – through acknowledgement of difference, similarity is apparent. To cut the individual off from his or her family members with the justification that if the family members wish to live together they should do so somewhere else is to deny a right to a personal identity. Identity politics based on social integration is used to justify punishing third country nationals for having foreign family members. Implicit is the argument that they should abandon their foreign identities (and families) abroad and start again with nationals of the host state. The European Union is Janus faced in this discussion. On the one hand it protects migrant nationals of the Member States from any suggestion that they should be required to integrate in their chosen host Member State or indeed that their families should have to do so while on the other hand it plays the identity politics game as regards third country nationals and their family reunification.

Identity Beyond Citizenship: the European Convention on Human Rights

The development of residence rights for foreigners through human rights in Europe is still quite a recent event. These rights have arisen from two main provisions of the ECHR: the right to protection against torture (article 3) and the right to respect for private and family life (article 8). The ECtHR has gradually interpreted the right to protection against torture as providing a wider right for asylum seekers than that provided in the Geneva Convention relating to the status of refugees 1951 and its 1967 protocol. Not only does it include all persons at serious risk of torture, inhuman or degrading treatment if returned to their country of origin, but there is no exception on grounds of national security. Article 3 protection may also extend to requiring a state to permit an individual suffering from a terminal disease (in the case, AIDS) to remain in the state if his or her return to the country of origin would mean the interruption of treatment which would be the equivalent of a death sentence.[18]

The right to family life in article 8, as interpreted by the ECtHR, has provided protection from expulsion for young men (the cases are all in respect of men) who have grown up in European states and subsequently become involved in criminal activity. Similarly, it has been interpreted as protecting the interests of wives (it is always wives) in the presence of their foreign husbands on the territory notwithstanding their criminal activities. The rights of parents and children has not only protected from expulsion foreign fathers of national children living with their mothers but also, in one case, the admission of a child who had been left abroad when her family moved to the member State.

In view of the contested nature of rights for foreigners in Europe, the degree to which member States have accepted and complied with the decisions of the ECtHR is impressive. This has extended to the changing of national law where the ECtHR has found it inconsistent with human rights of foreigners. O'Boyle suggests that there are three reasons why states submit to supranational interference in sensitive fields: first, the ECtHR has retained the confidence of the member States; secondly the system is constantly developing, engaging the member States in negotiations on new protocols, treaties etc; thirdly, the system reinforces the idea that the participating states are like-minded and have a common heritage of political traditions, ideals, freedom and the rule of law.[19] In the field of rights of foreigners, all three factors can be seen at work. The insistence of the ECtHR to review each case on its facts has encouraged member State confidence in the system. The reinforcement of the ECtHR's interpretation of foreigners' rights by the negotiation of new treaties and protocols engages member States in the acceptance of existing jurisprudence and encourages them to embrace it. The idea of a common heritage of rule of law which deserves to be upheld has been central to implementation of what, in some cases, have been rather unwelcome decisions.

Caporaso also provides a key to understanding the nature of the dynamic, returning always to the individual situated in his or her environment and struggling for various advantages.[20] As is apparent from a consideration of the cases, the complaints to the ECtHR are legal formulations of the hopes and fears of individuals seeking desperately (and at great personal cost) to establish rights. These individuals fill a certain space between transnational society and supranational institutions. As foreigners seeking identity recognition in a foreign state, they are a central part of transnational society. Their chance to achieve this recognition which is denied

---

18 *D v UK* 2 May 1997 Reports 1997-III.

19 M O'Boyle, 'Reflections of the Effectiveness of the European System for the Protection of Human Rights' in A Bayefsky (ed), *The UN Human Rights Treaty System in the 21st Century*, Kluwer Law International, the Hague, 2000 p 169.

20 J Caporaso, 'Integration Theory, Past and Future' in W Sandholtz and A Stone Sweet, *European Integration and Supranational Governance*, OUP, Oxford, 1998 p 349.

them at the national level is via the supranational institutions. As a result, the relationship of the ECHR and the EU has become increasingly complex as both supranational systems take on responsibilities for identity struggles contested at the national level. The role of the individual as the irritant between the national and supranational institutions is central. It is not least through this catalyst that the two supranational systems come face to face and must determine their articulation.

EU Identity? The Third Country Agreements

Just as the rule of law at the European supranational level began to have real consequences for foreigners in the 1990s, a theoretical battle began regarding immigration from third countries as a core part of national sovereignty. The challenge of EU law entering this field through specific arrangements based on nationality in the arena of international relations changed the dynamic between the Member States and individual foreigners on their territory. The insertion of EU law as a fixed element in the relations between the state and the individual is very different from the type of law which regulates migration at the national level. At national level this law is characterised by a suppleness and flexibility which does not give rise to a hard right of residence except after a substantial period of time in the state. At the international level, the traditional "invisibility" of the individual means that he or she is not envisaged by international agreements as an actor but as an object. Koskenniemi describes the relationship as one which places law as the handmaid of the diplomat or politician.[21]

A number of agreements settled by the EU with third countries include provisions regarding access to the territory, residence, economic activity and social security for third country nationals. The ECJ has found that a number of these provisions have direct effect, thus the individual is entitled to rely directly on them vis-à-vis the Member States to establish rights. However, there is a substantial difference in the ability to access rights for individuals under these agreements depending on whether the agreement protects residence rights or only social rights. The blunt reality from the cases which have come before the ECJ indicates that foreigners are not eager to challenge the state as regards rights they may have in the field of non-discrimination in working conditions or social security unless their residence right is really secure.

A change takes place only once the individual has a right of residence which derives from a source outside the state itself and which lacks a high degree of responsiveness to national sovereignty issues (including changes of legislation premised on the need to react against far right/anti-immigrant political parties). Once foreigners have a secure residence right from a supranational source, they are more

---

21 Koskenniemi, 'International Law Aspects of the Common Foreign and Security Policy' in M Koskenniemi, *International Law Aspects of the European Union*, Kluwer Law International, the Hague, 1998 pp 27–28.

willing to rely on their non-discrimination rights to achieve greater equality with nationals of the state. What had been symbolic law on non-discrimination becomes real law with consequences for allocation of resources, access to job security, protection in respect of disability etc. The claims to identity are no longer differentiated in practice around the issue of belonging as contained in the passport and liability to expulsion. If identity is formed in relationship, as Koskenniemi claims, the transformation of these relationships by the insertion of rights through third country agreements also transforms European identity.

Bringing Immigration and Asylum into the EC Treaty

The 1999 changes to the EC Treaty saw the insertion of a new Title VI containing wide powers in the field of immigration and asylum and a duty to adopt measures to implement these powers by 1 May 2004. These powers are aimed at a new objective: the creation of an area of freedom, security and justice. In the EU Treaty this area is stated to be for the citizen, thus giving rise to questions regarding the position of non-citizens as participants in the area of freedom, security and justice. The question which then arises, in light of the EU measures adopted to complete this new area, is the extent to which third country nationals are in fact the silent objects of national sovereignty in an area in which EU citizens have supranational rights or whether third country nationals are active participants acquiring rights themselves. Agamben's field of sovereignty as revealed in the exception as regards the foreigner provides an important perspective on the developments in this field at EU level.[22]

The relationship of the rule and the exception structured around the citizen and the state does not explain the transformation of law-making powers and their exercise in the field of EU immigration and asylum. Most symbolically important is, of course, the transformation of the meaning of borders and their control for persons in the EU. By applying a supranational law-making power to the definition of the border of the territory and with it a redefinition of the border from that of the nation state to the supranational entity which is not a state, the definition of the nation state itself crumbles. The relationship of the citizen to the state is transformed in that the citizen is no longer the measure of the scope of the law, the citizen and the state of exception are no longer bound together in opposition. Similarly, the foreigner is no longer the foremost subject of the exception. Instead, the antagonism of EU law (expressed most frequently by the ECJ) to measures which allow a different interpretation of the same legal provision in different Member States constitutes the basis for an alternative approach to the exception. The exception in EU law is not only a

---

22   G Agamben, *Homo Sacer: Sovereign Power and Bare Life*, Stanford University Press, Stanford, 1998.

field of sovereignty to be protected against judicial encroachment but, in principle, a threat to the integrity of the EU law system itself.

The struggle for control over the exception in the field of immigration and asylum will be played out at the EU level over the next 15 years. The role of the ECJ will be decisive in determining whether the EU in fact has a consistent immigration and asylum law which provides the same results across the Union or whether nation state sovereignty in the form of exceptionalism in the treatment of foreigners will manage to survive as the rule itself.

Identity in the EU Neighbourhood

The theory and practice of the EU internal market regarding the importance of the right of movement of persons for economic purposes finds expression in many central fields of EU policy but is also the subject of continuing resistance from JHA ministries. Nonetheless, in the vision of security for the European Union, the "Wider Europe" policy, announced by the Commission in 2003, the gradual extension of the internal market to the neighbouring states of the EU is the central feature.[23] In the development of a stability and security policy for the EU with its neighbours, the objective of free movement of persons is one of the four central planks. In addition, the policy of the EU in negotiations on liberalisation of trade in services with the rest of the world is to decrease restrictions on movement of persons for economic purposes related to service provision.[24] In both cases, the driving force is the European Commission, promoting a vision of expanding transnational governance directed by a core, the EU in the form of institutions with Member State participation, over the neighbourhood which will accept this form of governance without representation if enough incentives through internal market access are provided.

The approach of the JHA ministries in immigration negotiations at the EU level contrasts with that in other more EU-central policy fields. The JHA Council, which is limited to strictly immigration and asylum competences, emphases harder border controls to hamper the movement of persons from outside the Union. Even where the Commission proposes legislation which would enhance the position of third country nationals lawfully in the Union, the negotiations in the Council usually result in a lowering of standards which is then justified on the ground that these are just minimum standards thus maintaining the space for higher standards at the national level (see chapters 5 and 12). The fields in which the JHA Council is able to reach agreement are those which risk increasing the incidence of illegality among third country nationals in the Union by widening the category and limiting

---

23 European Commission, *Communication on the Wider Europe*, COM (2003) 104 final.
24 Brussels 29 April 2003 *WTO Services – EU proposes to improve trading opportunities giving developing countries a better deal.*

the protections. Thus the form is much more intergovernmental where the results of negotiations can be sold at home as national measures or requirements of the EU depending on the choices regarding national political concerns which JHA ministries make. This corresponds to an intergovernmental approach to rule making.

The JHA Council's insistence on expulsion and readmission agreements has knock on effects in policy fields dominated by an integrationalist vision of the EU. In the Wider Europe policy it undermines objectives of expanding integration by indicating to some surrounding countries that they are not really part of the project. Instead, they are responsible for illegal immigration, rather than on the way to free movement of persons. With some neighbours, such as Russia, Morocco and Ukraine, the JHA Council is demanding readmission agreements to simplify expulsion of their nationals (and others) from the EU. Other neighbours, such as Norway or Switzerland, are offered free movement of persons instead so that their nationals will not become illegally present in the Union.

The struggle in respect of competing theoretical principles at work in the EU is demonstrated with substantial clarity in the field of persons. Persons are part of a policy of stability, security and economic development in the form of widening integration in some areas of EU policy-making where the main actors are EU institutional and ministries other than JHA at the national level. In these areas, movement of persons is perceived as an opportunity to increase economic integration. In policy fields which are still struggling with a legacy of strong intergovernmental approaches such as JHA, movement of persons in general appears to be perceived as a threat. The incoherence between the two visions is problematic. The alignment of the development of the area of freedom, security and justice with the wider objectives of the Union is already clearly moving towards the integrationist principle. Persons, instead of being seen as a threat, are acknowledged as the means by which prosperity and security can be achieved not only in the region but beyond and they must be treated accordingly.

Racial Discrimination and EU Identity

There has been an impressive amount of legislative activity in the field of discrimination on prohibited grounds, including race and ethnic origin, in Europe at the turn of the millennium. Both at the EU and Council of Europe levels there have been serious efforts to enhance the protection of individuals against unjustified discrimination. This has included the opening for signature and ratification of a new protocol (number 12) to the ECHR which specifically extends protection against discrimination on prohibited grounds and the adoption by the EU of two directives prohibiting discrimination on the grounds set out in article 13 EC/article III-124 EU Constitution, directives 2000/43 and 200/78. However, what has been less apparent has been a willingness of EU Member States to give up their practices of arbitrary decision making which, justified on the basis of immigration and asylum laws, in effect discriminate on the basis of race, ethnic origin or religion hiding behind the justification of nationality.

In the EU legislation a very clear exception has been made regarding foreigners: first the directives do not prohibit discrimination on the basis of nationality; secondly they are "without prejudice to provisions and conditions relating to the entry into and residence of third country nationals and stateless persons on the territory of Member States, and to any treatment which arises from the legal status of the third-country nationals and stateless persons concerned."[25] Thus the Member States preserved their right to discriminate on the grounds of nationality, race and all other prohibited grounds so long as this discrimination is as regards the status of third country nationals and stateless persons. In the Council of Europe protocol, the exception is not so explicit. Instead it is noted in the memorandum on the new protocol against discrimination that only objective and reasonable justification can turn apparent prohibited discrimination into permitted distinction.

For the EU, Member State transposition of the new anti-discrimination legislation in directive 2000/43 had to be completed by July 2003. It is now up to the Member States to implement it and the courts to give effect to the spirit and letter of the law. As the International Council on Human Rights Policy has stated "Adequate laws, access to courts, a willingness to interpret the law broadly and effectively, and a determination on the part of the courts to enforce the law are all essential prerequisites for the eradication of racism".[26] The courts both at national and supranational level will be required to interpret the scope of the non-discrimination provisions. What is at stake cannot be underestimated in a Europe where extreme right wing parties have fed on anti-immigrant, anti-asylum seeker discourse, managing to increase their proportion of the popular vote in too many countries. The relationship between law and populism must be clearly delineated. The rule of law, particularly in the form of protection of minorities and enforcement of non-discrimination, is the institutional counterweight to inappropriate political behaviour. However, that law must not accept as a field of exceptionalism beyond its reach discrimination which has as an essential element differential treatment on grounds of race or religion merely because it has been formally categorised as nationality discrimination. Attempts by Member States to legitimise race discrimination in migration and asylum law and thereby remove the field from judicial supervision can only be detrimental to social cohesion both in the short and long term. What is at stake is the refutation or confirmation of what Amin starkly describes: "non-white residents and citizens of the European Union (EU) have no role to play in the 'Idea of Europe', which remains

---

25 The recital which was added states: "This prohibition of discrimination should also apply to nationals of third countries, but does not cover differences of treatment based on nationality and is without prejudice to provisions governing the entry and residence of third country nationals and their access to employment and to occupation."

26 International Council on Human Rights Policy, *The Persistence and Mutation of Racism*, 2000.

an ideal of unity drawing on a Christian-Enlightenment heritage to bridge the diversity of European national cultures."[27]

Integration and Identity: Long Resident Third Country Nationals

Žižek provides a challenging point of departure from which to understand the context in which the EU approaches third country nationals: "On today's market we find a whole series of products deprived of their malignant properties: coffee without caffeine, cream without fat, beer without alcohol ... And the list goes on: what about virtual sex as sex without sex, the Colin Powell doctrine of warfare without casualties (on our side, of course), the contemporary redefinition of politics as the art of expert administration, that is, as politics without politics, up to today's tolerant liberal multiculturalism as an experience of the Other deprived of its Otherness (the idealized Other who dances fascinating dances and has an ecologically sound holistic approach to reality, while practices like wife beating remain out of sight)?"[28] Žižek is examining the meaning of what he describes as the twentieth century's passion for the Real. He explains how this passion is a fake passion "whose ruthless pursuit of the Real behind appearances was *the ultimate stratagem to avoid confronting the Real*".[29] This pursuit of the Real which must be perceived as nightmarish leads to a categorization of third country nationals within the Union as necessarily Other. The Real Other which they represent is by definition, then, nightmarish or at least potentially nightmarish.

Žižek's contention can be measured against two EU directives in respect of third country nationals – directive 2001/40 on mutual recognition on the expulsion of third country nationals and directive 2003/109 concerning the legal status of third country nationals who are long-term residents. The first measure results in an objectification of third country nationals which results from their categorisation as potential or actual objects of an expulsion decision in one Member State. The individual becomes the object of a transnational "hunt" with the objective of expulsion. Into the framework of the "hunt" are placed a series of economic incentives for the officials of the Member States to carry out expulsion decisions for other Member States. The supranational mechanism which releases the individual from becoming potentially the object of such a search is the acquisition of an EU status of protected third country national. The willingness, or rather lack thereof, among the Member States to create a full and inclusive protected status for third country nationals has the

---

27   A Amin, 'Immigrants, Cosmopolitans and the Idea of Europe' in H Wallace, *Interlocking Dimensions of European Integration*, Palgrave, Basingstoke, 2001, pp 280–301.
28   S Žižek, *Welcome to the Desert of the Real*, Verso, London, 2002 pp 10–11.
29   S Žižek supra p 24.

consequence of leaving larger numbers of third country nationals in the limbo of potential objects of the "hunt".

The second measure, directive 2003/109, concerning the legal status of third country nationals who are long-term residents, is then critical to assessing the underlying assumptions of EU policy in respect of third country nationals. This directive sets out a status which is acquired by third country nationals after five years lawful residence in one Member State. The status provides rights of continued residence and economic activity as well as protection against expulsion. Once acquired, the status also allows the individual to take up residence and economic activities in other Member States. The legislative history of the measure is not reassuring for those who seek to defend the openness of the EU. When a comparison is made between the first proposal of the Commission for a directive on long-term resident third country nationals and the final directive as adopted it is difficult to avoid the conclusion that the Member States consider third country nationals, even after five years stable and lawful residence in the Union, an intrinsically suspect category. Asylum seekers, refugees and persons granted subsidiary protection are excluded entirely from any access to the free movement rights which are at the heart of the internal market. For them the borders remain as solid as if the objective of the original Treaty had been to achieve free movement of persons with the exception of anyone in need of protection against persecution. Article 14 EC/article III-14 EU Constitution, the abolition of intra-Member State border controls on persons, might just as well not exist for the JHA Council where the concept of borders is restrictive fences between the Member States which keep out the unwanted and potentially dangerous Other. For those who are admitted into one Member State the conditions which must be fulfilled before they will be able to acquire the status of long-term resident were augmented continuously throughout the negotiations in the Council, eventually including a requirement on integration.

The justification appears to be the tacit agreement among the Member States that third country nationals are potentially dangerous Others. Before they can be permitted to move in the Union and reside they must be subject to "integration". This is given a potentially wide social meaning even though the concept is strictly limited to the economic sector when the Member States consider activities of their own nationals. Article 151(4) EC/article III-280(4) EU Constitution proudly states "The Community shall take cultural aspects into account in its action under other provisions of this Treaty, in particular in order to respect and to promote the diversity of its cultures." Cultural diversity, it would appear, is only an asset when it is compatible with Žižek's world of the false Real which excludes the Other. The cultures of Europe which deserve respect and promotion in their diversity do not appear to include those of long-term-resident third country nationals.

Identity in Europe is in flux. The differentiation between the citizen and the foreigner as rights holders is the site of struggles at national and supranational levels. The result is a three-way tension in policy and law over the right to define identity among the Member States, the EU institutions and the Council of Europe.

The catalyst is the individual and his or her claim to legitimacy in the acquisition of rights. As an increasing amount of legislation is adopted, in particular at the EU level in this field (and the deadlines for transposition pass), the courts, including the national courts, the ECJ and the ECtHR, will be called upon to articulate the relationship of the individual to the territory and society in which he or she finds him or herself. In so doing, the clarification of the relationships of the judicial instances with one another will be unavoidable. Equally, the consequences of such a clarification are likely to determine the constitutional structure of Europe.

Bibliography

G Agamben, *Homo Sacer: Sovereign Power and Bare Life*, Stanford University Press, Stanford, 1998.

M Albert, D Jacobson, Y Lapid (eds), *Identities, Borders, Orders*, University of Minnesota Press, Minneapolis/London, 2001.

T Aleinikoff and D Klusmeyer, *Citizenship Policies for an Age of Migration*, Carnegie Endowment for International Peace, Washington, 2002.

A Amin, 'Immigrants, Cosmopolitans and the Idea of Europe' in H Wallace, *Interlocking Dimensions of European Integration*, Palgrave, Basingstoke, 2001, pp 280–301.

B Anderson, *Imagined Communities*, Verso, London, 1996.

M Anderson and E Bort, *Boundaries and Identities: The Eastern Frontiers of the EU*, University of Edinburgh Press, Edinburgh, 1998.

W B Arthur, *Increasing Returns and Path Dependence in the Economy*, University of Michigan Press, Ann Arbor, 1994.

R Badinter, *Une constitution européene*, Fayard, Paris, 2002.

W Bagehot, *The English Constitution*, OUP, Oxford, 2001.

M Banton, *International Action Against Racial Discrimination*, Clarendon, Cambridge, 1996.

C Barnard, 'Article 13: Through the Looking Glass of Union Citizenship' in D O'Keeffe and P Twomey (eds), *Legal Issues of the Amsterdam Treaty*, OUP, Oxford, 1999.

R Bauböck, 'The Crossing and Blurring of Boundaries in International Migration. Challenges for Social and Political Theory' in R Baubock & J Rundell, *Blurred Boundaries: Migration, Ethnicity, Citizenship*, Averbury, Aldershot, 1998.

D Beetham and C Lord, 'Legitimacy and the EU' in A Weale and M Nentwich, *Political Theory and the European Union*, OUP, Oxford, 1998.

D Beetham and C Lord, *Legitimacy in the European Union*, Longman, 1998.

M Bell, *Anti-Discrimination Law and the European Union*, OUP, Oxford, 2002.

R Bellamy, 'Constitutive Citizenship versus Constitutional Rights: Republican Reflections on the EU Charter and the Human Rights Act' in T Campbell, D Ewing and A Tomkins, *Sceptical Essays on Human Rights*, OUP, Oxford, 2001, pp 17–39.

J Bhabha, S Shutter et al, *Women's Movement, Women under Immigration, Nationality and Refugee Law*, Trentham Books, Stoke-on-Trent, 1994.

D Bigo, *Polices en Reseaux*, Presse de Sciences-Po, Paris, 1996.

D Bigo et E Guild 'Controller à distance et tenir à l'écart: le Visa Schengen' Cultures et Conflits, l'Harmattan, Paris, 2002 (4).

D Bigo and E Guild (eds) 'De Tampere à Seville: bilan de la sécurité européenne' Cultures et Conflits, l'Harmattan, Paris, 2002 (1 & 2).

D Bigo and E Guild, *Controlling Frontiers: Free Movement into and within Europe*, Ashgate, Aldershot, 2004 forthcoming.

T Bingham, 'Personal Freedom and the Dilemma of Democracies' International and Comparative Law Quaterly, Volume 52, Issue 4, October 2003, pp 841–858.

N Blake QC and R Husain, *Immigration, Asylum and Human Rights*, OUP, Oxford, 2003.

I Boccardi, *Europe and Refugees – Towards an EU Asylum Policy*, Kluwer Law International, The Hague, 2003.

A Böcker & E Guild, *Implementation of the Europe Agreements in France, Germany, the Netherlands and the UK: Movement of Persons*, Platinum, London, 2002.

P Boeles, 'An Area of Freedom, Security and Justice' in E Guild and C Harlow, *Implementing Amsterdam Immigration and Asylum Rights in EC Law*, Hart Publishing Oxford, 2001.

W R Böhning, *The Migration of Workers in the United Kingdom and Western Europe*, OUP, Oxford, 1972.

C Boswell, *European Migration Policies in Flux: Changing Patterns of Inclusions and Exclusion*, Royal Institute of International Affairs, London, 2003.

T Van Boven 'Discrimination and Human Rights Law' in S Fredman, (ed), *Discrimination and Human Rights: The Case of Racism*, OUP, Oxford, 2001, pp 120–121.

K Boyle and A Baldaccini, 'International Human Rights Approaches to Racism' in S Fredman (ed), *Discrimination and Human Rights: The Case of Racism*, OUP, Oxford, 2001, pp 135–191.

U Brandl, 'Distribution of Asylum Seekers in Europe? Dublin II Regulation determining the responsibility for examining an asylum application' in P de Bruycker & C de Souza, *European Immigration and Asylum Law*, Bruylant, 2003 (forthcoming).

G Brinkmann, 'Family Reunification' in E Guild & C Harlow, *Implementing Amsterdam: Immigration and Asylum Rights in EC Law*, Hart, Oxford, 2001, pp 241–266.

G Brinkmann 'An Area of Freedom Security and Justice: Five Years After its Creation: The Immigration and Asylum Agenda' ELJ 10:2 (2004).

E Brouwer, P Catz & E Guild, *Immigration, Asylum and Terrorism: A Changing Dynamic in European Law*, Recht & Samenleving, Nijmegen, 2003.

E Brouwer, 'Eurodac: Its Limitations and Temptations' EJML 2002 Vol 4, p 231–245.

M and A Geddes, *Migration and Welfare: Challenging the Borders of the Welfare State*, London, Routledge, 2000.

J Caporaso, 'Integration Theory, Past and Future' in W Sandholtz and A Stone Sweet, *European Integration and Supranational Governance*, OUP, Oxford, 1998.

S Castles with H Booth and T Wallace, *Here for Good, Western Europe's New Ethnic Minorities*, Pluto Press, London and Sidney, 1984.

S Castles, 'Globalisation and the Ambiguities of National Citizenship' in R Baubock, *Blurred Boundaries: Migration, Ethnicity, Citizenship*, Averbury, Aldershot, 1998.

D Chalmers, 'The Mistakes of the Good European' in S Fredman (ed), *Discrimination and Human Rights: The Case of Racism*, OUP, Oxford 2001, pp 202–203.

R Cholewinski, *The Conditions of Family Reunification in [8] Council of Europe member States*, Council of Europe, Strasbourg, 2001.

I Chopin & J Niessen, *Proposal for Legislative Measures to Combat Racism and to Promote Equal Rights in the European Union*, Commission for Racial Equality, London 1998.

S Collinson, *Beyond Borders: Western European Migration Policy Towards the 21st Century*, Royal Institute of International Affairs/Wyndam Place Trust, London, 1993.

R Cornelissen, '25 Years of Regulation (EEC) No 1408/71; Its Achievements and Its Limits' in, *25 Years of Regulation (EEC) No 1408/71 n Social Security for Migrant Workers*, Swedish National Social Insurance Board & European Commission, Stockholm, 1997.

J Crowley, 'The national dimension of citizenship in T H Marshall' Citizenship Studies 2(2) pp 165–178.

J Crowley, 'Where Does the State Actually Start? Territorial Control in the Contemporary Governance of Migration' in D Bigo and E Guild, *Controlling Frontiers: Free Movement into and within Europe*, Ashgate, Aldershot, forthcoming.

P David, "Clio and the Economics of QWERTY" (1985) American Economic Review 75:332-7.

C Dias Urbano de Souza, *The Emergence of an European Asylum Policy*, Bruylant, 2004 (forthcoming).

M Esposito, 'Libera Cirolazione e pubblica amministraione prassi nationale e prospettive' in B Nascimbene, *Le Libera Circolazione dei lavoratori*, Guiffre, Milan, 1998.

S E Finer, *Five Constitution: Contrasts and Comparisons*, Penguin, Middlesex, 1979.

L Fransman, *British Nationality Law*, 2nd ed, Butterworths, London, 2001.

S Fredman, (ed) *Discrimination and Human Rights: The Case of Racism*, OUP, Oxford, 2001.

E Gellner, *Nationalism*, Phoenix, London, 1997.

A. Giddens, *A Contemporary Critique of Historical Materialism*, vol 2, *The Nation-State and Violence*, University of California Press, Berkeley and Los Angeles, 1985.

C Gortazar; 'Spain: Two Immigration Acts at the End of the Millennium' EJML 2002 Vol 4: 1, pp 1–21.

K Groenendijk, E Guild, P Minderhoud, *In Search of Europe's Borders*, Kluwer Law International, The Hague, 2002.

K Groenendijk, 'New Borders Behind Old Ones: Post Schengen Controls Behind the Internal Borders and Inside the Netherlands and Germany' in K Groenendijk, E Guild and P Minderhoud, *In Search of Europe's Borders*, Kluwer Law International, The Hague, 2003, pp 131–146.

K Groenendijk, 'Regulating Ethnic Immigration: the case of the Aussiedler', New Community 23(4) 461 1997.

K Groenendijk, E Guild and H Dogan, *Security of Residence of Long Term Migrants: A comparative study of law and practice in European countries*, Council of Europe (English and French) Strasbourg, 1998.

G-R de Groot, 'The nationality Legislation of the Member States of the European Union' in M La Torre, *European Citizenship: An Institutional Challenge*, Kluwer Law International, the Hague, 1998, pp 115/147.

E Guild, 'Seeking Asylum: Storm Clouds between International Commitments and EU Legislative Measures' EL Rev 2004, forthcoming.

E Guild, 'Immigration, Asylum, Borders and Terrorism: the Unexpected Victims' in B Gökay and R B J Walker, *11 September 2001: War Terror and Judgement*, Cass, London, 2003, pp 146–194.

E Guild, *Immigration Law in the European Community*, Elspeth Guild, Kluwer Law International, The Hague, 2001.

E Guild and J Niessen, *The Developing Immigration and Asylum Policy of the European Union*, Kluwer Law International, The Hague, 1996.

E Guild and G Lesieur, *The European Court of Justice on the European Convention on Human Rights: Who said what when*, Kluwer Law International, The Hague, 1997.

E Guild, "How Can Social Protection Survive EMU? A United Kingdom Perspective", ELRev, 25:1(1999), pp 22–37.

E Guild, 'Exceptionalism and Transnationalism: UK Judicial Control of the Detention of Foreign "International Terrorists"' Alternatives (2003) forthcoming.

E Guild "The impetus to harmonise: asylum policy in the European Union", *Refugee Rights and Realities, Evolving International Concepts and Regimes*, Frances Nicholson and Patrick Twomey (editors), Cambridge University Press, Cambridge, 1999, pp 313–335.

E Guild "Between Persecution and Protection – Refugees and the New European Asylum Policy" in, *The Cambridge Yearbook of European Legal Studies Vol 3 2000*, A Dashwood, J Spencer, A Ward C Hillion, Hart: Oxford, 2001, pp 169–199.

E Guild, 'Equality as an EC Right' in G Moon (ed), *Race Discrimination: Developing and Using a New Legal Framework*, Hart, Oxford, 2000, pp 65–80.

E Guild "Entry into the UK: the changing nature of national borders", Immigration and Nationality Law and Practice, Vol 14 No 4, 2000, pp 227–238.

V Guiraudon 'Logiques et practiques de l'Etat délégateur: les companies de transport dans le contrôl migratoire à distance' Cultures et Conflits, 2/2002.

R Gutmann, *Die Assoziationsfreizügigkeit türkisher Staatsangehöriger, Ihre Entdeckung und ihr Inhalt*, 2 Auflage, Nomos Verlag, Baden-Baden, 1999.

R Gutmann, "Discrimination against own nationals: a brief look at European and German immigration law", Immigration and Nationality Law and Practice, Vol 9 No 3 1995.

J Habermas, 'Citizenship and National Identity: Some Reflections on the Future of Europe' in R Beiner, *Theorising Citizenship*, SUNY, New York, 1995, pp 255–281.

R Hofmann, 'German Citizenship and European Citizenship' in M Le Torre, *European Citizenship: An Institutional Challenge*, Kluwer Law International, the Hague, 1998, pp 149–166.

L Holmström, *Conclusions and Recommendations of the UN Committee against Torture*, Martinus Nijhoff, The Hague, 2000.

A Hurwitz 'The 1990 Dublin Convention: A Comprehensive Assessment' IJRL 1999 Vol 11, pp 646–677.

D Jacobsen, *Rights Across Borders: Immigration and the Decline of Citizenship*, John Hopkins University Press, Baltimore, 1996.

E Jileva, 'Insiders and Outsiders in the Enlargement of the EU borders: Bulgaria' in K Groenendijk, E Guild, P Minderhoud, *In Search of Europe's Borders*, Kluwer Law International, The Hague, 2003, pp 273–288.

K Kerber, 'The Temporary Protection Directive' EJML 2002 Vol 4 No 2, pp 193–214.

Koskenniemi, 'International Law Aspects of the Common Foreign and Security Policy' in M Koskenniemi, *International Law Aspects of the European Union*, Kluwer Law International, The Hague, 1998.

D Kostakopoulou, 'Floating Sovereignty: A Pathology or a Necessary Means of State Evolution?' Oxford Journal of Legal Studies Vol 22, No 1 (2002), pp 135–156.

D Kostakopoulou '"Integrating" Non-EU Migrants in the European Union: Ambivalent Legacies and Mutating Paradigms' Columbia Journal of European Law Spring 2002 Vol 8 No 2, pp 181–201.

D Kostakopoulou, 'Unweaving the Threads: Territoriality, National Ownership of Land and Asylum Policy' (2004) forthcoming.

M Krajewski & H Rittstief, 'Germany' in B Nascimbene, *Nationality Laws in the European Union*, Butterworths/Guiffè, London/Milan, 1996, pp 365–366.

I Macdonald & ors, *Immigration Law and Practice*, 5th ed. Butterworths, London, 2001.

C B MacPherson, *The Real World of Democracy*, Anansi, Concord, 1992.

P Magnette, *La Citoyenneté*, Bruylant, Brussels, 2001.

F Mancini, 'The Making of a Constitution for Europe' CMLRev 26:595 (1989).

F Mancini 'The Free Movement of Workers in the Case Law of the European Court of Justice' in Curtin, D, O'Keeffe, D (eds), *Constitutional Adjudication in European Community and National Law: Essays in Honour of Mr Justice T. F. O'Higgins*, Butts, Dublin, 1992.

T H Marshall, *Citizenship and Social Class*, CUP, Cambridge, 1950.

D Martin & E Guild, *Free Movement of Persons in the European Community*, Butterworths, London, 1996.

D Martin, 'Association Agreements with Mediterranean and with Eastern Countries: Similarities and Differences,' in Antalovsky, K Konig, B Perchinig, H Vana, *Assoziierungsabkommen de EU mit Drittstaaten*, 1998.

P Martin, *Germany Reluctant Land of Migration*, American Institute for Contemporary German Studies, John Hopkins University, Baltimore, 1998.

A van der Mei, *Free Movement of Persons within the European Community: cross border access to public benefits*, Hart, Oxford, 2003.

H Mikkeli, *Europe as an Idea and Identity*, Macmillan, London, 1998.

J S Mill, *On Liberty and Other Essays*, OUP, Oxford, 1998.

P Minderhoud 'The Dutch Linking Act and the Violation of Various International Non-Discrimination Clauses' EJML 2 (2000), pp 185–201.

A Moravcsik, 'Negotiating the Single European Act: National Interests and Conventional Statecraft in the European Community' International Organisation (1991) 45:19–56.

B Nascimbene, *Nationality Laws in the European Union*, Butterworths/Giuffre, London/Milan, 1996.

B Nascimbene (ed), *Expulsion and Detention of Aliens in the European Union Countries*, Guiffre Editore, Milan, 2001.

F Nicholson, 'Implementation of the Immigration (Carriers' Liability) Act 1987: privatizing immigration functions at the expense of international obligations?' ICLQ 46:586, 1997.

G Noiriel, *Etat, nationalité et immigration vers une histoire du pouvoir*, Belin, Paris, 2001.

M O'Boyle, 'Reflections of the Effectiveness of the European System for the Protection of Human Rights' in A Bayefsky (ed), *The UN Human Rights Treaty System in the 21st Century*, Kluwer Law International, The Hague, 2000.

S O'Leary, *The Evolving Concept of Community Citizenship*, Kluwer Law International, The Hague, 1996.

C Offe, 'Homogeneity' and Constitutional Democracy: Group Rights as an Answer to Identity Conflicts?' in S Saberwal and H Sievers (eds), *Rules, Laws Constitutions*, Sage, New Delhi, 1998.

C Ovey & R White, *Jacobs & White: The European Convention on Human Rights*, 3rd Ed, OUP, Oxford, 2002.

A di Pascale 'The New Regulations on Immigration and the Status of Foreigners in Italy' EJML 2002 Vol 4: 1, pp 71–77.

S Peers, 'Readmission Agreements' in S Peers and N Rogers, *Immigration and Asylum in EU Law afvter Amsterdam*, Kluwer Law International, The Hague, forthcoming.

M Piore, *Birds of Passage: Migrant Labour and Industrial Societies*, CUP, Cambridge, 1979.

O Potemkina, 'Some Ramifications of Enlargement on the EU-Russia Relations and the Schengen Regime' EJML 2003 Vol 1 No 1.

U Preuss, 'Constitutionalism – Meaning, Endangerment, Sustainability'in S Saberwal and H Sievers (eds), *Rules, Laws Constitutions*, Sage, New Delhi, 1998.

V Robinson 'Marching into the Middle Classes? The long term resettlement of East African Asians in the UK' Journal of Refugee Studies Vol 6: 3 (1993), pp 230–248.

R Manuel Moira Ramos, 'Le droit portugais de la nationalité' in B Nascimbene (ed), *Nationality Laws in the European Union*, Butterworths/Giuffre, London/Milan, 1996.

W Sandholtz 'Choosing Union: Monetary Politics and Maastricht' International Organisations (1993) 47: 1–39.

W Sandholtz and A Stone Sweet, *European Integration and Supranational Governance*, OUP, Oxford, 1998.

C Saas, 'Les refus de deliverance de visas fondés sur une inscription sur le Système Information Schengen' Cultures et Conflits 2002 (4), Paris, Harmattan.

M Sakslin 'The Concept of Residence and Social Security: Reflections on the Finnish, Swedish and Community Legislation' EJML 2 (2000), pp 157–183.

S Sachdeva, *The Primary Purpose Rule in British Immigration Law*, Trentham Books, Stoke-on-Trent, 1993.

S Sassen, *Losing Control? Sovereignty in an Age of Globalisation*, Columbia University Press, New York, 1996.

M Schieffer, *Community readmission agreements with third-countries – objectives, substance and current state of negotiations*, EJML, 3(2003).

P Shah, *Case note on Kaur*, European Journal of Migration and Law, Vol 3 No 2 2001, pp 271–278.

J Shaw, *Citizenship of the Union: Towards Post-National Membership?*, Jean Monnet Working Paper, Jean Monnet Center, NYU School of Law, New York, June 1997.

N Shuibhne, 'Free Movement of Persons and the Wholly Internal Rule: Time to Move On?' CMLRev 39 (4): 731–771, Aug. 2002.

K Sieveking, 'The Significance of the Transborder Utilisation of Health Care Benefits for Migrants', EJML 2 (2000), pp 143–155.

A Skordas 'The New Immigration Law in Greece: Modernization on the Wrong Track' EJML Vol 4: 1 (2002), pp 23–48.

SOPEMI 2000, *Trends in International Migration*, OECD, Paris, 2000.

Y Soysal, *Limits of Citizenship, Migrants and Post-national Membership in Europe*, University of Chicago Press, Chicago, 1994.

H Staples, 'Adjudicating the Schengen External Border' in K Groenendijk, E Guild and P Minderhoud, *In Search of Europe's Borders*, Kluwer Law International, The Hague, 2003, pp 215–250.

E Szyszczak and R Cholewinski, *Irregular Migration in the European Union*, Kluwer Law International, The Hague, 2004.

C Tilly, *The Formation of Nation States in Western Europe*, Princeton University Press, Princeton, 1975.

N Timmins, *The Five Giants: A Biography of the Welfare State*, Fontana Press, London, 1996.

J Torpey, *The Invention of the Passport*, Cambridge University Press, Cambridge, 2000.

A Tyson 'The Negotiation of the European Community Directive on Racial Discrimination' EJML Vol 3 No 2 2001, pp 199–229.

R B J Walker, 'Europe is not where it is Supposed to be' in M Kelstrup and M Williams, *International Relations and the Politics of European Integration*, Routledge, London, 2000.

N Walker, *Beyond the Unitary Conception of the United Kingdom Constitution?*, PL 384 (2000) 394.

H & W Wallace, *Policy Making in the European Union*, 4th Edition, OUP, Oxford, 2001.

M Weber, *Economy and Society*, vol 1, Ed Roth G & Wittich C, University of California Press, Berkeley, 1978.

P Weil & R Hansen, *Nationalité et citoyenneté en Europe*, La Decouverte, Paris, 1999.

J H H Weiler, 'Thou Shalt Not Oppress a Stranger: On the Judicial Protection of the Human Rights of Non- EC Nationals,' 3 EJIL (1992) 65.

A Wiener, *"European" Citizenship Practice: Building Institutions of a Non-State*, Westview, Boulder, 1999.

R Wintemute & M Andenas, *Legal Recognition of Same Sex Partnerships: A Study of National, European and International Law*, Hart, Oxford, 2001.

C Urbano de Sousa, 'The New Portuguese Immigration Act' EJML Vol 4: 1 (2002), pp 49–69.

S Zizek, *The Ticklish Subject: The Absent Centre of Political Ontology*, Verso, London, 2000.

S Žižek, *Welcome to the Desert of the Real*, Verso, London, 2002.

Index